ENCOUNTERS WITH KARL RAHNER

To Bob,

With prayers
and best wishes!

Mel

May 24, 2009

ENCOUNTERS WITH KARL RAHNER

REMEMBRANCES OF RAHNER
BY THOSE WHO KNEW HIM

EDITED & TRANSLATED BY
ANDREAS R. BATLOGG & MELVIN E. MICHALSKI

TRANSLATION EDITED BY
BARBARA G. TURNER

MARQUETTE
UNIVERSITY
PRESS

MARQUETTE STUDIES IN THEOLOGY
NO 63
ANDREW TALLON, SERIES EDITOR

Library of Congress Cataloging-in-Publication Data

Begegnungen mit Karl Rahner. English.
Encounters with Karl Rahner : remembrances of Rahner by those who knew him
/ edited & translated by Andreas R. Batlogg & Melvin E. Michalski ; translation
edited by Barbara G. Turner.
p. cm. — (Marquette studies in theology ; No. 63)
Includes bibliographical references and index.
ISBN-13: 978-0-87462-740-4 (pbk. : alk. paper)
ISBN-10: 0-87462-740-0 (pbk. : alk. paper)
1. Rahner, Karl, 1904-1984. 2. Rahner, Karl, 1904-1984—Friends and associates--
Inteviews. I. Batlogg, Andreas R. II. Michalski, Melvin, 1943- III. Turner, Barbara,
1941- IV. Title.
BX4705.R287B4313 2009
230'.2092--dc22
2009005071

The original German edition of this book is entitled *Begegnungen mit Karl Rahner: Weggefährten erinnern sich (Freiburg im Breisgau: Herder 2006).* We are grateful for permission to publish this translation. We also acknowledge permission to use the cover photo of Rahner and Metz from the original edition.

♾The paper used in this publication meets the minimum requirements of the
American National Standard for Information Sciences—
Permanence of Paper for Printed Library Materials, ANSI Z39.48-1992.

Association of American
University Presses

MARQUETTE UNIVERSITY PRESS
MILWAUKEE

The Association of Jesuit University Presses

CONTENTS

PREFACE

Twenty-five years ago, on March 30, 1984, Karl Rahner, SJ, died in Innsbruck, Austria, a few weeks after reaching the age of 80. As influential as his theology still is, and (for this one does not have to be a great prophet) will be, far beyond the 20th century, the memory of Karl Rahner himself, the human being, the Jesuit, the scholar and professor, the conciliar theologian, the priest and pastor, is gradually fading, if not, disappearing. Theology, however, will always be done contextually and to a context there belongs the life history and the faith history of this theologian—a prominent member of the Society of Jesus.

The aim of this book, which first appeared in German in June 2006[1] and which is now being made available in English translation, is to give life to and to preserve for future generations remembrances of Karl Rahner. The process in producing this book was as follows: first a rough translation from the German into English was done by Fr. Melvin Michalski. This translation was then painstakingly, significantly reworked and edited by Dr. Barbara G. Turner, who worked closely with Fr. Michalski, constantly comparing the translation with the German original. To Dr. Turner we owe our heartfelt thanks. We are also very grateful to Fr. Andrew Nelson for his extensive work and expertise in helping edit the English translation. We also thank Sister Virginia Handrup for her help in editing the endnotes. We also wish to thank Dr. Pieter von Herrmann for his feedback and input.

At the annual convention of the Catholic Theological Society of America (CTSA) in June 2008 and during a two week period in Vorarlberg, Austria, the two editors (Fr. Andreas R. Batlogg, SJ, and Fr. Melvin E. Michalski) reworked the translation, or to be more precise, "polished" it. It took a further two and a half months until the work could be completed and in October 2008 the manuscript was delivered to Dr. Andrew Tallon of Marquette University Press who agreed to publish the English edition. We thank him for both his competent as well as friendly cooperation.

That the English edition is being published by a Jesuit institution which presented Karl Rahner with the "Père Marquette Discovery

Award" in March 1979, an award which until then had only been given to the team of astronauts of Apollo 11,[2] makes us exceedingly happy.

The editors of this book owe the reader some background information on the somewhat complicated history of the origin of the book, which reaches all the way back to the beginning of this decade. Fr. Melvin E. Michalski, then an Assistant Professor of Systematic Theology at Saint Francis de Sales Seminary in Milwaukee, WI, now Professor of Systematic Studies at Sacred Heart School of Theology in Hales Corners, WI, began a sabbatical project in 2001 in which he conducted interviews with more than two dozen individuals in Germany and Austria who had significant encounters with Karl Rahner. Originally the plan was to translate the transcripts of the tape recorded conversations conducted in German into English and to publish them in the year commemorating the 100th year of Rahner's birth and the 20th anniversary of his death (2004), but for a variety of reasons that did not happen.

The question as to the fate of these interviews arose at the annual meetings of the American Karl Rahner Society. The Karl Rahner Society Bulletin, which Michalski edited and which concluded with some anecdotes about Rahner and some shorter texts of Karl Rahner in English translation, served to raise further interest. As opposed to the German speaking world, in the Anglo-Saxon countries, interest in "oral history" is much greater.

The Austrian Jesuit, Andreas R. Batlogg, a member of the editorial board of the periodical, *Stimmen der Zeit*, came to the USA for an eleven month stay and met with Fr. Michalski. The two Rahner researchers, who knew each other from their years of study in Innsbruck, recognized, after looking at the documentation that they had gathered from the interviews, that it would be a shame, indeed a loss, to keep the remembrances, observations and assessments contained therein, under lock and key and to refrain from publishing them. Thus it was decided to make another attempt to publish the interviews in an edited version. Throughout the year they met to work on the project.

In August 2005 Fr. Michalski met with Herbert Vorgrimler in Münster/Westphalia and interviewed him about his relationship with Fr. Karl Rahner. Batlogg, after his return to Europe, interviewed two additional contemporaries of Rahner: Walter Strolz and Irmgard Bsteh. An appendix was added that included two texts, the first providing part of a longer letter Hugo Rahner (1900-1968) wrote to his brother Karl in 1955, which is contained in an editorial report from vol. 9 of *Sämtliche Werke*. The letter throws significant light on the heartfelt relationship of the two scholarly brothers and reveals how they related to each other. The second text is a reprint of Roman A. Siebenrock's article, *"Erfahrungen im Karl-Rahner-Archiv,"* which was first published in 2004.

There followed months of long, painstakingly detailed work in which the tape recordings were listened to over again, newly transcribed, considerably edited and further notes were added to direct one to further research. Eliminated were repetitions, apparent contradictions or mistakes (names, dates), duplication of events or statements which, due to the developments that occurred since 2001, were outdated, for example, references to the Complete Edition of Karl Rahner's works (*Sämtliche Werke*), which in 2001 consisted of 5 volumes, but which grew by 9 volumes to a total of 14 by the fall of 2005. Since then, by the spring of 2009, the edition will stand at 24 volumes (of the 32 planned). All the endnotes are the work of Andreas R. Batlogg. They explain things hinted at, recall names and point to texts by Karl Rahner, or to be more precise, lead one to them. Meanwhile, Batlogg replaced Karl H. Neufeld, SJ, as a Co-editor of Karl Rahner's *Sämtliche Werke* [3] in 2005 and was appointed the new Director of the "Karl-Rahner-Archiv" in 2008 (see http://www.karl-rahner-archiv.de/), which has been moved from Innsbruck, Austria, to Munich, Germany.

All of the interviews were expressly authorized in the fall of 2005; those interviewed having been given the opportunity to delete one or another remark, or to amplify their comments, without, however, changing the character of a conversation that had been conducted four years earlier. Karl Rahner's sister, Elisabeth Cremer, Franz Cardinal König (the emeritus Archbishop of Vienna), Professor Adolf Darlap, as well as Hans Bernhard Meyer, Raymund Schwager, and Emerich Coreth have since died. Elisabeth Cremer died shortly before the 100th birthday of her famous brother at the age of 95 on February 14, 2004. Cardinal König died one month later on the 14th of March, at the age of 99.

The editors want to thank first of all their 28 interview partners. Then, for their helpful tips and advice, we want to thank Professor Dr. Thomas F. O'Meara, OP, (Chicago, IL), as well as Professor Dr. Michael A. Fahey, SJ, (Boston, MA), and Professor Dr. David G. Schultenover, SJ, (Milwaukee, WI), Professor Leo J. O'Donovan, SJ,

(New York, NY), as well as Professor Dr. Albert Raffelt (Freiburg). Professors Dr. John Gallam and Dr. Daniel T. Pekarske, SDS, (Sacred Heart School of Theology), as well as Dr. Paul Misner, (Professor emeritus, Marquette University), and Professor Dr. Peter C. Phan, (Ignacio Ellacuria Chair of Catholic Social Thought, Georgetown University), also provided much encouragement along the way and we thank them. Hospitality was offered to us during the weeks of intensive work by colleagues at Saint Francis de Sales Seminary and then Rector, Professor Dr. Michael E. Witczak, as well as by Dr. Patrick J. Burns, SJ, and the Jesuit Community "Holy Rosary Mission," of the Red Cloud Indian School in Pine Ridge, (SD). In July 2008, Pfarrer Edwin Matt hosted us in his rectory in Andelsbuch, Bregenzerwald, (Vorarlberg, Austria). Last, but not least we are grateful to Dr. Peter Suchla, Freiburg i. Br. (Germany), from Herder Publishing for obtaining the rights for translation of this book into English.

A word about the translation: it is not a strictly literal translation. So, a few titles, which only made sense in the German version, were changed in the English version (Lehmann, Neufeld, Coreth, Klein, Rotter), because the play on words found in the original could not be understood in translation. Furthermore, emendations were made to the endnotes which take into consideration the ongoing research, as well as the latest volumes of Karl Rahner's *Sämtliche Werke*. The Afterword in the German edition (*"Was heisst es heute: Karl Rahner erfahren?"*) appeared to us, to be better suited as an Introduction: ("What does it mean: To encounter Karl Rahner?") as it analyzes the interviews and the two texts in the appendix and so offers guidance to the reader.

In the preface to the new translation of his famous book, *Night*, which recalls his experiences in Auschwitz as a child, Nobel Prize winner Elie Wiesel, writes: "If in my lifetime I was to write only one book, this would be the one."[4] Comparisons, of course, always limp, but we are convinced that our book, perhaps, more than some scholarly treatises about Karl Rahner, demanded to be published. Robert A. Krieg, in his short book review in *Theological Studies*, stated: "Although Karl Rahner (1904-1984) held that the details of his life were unremarkable, these portraits help clarify key aspects of the Jesuit's thought and shed light on personal, cultural, and institutional factors that shaped his ideas and writings." And he ended his reflections with this assessment: "This book is a helpful resource for understanding Rahner's theology and its context."[5]

Karl Rahner did not make a great fuss about his person. Today's forms of autobiographical attention to self or self-absorption were foreign to him. Increasingly, younger generations of theologians and those "newcomers" to theology are as much interested in the person who stands behind such an imposing body of theological work as in the work itself. Karl Rahner, the person, "reveals" himself in the present book. He almost comes within the hand's reach. The person and the work of Karl Rahner do not allow themselves to be separated from each other, as the attentive reader of this book will recognize, just as the "pious Rahner" and the "scientific Rahner" cannot be seen as if two different persons. We invite you to experience Karl Rahner in such a way that you get to know him and above all are motivated to read him. In the last analysis it is about having one's own unique encounter with him. It's worth it.

Munich / Milwaukee, March 30, 2009,
Karl Rahner's 25th anniversary of death

Andreas R. Batlogg, SJ – Melvin E. Michalski

NOTES

1   Cf. Andreas R. Batlogg, Melvin E. Michalski (eds.), *Begegnungen mit Karl Rahner*. Weggefährten erinnern sich (Freiburg: Herder, 2006), 377 pages.

2   Cf. anecdote no. 7 of "Rahner –Worte und Geschichten," in: K. Rahner, *Sämtliche Werke*, vol. 25: Erneuerung des Ordenslebens. Zeugnis für Kirche und Welt. Bearbeitet von Andreas R. Batlogg (Freiburg, Herder: 2008), 42-46, 44 f.

3   Cf. Andreas R. Batlogg, "Karl Rahner's *Sämtliche Werke*: a new revised and edited collection of his works. A major project of lasting significance?" in: *Philosophy & Theology* 19, 1-2 (2007), 347-354.

4   Elie Wiesel, *Night* (New York: Hill and Wang, 2006) vii.

5   Cf. *TS* 68 (2007) 474 f.

INTRODUCTION

ANDREAS R. BATLOGG, SJ

WHAT DOES IT MEAN TODAY: TO ENCOUNTER KARL RAHNER?

This book contains interviews in which twenty-eight people reflect on their "Encounters with Karl Rahner." In addition, there are excerpts from a long letter which Hugo Rahner wrote to his younger brother, Karl, in 1955, as well as a report, spanning two decades of "Experiences in the Karl-Rahner-Archiv" in Innsbruck, by Roman A. Siebenrock, which was published in 2004. The subtitle of this book is "Remembrances of Rahner by those who knew him." The interviews contain remembrances, reflecting the encounters of both women and men who were involved in one way or another with Karl Rahner, one of the most important theologians of the twentieth century, at various stages in his life and work. Among them are Elisabeth Cremer, his sister, as well as Jesuit colleagues, assistants and co-workers, some who were close friends, some who even became lifelong companions, theologians, and also "very normal" people, who remained part of the life of this Jesuit theologian.

I

The interviews are divided into five categories: "Karl Rahner as scholarly researcher and editor;" "Karl Rahner's assistants and co-workers;" "Karl Rahner as a Jesuit colleague;" "Karl Rahner's personality;" and "Karl Rahner as teacher and author." These categories are not arbitrary, but the boundaries between them are fluid. Some could easily be placed in a different category with good reason. For example, some Jesuits were also fellow teachers or intimate co-workers with Karl Rahner (*Emerich Coreth, Albert Keller, Peter Knauer, Hans Bernhard Meyer, Otto Muck, Karl H. Neufeld, Hans Rotter, Raymund Schwager, Wolfgang Seibel, and Georg Sporschill*). Some Jesuits, his former students, later became his religious superiors (*Emerich Coreth, Alfons Klein, and Otto Muck*). Other Jesuits knew him only in the later years of his life or entered the Society of Jesus after 1984 (*Andreas R. Batlogg, Johannes Herzgsell*). Whoever came into contact with him professionally or experienced him as a speaker by attending his lectures and seminars never encountered only a famous professor, who lived apart in a scholarly ivory tower and who had developed an off-putting privileged demeanor (*Irmgard Bsteh, Klaus Egger, Józef Niewiadomski, Gerhard Ruis, and Paul Wess*). Elfriede Oeggl was Karl Rahner's last secretary in the capital of Tirol, and from the fall of 1981 she encountered him as her boss in that capacity, but in the two and a half years that she served him, she became more than that: she not only organized his appointment calendar, took dictation and typed his lectures and articles, but also became his helper in all things, from chauffeur to housekeeping duties. She became a discreet companion and developed a close relationship with him that some Jesuits came to envy. What would this increasingly aging, exhausted Karl Rahner – who could only, with great difficulty, say "no" to someone's appeal and therefore accepted the most unusual requests – do without her, her competency, as well as her charm, her thoughtfulness and her support?

Franz König and Karl Rahner met for the first time in 1937 at the Summer School, *Salzburger Hochschulwochen*, and from that time were always in contact with one another. In 1956, Franz König became Archbishop of Vienna and a few years later, when a Council was convoked, the cardinal immediately had recourse to Karl Rahner and invited him, not only to look at and comment on the preparatory schemata of the Curia officials but also to accompany him to Rome as his personal theological advisor – something that the Archbishop of Munich and Freising, Cardinal Julius Döpfner, would gladly have done. What had begun with some people as a helping hand, at a given moment, could develop into very intensive collaboration over the years and not everyone of these persons needed to have an official position as an assistant (*Karl Lehmann,*) or research assistant (*Karl H. Neufeld, Adolf Darlap, Albert Raffelt, Herbert Vorgrimler.*)

Elisabeth Cremer, his younger sister by five years, who outlived him by almost two full decades, was for Karl Rahner, on the one hand, "only the little sister with whom one could not carry on an intelligent conversation," and on the other hand, someone who experienced him her entire life long as someone who was greatly interested in family matters; who was not unconcerned about activities and events in her children's lives; who could be proud of them, even though he could not express that with great emotion, and who could be helpless and insecure in things involving everyday life. Some people came to know Karl Rahner because their relatives were in contact with him; because he became interested in their children; or he became their advisor or, as priest, became their friend and even went on short vacations with them (*Friedrich* and *Harald Röper*). Karl Rahner did not only have professional contact with his publisher at Herder (*Franz Johna*), but also became a part of his family life and went on excursions together with him. Thus, even though Karl Rahner did not seem prepared for such familiarity or even capable of that as "a Jesuit of the old school," close and trusting relationships occurred. For *Walter Strolz* the encounter with the Jesuit served as a wake-up call, because he found in it something like a "force penetrating to the depths of one's soul with existential relevance." Toward the end of the 1950's he completed a compilation of articles for Tyrolia publishing company (Innsbruck) "Mission and Grace" (*Sendung und Gnade*), which was translated into many European languages and played a significant role in furthering Karl Rahner's international reputation in the time immediately prior to the Council.

II

What does it mean today: to encounter Karl Rahner? To encounter him, to meet him, can be done in a variety of ways, as the texts collected here reveal. Some interviewees were contemporaries; they experienced him first hand, immediately, directly. Others did not have this privilege or this "advantage;" they were not able to know him personally, "live," as a professor, as a preacher, or as a priest. But they did come in contact with him indirectly; by means of his books, his articles, his meditations, perhaps by means of recordings or CD's. Such encounters were not less meaningful and for many people this form of encounter had a lasting impact: they were transformative, they made one reflective, they enabled "aha" experiences, and they took hold and stayed in one's being.

Some spent years of their formation or later their teaching years in the same college or university with Karl Rahner: they lived together with him in a Jesuit community, encountered him, who, in the mean-

time, had become a famous professor and conciliar theologian; as a
scholarly teacher, they worked for him, either officially as assistants or
voluntarily, selflessly, united with him out of respect or entirely out of
friendship. There were Jesuits from Austria, Germany, but also from
non-European countries and Jesuit provinces. There were students
from all parts of the world, assistants, secretaries – or also people,
who could experience Karl Rahner, Sunday after Sunday, as a preacher, in the Hospital Church or the Church of the Holy Spirit (*Heilig-
Geist-Kirche*), in the Jesuit Church or the Church of the Blessed Trinity (*Dreifaltigkeitskirche*), which is also the University Church. Some
could "look behind the curtains" and in doing so met a thin-skinned,
vulnerable, playful, helpless, aggressive, moody, or contradictory Karl
Rahner.

The interviews narrate – some more directly, others more indirectly – something of that which was not always so visible or widely
experienced. They uncover the "inside" of Karl Rahner, which appears,
carefully revealing itself, without catering to the need for exposure or
sensationalism, as is so customary today, in order to produce an artifi-
cial authenticity. So there emerges here, for example, a tearful and exhausted Karl Rahner, who flees from the telephone and would sit for
awhile (*"auf der Bude hocken"*) in the room of a young Jesuit student
(*"Scholastiker"*) simply to look out the window and to be inaccessible;
an impatient Karl Rahner, who attempts to grab the gear shifter of
his secretary's car and orders her to exceed the speed limit; a reflective
Karl Rahner, who does not have a ready answer prepared, when he, at
the spur of the moment, is asked to provide a wise theological commentary or pastoral advice; a priestly Karl Rahner, who asks a young
Jesuit colleague, while they are walking together under a bridge, following a long conversation, whether he should give him absolution; a
playful Karl Rahner, who, while at dinner at the home of his publisher
at Herder, has fun with the children and jots on a paper napkin and
challenges them with little puzzles; a Karl Rahner, possessed by the
need to write, who puts the pressure on himself, although at the same
time, he grumbles about stupid Herder (*"blöder Herder"*) – strong language that was not meant to be vicious or offensive, but could spontaneously be uttered if one pressured him – as though he would be able
to endure not being asked when the next manuscript would be ready;
a naïve Karl Rahner, who could reproach the publishing company, saying that it only sought to make money on him, as though he would

not have also benefited from the productivity of the publishing house
and had no idea that profitability had to be taken into account, apart
from the fact, that he liked to depend on the generosity of others; a
demanding Karl Rahner, who, not only to himself, but also to his closest female and male co-workers, granted no privileges and was quick
to decline the need for vacation or pauses; a despairing Karl Rahner,
who could feel persecuted by Rome and who consequently threatened
to cease writing and teaching.

All these are facets of a personality, which can mislead one into
crafting an image that is false by exaggerating only one aspect. They
are and remain facets of a personality, nothing less, but nothing more.
Karl Rahner ends up all too quickly – as does everyone who publishes
something – in the Procrustean bed of his interpreters. Then, depend-
ing on one's interest or pleasure, exaggeration or curtailment occurs,
until one is left with a variation of the question posited by the famous
television quiz show hosted by Robert Lemke: "Which Rahner would
you like to have?" From the published encounters, observations, experiences and impressions, can one actually draw an accurate, typical
image or profile of the theologian Karl Rahner, so as to avoid fashion-
ing or constructing one? That was not intended, nor is that something
that the interviews provide. They remain commentaries, sometimes
perhaps explanations, or even interpretations. But it must be granted
to Karl Rahner, that which remains true of every human being: he
remains, not only to himself, a mystery.

III

Whatever aspects, whatever talents, and whatever rough edges he always may have had – Karl Rahner exuded something particularly fascinating and it has endured more than 100 years, from his birth (March
5, 1904), to over twenty years after his death (March 30, 1984). No
matter what one's perspective in relation to Rahner, this fascination,
perhaps has to do with what Albert Görres (1918-1996), from his
perspective as a psychotherapist, suggested: "What is different about
the theology of Rahner as compared to other important theologians?
It appears to me, that he begins, in a unique sense, with the human
person. He strives, as deeply as he possibly can, to penetrate to the
very roots of his conversation partner, to understand why and what
a Marxist, an atheist, a natural scientist, a psychoanalyst, or whoever

the person is, thinks, how he thinks and feels and what he feels. He does not attempt to contradict or correct, but rather tries to follow this alien way of thinking and striving to where it has its kernel of truth, its existential core. From there, he tries to reach, in everyone, the openness to the whole, which every worldly human experience, and every individual subject, carries within. It is not so important to me, whether one calls that the transcendental-anthropological method. What is important to me is that after every conversation with Rahner, I could understand my own questions better: specialized, professional, religious, and better understand myself."[1] Görres first met Karl Rahner in 1942 when Görres was a medical student in Vienna. Later he became a Jesuit and continued to maintain a friendly relationship for decades with Rahner, along with his entire family, even after leaving the Society of Jesus.

Hans Küng did not always agree with Rahner, most especially on the question of infallibility which provoked a fierce battle between them. Küng introduced his article on this topic, a reply to Karl Rahner in 1971, in the January issue of *Stimmen der Zeit*, which began with almost hymn-like praise, more of a *captatio benevolentiae* for the harsh criticism which followed it: "I would give anything if I did not have to write this reply ... I view Karl Rahner, although I was never his student, as one of my teachers in theology. He has opened, with a strong hand, innumerable doors, the untiring pioneer, for our generation. He addressed questions which no Catholic theologian dared to address; rearranged what did not appear to him to be in its proper place; pointed the way to the future, beginning from the sublime heights of the doctrine of God and Christology all the way to completely practical questions of parish life and personal spirituality; boldly gave new answers, which were then branded as heretical. In all of this he mediated to us young theologians a joy in theology, he encouraged us to have the courage to think, allowed us to break out of the rigid and grey enclosure of Neo-scholasticism, and along with others of the sacred legion of Catholic theology today, (Hans Urs von Balthasar, Yves Congar, Otto Karrer, Henri de Lubac), he enticed several of us who wanted to go into parish ministry, to be open to the great adventure of Catholic theology at the time of the beginning of radical change and to become theologians."[2] Rahner responded to Küng's questions as early as the March issue of *Stimmen der Zeit* in terms of their content, although not without some restrained criticism for the editors, since the article of the Tübingen theologian was "almost twice as long as my own essay."[3] Certainly, Küng's passage praising Rahner did not stem purely from a political motive and reveals how much he had been influenced by him. What personal charisma ("*Ausstrahlung*,") as one says today, Rahner had on the young theologians, and not only on them.

IV

What does it mean today: to encounter Karl Rahner? In this book several aspects and sides of one and the same human being come to light. Perhaps, it would be more accurate to say that various aspects and sides of one and the same human being flash before our eyes, and taken together, they still do not provide a well-rounded portrait. Does one need that? Is such a thing even possible? These diverse perceptions show either close up or from a distance a *human being*, not only a professor, a priest, a Jesuit, and a theological author. Has not Karl Rahner, the human being, sometimes been forgotten by the fans of his theological works, as well as by his opponents? He almost disappears behind his work. What is a customary saying in the German speaking world (although in many ways strange and in any case problematic): "Scholars do not have a biography, but rather a bibliography" appears to be true for Karl Rahner and to fit him perfectly. Behind the more than 4000 entries in his bibliography – which, when one subtracts the numerous editions and translations, still remains at almost 1800 entries – there is a human being in the background, even if the observation by Johann Baptist Metz is accurate, that Karl Rahner "apart from his life-long work in theology, does not have a biography." His life is "not only one dedicated to theology, but one invested in it, a life spent in selfless service to it."[4] So much so, that he heard his teacher himself say, there is "actually nothing for me to say, that I have not written."[5] That all may well be true. Still there is always the human being, the Jesuit of flesh and blood, who stands behind it. Today, I feel differently and I read with more critical eyes a sober statement made by Rahner, who avoids any hint of emotion. It has impressed me greatly over a period of many years, because in it, in retrospect on the eight decades of his life – when asked what the founder of his Order, Ignatius of Loyola, means for his "personal life," Rahner responded, revealing either a flaw or a deficit: "I have not led a life; I worked, wrote, taught, sought to do my duty, to earn my bread. I tried in this banality of everyday life, to serve God, period."[6]

It may well be, that Karl Rahner's "life-long dogmatic ... of a decidedly antibiographical type"[7] was so. And, it cannot be denied that Karl Rahner belonged to a generation of Jesuits that was not accustomed to place something personal of a biographical nature in the foreground. That is why it is not coquettish or false, merely rhetorical modesty, when he perceives his life as average, uneventful or not really exciting. Only in his later years and at the persistence of others did Karl Rahner provide any information about what we today speak about as "biography sharing" and "faith sharing" ("Glaubenssozialisation"). One then might stumble on some late recollections of this highly honored and distinguished person. By nature he was withdrawn and introverted, yes, even somewhat melancholy by disposition. According to his own admission he had "a certain skeptical melancholia,"[8] which, according to the observations of others, was coupled "with an impetuous temperament."[9] Karl Rahner's religion teacher, Meinrad Vogelbacher (1879-1965), perceived him to be so "unsociable and so grumpy" that when he learned of Karl's intention to join the Society of Jesus, he judged him to be "not suitable."[10] This characterization, at any rate, impressed itself deeply in Karl Rahner's memory for the rest of his life. But he also had feelings, desires, dreams, ideas, which – even if unarticulated or in any case not recognized – flowed into his thinking and writing. Life and work remain inseparably united within Karl Rahner.

At the end of his life, Karl Rahner did not have the modern, urgent need for "revelations," "confessions," or the need to avail himself of details from his life-history. The modern, widely disseminated interest in indiscretion, in private statements, which do not belong in the public forum, but which allegedly allow the work of a great person to appear "more human," would have been repugnant to him. There is a very naïve side to Karl Rahner, a carefree attitude, which could, as some of his co-workers, or close Jesuit colleagues report, sometimes easily and quickly compromise him. The mere mention of "Rahner – Rinser," that now, as before, causes these feelings to surface, and, at least in the USA is still virulent, as I myself often experienced, is the reason why this topic is mentioned several times in this book. Karl H. Neufeld asserts in a retrospective in the second edition of his double biography that "the more famous both Rahner brothers became the more often people pressured them and sought from these relationships benefits of various kinds. To fend that off, in an acceptable way, was sometimes difficult, especially if someone felt entitled to this or that favor. Who protects one from such 'friends'"?[11]

Whoever was close to Karl Rahner, whoever belonged to his staff of co-workers, whoever encountered him or sought an encounter with him, would profit from that. It was a seal of approval to have been accepted as a colleague of Karl Rahner's and not because it was a statement about one's ability to drive or that one possessed other skills that one later recalled. Did some seek to benefit from such a close relationship? How "objective" are recollections and observations, which also say something about or refer to those being interviewed? Are what one remembers and what one chooses to reveal to be put into the category of "work relationship," or rather is it more appropriate to be categorized as something "private?" Where are the boundaries to be drawn? Is it meaningful or possible to draw them at all? Some Jesuits encountered Rahner in many different ways: as Jesuit colleague, as well as a faculty colleague, or as an assistant, officially (through the university) or appointed by the Order. It is impossible to make these distinctions with exactness. Being close to Rahner also brought with it, of course, knowledge of his weaknesses and his limitations, but it also revealed his strengths and his preferences. The editors of this book found that some passages of the recorded conversations had to be struck from the record or were formulated differently because when seen in print what was recorded seemed as if it would be perceived differently from what was said spontaneously, without having had one's guard up. This is especially true with material that arises from a free-flowing speech where one has first to get the conversation started and some of those interviewed were as yet unaware of the intention to publish the interviews. For understanding Rahner such corrections are irrelevant. It is indeed not the intention of these conversations to create some sort of Rahner-"Fioretti:" legends, stories and anecdotes, which belong to "oral history."

Naturally, it is amusing to learn how Elisabeth Cremer, nee Rahner, remembered her older brother. She remembered that already as a high school student he had his sacred times and on Sunday afternoons did not want to be disturbed, when at the last minute, he got to work on an essay that still needed to be written. It is touching to learn from Harald and Friedrich Röper, that their mother, who maintained a relationship for decades with Karl Rahner through letters as well as personal contact, whenever she and her sons went for a walk with Rahner, would stay some meters behind as Karl Rahner talked with her two boys – not only, so that these two would have an opportunity to have a conversation with him – but also in order to protect Karl Rahner from any possible ambiguity. Such remembrances and circumstances say something about the association with Karl Rahner.

That he, like every human being, had limits and weaknesses, cannot really surprise anyone. The issue is: what conclusions one reaches as a result of recognizing them and whether one then connects them, in an inadmissible way, to his work. Karl Rahner was also a workaholic. The editor-in-chief of Benziger Publishing, in July 1964, felt that he had to warn the young Karl Lehmann, whom the prominent conciliar theologian wanted to engage as an assistant for his work as occupant of the Romano Guardini chair in Munich. He told him: "He will use you completely. You must know that already today when you go. He has burnt out many."[12] Four years after that, Lehmann, later a Bishop and Chairman of the German Bishops' Conference – carrying an appointment to be Professor of Dogmatic Theology at the University of Mainz in his possession – endured an adventurous trip to Rome in the height of the summer, that he characterized as "the trip from hell."[13] Karl Rahner, during a (working) vacation on the Yugoslavian Adriatic coast, ordered a quick trip be made to the Jesuit curia for a conversation with the Superior General of the Society of Jesus, Pedro Arrupe, SJ, (1907-1991), on the issue of "*Humanae vitae.*" The following morning Karl Lehmann and Roman Bleistein, SJ (1928-2000), who had never before been to Rome, were ordered to immediately begin the return trip.

The aim of this book is not to obtain new factual knowledge about the theology of Karl Rahner. Individual observations, which are more of a personal nature and rest on personal judgments, cannot accomplish that. The events and encounters recalled here bring to the fore Karl Rahner, the human being, who stands behind an imposing work of almost incalculable worth. This human being could be impatient, not only at meals, as many are able to verify, or when riding in the car; but also at other times. He could be vulnerable, tired and exhausted, restless and indefatigable, depressed … The interviews have more to do with such observations and aspects than with new or even sensational pieces of material. Whoever was asked – often about the same events and issues – had his or her own remembrances. These memories are recorded here to reveal the more human and endearing aspect of Karl Rahner. Is he, therefore, to be seen as childish because he could take pleasure in childlike things? The "great" Rahner appears in these pages at times as very small, sensitive, vulnerable – human.

V

On the 10th anniversary of Karl Rahner's death (1994), Karl Lehmann said: "There is no bizarre Rahner cult that concerns itself more with his person than with his work, although many contemporaries could still throw light upon the life and the work of this selfless and rather hidden hard-working Jesuit."[14] This, too, this book does not claim to do; the individual encounters and observations presented here should lead one to the writings of Karl Rahner, awaken an interest in his work and not lead to the creation of an uncritical personality cult. Lehmann's reference to the charisma of the Jesuit is noteworthy: "Karl Rahner has not become a mummy, who can only be viewed from the distant perspective of history, to be dissected in all different ways. Also, the present, young generation, who could hardly have come to know the human, personal side of Karl Rahner can be energized and identify with his concerns. For that to occur, they must naturally not shy away from the effort required for conceptual thinking and strict reasoning."[15]

The fact is that there has been a continuous, ongoing interest in the theology of Karl Rahner and not only in the German-speaking world, as a look at the bibliography of secondary literature shows.[16] Karl Rahner did not build a "community of kindred spirits, an intimate group of supporters: He did not even found a theological school, in the traditional sense, around himself."[17] He wanted to serve theology and the Church, and he did not focus on establishing his own theology, even when it must be recognized that much of what today passes for the common heritage of theology – one thinks, for example, of the understanding of grace as "God's self-communication" – comes from Karl Rahner, a fact that his critics may not always clearly see. Again and again students were surprised, for example, when they found at their oral exams Rahner tested them on their factual knowledge for which they needed to know "Denzinger" or other compendiums of Church documents. Oral exams as occasions for a theological chat were not his style.

The "industry" of Rahner-interpretations has long been controversial and has not come to an end by far. Do these authors, at any
time, think sometimes also about the one who gave them their name?
The commemorative year, 2004, revealed that some intellectuals are
working against the spirit of Karl Rahner and probably generations of
scholars still will work like crazy in such a way that there will be misunderstandings and intractable prejudices will be passed on – as well as
assertions that simply and shockingly miss the point of the text. That
differences of opinion exist about Karl Rahner should no longer surprise anyone. These opinions vary greatly among intellectuals: while
some want to see in Karl Rahner a kind of "Doctor of the Church
for modern times"[18] ("*Kirchenlehrer der Moderne*") and attest to his
unconditional loyalty to and his love for the Church, others deny this
vehemently. The year 2004 was a graphic example of that. There were
completely positive, sometimes, almost hymn-like acknowledgements
and thanks for a gigantic, theological life-long achievement. Cardinal
Joseph Ratzinger himself, as Prefect of the Congregation for the Doctrine of the Faith (CDF), said in an interview: "One must understand
Rahner in the fullness of his will and thought and purely and simply
recognize that it was his will not to violate the faith of the Church …
his will to remain within the doctrine of the Church – to interpret the
faith of the Church and not to alter it or turn it around – is undisput-
ed."[19] There were also destructive criticisms, polemics and suspicions
that resulted in absurd and strange accusations that parts of Rahner's
theology are heretical and "Rome" must once more thoroughly concern itself with the work of the Jesuit theologian.[20] Karl Rahner was
seen as a pioneer for the post-conciliar decline of the Church and
gravedigger of Neo-scholasticism, whose unstoppable collapse after
the Council is attributed to him as its source. Such allegations which
contained specific false statements and misinformation violated every
academic standard with crude assertions which turned a blind eye to
what is to be found in the text.[21] A recent, and from my perspective
tragic example, is the biting and insulting presentation of Karl Rahner
in a biography of Ignatius by an historian, who in less than five pages,
attempts a scholarly, but dishonest account.[22]

Even "those who criticize or reject him," writes Johann Baptist Metz,
"still draw on his insights, on his acute as well as gentle perceptions in
the world of life and faith. And those who ignore him ignore much
more than one theological opinion among others. Karl Rahner has re-

newed the face of theology. Nothing is any longer the way it was prior to him."[23] Are the sharp critics of the theology of Karl Rahner, if they want to be fair, unaware of that? It is necessary to move from Rahner jargon to Karl Rahner himself. It is not enough to know a lot about Karl Rahner's life or to have studied his theology conscientiously. It is not a matter of parroting him, repeating a Rahner catchword for every theological problem and casting it into the academic arena and into databanks, which insinuate that one has a complete understanding of Karl Rahner.

It comes down to getting to know the life source of his kind of theology, to discover it, and to make it fruitful for oneself and one's work, to think with Karl Rahner and beyond Karl Rahner – not as an intellectual exercise, gazing into a crystal ball, but in order to live Church today. To do that it takes, certainly, theology and theological discourses – *"Quaestiones Disputatae"* – and not only McKinsey strategies. Karl Rahner's *Strukturwandel der Kirche als Aufgabe und Chance,* (1972) ("The Shape of the Church to Come") is not, by far, for all its drama, a recognized alternative to the complacent Church – which, at least in Germany – without doubt must trim down. (Would it do so freely, if she were not compelled?) "It is profitable," according to Karl Lehmann, "to listen to Karl Rahner as an independent observer of our situation, who is at once an unerring and sober diagnostician and pastor, who radiates much courage and confidence in an often miserable situation. Whoever goes to school with Karl Rahner does not stop at self pity, self contemplation and resignation, but rather remains open to be grasped, again and again, by mission and grace ('Sendung und Gnade')."[24]

Karl Rahner, as theologian, was not only there for men and women theologians. His work is also capable of making connections today (*"anschlussfähig"*). He was also a bridge builder: he thought and worked in a way which today would be called interdisciplinary. Such a theology does not emerge without a context, and it is not insignificant or simply a biographical footnote that he did theology as a Jesuit, within the context and spirit of the *Spiritual Exercises.* Hence, it is not an exaggeration to say: "New generations, who naturally must overcome a certain hesitation to begin, will find here much that is valuable, which in our time was lost or disfigured. Karl Rahner is a person for the day after tomorrow."[25]

VI

Herbert Vorgrimler, probably the person who was closest to Karl Rahner and knew him the best, who over decades (without having the position as an assistant) worked selflessly with Karl Rahner, presented his teacher with a *Festschrift* in 1979, whose title and subtitle express something important: *Wagnis Theologie. Erfahrungen mit der Theologie Karl Rahners* ("'Venture' Theology. Experiences with the Theology of Karl Rahner"). Students and co-workers of Karl Rahner contributed to this *Festschrift*; their knowledge as female and male theologians cannot be separated from their personal encounters, impressions, and experiences. Vorgrimler also emphasized this, in a sophisticated way, in his letter of introduction: "It is correct, that you did not raise technical ability or knowledge to a goal in itself; it is also correct that you did not want to form a 'school.' Anyone who follows you along the way of mystagogy can be your student; however, he must have his own experience of God and practice his own concrete form of love."[26]

It is this "art of being a midwife of questions," which, according to Metz, made him a graced maieutic, who therein "cannot successfully be imitated."[27] That must have been something others sensed when they listened to him: in courses and seminars, in homilies, in lectures, perhaps also in the counseling room, into which the great scholar did not find it beneath him to go. There are private or discreet activities that Karl Rahner did not speak about publicly because they were an essential aspect of being a priest or a religious, and had to do with discretion and privacy. There were also matters that can fade into oblivion and be lost in a time of autobiographical craving. Can one say anything more wonderful about a teacher of theology than that he had become "the father of my faith"?[28] Karl Rahner, once observed, a little bitterly, that he did not have "disciples." "Good, but he must allow himself to be told today by me that he became much more than a teacher of theology for us."[29] Why? "There was someone who spoke of God and grace, of salvation, and of the sacraments, not only in the language of subtle dogmatic instruction and argumentation, but in language pointing to and demonstrating, the experience of faith. Here not only was a preconceived faith taught and instructed, but also faith for daily life awakened."[30]

VII

One of the most quoted sentences of Karl Rahner, often taken out of context, which is reduced to a pious aphorism and often misrepresented – and thereby exploited and trivialized and then passed on, comes from the article "*Frömmigkeit früher und heute*" 1966: "Only in order to make it clear what is meant here, and with the understanding that the concept of 'mysticism' is a loaded one, (rightly understood it is not the opposite of belief in the Holy Pneuma but rather identical with it), it might be asserted that: the devout Christian of the future will either be a 'mystic,' one who has 'experienced' something, or he will cease to be anything at all. For devout Christian living as practiced in the future will no longer be sustained and aided by the unanimous, manifest and public convictions and religious customs of all, which summon each one from the outset to a personal experience and a personal decision. Because of this, the Religious education which has been practiced can only provide a very secondary kind of formation or preparation for the institutional element in the religion of the future."[31] The pious person of tomorrow ("*Der Fromme von morgen*"), who becomes characterized in some vague way as "a mystic," is "one, who has experienced something." Whoever encounters Karl Rahner, his theology, his struggles, his person, will find someone with whom to make his or her own encounters.

That is precisely the aim of this book: to bring about an encounter with Karl Rahner himself, to read him, to consider him and from that also, perhaps to learn something for one's own life as a Christian. The interviews are meant, at the same time, to lead to Karl Rahner himself, through stirring up interest, to show that behind the intellectual and prolific writer a human being was concealed, whose work will continue to have an impact for a long time. It remains a phenomenon: this universally accepted as difficult to read dogmatic theologian's writings have long since become a theological and surprisingly, at the same time, a spiritual classic. Much of the best of this long seller, in the meantime belongs, as already stated, to the common heritage of the Church.[32] The meditations, *Worte ins Schweigen*, 1938, (*Encounters with Silence*), or the Lenten homilies in the lean year, 1946, first published in 1949, with many editions, *On the Need and the Blessing of Prayer*, were "pious things," but for Karl Rahner "at the very least were just as important as the actual theological works," because therein "at least as much theol-

ogy, intellectual, laboriously assimilated theology, is invested in it."[33]
These have become for innumerable people a help for their faith and
their life. His *Foundations of Christian Faith* (1976) made generations
of questioners and seekers curious about Christianity.

There is something full of vigor in Karl Rahner's work, something
that endures in a time which is lacking in theological depth, which is
more interested in quick advice and which has produced a market for
wellness-spirituality, which comes with a superficial theological foundation. In contrast to superficial spiritual "prescriptions," which promise help for one's life, which they are not truly and (effectively) able to
provide, one is reminded once again of the words of Albert Görres:
"For innumerable exhausted minds and wounded hearts, for legions
of those injured by the Church and those disappointed in God, Karl
Rahner found words of help which opened for them the blocked access to a lost God, to his creation filled with atrocities, to a bloody
history and to his tormenting gospel, to his burdensome Church, and
once again, made it loving. He consoled the mourning, instructed the
ignorant, reprimanded the wayward, and advised those in doubt. He
reconciled those who were troubled and in all that he reached the pin-
nacle of what psychotherapy after Freud can on the whole achieve: reconciliation with a seemingly intolerable reality, consent to everything
which is worthy of consent; resistance against all, which cannot be
accepted ... So is Karl Rahner one of the most salutary psychothera-
pists for all those people who turn away from the unbearable reality of
their lives because he is an exceptional teacher with total dedication to
a reality capable of being healed."[34]

The encounters with Karl Rahner collected here, tell us that. Perhaps they help a little to overcome what Karl Lehmann diagnosed
as the "initial fear to approach him," which may develop when people
think of the theology of Karl Rahner. Shortly before Christmas in
1968 Hugo Rahner was released by death from years of suffering with
Parkinson's disease. Hugo and Karl were united not only through
theological interests and the usual amusing stories which were told
about them, but also in their insufficiently appreciated effectiveness.
Karl Rahner concluded his eulogy for his brother Hugo with a sentence that could also be applied to his own life: "to act important and
to take himself to be particularly important, that he could not do. But
behind his life, there was something."[35]

NOTES

1 Albert, Görres, Wer ist Karl Rahner für mich? – Antwort eines Psychotherapeuten, in: Paul Imhof, Hubert Biallowons (eds.), *Karl Rahner – Bilder eines Lebens* (Freiburg: Herder, 1985) 78-80, 80.

2 Hans Küng, Im Interesse der Sache. Antwort an Karl Rahner, in: *Stimmen der Zeit* 187 (1971) 43-64, 43. The second part is a continuation (therefore with the same title) of the issue appearing the following month: *Stimmen der Zeit* 187 (1971) 105-122. Küng reacted to the critical comments in the December issue: Karl Rahner, Kritik an Hans Küng. Zur Frage der Unfehlbarkeit theologischer Sätze, in: *Stimmen der Zeit* 186 (1970) 361-377.

3 Karl Rahner, Replik. Bemerkungen zu: Hans Küng, Im Interesse der Sache, in: *Stimmen der Zeit* 186 (1971) 145-160; cf. Andreas R. Batlogg, Karl Rahner als Autor der "Stimmen der Zeit," in: *Stimmen der Zeit*, Spezial 1-2004, 16-30, 27.

4 Johann Baptist Metz, Karl Rahner – ein theologisches Leben. Theologie als mystische Biographie eines Christenmenschen heute, in: *Stimmen der Zeit* 192 (1975) 305-316, 315.

5 Ibid.

6 K. Rahner, *Bekenntnisse. Rückblick auf 80 Jahre*, edited by Georg Sporschill (Vienna: Herold,1 984)5 8. Now in: ibid., *Sämtliche Werke*, vol. 25: *Erneuerung des Ordensleben. Zeugnis für Kirche und Welt*. Bearbeitet von Andreas R . Batlogg (Freiburg: Herder, 2008) 84.

7 Johann Baptist Metz, Karl Rahner – ein theologisches Leben, 309.

8 K. Rahner, Der Werdegang eines Theologen, in: ibid., *Im Gespräch*, vol. 2, edited by Paul Imhof, Hubert Biallowons (Munich: Kösel, 1983) 146-153, 147. – English translation: ibid., On Becoming a Theologian, in: *Karl Rahner In Dialogue*. Conversations and Interviews, 1965-1982. Translation edited by Harvey D. Egan (New York: Crossroad, 1986) 253-258, 254.

9 Herbert Vorgrimler, *Karl Rahner verstehen*. Eine Einführung in sein Leben und Denken (Freiburg: Herder, 2nd edition, 1988) 54.

10 K. Rahner, *Erinnerungen im Gespräch mit Meinold Krauss* (Freiburg: Herder, 1984) 24. Now in: ibid., *Sämtliche Werke*, vol. 25, 94.

11 Karl H. Neufeld, *Die Brüder Rahner. Eine Biographie* (Freiburg: Herder, 2nd edition 2004) 414.

12 Quoted from Daniel Deckers, *Der Kardinal. Karl Lehmann. Eine Biographie* (Munich: Pattloch, 2002) 127.

13 Cf. ibid., 145-150.

14 Karl Lehmann, Karl Rahner zum Gedächtnis. Neunzigster Geburtstag – Zehnter Todestag, in: *Stimmen der Zeit* 212 (1994) 147-150, 148. One

could accuse the former assistant of Karl Rahner and Co-editor of the Complete Works (*Sämtliche Werke*) of Karl Rahner of being partisan, but he spoke here as the Chairman of the German Bishops' Conference.

15   Ibid.

16   Cf. www.ub.uni-freiburg.de/referate/04/rahner/rahnerli.htm

17   Johann Baptist Metz, *Den Glauben lernen und lehren*. Dank an Karl Rahner (Munich: Kösel, 1984) 26.

18   Günther Wassilowsky, Kirchenlehrer der Moderne: Ekklesiologie, in: Andreas R. Batlogg, Paul Rulands, Walter Schmolly, Roman A. Siebenrock, ibid., Arno Zahlauer, *Der Denkweg Karl Rahners*. Quellen – Entwicklungen – Perspektiven (Mainz: Grünewald, 2nd edition 2004) 223-241.

19   Cf. The Interview with Radio Stephansdom/Wien (April 4, 2004), documented in: www.ub.uni-freiburg.de/referate/04/rahner/rahnerlineu.htm (= the catalogue of secondary literature for Karl Rahner).

20   Cf. e.g., David Berger, Editorial: 100. Geburtstag und 20. Todestag Karl Rahners, in: *Theologisches* 34 (2004) 186-190; cf. Herbert Vorgrimler, Zur bleibenden Akualität Karl Rahners, in: *Theologische Revue* 100 (2004) 91-100, esp. 91; ibid., *Karl Rahner*. Gotteserfahrung in Leben und Denken (Darmstadt, Primus, 2004) 15 ("Bösartige Polemik").

21   *Karl Rahner*, Kritische Annäherungen, edited by David Berger (Siegburg: Schmitt, 2004); earlier: ibid., Karl Rahner. Ketzer oder Kirchenleher? Zugleich eine Antwort an die neueren Rahnerapologeten, in: *Theologisches* 32 (2002) 287-327.

22   Cf. Helmut Feld, *Ignatius von Loyola*. Gründer eines Jesuitenordens (Köln: Böhlau, 2006) 327-331 ("Karl Rahner").

23   Johann Baptist Metz, Den Glauben lehren und lernen, 13.

24   Karl Lehmann, Karl Rahner zum Gedächtnis, 149.

25   Ibid.

26   Herbert Vorgrimler, Ein Brief zur Einführung, in: *Wagnis Theologie*. Erfahrungen mit der Theologie Karl Rahners, edited by Herbert Vorgrimler (Freiburg: Herder, 1979) 11-17, 16.

27   Johann Baptist Metz, Karl Rahner – ein theologisches Leben, 312.

28   Ibid., Den Glauben lernen und lehren, 24.

29   Ibid., 26.

30   Ibid., 15.

31   K. Rahner, Frömmigkeit früher und heute, in: ibid., *Schriften zur Theologie*, vol. 7 (Einsiedeln: Benziger, 1966) 11-31, 22 f. – Now in: ibid.,

Sämtliche Werke, vol. 23: Glaube im Alltag. Schriften zur Spiritualität und zum christlichen Lebensvollzug. Bearbeitet von Albert Raffelt (Freiburg: Herder, 2006) 31-46, 39 f. – See ibid., Christian Living Formerly And Today, in: ibid., *Theological Investigations*, vol. 7, translated by David Bourke (London: Darton, Longman & Todd, 1971), 3-24, 15.

32   Cf. Andreas R. Batlogg, Von Karl Rahner lernen, in: *Stimmen der Zeit*, 222 (2004) 145-146; Nikolaus Klein, Karl Rahner (1904-1984), in: *Orientierung* (2004) 37-39; Magnus Striet, Ein bleibendes Vermächtnis. Was die Theologie heute von Karl Rahner lernen kann, in: *Herder Korrespondenz* 58 (2004) 559-564; Albert Raffelt, Nach wie vor starke Resonanz. Ein Rückblick auf das "Rahnerjahr" 2004, in: ibid., 564-568; Leo J. O'Donovan, Losing Oneself and Finding God, Karl Rahner (1904-1984), in: *America* 191 (2004) Nr. 14, 12-15; Bernhard Nitsche, Bilanz – Umbrüche – Desiderate. Rahner-Forschungsbericht 1995-2004/05, in: *Theologische Quartalschrift* 185 (2005) 303-319 and 186 (2006) 50-65.

33   Gnade als Mitte menschlicher Existenz. Ein Gespräch mit und über Karl Rahner aus Anlass seines 70. Geburtstages, in: *Herder Korrespondenz* 28 (1974) 77-92, 81. – Now in: K. Rahner, *Sämtliche Werke*, vol. 25, 10; similarly in: [K. Rahner], Lebenslauf, in: W. Ernst Böhm (ed.), *Forscher und Gelehrter* (Stuttgart: Battenberg, 1966) 21; as well as in: Ein Brief von P. Karl Rahner, in: Klaus P. Fischer, *Der Mensch als Geheimnis*. Die Anthropologie Karl Rahners (Freiburg: Herder, 2nd edition 1974) 400-410, 403.

34   Albert Görres, Wer ist Karl Rahner für mich – Antwort eines Psychotherapeuten, 80.

35   Karl Rahner, Ein spielender Mensch. Gedenkwort für Hugo Rahner, in: ibid., *Chancen des Glaubens*. Fragmente einer modernen Spiritualität (Freiburg: Herder, 1971) 150-152, 152. – Now in: ibid., *Sämtliche Werke*, vol. 25, 161f., 162.

PART ONE

KARL RAHNER AS SCHOLARLY
RESEARCHER AND EDITOR

I

THIS LANGUAGE DIRECTS US TO INSIGHT

A CONVERSATION WITH JOHANNES HERZGSELL, SJ, MUNICH

Johannes Herzgsell, SJ, Dr. phil., born in 1955, a Jesuit since 1979, is a Lecturer in the Philosophy of Religion and the Foundation of Systematic Theology at the Jesuit Hochschule für Philosophie in Munich.

Where did you meet Karl Rahner for the first time?

I first met Karl Rahner when I was a novice living in Berchmans College. At that time Fr. Rahner also lived here in quarters above the Hochschule. I was doing my practicum in a hospital in Munich and Karl Rahner came on the weekend to have supper with our group. I got to see him there occasionally. He was rather reserved and did not speak very much at the table. He listened, and he seemed at ease, but he seldom said anything. I remember that once he admired a cigarette lighter that belonged to a scholastic and took it in his hand, and tried it out. Fr. Rahner had smoked for many years and wanted to know how the lighter functioned. He seemed much taken by the lighter, almost as if in awe: he could be amused like a child.

In your doctoral dissertation you discussed Karl Rahner's work intensively, emphasizing especially the concept of *memoria*. Would you elaborate on this?

My doctoral dissertation examined Karl Rahner's concept of Transcendence.[1] He postulates that transcendence always resides in knowing and willing or, respectively in freedom, and also in memory – "*memoria.*" This triad of understanding, willing and memory is also found in Augustine and many others in the Middle Ages. It struck me, that in the places where Rahner speaks of transcendence, memory does not play a role; he mentions only understanding and the ability to know. In *Foundations of Christian Faith*, and maybe in a few other places, he refers only once, and very briefly, at the end of the section on Christology, to Plato and Augustine's teaching on *memoria*.[2] With Augustine, he emphasizes that there is such a thing as an historical sense that enables us to anticipate salvation in history, and an understanding of the Savior, of Jesus Christ, as an historical figure.[3] Later in my studies, I found out, as he sometimes excitedly states, that this is one of the few places that he knows of where the idea of *memoria* appears as that historical sense and with it, in the end, the meaning which Jesus Christ has in the history of humanity.

You have written that Fr. Rahner in *Spirit in the World* and in *Hearer of the Word* switched very quickly from "*ens commune*" to infinite being. Is that a problem?

I determined that, for him, the concept "*ens commune*" stands for finite being, and that all ordinary being is finite and from that premise he proceeds, almost as if it were self-explanatory, to infinite being. For many that is too big a jump. They might agree that one can grasp being (whatever is) as the embodiment of Being, but then to proceed, without further ado to infinite being and then immediately to God, that I believe must be done with more nuance.

The problem for him in *Hearer of the Word* was apparently, to where does transcendence tend? What was relatively unproblematic for him was the issue that persons in their knowing and their willing somehow surpass their finitude. But then we have the question: to what does transcendence tend? Here he distances himself from Heidegger. Transcendence does not tend toward nothingness, but toward Being. For today's reader the act of transcendence is itself a problem – namely, that the human person somehow tends beyond the finite.

In your dissertation you have a chapter in which you examine the development of Fr. Rahner's spiritual-theological ideas and you do not do this exclusively from an academic perspective. Why is that so?[4]

I believe that Rahner does theology starting from a spiritual experience: that is what always motivated me to concern myself with his thought. I received this impression from everything that I had read by him and this was confirmed when I got to know him personally – in lectures and by personal encounters. It is more than supposition on my part; Karl Rahner theologizes truly out of experience.

You mentioned that Fr. Rahner was not very communicative. I assume that despite that his presence in the Berchmans College was appreciated?

That's completely true. Once, by accident, I came upon him sitting in a circle of mostly young colleagues – it was in the refectory – and it was apparent that he felt at home with these young Jesuits and they were happy that he was among them and that he enjoyed being there. He sat with his arms outstretched, behind his head, at the table and when I came into the room he looked at me and thought: I don't know him at all. He became interested in me immediately. He was open, in fact, he was very open. That's the impression he made on me – even then when – let me put it this way – he found it difficult to simply speak about everyday things. He was much too complex a thinker, so what we call "small talk" did not come easily to him.

Did he live long at the Berchmans College?

When he got the call to the Romano Guardini chair (1964), he belonged to the Jesuit community of writers in the Veterinärstrasse and later in the Zuccalistrasse and then later he went to Münster as a Professor. When he was no longer teaching he felt lonely in the writer's house in Nymphenburg and because there were more Jesuits in residence at the Berchmans College he came here. After a few years he moved to Innsbruck.[5]

Did he say why he wanted to change to another community?

Indirectly, I took it to mean that he was drawn back home. He had taught for many years in Innsbruck; that's where he began his theological career, and he apparently felt more at home there than in Munich. Perhaps, he also was more comfortable with his colleagues there. In the refectory here, he always ate at the same place for lunch and it seemed to him that it took too long. After half an hour he wanted to take his midday rest or continue to work. In his impatience he would begin to rock back and forth in his chair and after he moved out I noticed a spot on the wall where the back of his head always rubbed up against it. His impatience was well-known and these idiosyncrasies belong even to those who are great.

What do you miss most about Karl Rahner, both personally and theologically?

What I miss theologically, is his loyalty. I always understood that Fr. Rahner truly sought to be completely loyal in relationship to the magisterium. I am amazed at how he attempted to "save" magisterial teaching and to translate it, in any event to hold fast to it, and not simply to bypass Church teaching or ignore it. On the other hand, he sought, in the same way, to be up to date in his thinking. I always had the impression that it was a fundamental concern of his to be able to speak to the contemporary person, to meet the reader where he was at that moment in time with his own problems, within the context of his own horizon. That is also his fundamental concern in theology and the subject of his many theological essays leading up to his *Foundations of Christian Faith*. He tries to have theology make sense to the people of today. I miss such theologians: teachers, who can sustain the tension between an awareness and appreciation for the tradition and a concern and an ability to bring the deposit of faith into the situation of the world today.

Did you ever encounter a humorous side to Fr. Rahner or any special human characteristics?

I did not really have any direct experience of that. Naturally he laughed. He could, I believe, be self-deprecating, but I did not experience that directly. I did see a filmed interview with him recently on Austrian television. It was about an hour long and the reporter asked him at the end something like: "Fr. Rahner, what do you think people will say of you after you have died?" He replied: "What people will say after I am gone is totally meaningless. Completely without importance, one way or the other." I find that to be humorous. And this reaction was typical of him. He was not self-absorbed.

Fr. Grom, a religious psychologist in the community,[6] has a very easy
going personality without being superficial. He is simply an optimist
and finds it easy to be among people. He told me this story about Fr.
Rahner. He said that Fr. Rahner said to him: "My dear Bernhard, I
envy you your easy going personality. You are so easy to be with, so optimistic, and I have such a dour personality." I believe that says something about Rahner. It was something that he had observed about
himself, that he could be rather serious about himself with a tendency
to grumble. He could be self-deprecating.

**What do we owe Fr. Rahner? Why do you think that it's worth-
while to concern ourselves with him?**

I find that reflecting on his understanding of what it means to be human and his relationship to the world is very worthwhile. He basically
has a positive attitude towards the world and is open to modernity.
He never thought of theology as something that took place only in the
stillness of one's room, far away from the world. For him, theology had
to take into account what was happening in the world and it meant
having an active engagement with the world. That does not mean that
it should be uncritical. There are essays in which he writes about the
world as God's creation and that God reveals himself in the world.[7]
In Freiburg, at his last public lecture, around his eightieth birthday,
he addressed this very topic.[8] He stated that he regretted that he, as a
theologian, did not interact more with other scholars and that he knew
too little of the world of art. He went on to say that this was important
in order to understand God better, because God was to be found in
the world. I believe, in this regard, he thought and lived out of a very
Ignatian perspective: that God lets himself be found in the world.
    He also always emphasized that the human person realized his re-
lation to God in everyday actions.[9] A colleague told me that Rahner
once said that a nurse who does her duty every day tending to the sick
accomplishes the work of manifesting truly the love of God and neighbor. God can be met in all our daily actions in the world.[10]

**The transcendental orientation of the human person towards the
holy mystery also has to do with Fr. Rahner's strong emphasis on
the unity of the love of neighbor and the love of God. You address
that in your dissertation.[11] Why?**

Some have criticized Karl Rahner, raising the objection that in his early great philosophical works, *Spirit in the World* and *Hearer of the Word*, he thought too much about the subject before God and neglected the interpersonal dimension: the concrete human "you." I believe that there is something to this; I also think that Rahner was capable of learning and that in his later writings he made up for that. In *Foundations of Christian Faith* he begins, in fact, with the individual subject that transcends himself in his movement towards the absolute.[12] But then there are some passages where he clearly points to the relationship among persons. He emphasized the unity of love of neighbor and the love of God more clearly in his later works than in those in his early period.

Early in the 1980's we invited Karl Rahner to the novitiate in Nürnberg in order to get to know this famous Jesuit colleague and he accepted our invitation gladly. He felt at home in this circle of younger Jesuits. He took a second chair in the community room and propped his legs up on it. He actually was lying down more than sitting. We asked him a few questions that we had prepared in advance. It seemed to me at that time that his answers were almost word for word what he had already published somewhere. His thought processes were so ingrained in him that he could recall them at any time and so there was practically no difference between his spontaneous responses, his lectures and what he had written.

As to Karl Rahner's language: he dictated and composed long sentences with "if" and "to a certain degree." Everything was carefully, precisely and clearly formulated. His *Foundations of Christian Faith* was dictated. When someone has such command of the language does he deserve admiration because of that?

I believe that one must really read one's way into Karl Rahner. He does not speak in a way that is easily accessible and understandable. Many have said that he is too complicated and difficult. I have heard this many times. Many have also said that they never found a way to connect with him, but when one first reads one's way into Rahner then, with time, it becomes clear as to how he thinks and why he thinks that way. I believe that he could not express himself in any other way, because that was how he really thought. Thus, some assert it is authentic and rings true. He knows the tradition; he was totally at home with it and had to articulate it in that way. I share your impressions completely. I believe that one must work to learn his language which is idiosyncratic. That is indisputable! But this language leads to insight. I never had the impression that he spoke elegantly just for the sake of eloquence, but rather it was always to address the matter at hand. He always focused on the issue and the complexity of the language mirrored the complexity of the issues he was dealing with. It was a matter of becoming accustomed to the language, and then the matter at hand became clear.

By way of conclusion are there any recollections of the "human side" of Rahner?

There was an interview in which he killed two birds with one stone, so to speak. To a question put to him he answered – to paraphrase: "Well, you should really ask Hans Urs von Balthasar. He has read a lot more about that than I." Then he proceeded to answer the question. I found that to be very revealing – very human. On the one hand he exhibited humility by admitting that Balthasar had a better grasp of the issue than he, as Balthasar had read more about it, but on the other hand, by then going on to respond at length he appeared to inject a note of irony into his praise. But he meant it all to be taken seriously and that fits with his ability to speak humorously about himself. He did not take himself too seriously and was not vain.

NOTES

1   Cf. Johannes Herzgsell, *Dynamik des Geistes*. Ein Beitrag zum anthropologischen Transzendenzbegriff von Karl Rahner (Innsbruck: Tyrolia, 2000).

2   Cf. K. Rahner, *Foundations of Christian Faith*. An Introduction to the Idea of Christianity (1976) (New York: Seabury Press, 1978) 318 f.: "But if we recall Plato's teaching about *anamnesis* or Augustine's teaching about *memoria*, which we cannot go into here ..."

3   Ibid., 319-320: "We can only give here brief indications of what this theory of memory is about. The main point is that memory involves most specifically the anticipation of the absolute savior in terms of searching and watching in history. It is a formal anticipation, not anticipating the specifics of history, but rather an awareness of our historical reality, which allows us to remain open to the experience."

4 Cf. Johannes Herzgsell, *Dynamik des Geistes*, chapter 3: Die spirituell-theologische Gedankenentwicklung: Der Mensch als Wesen der geistlich erfahrbaren Transzendenz,": ibid., 256-339.

5 For about ten years Karl Rahner belonged to the so-called "writer's community." He moved December 1963 to Munich holding onto his residence there during the years he was Professor in Münster (1967-1971). In 1973 he moved to the Berchmans College, not far from the English Gardens. In the fall of 1981 he moved to Innsbruck. Cf. Andreas R. Batlogg, Karl Rahner als Autor der "Stimmen der Zeit," in: *Stimmen der Zeit* spezial, 1-2004, 16-30; Karl H. Neufeld, *Die Brüder Rahner*. Eine Biographie (Freiburg: Herder, 2nd edition 2004) 370.

6 Bernhard Grom, SJ, born in 1936, Professor for Psychology of Religion and Catechetics, staff member of *Stimmen der Zeit*.

7 Cf. K. Rahner, *Everyday faith* (New York: Herder and Herder, 1968); ibid., *Everyday things* (London: Sheed and Ward, 1965).

8 Cf. K. Rahner, SJ, Experiences of a Catholic Theologian. Translated by Declan Marmion, S. M., Gesa Thiessen, in: *Theological Studies* 61 (2000) 3-15, 13: "As a theologian, I maintain that God created the world, but since I know so little about the world, the notion of creation remains strangely empty. As a theologian, I also proclaim that Jesus, as well as being human, is Lord of all creation. Then I read that the cosmos extends thousands of millions of light-years and I ask myself, somewhat fearfully, what my precious statement actually means. St. Paul still knew which sphere of the cosmos belonged to the angels. This is something I do not know. I ask myself with trepidation whether about half the souls in the Kingdom of God have ever had a personal history. I ask this since authentic church teaching holds that a personal, spiritual, and eternal soul exists from the moment of an egg's fertilization by sperm and that any other view is simply not acceptable. How is the fact of countless number of abortions reconciled with this notion of a personal history of freedom right from the start? I find no clear answer when I ask myself what is the precise meaning of the claim that the first humans over two million years ago constitute the first subjects of salvation history and revelation. I let secular anthropology teach me to be more careful about differentiating between body and soul – something that continues to be problematic. This implies that I can no longer interpret the teaching contained in the encyclical, *Humani Generis*, namely, that the human body derives from the animal kingdom whereas the soul is created by God, as dualistically as it initially appears."

9 Cf. Johannes Herzgsell, Karl Rahners Theologie der Mystik, in: Andreas Schönfeld (ed.), *Spiritualität im Wandel*. Leben aus Gottes Geist. Festschrift zum 75. Jahrgang von „Geist und Leben" – Zeitschrift für christli-

che Spiritualität begründet als Zeitschrift für "Aszese und Mystik" 1925-2002 (Würzburg: Echter, 2002) 65-76.

10   Cf. K. Rahner, Reflections on the Unity of the love of neighbor and the love of God, in: ibid. *Theological Investigations*, vol. 6 (New York: Crossroad, 1969) 231-249.

11   Cf. Johannes Herzgsell, *Dynamik des Geistes*, 321-331.

12   Cf. K. Rahner, *Foundations of Christian Faith*. An Introduction to the Idea of Christianity (New York: Crossroad, 1978) 296: "But a love whose absoluteness is experienced, even though it becomes fully itself not by virtue of itself, but only by virtue of its radical unity with the love of God through Jesus Christ, this love wants more than just a divine guarantee which remains transcendent to it. It wants a unity between the love of God and love of neighbor in which, even though this might merely be unthematic, love of neighbor is love of God and only in this way is completely absolute." Cf. ibid., 309-310; Andrea Tafferner, *Gottes-und Nächstenliebe in der deutschsprachigen Theologie des 20. Jahrhunderts* (Innsbruck: Tyrolia, 1992) esp. 220-228.

2

MY CONCILIAR THEOLOGIAN

IN CONVERSATION WITH FRANZ CARDINAL KÖNIG, VIENNA

Franz König (1905-2004), Dr. phil., Dr. theol., 1948 Professor of Moral Theology at the University of Salzburg; 1952 Auxiliary Bishop and Coadjutor Bishop in Sankt Pölten (Lower Austria); 1956-1985 Archbishop of Vienna, 1965-1985 founder and first President of the Vatican Secretariat for Non-Believers (now: Pontifical Council for Culture).[1]

Your Eminence, you were a facilitator at the Salzburg lecture series (Salzburger Hochschulwochen) in August of 1937. One of the presenters was a young theologian, Karl Rahner. What was your relationship with him at that time?

My role at that time was to summarize Fr. Rahner's presentations on the relationship between the Philosophy of Religion and Theology.[2] These lectures were later published in book form in 1941 under the title *Hearer of the Word*.[3] But at that time I only had a casual relationship with Fr. Rahner. He told me that he studied philosophy in Freiburg with a special interest in existential philosophy. He was most influenced by his encounter with Martin Heidegger.

When did you next meet him?

I next met Fr. Rahner at what turned out to be his last theology lecture series before the war because the series was forbidden by the Nazi authorities from continuing. I did meet Fr. Rahner now and then after the Nazis occupied Austria and the Church was almost forced to go underground. The Theology Faculty in Innsbruck was closed down[4] and the Church encountered difficulties everywhere. After the Jesuits were expelled from Tirol, Fr. Rahner came to Vienna. In Vienna Fr. Karl Rudolf[5] was the head of the Office for Pastoral Ministry, known today as Pastoral Services. Fr. Rudolf was a very actively engaged Pastoral Theologian, a diocesan priest and friend of Michael Pfliegler,[6] who at that time was a Professor of Pastoral Theology and who had introduced many new ideas into this area. These ideas interacted with another phenomenon, not so well known today, that was influential at the time: the German youth Movement.

What role did this most influential reform movement, the German youth Movement, play alongside the Liturgical Movement and the Biblical Renewal Movement in the development of Karl Rahner?

The Youth Movement represented in Germany by the *Quickborn*, the *Bund Neudeutschland*, and in Austria the *Bund Neuland* was a form of a *Movimento*, as we would say today, a meaningful movement of the young generation.[7] After World War I everything was destroyed. The young generation wanted to begin anew. A new movement sprang up that was essentially a spiritual movement, a turn away from bureaucracy, formality and authority. "Away with the Middle Class!" "Back to the simple life!" was a kind of motto for that young generation. The *Wandervogel* was a particular form of the movement of the liberal youth, mostly Protestant, mostly critical, with a Catholic counterpart in Germany and Austria. The popularity of this Youth Movement was felt in Vienna and Prelate Rudolf, as well as Fr. Michael Pfliegler, were connected with this Youth Movement. They had, as intellectuals, helped to propagate these ideas to some extent. Well – that's the story of the rise of the Youth Movement. Fr. Rahner told me about his being a member of the *Quickborn*,[8] when he was a high school student. The leading intellectual figure of *Quickborn* was Romano Guardini. Fr. Rahner from his youth had been a person open to new ideas and with the rise of the Youth Movement he discovered a new vision; windows were opened for him, so to speak.

What influence did Hugo Rahner have on his brother Karl in those early years?

The two were very different in temperament: Hugo was open and socially adept, Karl was reserved and almost shy – showing emotion was difficult for him. You most certainly have heard that Hugo Rahner allegedly said that when he retired, he would translate his brother Karl's books into German. What he meant was that Karl writes sentences that are too long, often more than one entire page. They were difficult to understand, involving many new and complex thoughts. But a Professor of Dogma has a different style than an historian. Apparently, both of them in the early years of their religious life, did research together on the life of their Order's founder, Ignatius, and published together.[9] Fr. Neufeld always makes a point of saying that there was a lifelong mutual cooperation.[10]

You decided before the Council began to take Karl Rahner with you to Rome as your theological advisor. Wasn't this decision at odds with your observation that while Karl Rahner was highly intelligent, he was also difficult to understand?

I viewed the proclamation of Pope John XXIII to convoke a Council with skepticism. The entire world had responded with skepticism as well, by saying that this man is 78 years old. Can he actually bring this Council to pass? Many cardinals and bishops had these same reservations. It appeared comical that a few months after his election, which occurred in October 1956, the Pope surprised everyone with his plan to convoke a Council. One year later – I had a good relationship with John XXIII – he told me in a private audience that the thought came to him during the liturgical week of Prayer for Christian Unity, that he must as pope convoke an Ecumenical Council. He was shocked by that thought and said to himself: "That's something difficult. I can't do that; that's an idea that comes from the devil. The devil wants to create difficulties for me and gives me these thoughts. No, I'm not going to do that." But the thought continued to come to him again and again. He prayed: "Dear God, help me! If you want this, I will do it, but I don't believe that you want it – the devil wants it." He prayed for clarity. On the last day of the Week of Prayer for Christian Unity, he became convinced that the idea came from God and decided to do it. On the next day, the 25th of January 1959, he told a small group of cardinals that he would convoke a Council. The cardinals were in shock; the entire world was in shock, not only the Catholic Church. But then the preparations began and the interest outside the Church began to grow as well.

I knew that I would participate in the Council. I learned – I did not know this in advance – that every bishop had the right to bring a theological advisor with him, if he so desired. I looked around and thought, Karl Rahner is interesting; he is a very flexible theologian and has new ideas. I called him on the phone and asked him to accompany me. His reaction is now well known; he hesitated because he thought that he did not have a good reputation in Rome. He wanted to remain in Innsbruck. I asked him to consider my invitation and said that I understood his reluctance. At the same time, I made it clear to him that he should trust me. I assured him that I would do everything so that nothing would happen to him. He finally said yes.

Did you find that Fr. Rahner's fears regarding the curial offices were confirmed?

Cardinal Alfredo Ottaviani, Prefect of the Holy Office, the institution preceding the Congregation for Doctrine of the Faith (CDF), responded with skepticism and mistrust when he learned that Fr. Rahner was coming to Rome. Fr. Rahner was curious as to what would happen. Right from the beginning he spoke with Ottaviani and we could all see that there was no conflict. They spoke quite openly. I once asked Cardinal Ottaviani directly, "Are you against Karl Rahner?" "Yes," Ottaviani replied: "Rahner is modern and always bringing untested ideas into theological discussions." I recommended that he listen to Fr. Rahner and talk to him and this resulted in a completely cordial relationship between the Holy Office and Fr. Rahner. I saw to it that Fr. Rahner came to work on the Theological Commission. The Council had ten commissions to accomplish all the work: a Liturgical Commission, a Dogmatic and a Theological Commission. These were the core commissions. Fr. Rahner came to work on the Theological Commission and was quite influential there.[11]

And that was due to your efforts?

I did lobby a bit to get him onto the commission, mostly with the bishops of central Europe: France, Belgium, Holland, Germany, Austria and some in Italy. The really important problem was which themes the Council should address. We had about one year before the Council began. An international commission was to prepare the Council. I, myself, belonged to this commission. It was very interesting. About 60 themes were proposed to the Council and they were of a traditional nature, very conventional, for example, the Divine Office, or liturgical questions – all very traditional! The Preparatory Commission suggested that they would present all the new proposals that were coming from every direction and the Council could choose from among them. The Council then said: We can only consider a few topics!

So the Council along with the Theological Commission came together to decide which themes were important for the Church today? That must have been difficult at the beginning of the Council because the opinions coming from the United States were very different.

The Council experienced its first crisis. It simply did not know which theme was more urgent or necessary. The most significant questions that surfaced came to be the ones that asked: What does the Church want today; What does the Church have to say to the world? Above all, what was most interesting was the ecumenical dialogue. John XXIII wanted a conversation; he did not want to aggressively defend the faith. He wanted to open up the windows. The Roman Catholic Church in Europe – this is my personal opinion – was defensive: afraid of the sciences, afraid of the Protestants, afraid of modern movements, of the historical method, the struggle with the liberals and so on. The Church somehow limped long; she lagged behind recent developments. This was the situation in which Fr. Rahner began his theological career. His work met with approval in circles that were ready for reform. As a matter of fact he did what the pope had expressed in his metaphor, open windows. He did not respond with anxiety and defensiveness. "Dialogue" is, perhaps, today a much overused word, but at that time it was new.[12] The dialogue with the separated Christians, for instance, was very much in its beginning stages. The Catholic Church viewed the Ecumenical Movement, which began in England and was connected with the founding of the World Council of Churches (1948), rather critically. The Church had refused to participate, but the Council said that while we will not become a member of the World Council of Churches, we want very much to work together. These were the two most significant events for the Ecumenical movement – for the Protestants, the establishment of the World Council of Churches, and for the Catholics, the Second Vatican Council which produced a document on Ecumenism,[13] which created a completely new atmosphere of good will and cooperation.

A third point, for me, is the interreligious dialogue. To seek conversation with other religions, not to push them away, not to be aggressively defensive, that was, after a century of oppressive history, something wonderfully new. The so-called "Jewish question" which was a hot-button issue, the question of conversation with Muslims, and the great religions of Asia – those were milestones. It was clear to Fr. Rahner: the world is becoming smaller, everything is drawing closer together, and we cannot isolate ourselves; we must speak with one another. New directions emerged from the Council.

And Fr. Rahner contributed to all this?

The Theological Commission of the Council endorsed those powerful impulses for liturgical renewal, the new idea of the Catholic Church in general, the apostolate of the laity, the conversations within the Ecumenical Movement, and not just conversations, but cooperation with other religions, as well as advocating for freedom of religion. Fr. Rahner introduced many of these recommendations and helped bring them to fruition.

It was something entirely new for a Council to address the topic of Church! What is the Church? What tasks does the Church have? What does she have to say to the world and why is there a Church? There were many positions, conservative and otherwise. Fr. Rahner felt that we must speak in a new way to one another; we should not be afraid, or defensive or overly careful. He had a very positive and fundamentally enabling attitude and encouraged others to be open. At that time the major work was to be the Dogmatic Constitution on the Church. There were many stages in this discussion and often the entire day was spent in the Aula debating the pros and cons of certain positions. The results then went back to the Theological Commission which had to synthesize everything. Then the whole business went back to the Council again. It was a back and forth process. Fr. Rahner knew many of the other *periti*, as well as many bishops. He had a large number of personal contacts and so he had a great influence on the outcome of these deliberations. And as I have said, he was someone who brought a whole new approach to things.

How did that occur specifically: for example did you write your comments and show them to Fr. Rahner or did you say: Fr. Rahner, I would like to have a draft of your thoughts on this or that topic?

It happened this way – I made my presentation in the Aula and then after the debate I said to Fr. Rahner, we should speak about this. The Mother of God, for instance, was a very important topic. The issue that arose in this regard was: should the document on the Church have a chapter on the Mother of God or not? Many said: No – it would be better if there were two separate texts, one on the Church and one on the Mother of God. I said: "No – one document for everything, the Mother of God belongs in the document on the Church!" Those who were extreme defenders of Mariology rapidly argued for two distinct documents. My concern was that there was a danger that Mary would become almost more important than the Church. The climate in the Aula was tense. Then the moderator said: "Well, we must vote – two documents or one?" Two speakers were to make their presentation before the vote. The Cardinal of Manila spoke on behalf of having two different documents and I spoke on behalf of one. Prior to doing that I asked Fr. Rahner to make an outline for me.[14] I also asked other theologians to give me their thoughts. I then discussed the arguments with Fr. Rahner, asking him what he would say to this or that statement. Fr. Rahner had influence in the Theological Commission and he also had an impact whenever I spoke at the Council (everything was in Latin) and I needed to have a written position statement. Most often he made an outline of the talk, or I went over my notes with him.

You said once, that you were afraid that some other bishop would take Fr. Rahner as his _peritus_. Was that something that could have been possible?

The entire German Bishops' Conference wanted to have him! I was with Cardinal Julius Döpfner (Munich and Freising) and I said to him, "My dear friend, Fr. Rahner is my Conciliar Theologian! You can have him for discussions, but he remains my Conciliar Theologian." Thus, he was often invited by the German Bishops' Conference to speak, but as my Conciliar Theologian. It is not true, as is sometimes asserted, that Fr. Rahner was both my Conciliar Theologian and that of the German Bishops' Conference as well. I had the good fortune to ask him, shortly before he was asked by Cardinal Döpfner, to accompany me to Rome and because he taught in Innsbruck, he felt more obliged to me than to Döpfner, although Rahner was a German.

Cardinal Lehmann, a student at the Germanicum during the Council, served Karl Rahner in many small ways, but was not always in agreement with him. He thought that Rahner sometimes spoke without sufficient prior reflection. In your opinion should Fr. Rahner have been more careful, more circumspect in his statements?

Fr. Rahner, could be – how shall I put this – quite explosive. Sometimes his emotions were stronger than his reason. He could be very direct and sometimes I had to tell him that he should not provoke the opposition. But one could speak freely to him and he could be reasoned with. He was a man who always had new ideas, new suggestions. He also recognized when he had to reflect on and consider matters more precisely.

You also said once that Fr. Rahner contributed much to the Council. I believe that you were referring especially to the question of salvation in _Lumen Gentium Nr. 16_ that "Those who through no fault of their own, do not know the Gospel of Christ, or his Church, but who nevertheless seek God with a sincere heart, and moved by grace, try in their actions to do his will as they know it through the dictates of their conscience – those too may achieve eternal salvation."

That's a famous passage, yes; it's also a difficult passage. It shows Fr. Rahner's great influence. The universal saving will of God is the firm foundation of his entire theology – with wide reaching consequences, which finds expression in his theorem about the unconscious or anonymous Christian. Many are Christians without being aware that they are on the way, so to speak, to Christianity. He always had this idea. Later when the designation "anonymous Christian" arose, it found much support, but also much opposition.

The debate on this topic continues still; I think of the difficulties which the Jesuit Jacques Dupuis of the Gregorian University, has at this time.[15] I defend his position and I am in the process of writing a positive evaluation of his work for "The Tablet."[16] In the background is the conflict surrounding the interpretation of *Dominus Iesus* (2000), the document of the CDF. I, for one, don't believe that Dupuis is spreading dangerous heresies. It is a kind of tragedy that a Jesuit Professor who has dedicated his entire life to theology and during his professorship in India was never denounced as a progressive, now is in the "cross hairs" of the CDF. I know that these accusations are personally very disheartening for him. Fr. Gerald O' Collins, SJ, Fundamental Theologian at the Gregorian University, is of the opinion that the alleged heresies cannot be found in the book. However, one can read them in, naturally, if one wishes to. The manner of the CDF should be a little flexible. The world is becoming smaller, religious pluralism is an everyday reality – so that as a Christian I must find a response. Naturally, the CDF must control and critically examine what is being said, but the issue is also a human problem.

Does Karl Rahner's theology have a future?

I am of the opinion that Karl Rahner is almost better known in the USA than here. There is more concern with his theology there than here. That is a pity. The *Collected Works* (*Sämtliche Werke*) may be able to correct a number of prejudices against him.

What is your opinion: Is it to be expected or do you regret that the same could be said about Hans Urs von Balthasar?

That one speaks too little about Balthasar, just as one speaks so little about Fr. Rahner? The public discussion in Austria and for Western Europe in general is, in my opinion, tired. The Church is tired as well; she is too much head and too little heart. The Church is critical; she also finds her critics everywhere as well. That's why the general climate here at this time is not very good. The USA is healthier, the Church in the USA is open, it discusses issues and it seeks dialogue. There is not so much skepticism, so much resignation. The intellectuals there debate more. At least that is my impression.

You never regretted taking Karl Rahner with you to the Council?

No! – Absolutely not. I believe that it was good for me, but also for the Council. Fr. Rahner was, despite all his temperamental outbursts, very stimulating. You could not accept everything he said, his emotions often outran his reason. But he was always open to the arguments of others in the conversation; then he would modify his positions. He was a great, creative thinker and he was a pious man, in his way a very pious man, very intellectual, but he could write very simple prayers. He was afraid of being thought of as not as orthodox as he really was. He always wanted to remain faithful to the Church.

Did you attend his funeral?

No, unfortunately I was prevented from doing so. But let me repeat: One often forgets that Fr. Rahner also composed prayers, simple, almost child-like pious prayers. He was both a complex theologian and a graced author.

NOTES

1 Cf. Franz König, "Die Gottesfrage verbindet die Menschen aller Religionen und Kulturen," in: Eugen Biser, *Der obdachlose Gott*. Für eine Neubegegnung mit dem Unglauben (Freiburg: Herder, 2005) 115-124. – This memorandum is dated February 28, 2004. Two weeks later, on March 12, 2004, the Cardinal died.

2 Cf. K. Rahner, Religionsphilosophie und Theologie, in: Georg Baumgartner (ed.), *Die siebenten Salzburger Hochschulwochen. 10. bis 28. August 1937. Aufriss und Gedankengänge der Vorlesungen, Seminare und Vorträge* (Salzburg: Pustet, 1937) 24-32; now in: K. Rahner, *Sämtliche Werke*, vol. 4: Hörer des Wortes. Schriften zur Religionsphilosophie und zur Grundlegung der Theologie. Bearbeitet von Albert Raffelt (Freiburg: Herder, 1997) 285-293.

3 K. Rahner, Hörer des Wortes. Zur Grundlegung einer Religionsphilosophie (München: Kösel, 1941, 2nd edition 1963); now in: K. Rahner, *Sämtliche Werke*, vol. 4, 1-282.

4 Cf. Karl H. Neufeld, "Aufhebung" und Weiterleben der Theologischen Fakultät Innsbruck (1938-1945). Fakten, Reaktionen und Hintergründe während des Zweiten Weltkriegs, in: *Zeitschrift für Katholische Theologie* 119 (1997) 27-50, as well as Andreas R. Batlogg, Die Theologische Fakultät Innsbruck zwischen "Aufschluss" und "Aufhebung" 1938, in: *Zeitschrift für Katholische Theologie* 120 (1998) 164-183.

5 Karl Rudolf (1886-1964), Pastoral Theologian and Pastor, renewer of Pastoral Ministry and paved the way for the Second Vatican Council; cf. Andreas R. Batlogg, In die Pflicht genommen: Im Wiener Seelsorgeamt,

in: ibid., Paul Rulands, Walter Schmolly, Roman A. Siebenrock, Günther Wassilowsky, Arno Zahlauer, *Der Denkweg Karl Rahners*. Quellen – Entwicklungen – Perspektiven (Mainz: Grünewald, 2nd edition 2004) 144-157; Karl Rudolf, *Aufbau im Widerstand*. Ein Seelsorge-Bericht aus Österreich. 1938-1945 (Salzburg: Pustet, 1947).

6   Michael Pfliegler (1891-1972), 1935-1938, Instructor, 1945-1961 Professor for Pastoral Theology at the University of Vienna.

7   Cf. Franz Henrich, *Die Bünde Katholischer Jugendbewegung*. Ihre Bedeutung für die liturgische und eucharistische Erneuerung (Munich: Kösel, 1968).

8   Cf. K. Rahner, Erinnerungen im Gespräch mit Meinhold Krauss (Freiburg: Herder, 1984) 27: "At that time I was a member of Quickborn. It was a more open movement, emerging from the grassroots, not so explicitly church controlled, but still Catholic and religious, thoroughly alive and intensely active. From that movement I received fruitful directions for my future life. I also made the acquaintance of Romano Guardini at the Rothenfels Castle." – Now in: K. Rahner, *Sämtliche Werke*, vol. 25: Erneuerung des Ordenslebens. Zeugnis für Kirche und Welt. Bearbeitet von Andreas R. Batlogg (Freiburg: Herder, 2008) 95.

9   There is a Festschrift for Hugo and Karl Rahner's father in honor of his 60th birthday, containing essays and articles of both Hugo and Karl from their early years in the Society of Jesus. Of the twelve contributions, five are from Karl, and seven are from Hugo Rahner. The contributions of Karl Rahner will be published in volume 1 of *Sämtliche Werke*; cf. Karl H. Neufeld, *Die Brüder Rahner*. Eine Biographie (Freiburg: Herder, 2nd edition 2004) 40-41, as well as Arno Zahlauer, *Ignatius von Loyola als "produktives Vorbild"* der *Theologie Karl Rahners* (Innsbruck: Tyrolia, 1996) 97.

10   Cf. Karl H. Neufeld, *Die Brüder Rahner*; ibid., Unter Brüdern. Zur Frühgeschichte der Theologie K. Rahners aus der Zusammenarbeit mit H. Rahner, in: Herbert Vorgrimler (ed.), *Wagnis Theologie*. Erfahrungen mit der Theologie Karl Rahners (Freiburg: Herder 1979) 341-354; ibid., Abraham P. Kustermann (eds.), "Gemeinsame Arbeit in brüderlicher Liebe." Hugo und Karl Rahner. Dokumente und Würdigung ihrer Weggemeinschaft (Stuttgart: Akademie der Diözese Rottenburg-Stuttgart 1993); Karl Rahner, Hugo Rahner, Die aszetischen Schriften in den *Monumenta Historica SJ* Introduced and edited by Karl H. Neufeld, in: *Zeitschrift für Katholische* Theologie 108 (1986) 422-433; in honor of K. Rahner's centennial there was a special issue of *Zeitschrift für Katholische* *Theologie* 122 (2004) 113-196.

11   Cf. Karl H. Neufeld, Theologen und Konzil. Karl Rahners Beitrag zum Zweiten Vatikanischen Konzil, in: *Stimmen der Zeit* 202 (1984) 156-166; Roman A. Siebenrock, "Meine schlimmsten Erwartungen sind weit über-

troffen," in: Klaus Wittstadt, Wim Verschooten (eds.), *Der Beitrag der deutschsprachigen und osteuropäischen Länder zum Zweiten Vatikanischen Konzil* (Löwen: Bibliotheek van de Faculteit Godgeleerdheid, 1996) 121-139; Andreas R. Batlogg, Karl Rahners Mitarbeit an den Konzilstexten, in: Franz-Xaver Bischof, Stephan Leimgruber (eds.), *Vierzig Jahre II. Vatikanum*. Zur Wirkungsgeschichte der Konzilstexte (Würzburg: Echter, 2nd edition 2005) 355-376; Günther Wassilowsky, *Universales Heilsakrament Kirche*. Karl Rahners Beitrag zur Ekklesiologie des II. Vatikanums (Innsbruck: Tyrolia 2001).

12   Cf. Karl H. Neufeld, Dialog. Herausforderungen, Möglichkeiten und Grenzen im Anschluss an Karl Rahner, in: Matthias Lutz-Bachmann (ed.), *Und dennoch ist von Gott zu reden* (Festschrift Herbert Vorgrimler) (Freiburg: Herder 1994) 246-261.

13   Cf. Peter Neuner, Das Dekret über die Ökumene *Unitatis redintegratio*, in: Franz-Xaver Bischof, Stephan Leimgruber, Vierzig Jahre II. Vatikanum, 117-140; Bernd Jochen Hilberath, Theologischer Kommentar zum Dekret über den Ökumenismus *Unitatis redintegratio*, in: Peter Hünermann, ibid., (eds.), *Herders theologischer Kommentar zum Zweiten Vatikanischen Konzil*, vol. 3 (Freiburg: Herder, 2005) 69-223.

14   K. Rahner's writings on Mary are readily available in: K. Rahner, *Sämtliche Werke*, vol. 9: Maria, Mutter des Herrn. Mariologische Studien. Bearbeitet von Regina Pacis Meyer (Freiburg: Herder, 2004). His drafts with regard to the Council are reserved for the first volume on the Council, *Sämtliche Werke*, vol. 21.

15   Cf. Franz König, In defense of Fr. Dupuis, in: *The Tablet*, Jan. 16, 1999, 76-77; cf. also Hans Waldenfels, Unterwegs zu einer christlichen Theologie des religiösen Pluralismus. Anmerkungen zum "Fall Dupuis," in: *Stimmen der Zeit* 217 (1999) 597-610.

16   Cf. Franz König, Let the Spirit breathe, in: *The Tablet*, April 7, 2001, 483-484; Hans Waldenfels, Jacques Dupuis – Theologie unterwegs, in: *Stimmen der Zeit* 219 (2001) 217-218. – See also Franz Kardinal König, *Offen für Gott – Offen für die Welt*. Kirche im Dialog. Translated and edited by Christa Pongratz-Lippitt (Freiburg: Herder, 2006); cf. Andreas R. Batlogg, Das Vermächtnis des Kardinals. Franz Königs postumes Plädoyer für Dialog, in: *Stimmen der Zeit* 224 (2006) 344-348.

3

ETHOS OF PROCLAMATION

IN CONVERSATION WITH FR. HANS BERNHARD MEYER, SJ, INNSBRUCK

Hans B. Meyer, SJ (1928-2002), lic. phil., Dr. theol., a Jesuit since 1946, Lecturer in Pastoral Theology at the University of Innsbruck from 1964, 1966-1969 Professor of Moral Theology and Social Ethics and from 1969-1995 in Liturgy, (succeeding Josef A. Jungmann, SJ), Dean of the Theology Faculty in 1967-68 and 1970-81 and in addition Editor-in-chief of the Innsbruck periodical "Zeitschrift für Katholische Theologie."

The philosopher Josef Pieper (1904-1997) met Karl Rahner during a conference and saw Rahner celebrating a private Mass with his back to the people. Pieper was somewhat surprised by this particularly since this took place after the Second Vatican Council. Did you know about this?

Pieper writes about this in his autobiography, not without a certain degree of irony.[1] But it is understandable in light of the fact that Rahner grew up with the pre-Vatican II liturgy and he was not himself a liturgist. Before the Council it was the practice for priests to have private Masses as a form of personal piety and I am sure that this appealed to him more than the community Mass as it was celebrated after the Council. Here in Innsbruck he always celebrated Mass alone – very early – about 5 a.m. He was an early riser. His personal piety had been shaped by the pre-conciliar period and that tradition remained with him even after the Council.

Karl Rahner was a very pious, spiritual person, a man of prayer – was he not?

Certainly! That personal piety with which he grew up continued to shape him throughout his entire life – it sustained him. Leaving aside his personal idiosyncrasies, he was, without a doubt, a deeply pious person, who, for example, spoke about prayer in his writings, and continued to do so as well in his lectures. I heard him preach many times. His preaching was noticeably permeated with a deep personal conviction and piety. The person and the message which he proclaimed were, so to speak, a unity, which could not be separated, one from the other.

Despite that Rahner could also be very impatient?

Yes he could. I can remember an incident which reveals both his piety and his impatience and his excitability. He always worked to the limits of his strength. Once on the morning of one of his birthdays, I knocked on the door of his office and went in to congratulate him. He had already begun his work and when I entered, he abruptly and angrily pushed me out because I had not been given an appointment to see him by his aide, who at that time was Adolf Darlap. He practically threw me out. I didn't even get to congratulate him, but that evening he came to me and apologized.

Did you have Fr. Rahner as a Professor?

Yes. I heard both Karl and Hugo Rahner lecture and also Josef Andreas Jungmann, who was rather a boring lecturer with a soft voice and few oratorical flourishes. That was not his style, but I came to realize over time his worth. It was not like that with Karl Rahner; his lectures were truly exciting. He was extemporaneous and thought out loud as he walked back and forth as we tried to follow his thought. This ethos of proclamation was characteristic of him, as can be seen in his entire thought. He could with one step alternate between the most difficult speculative reflections and the practical ecclesial pious life, so that one saw how one was connected to the other. That was a great talent and it deeply impressed us.

Does this interaction also take place in *Theological Investigations?*

There are works in which more of the second aspect dominates, as for example in his small book on prayer.[2] I wouldn't be able to name anything specifically in which both aspects were equally present. His

Theological Investigations are mostly theoretical: not in a negative, but in a completely positive sense. There are other writings that are directed more to the practical Christian life of the individual, of the Church and her communities. In this regard he wrote the *Handbook of Pastoral Theology*, but not all of the articles in that book were always entirely practical. Some things are a bit too utopian, for example, his concept of the diocese as a "particular Church" – the fullness of the Church as it exists in a specific locale. He says: each diocese needs to have everything that makes up Church in its completeness, beginning with a discriminating theology down to the daily pastoral functions.[3] I believe that is not totally realistic; many dioceses in Italy for instance and elsewhere would find it hard to comply with that concept. There were areas where he worked very intensively to try to accommodate the core truths of his theological-theoretical approach to Church practice, but he was not familiar enough with the concrete practice of local Churches.

Herbert Vorgrimler, in his introductory book on Karl Rahner, published Rahner's letters from the time of the Council.[4] In these letters Rahner goes on at length about his complaints. I can understand that these complaints can spontaneously arise from impatience, frustration and disappointment, but do you think it was necessary to publish them?

Your impression is certainly correct. One has to take into account that in this phase of his life he was severely overworked. He, himself, set the standard for his work, which was inhuman with regard to his mode of life. For example, he believed that a certain number of lines had to be written each day; it was an unbelievable number – about 30 pages or so. But that came from his love for the Church, which was very intense, for the mystery of the Church. At the same time, he also had a tendency to view the institutional Church critically and to make statements where one might later say: they are only human beings, with their strengths and weaknesses. One must learn to live with that!

Was there no one in the house who could have said to him: Fr. Rahner, it can be 10 pages a day, not 30? Could his brother, Hugo, have said that to him?

Perhaps, he might have accepted that from him, but, of course, that would place an enormous amount of stress on him.

This pressure did not come from without then – from a publisher – but was self-imposed?

The stress came from within Fr. Rahner himself. Naturally, he received many invitations which he could not easily refuse. He gave innumerable lectures, and wrote books and articles when he was asked to do so. It was simply a necessity for him to contribute to the Church and when he detected a mistake, or an omission he felt compelled to suggest, if possible, a better way of proceeding. That was a priority for him. In this sense he was much more pastoral than one might have believed.

He had a secretary during his final years in Innsbruck. How was that in the 1950's and 60's?

At the end he had Ms. Oeggl, but prior to her, there were no secretaries. Different students worked for Fr. Rahner – Adolf Darlap or Franz Mayr. There were no assistants in today's sense, at that time, on the faculty. Fr. Rahner, however, always found some aides who worked for him. He could, for instance, give Darlap a manuscript and say: "Now add a few footnotes to this."

Was Rahner often overworked?

There were periods when he was exhausted. The Council took a lot out of him. He did not return to Innsbruck after the Council, but instead went to Munich. He was not happy with some of his Jesuit colleagues from whom he had expected more assistance. There were also some tensions in the community, with Fr. Engelbert Gutwenger, SJ,[5] and some others. That's the origin of the often quoted expression which arose during a heated discussion between Fr. Felderer and Fr. Rahner. Fr. Rahner got rather worked up during the discussion with Fr. Josef Felderer, SJ,[6] who was a very conservative theologian, more scholastic in the old sense and completely different in his style from Fr. Rahner. They could not come to an agreement. Finally, Fr. Rahner said to Felderer, "Stay with your opinion, for you it is good enough." The mild mannered Felderer's face turned red and he stood up and left. There were some remarkable instances when Fr. Rahner could not control himself. For example, he invited a Professor from another faculty to lecture at an evening colloquium. The colleague was a philologist and he had either a prosthesis or a stiff leg. The Professor stood next to the podium, waiting for the moment when he could begin his lecture. Rahner introduced him and then proceeded to explain what the topic was. Rahner then began to reflect on the topic and he spoke and spoke. That went on for about 45 minutes and the poor man stood there waiting. Finally, Rahner stopped and invited the guest to the podium. The Professor then simply said: "Much of what I was going to say, Professor Rahner has already spoken about. I can't add much to that." Then he returned to his seat. Rahner never even realized how much he had offended his guest.

Fr. Sporschill's work with young people was fascinating for Rahner, was it not?

Georg Sporschill was one of those kinds of people that greatly impressed Fr. Rahner. He was my assistant for a long time and then he went to Vorarlberg to be involved in Adult Education. He was a very restless person. He could never stay in one place for very long; he couldn't sit still, as we say. Then he became a Jesuit and though I would have liked to have seen him go into Pastoral Theology and eventually become the successor to Fr. Walter Croce, SJ,[7] that didn't work out. Fr. Sporschill then did what he wanted in the Order. At that time I held it against the Order that they did not exercise more control over him.[8] But with his dynamic style and his talent he was able to attract young people to himself and recruit them as volunteers for all kinds of things; that was very demanding for him – it certainly was. Some of them joined the Jesuits because they were so impressed with him. That impressed Fr. Rahner enormously and he supported Sporschill whenever he could. In 1984 Fr. Sporschill edited a small book of memories of Rahner's life.[9]

What should unquestionably be passed on of Rahner's theology? What would you say spontaneously? Why is he still important?

It seems to me that his transcendental starting point is the critical systematic motor that drives his thinking that led him to proclaim the Mystery of God: the transcendence of God and at the same time God's immanence in human life. That is also the reason why he had such an influence, not only on seminarians, but also on the great masses of lay people. He brought a dimension into their lives that they were not conscious of: the hidden congruence of God and creation. I believe that this is a critical point in terms of his effectiveness in theology as well as his enlightening power in the Church. Many laity had the feeling: there is someone who recognizes who we actually are and what is life giving to us and expresses it in a way that we can understand.

Are you thinking of a specific text or book?

That's something that I would find difficult to be specific about, because that tends to be present more in the background of his work, both in his lectures and homilies as well as in his more pastorally centered works. Whether we are speaking about *Foundations of Christian Faith* or whatever it might be, there is always this hidden structure that supports everything. That is something that not only his theology students could recognize, but also all those who heard his sermons or talks.

What did you like the most about Karl Rahner?

I liked his theology very much. He could also be quite human. For example, he preached at my First Mass, about which I remember nothing. But I do recall that my sister and I were concerned about where we could sit Fr. Rahner at the First Mass banquet so that he would have a good conversation partner. I sat opposite him with my sister and the pastor. We thought this would make for the possibility of conversation. We went to the table and he took his place and was rather silent. At that time my nephew, who was also at the table, was a little boy and he started to run around the table. Fr. Rahner scooped him up and sat him on his lap and then proceeded to collect the folded place cards and group them so that they formed a tunnel. He then took out his rosary from his pocket and started to play choo-choo train with my nephew, using the rosary as a train going through the tunnel. The question about who would carry on a conversation with him was thus solved.

That's so wonderful that he could be so imaginative and think of something to amuse the child. Do you have any other recollections?

This is an anecdote that was typical of him. He often used a young scholastic, who had a driver's license, to look after his needs. One morning, at around 4 a.m. he knocked on the scholastic's door. The scholastic answered: "Yes, what's wrong?" From the hall came Rahner's voice: "Are you awake yet?" "Yes," came the reply, "what is it?" Rahner asked: "Can I come in?" "Yes," came the answer. Then, Rahner entered the room, holding up his pants with his hand and said: "I have to leave now to travel to a lecture and the buttons are missing from my pants in a most important place. Do you know how to sew on buttons?" The scholastic said: "Yes, I do." Rahner took off his pants and sat down in his underwear on the bed and the scholastic took out a needle and thread and sewed on the buttons while Rahner watched him. And suddenly in this meditative silence Fr. Rahner said: "It's really a pain, isn't it, when one doesn't have a wife!"

NOTES

1 See Josef Pieper, *Eine Geschichte wie ein Strahl*. Autobiographische Aufzeichnungen seit 1964 (Munich: Kösel, 2nd editon 1996) 153: "At a meeting in the Leo-Konvikt in Paderborn, I arrived late in the evening. The next morning I greeted in the chapel this or that person in silence, shaking his hand. Two candles were already lit on the altar, which had been set up in front of the chapel, where Mass would be celebrated. Then both candles were extinguished, and instead two candles were lit at the main altar. The house prefect came from the sacristy, passed by close to me and whispered, 'Professor Rahner is going to celebrate Mass in an entirely new form.' In reality he went to the altar, turned his back to us, as was the age old custom, and celebrated in hardly audible dialogue with the altar servers, a 'Silent Mass.' When he sat down at my table for breakfast, I congratulated him, laughing: 'Now that was a truly postconciliar Mass!' [Rahner replied:] 'But don't you like that way of celebrating Mass as well?'"

2 K. Rahner, *Von der Not und dem Segen des Gebetes* (1949); English translation: *The Need and the Blessing of Prayer*.

3 See K. Rahner, Die Träger des Selbstvollzugs der Kirche in: ibid., *Sämtliche Werke*, vol. 19: Selbstvollzug der Kirche. Ekklesiologische Grundlegung praktischer Theologie. Bearbeitet von Karl H. Neufeld (Freiburg: Herder 1995) 80-147, esp. 99-110 ("Bischof and Bistum").

4 See K. Rahner, Kleine Brieffolge aus der Konzilszeit, in: Herbert Vorgrimler, *Karl Rahner verstehen*. Eine Einführung in sein Leben und Denken (Freiburg: Herder, 2nd edition 1988) 171-220; English translation: *Understanding Karl Rahner*. An Introduction to his life and thought (New York: Crossroad, 1986).

5 Engelbert Gutwenger, SJ, (1905-1985), 1939 teaching position in Innsbruck, 1939-1946, teacher at Heythrop College, Oxford, 1946-47, Professor at the Seminary, St. Georgen am Längsee, Carinthia, then teaching position again in Innsbruck (Fundamental Theology, Dogmatic Theology, Philosophy), 1954 a. o. Professor, 1958 Professor for Fundamental Theology, 1949-50 Dean of the Theology Faculty, 1961-62 Rector of the University of Innsbruck, 1949-1950,Vice Rector of the Canisianum; See Emerich Coreth, In memoriam P. Engelbert Gutwenger, SJ, in: *Zeitschrift für Katholische Theologie* 107 (1985) 249-251.

6 Joseph Felderer, SJ, (1919-2006), 1953 Assistant Professor for Fundamental Theology at the University of Innsbruck, 1970 tit. a. o. Professor.

7 Walter Croce, SJ, (1912-2004), 1957-1977 Professor for Pastoral Theology at the University of Innsbruck.

8 See the interview with Georg Sporschill, SJ in this book.

9 See K. Rahner, *Bekenntnisse*. Rückblick auf 80 Jahre, edited by Georg Sporschill (Vienna: Herold 1984); now in: K. Rahner, *Sämtliche Werke*, vol. 25: Erneuerung des Ordenslebens. Zeugnis für Kirche und Welt. Bearbeitet von Andreas R. Batlogg (Freiburg: Herder 2008) 61-84.

4

NOT ONLY FOR OPPORTUNISTIC REASONS

IN CONVERSATION WITH FR. OTTO MUCK, SJ, INNSBRUCK

Otto Muck, SJ, Dr. phil., lic. theol., born 1928, a Jesuit since 1951, 1962-1965 a University Lecturer, 1965-1970 a. o. Professor, 1969-1970 Dean of the Theology Faculty, 1971-1997 Professor of Christian Philosophy at the University Innsbruck, 1975-1977 Rector of the University of Innsbruck and from 1969-1973 Rector of the Jesuit Residence at Innsbruck.

What memories do you have of Karl Rahner as a teacher?

I studied Dogmatic Theology in Innsbruck for three years with Rahner from 1956 to 1959. That was very interesting. Part of the time he taught in Latin and at other times in German. It is not absolutely clear in my memory, but I think he taught History of Dogma and Biblical Theology in German, and Systematic Theology in Latin. I also took Dogmatic Theology from Franz Lakner, Engelbert Gutwenger and Josef Felderer. Lakner taught more often in Latin than did Rahner. Even before I became a Jesuit, when I was a student in Vienna studying philosophy, mathematics and physics, I was interested in theology and philosophy. I can still recall how we college students discussed Rahner's article about "The one sacrifice and the many Masses,"[1] as well as his articles on Mary.[2]

Which of Rahner's philosophical writing interested you the most?

In 1953-54 I studied his book *Hearer of the Word* very intensively. We met in a small group to discuss it, debating to what degree this book was a type of anthropology. The more intensively one gets involved in studying Rahner's work, the clearer the need for understanding his methodology becomes. If the approach to Rahner remains superficial it can only result in unsubstantiated associations. What results is a hodge-podge of phrases taken out of context. I have the impression that some people quote Rahner only for opportunistic reasons in order to support their own theory or in order to prove him wrong. What results are different groups that set themselves up as being either for or against Rahner based not on what he actually said or meant, but on what they think.

How do you understand his methodological approach?

First of all, to really understand Karl Rahner, one must clearly understand scholasticism and scholastic concepts as well as their neo-Scholastic expressions. Fr. Rahner was formed by this tradition. Secondly, it's also very important to recognize that Fr. Rahner reinterpreted this scholastic and Aristotelian legacy following in the footsteps of Joseph Maréchal. Most students today are not aware of the basic ideas of Scholastic Philosophy, or how they were used in theology with its background of an antiquated cosmological view of the world. They have studied scholasticism only superficially and thus tend to denigrate and dismiss it. Karl Rahner studied the transcendental analysis of Maréchal intensively.[3] The term "Transcendental Method" or "analysis" first appeared in the second half of the 19th century, but Maréchal took transcendental analysis to a new stage. Karl Rahner built on Maréchal and further developed his thought through the use of the existential terminology of Martin Heidegger. Experience is understood not only in an empirical sense. Thus, the transcendental philosophical starting point of Maréchal, upon which Rahner intensively reflected during the course of his studies, he wedded to an existential-phenomenological element. The approach to the question of being, Rahner worked out using Heidegger. So one must always be mindful of these three roots when one is studying Rahner's methodology: Scholasticism, Maréchal and Heidegger.[4]

If someone were to say today "I doubt whether it's possible for me to understand Karl Rahner's presuppositions if it is so complicated" – what would you say?

Then I would recommend that one turn for help to other authors who have worked through the presuppositions of Karl Rahner's theology.

Was Karl Rahner also influenced, in some way, by his brother Hugo?

That I don't know. It is interesting that Karl Rahner also was engaged in the study of Patrology, at least in the beginning. He also had a great interest in spirituality. But Hugo Rahner was the one who was most familiar with the Patristic period and who had a sense and appreciation for literary forms and symbolism. Karl Rahner may have gained from him an understanding of the importance of symbolism and for such primal terms as "The Sacred Heart of Jesus," but Hugo Rahner was more gifted linguistically and a better speaker. For Karl Rahner his paramount concern was not rhetoric, but the precision and logic with which an issue was addressed. As a result it was very difficult to listen to him, but for someone who was able to follow his thinking it was very fruitful. Some of his sentences are, unfortunately, very long and difficult to understand. Sometimes his sentences have to be reformulated, shortened.

Do you think, perhaps, that what is revealed in Fr. Rahner's long convoluted sentences is his concern for logic over rhetoric?

What was important to Fr. Rahner was developing his thought; he thought out loud and did not take the time to edit his writing.

A question regarding Karl Rahner the person: what did you most admire about him?

His entirely simple, uncomplicated style! He was difficult at times in that when he was developing his thoughts he could be grouchy when anyone interrupted him, but normally he was very approachable.

In addition to his speculative theological writings, he also produced a series of simple, pious books, *Heilige Stunde und Passionsandacht* (1949), which he published under the pseudonym Anselm Trescher, the family name of his grandmother. Can you speak about that?

In 1939 his book *Spirit in the World* was published. The publishing house did so on the condition that he would write a more popular work which could be sold more easily. He gave them ten meditations, which had already been published individually and they published them as a collected work, *Encounters with Silence*. This, in essence, was his doctrine of God. This small book is challenging and contains the very personal, existential foundation of his thought. What he then developed theologically he wished would always lead to the core of the Christian faith. That's something that should not be overlooked when one considers the critical comments Fr. Rahner made about the Church in the later years of his life.

NOTES

1   Cf. K. Rahner, Die vielen Messen und das eine Opfer, in: *Zeitschrift für Katholische Theologie* 71 (1949) 257-317. – This article appeared as an independent publication in 1951 (Freiburg: Herder). Cf. später: ibid., Die vielen Messen als die vielen Opfer Christi, in: *Zeitschrift für Katholische Theologie* 77 (1955) 94-101; ibid., Die vielen Messen und das eine Opfer. Eine Untersuchung über die rechte Norm der Messhäufigkeit (Quaestiones Disputatae 31) (Freiburg: Herder, 1966).

2   Cf. now: K. Rahner, *Sämtliche Werke*, vol. 9: Maria, Mutter des Herrn. Mariologische Studien. Bearbeitet von Regina Pacis Meyer (Freiburg: Herder, 2004).

3   Cf. Otto Muck, Thomas – Kant – Maréchal. Karl Rahners transzendentale Methode, in: Harald Schöndorf (ed.), *Die philosophischen Grundlagen der Theologie Karl Rahners* (Quaestiones Disputatae 213) (Freiburg: Herder, 2005) 31-56; see also Otto Muck, Die deutschsprachige Maréchal-Schule – Transzendentalphilosophie als Metaphysik: J. B. Lotz, K. Rahner, W. Brugger, E. Coreth u. a., in: Emerich Coreth, Walter M. Neidl, Georg Pfligerdorffer (eds.), *Christliche Philosophie im katholischen Denken des 19. und 20. Jahrhunderts*, vol 2 (Graz: Styria, 1988) 590-622; Johann Baptist Lotz, Joseph Maréchal (1878-1944), in: ibid., 453-469; Klaus Müller, Zur Bedeutung Kants für die gegenwärtige Katholische Theologie in Deutschland, in: Norbert Fischer (ed.), *Kant und der Katholizismus*. Stationen einer wechselhaften Geschichte (Freiburg: Herder, 2005) 515-528, esp. 425-427 (Karl Rahners Projekt transzendentaler Theologie); François Marty, Joseph Maréchal (1878–1944). Kritische Philosophie und Neuscholastik. Eine transzendentale Theologie, in: ibid., 515-528, esp. 520-524 (Karl Rahner, eine transzendentale Theologie). See also Otto Muck, *The Transcendental Method* (New York: Herder and Herder, 1968).

4   Cf. Otto Muck, Heidegger und Karl Rahner, in: *Zeitschrift für Katholische Theologie* 116 (1994) 257-269.

5

HE TOOK HIS STUDENTS SERIOUSLY

IN CONVERSATION WITH ALBERT RAFFELT AND
FRANZ JOHNA, FREIBURG

Albert Raffelt, Dr. theol., born 1944, is the Assistant Director of the University Library and Honorary Professor of Dogmatic Theology at the University of Freiburg. He is co-editor of the Collected Works (Sämtliche Werke) of Karl Rahner.

Franz Johna, born 1929, Translator and Editor of spiritual books, was an Editor at Herder Publishing, Freiburg, until 1994.

Professor Raffelt, you play a major role in the publication of Karl Rahner's works with the Herder Publishing Company. Tell us about this.

First let me tell you something about myself. In 1964 I began to study theology in Münster. It was the time of the Second Vatican Council and any student who was interested in theology inevitably came to know the name Karl Rahner. At that time there was a series of Herder paperbacks consisting of selections of articles from *Theological Investigations* (*Schriften zur Theologie*). I purchased these, one of which was *Gegenwart des Christentums*.[1] I read some of these books in addition to those of Hans Küng who was, perhaps, the most prominent theologian in the pre-Vatican II period, who traveled a lot giving speeches. Fr. Rahner, however, was the name that was most respected. I have to add, though, that at the time Fr. Rahner was considered somewhat passé. We young people thought: "That's the theology of the past." I also must admit that at the beginning of my studies I was much more interested in Protestant theologians such as Paul Tillich. "They are more modern," I said to myself: "Karl Rahner is indeed important and respectable, but modern theology is to be found elsewhere."

Then I continued my studies in Munich where Fr. Rahner held the Romano Guardini chair in Christian Philosophy at that time. I must admit that I did not attend his lectures. I went once to a class and he held up the first volume of the *Handbuch der Pastoraltheologie* (Handbook of Pastoral Theology) and said: "What I am now going to lecture on will appear in the second volume." The class was so difficult that I thought: "It would be much easier to read that." So I no longer attended his class and instead attended the lectures of Heinrich Ott, a Protestant theologian, who was a visiting professor.[2] As chance would have it, Fr. Rahner moved to Münster in 1967. I returned to Münster as well, and he was my teacher in my required courses. Then I had to study Karl Rahner very intensively for the entire semester. I also read only Rahner during my vacation. That was when I experienced a breakthrough because I occupied myself with him so intensively. I was in close contact with Karl Lehmann who lived at the Seminary, *Collegium Borromaeum*, and so I became more acquainted with Fr. Rahner's work.

After I completed my master's degree, I wanted to go to Tübingen to begin doctoral studies. Through Karl Lehmann's intervention, I stayed in Münster and began a doctoral dissertation with Karl Rahner, but I did not complete it with him because I went to Mainz in 1969 with Lehmann.

You then did your doctoral dissertation on Maurice Blondel under Karl Lehmann's direction?

I had a conversation with Fr. Rahner at the *Collegium Marianum*, a student residence where he lived. His room was modestly furnished; there were only a few books. That impressed me. Rahner told me that he did not have much familiarity with Blondel. He remembered when he was an editor for *Zeitschrift für Katholische Theologie*[3] in the 1930's that there was an article by Walter Warnach[4] that he was familiar with and he learned some things from Robert Scherer,[5] an expert in Blondel. But he was not a Blondel specialist as Lehmann was. What took me by surprise was the fact that Fr. Rahner took me so seriously. He wanted to know what I thought about different things. I had not encountered such interest even from my theology professors. He had many doctoral students at the time so at the next meeting he had trouble remembering who I was. So I decided that it was better to go to

Karl Lehmann with whom I had direct contact. But through Lehmann I met Fr. Rahner again when he came to Mainz with Eberhard Jüngel for a guest lecture.[6] In Freiburg Fr. Rahner frequently came to the Institute when I was an assistant there. Mr. Johna can better explain how it came about that I began to work on Fr. Rahner's publications.

(*Franz Johna:*) As far as I can recall, Fr. Rahner, as well as Karl Lehmann, brought Albert Raffelt to the attention of the editorial board at Herder. Lehmann had great confidence in Mr. Raffelt when it came to precision and a scholarly approach. The relationship between Raffelt and Herder publishing grew deeper and closer. Fr. Rahner, in my estimation, always placed a great value on his relationship with you, Mr. Raffelt.

In 1976 Herder published *Foundations of Christian Faith*. How did this come about?

(*Franz Johna:*) The *Foundations of Christian Faith* was a real problem.[7] Fr. Rahner made several attempts at it, but without success at first. He had various competent people assist him with the preparation of the manuscript.

(*Albert Raffelt:*) My recollection is that Karl Lehmann would be the first person to examine the initial preparatory drafts. Fr. Rahner's approach consisted of his providing the fundamental ideas and Lehmann doing the exegesis and everything else. That, of course, was somewhat difficult, but in many cases Lehmann did exactly that. For example the article "Jesus Christ" in *Sacramentum Mundi*[8] is primarily Lehmann's work. Lehmann also contributed greatly to *Mysterium Salutis*.[9] The way they worked was that Rahner would initially prepare the treatise and Lehmann would add the historical research. Rahner, probably, thought that this would work for *Foundations of Christian Faith* as well.

(*Franz Johna:*) Lehmann had direct access to the data and was also, with regard to editorial work, very accomplished.

(*Albert Raffelt:*) Furthermore, he was more at home with exegesis than Fr. Rahner. Then in 1968, Lehmann received a call to be Professor of Dogmatic Theology in Mainz, so the project *Foundations of Christian Faith*, actually died at that time.

(*Franz Johna:*) Fr. Rahner was left without any support. As far as I know, he made various attempts to work on it himself. Elisabeth von der Lieth gave him a hand by sorting out the material. The Jesuit Fathers, Schöndorf and Neufeld, also helped him.

(*Albert Raffelt:*) To put it bluntly, the final *Foundations of Christian Faith* manuscript is a compilation of the Münster lectures because that was the last stage of the project. The Munich lectures contained more material and he continued to expand on those. Fr. Rahner had taught Christology in Münster.[10] Those lectures were expanded upon and transcribed together with some missing parts from Rahner's other essays, as accurately as possible. Rahner practically dictated the small section on the Sacred Scriptures.

(*Franz Johna:*) I would like to add something, speaking from the perspective of the publishing house. We urged Fr. Rahner to create a large, comprehensive foundational work which would be seen as the crown of his theology and so to complete the *Foundations of Christian Faith*. We were concerned that it proceed on track so that it would actually come to publication. Fr. Rahner was worried about this. He wanted to write something, but he knew that he could not do it alone. The last phase of the preparation for publication was actually the most fruitful when Albert Raffelt received the manuscript. We had reserved a room for Fr. Rahner in the Karlshotel in Freiburg, which was located not far from the publishing house, and we engaged the services of a secretary, Ms. Schwab, who met with Fr. Rahner daily and to whom he dictated the missing parts. Fr. Rahner very much appreciated when he could be alone and work. It was important for him to be able to see that progress was being made and the project was moving forward. He operated on a very strict work schedule.

Specifically what did his work schedule look like?

(*Albert Raffelt:*) Fr. Rahner examined all the material and made some corrections. Ms. Schwab retyped whatever was illegible. When it was finished, I was given the draft. At first, I was very, very cautious. Franz Johna and Gerbert Brunner[11] also went over the manuscript and agreed that I had to be more aggressive in the editing. I had to get accustomed to doing that, to deleting the texts of Karl Rahner. The main thing was to have a text that flowed smoothly. That, of course, changed the style; some sentences needed to be shortened; some conclusions needed to be formulated differently and above all put into subsections. Fr. Rahner then read everything one more time.

What did Fr. Rahner say to that? Was he satisfied or did he object to some of the changes?

(*Albert Raffelt:*) Actually, he didn't say anything and in essence accepted everything. I don't recall that he demanded many changes. One thing that I remember was that I had more things underlined and I italicized the Latin expressions. He did not like that very much, so we took that out. One section that he wanted to change was on the scriptures as the Book of the Church.[12] He told me that when he was in my home. I took his book *Inspiration in the Bible*[13] from my bookshelf and similar works, and he looked through the books, but was not satisfied. He then came upon the Latin dogmatic text *Sacrae Theologicae Summa*; it is very traditional. He looked at the table of contents and the organization and he dictated his thoughts according to the divisions.[14] That same night I typed up his dictation and reworked it. He looked at the text the next morning and approved it. That was the last part of the *Foundations of Christian Faith*.

You can see that the work has several levels. Later, I noticed something that I had overlooked earlier: that, for example, the terms *Grundsakrament* and *Ursakrament* were used interchangeably. Nikolaus Schwerdtfeger also notes some inconsistencies in volume 26 of the *Collected Works*.

What is the importance of the *Collected Works* of Karl Rahner? Are they relevant only for Rahner research?

Let me first say something about how this came about.[15] The Karl Rahner Foundation came to me and asked me if I thought such a project was worthwhile and what it should look like. They asked the same question of Fr. Neufeld, the director of the Karl Rahner archives in Innsbruck. I recommended a stronger, systematic approach. I had wanted to arrange the material in such a way that the book would be first and foremost a systematic division of his thought, and then the material within those systematic sections would be organized chronologically. Adopting that plan would have meant that Fr. Rahner's desire to distinguish between his "academic" and "spiritual writings – he called them his "pious" writings – would have been accepted. But Fr. Neufeld's suggestion to make a strictly chronological edition was accepted. That, however, was very difficult to achieve because the Rahnerian corpus is very scattered and exists in distinctly individual pieces which makes a purely chronological approach impossible to achieve. Thus, a kind of patch-work quilt results.

The basic structure is, therefore, chronological and within that structure, various topics are summarized. Although I originally had a different opinion, I see now that this plan is a good one. It has great advantages, for example, when I think of volume 4 which I edited: the monograph *Hearer of the Word*. Normally this would be placed under the heading "Philosophical writings." Now it stands in relation to other writings which were written at the same time regarding the foundation of theology. At the time Fr. Rahner made a decision to turn from a career in philosophy to that of theology and that's the reason the subtitle is "Writings about the Philosophy of Religion and the Foundation of Theology."[16] The volume also contains scientific reflections regarding theology, problems surrounding a Theology of Proclamation, etc.

With volume 2, one can see the effect of Heidegger on Rahner's thought which was not apparent before. Karl Rahner's essay on Heidegger had only been available in French,[17] so this was the first time that it appeared in a German translation. There is also, in this volume, material that had not been previously published: outlines from his time as a student, seminar records and similar things so that *Spirit in the World* can be viewed in a broader context. That I believe is the great advantage of the edition.

The question comes to mind as to why, for example, *Encounters with Silence* is not found in the same volume as *Spirit in the World*, since it too is an early work of Rahner's.

That reveals a problem with the entire approach, but when his work is viewed in terms of phases, that is the early phase and it is better to have the writings placed as closely together as possible, better than if they had been categorized systematically – even if everything does not fit into one volume. That is the advantage of the chronological approach.

Everything can be found in the *Collected Works*, both very famous works such as *Spirit in the World* or *Hearer of the Word* as well as lesser known works. Volume 3 (*Spirituality and the Theology of the*

Church Fathers) could easily be overlooked. Would you comment on this?

Some facets of Karl Rahner's work are not well known. Very few realized that he did extensive work in the Church Fathers. Volume 1 which contains his very early essays will reveal this. Rahner's doctoral dissertation,[18] which was totally unknown, as it was never published while he was alive, is included in volume 3. There are also largely unknown texts, some on the Theology of Proclamation,[19] that are included in volume 4.

Mr. Johna, have you been asked why the smaller publications of Rahner haven't been republished?

(*Franz Johna:*) Fr. Rahner had a very close relationship with Herder Publishing, both on a personal and professional level. The publishing house became an important instrument in the dissemination of his ideas. He also had a close professional relationship with the people in the company who assisted him. Some of these professional relationships became personal, as was true in my case. With all due respect to this great theologian I believe we developed a friendship. I could speak openly and unguardedly with him, if I had a problem or a request. An editor has the task, twice a year – in spring and in autumn – to come up with a workable program. Publishing is a business and you have to have a certain number of books to publish to make a living. You establish a collection of titles with points of emphasis: there are the *Quaestiones Disputatae, the Theological Commentary to the New Testament* and so on. Now and then I would say to Fr. Rahner that we need a new volume for the *Quaestiones Disputatae*, a scholarly theological series, which Rahner had founded along with Heinrich Schlier.

Fr. Rahner was always very approachable. He offered suggestions and was open to receiving them from others. We introduced a so-called "small meditation" series. We had a series of well- known theologians writing for the series, but in a more immediately spiritual, somewhat kerygmatic fashion. The series was not only for clerics or for the theologically educated, but also for the general public that was interested in theology, but above all in spirituality. He was amenable to this and took an active role. We published it as *Theological Reflection and Faith-filled Meditation*. When you begin such a series you must publish at least two booklets a year for it to be successful. Fr. Rahner was always a much sought after speaker and when he gave a lecture he would send it to me: "Dear Mr. Johna, if you are interested in this ..." I would then contact Albert Raffelt. Not all, but many of the smaller publications in the theological series were the results of the publishing house's need to have number of books in print.

(*Albert Raffelt:*) I would agree with that. In addition we published *Theological Meditations* with Benziger.[20] It's unfortunate, but all of this is no longer readily available. I am at a loss to understand why, for example, the large reader *Rechenschaft des Glaubens (The Context of Faith)* is no longer available. It contains a selection of the best of Karl Rahner. Maybe it will be reprinted in the "Rahner Year 2004."[21] Karl Lehmann has, in the meantime, become a Cardinal, so that helps to make the work more prestigious. The marketing division of Herder must do more in this regard. Karl Rahner is no longer on the radar screen for today's students, but he is a classic. Even if it appears that certain meditations seem a bit outdated, they are nonetheless profound. Whoever makes the effort to read them would be well rewarded.

What role did the interviews play which Fr. Rahner gave for *Entschluss*, as well as those he did on Television and radio?

(*Albert Raffelt:*) Naturally those interviews must be part of the *Collected Works*. One major problem is that some of the editions are not very good because Fr. Imhof altered some texts too freely. I noticed that in a text that I had given to him (in my Proseminar on Karl Rahner) Imhof altered the headings and changed the context. One has to be very careful in reading this edition.[22]

Mr. Raffelt, one final question: do you recall anything particularly noteworthy that you spontaneously associate with Karl Rahner?

(*Albert Raffelt:*) I am not going to pass on gossip. Above all, I remember his great objectivity. Fr. Rahner never despised anyone; he was not an elitist. He was very direct in his dealings with people and spoke to them very unpretentiously even about theological topics. That is a trait not found in many people. He listened to his students' comments and took them very seriously. His directness impressed me deeply. Fr.

Rahner was not someone to seek acclaim. It was not important to him to be regarded as a learned speaker.

Since Karl Rahner was in Freiburg at the time, I invited him to come to my Proseminar on his theology to answer the students' questions directly. Hans Urs von Balthasar had criticized Rahner's work for its alleged absence of a "Theology of the Cross," and one of my students asked him about this. Fr. Rahner replied that he most certainly did have a Theology of the Cross and Anselm Grün had written a thick monograph about this very subject.[23] And then the famous sentence surfaced in the form of a little attack and he said, without mincing words: "If I wanted to counter-attack I would have to say that there exists a modern tendency (and I intentionally call it a tendency rather than a theory) that conceptualizes a Theology of the Death of God which appears to me to be a rather gnostic position. This tendency can be observed not only in the writings of Hans Urs von Balthasar, but also in those of Adrienne von Speyr, and quite independently, in those of Moltmann. To express it quite crudely: 'If I want to escape from my filth, mess and despair, it doesn't help me one bit if, to put it bluntly, God is in the same mess.'"[24] That was said spontaneously and without any ill will, but it had the effect of upsetting Hans Urs von Balthasar terribly.

That statement by Rahner can be found somewhere in his *Theodramatic*. It was a much quoted sentence. From what was to be a harmless theological conversation something completely different ensued. I only want to say that the colloquial tone Karl Rahner used was sometimes a little flippant or unguarded. When he was visiting someone he could become interested in the smallest thing from the hanging fuchsia plant on our terrace to the cats in the Black Forest that we saw on a trip.

(*Franz Johna:*). I can confirm that. Fr. Rahner was always very aware of and interested in his surroundings. Once when I was with him in Colmar in Alsace, in the "Unterlinden Museum," which is home to the Isenheimer Altar of Matthias Grünewald, he was in and out within a span of 10 minutes. But as we walked down the street he stopped at the doors of the houses we passed, looked at the names on the doors and took delight in the typical Alsacian names which have a definite ring to them. Such things interested him immensely.

NOTES

1 Cf. K. Rahner, *Gegenwart des Christentums* (Freiburg: Herder, 1963).

2 Heinrich Ott, Dr. theol., born 1929, Professor for Systematic Theology at the University of Basel (successor of Karl Barth).

3 Karl Rahner was an associate editor from 1936 to 1938 and then, for a short time, editor-in-chief of the *Zeitschrift für Katholische Theologie* (*ZKTh*); cf. Karl H. Neufeld, Karl Rahner und die "Zeitschrift für Katholische Theologie:" Schreiber and Schriftleiter, in: *Zeitschrift für Katholische Theologie* 126 (2004) 131-148.

4 Walter Warnach, *Sein und Freiheit*. Blondels Entwurf einer nornmativen Ontologie, in: *Zeitschrift für Katholische Theologie* 63 (1939) 273-310, 393-427.

5 Cf. the review by Robert Scherer (1904-1997), who from 1923-1928 was a member of the Society of Jesus and was a life-long friend of Karl Rahner, e.g., the book review, in: *Zeitschrift für Katholische Theologie* 61 (1937) 108-119.

6 Cf. Karl Rahner, Eberhard Jüngel, *Was ist ein Sakrament?* (Freiburg: Herder, 1971).

7 Cf. K. Rahner, *Foundations of Christian Faith*. An Introduction to the Idea of Christianity (New York: Seabury Press, 1978); now in: ibid., *Sämtliche Werke*, vol. 26: Grundkurs des Glaubens. Studien zum Begriff des Christentums. Bearbeitet von Nikolaus Schwerdtfeger und Albert Raffelt (Freiburg: Herder, 1999). The comprehensive commentary by Schwerdtfeger and Raffelt (ibid., XI-XXXIX) provides information on the background and on the history of the text's creation (esp. XXV-XXVII: "Von der 'Einführung' zum 'Grundkurs': Auf dem Weg zur Publikation.")

8 Cf. K. Rahner, Jesus Christus, in: *Sacramentum Mundi*, vol. 2 (1968) 920-957; now in: K. Rahner, *Sämtliche Werke*, vol. 17: Enzyklopädische Theologie. Die Lexikonbeiträge der Jahre 1956-1973. Bearbeitet von Herbert Vorgrimler (Freiburg: Herder, 2002) 1109-1136.

9 Cf. Karl Rahner, Karl Lehmann, Kerygma und Dogma, in: , vol. 1 (1965) 622-703; ibid. Geschichtlichkeit der Vermittlung. Das Problem der Dogmenentwicklung, in: ibid., 725-775; ibid., Die Bedeutung der Dogmengeschichte, in: ibid., 776-787; Karl Rahner, Der dreifaltige Gott als transzendenter Ursprung der Heilsgeschichte. Methode und Struktur des Traktats "De Deo Trino," in: , vol. 2 (1965) 317-347; ibid., Grundzüge der kirchenamtlichen Trinitätslehre, in: ibid., 348-368; ibid., Systematischer Entwurf einer Theologie der Trinität, in: ibid., 369-401; ibid., Grundsätzliche Überlegungen zur Anthropologie und Patrologie im Rahmen der Theologie, in: ibid., 406-420.

10   Cf. Karl Rahner, Wilhelm Thüsing, *Christologie – systematisch und ex-egetisch* (Quaestiones Disputatae 55) (Freiburg: Herder, 1972).

11   Gerbert Brunner (1933-2005), from 1955-1973 a Jesuit, he was an edi-tor at Herder Publishing from 1973-1996 and, until volume 5 appeared, director of the publishing company's publication of the 3rd completely re-vised edition of the *Lexikon für Theologie und Kirche*.

12   Cf. Albert Raffelt, "Grundkurs des Glaubens" – ein einzigartiges Rah-nerwerk, in: Paul Imhof, Hubert Biallowons (eds.), *Karl Rahner – Bilder eines Lebens* (Freiburg: Herder, 1985) 89-90.

13   Cf. K. Rahner, *Über die Schriftinspiration* (Quaestiones Disputatae 1) (Freiburg: Herder, 1957); now in: K. Rahner, *Sämtliche Werke*, vol. 12: Menschsein und Menschwerdung Gottes. Studien zur Grundlegung der Dogmatik, zur Christologie, Theologischen Anthropologie und Eschato-logie. Bearbeitet von Herbert Vorgrimler (Freiburg: Herder, 2005) 3-58.

14   Cf. *Sacrae Theologiae Summa*, 4 volumes (Madrid: Biblioteca de Autores Cristianos, 1958 ff.).

15   Cf. Albert Raffelt, Was will die Karl Rahner Gesamtausgabe?, in: *Zeit-schrift für Katholische Theologie* 121 (1999) 413-430.

16   Since the beginning of 1927, Rahner was designated by the Society of Jesus to be a Professor of the History of Philosophy at the Jesuit Institute for Philosophy in Pullach near Munich. Karl Rahner came to Innsbruck in the middle of 1936, was promoted to Doctor of Theology, and in 1937 he was named an Instructor for Dogmatic Theology and the History of Dogma at the University of Innsbruck.

17   Cf. K. Rahner, Introduction au concept de philosophie existentiale chez Heidegger, in: *Rechererches de sciences religieuse* 30 (1940) 152-171, now in: K. Rahner, *Sämtliche Werke*, vol. 2: Geist in Welt. Philosophische Schriften. Bearbeitet von Albert Raffelt (Freiburg: Herder, 1996) 319-346 (French original and translated back into German).

18   K. Rahner, *E Latere Christi*. Der Ursprung der Kirche als zweiter Eva aus der Seite des zweiten Adam. Eine Untersuchung über den typologi-schen Sinn von Joh 19, 34, in: ibid., *Sämtliche Werke*, vol. 3: Spirituali-tät und Theologie der Kirchenväter. Bearbeitet von Andreas R. Batlogg, Eduard Farrugia, Karl H. Neufeld (Freiburg: Herder 1999) 3-84; cf. the commentary, in: ibid., XVII-XLIII; Andreas R. Batlogg. Karl Rahners theologische Dissertation "E Latere Christi." Zur Genese eines patristi-schen Projekts (1936), in: *Zeitschrift für Katholische Theologie* 126 (2004) 111-130.

19   Cf. K. Rahner, Über die Verkündigungstheologie. Eine kritisch-sy-stematische Literaturübersicht, in: ibid., *Sämtliche Werke*, vol. 4: Hörer des Wortes. Studien zur Religionsphilosophie und zur Grundlegung der

Theologie. Bearbeitet von Albert Raffelt (Freiburg: Herder, 1996) 337-345. – This essay was originally published (in German) in a Hungarian periodical.

20   Cf. K. Rahner, *Alltägliche Dinge* (Theologische Meditationen 5) (Einsiedeln: Johannes Verlag, 1964), now in: K. Rahner, *Sämtliche Werke*, vol. 23: Glaube im Alltag. Schriften zur Spiritualität und zum christlichen Lebensvollzug. Bearbeitet von Albert Raffelt (Freiburg: Herder, 2006) 475-487; ibid., *Im Heute glauben* (Theologische Meditationen 9) (Einsiedeln: Johannes Verlag, 1965), now in: K. Rahner, *Sämtliche Werke*, vol. 14: Christliches Leben. Aufsätze – Betrachtungen – Predigten. Bearbeitet von Herbert Vorgrimler (Freiburg: Herder, 2006) 3-25; ibid., *Ich glaube an Jesus Christus* (Theologische Meditationen 21) (Einsiedeln: Johannes Verlag, 1968); ibid., *Mitte des Glaubens*, in: Karl Rahner, Adolf Exeler, Johann Baptist Metz, *Hilfe zum Glauben* (Theologische Meditationen 27) (Einsiedeln: Johannes Verlag, 1971) 39-56, now in: K. Rahner, *Sämtliche Werke*, vol. 26, 498-506; ibid., *Glaube als Mut* (Theologische Meditationen 41) (Einsiedeln: Johannes Verlag, 1976), now in: ibid., *Sämtliche Werke*, vol. 23, 281-294.

21   That was the case. Cf. Karl Lehmann, Albert Raffelt (eds.), *Karl-Rahner-Lesebuch* (Freiburg: Herder, 2nd edition 2004). English edition, *The Content of Faith*, translation edited by Harvey D. Egan, SJ (New York: Crossroad, 1994).

22   Cf. K. Rahner, Zugänge zum theologischen Denken, in: ibid., *Im Gespräch*, vol. 1, edited by Paul Imhof, Hubert Biallowons (Munich: Kösel, 1982) 240-256, 245 f.

23   Cf. Anselm Grün, *Erlösung durch das Kreuz*. Karl Rahners Beitrag zu einem heutigen Erlösungsverständnis. (Münsterschwarzach: Vier-Türme-Verlag, 1975).

24   K. Rahner, Zugänge zum theologischen Denken, 245 f.

6

A TOWERING FIGURE OF THEOLOGY IN
THE 20TH CENTURY

IN CONVERSATION WITH FR. RAYMUND SCHWAGER, SJ, INNSBRUCK

Raymund Schwager, SJ, (1935-2004), lic. phil., Dr. theol., a Jesuit since 1955. He served on the editorial board of the periodical "Orientierung" in Zurich. In 1977 he was appointed a Professor of Dogmatic Theology at the University of Innsbruck and served as Dean of the Theology Faculty in 1985-1987 and in 1999-2003. He is the founder of the school of Dramatic Theology which has its roots in the analytical work of René Girard. In 1995 he founded the international "Colloquium on Violence and Religion" which was based at Stanford University in the USA and served as its first president.

What was your experience of Karl Rahner?

I only came to know him in the final years of his life when he returned to Innsbruck from Munich. He was, of course, always very busy, but he loved to go on trips and have people go out and share an ice cream with him. The young Jesuits often drove him to South Tirol (*Südtirol*). He simply wanted to get away. He was able to relax when he took a ride with them in a car. He was then at an age when his ability to work was somewhat limited.

I did once meet him at a Dogmatic Theology workshop in Lucerne, Switzerland, before this. We went for a walk together, and he would stop and look at every department store window. He was like a child; he relished looking at the window displays.

What did this personal relationship mean to you?

As I said, I knew him only when he was already at an advanced age and he was surrounded by people who admired him. I also found him to be someone who had little patience. At mealtimes he seemed to be constantly agitated. Communicating with him was not easy because he was hard of hearing; this was made even more difficult when he was surrounded by larger groups of people. It was a happy occurrence for us that he returned to Innsbruck in the fall of 1981 and he seemed to be pleased by that. He appeared to regard Innsbruck as his home. I visited him at the hospital a few days before he died. He had received a call from Germany, inviting him to give a lecture. He immediately agreed to that, but I later telephoned them and emphasized that this was only a provisional agreement.

What does Karl Rahner, the theologian, mean to you?

Of course, I read Rahner at various times, but I never fully found myself in accord with the positions of Transcendental Theology. I studied philosophy in Pullach, but went to Fourvière in Lyon (France) for theology. There they were rather skeptical about the transcendental theological and philosophical approach. They advocated a more empirical approach. Phenomenology was much more important, even as a way of dealing with biblical narratives. Everything was referred to experience. I did a lot of exegesis, which Rahner did not do; this was an area in which he was rather weak. But I did find time to read Rahner.

What would you particularly recommend that people read to learn more about Rahner?

I am, naturally, influenced by the dissertations that have been written under my direction on Rahner. Walter Schmolly wrote on the early Rahner.[1] The predominant opinion among the younger Rahner scholars is that the early Rahner has not been sufficiently recognized. They stress the importance of the early Rahner, especially his tract on grace and in connection with that the universal hope of salvation.

Secondly, it is important to know that the early Rahner was constantly working with neo-Scholastic categories. Those who later wrote about Rahner and who had never learned about neo-scholasticism miss much of significance. Rahner was much more of a scholastic theologian than many were willing to admit. Schmolly's work clearly identified the connection that Rahner's thought always had with the ecclesial problems of a given period. The challenges of the 1930's and 40's often played an important role in his work which cannot be clearly understood without knowing this background. Willibald Sandler,[2] who also wrote a doctoral dissertation under my direction, strongly emphasizes the transcendental method which many Rahner critics ignore.

What do you personally find important in Rahner?

For me personally, an important article is the article on salvation history. It is a longer passage in which he gives a short outline of salvation history. He says there – and I paraphrase – the action of God is always to be understood as an answer to the actions of human beings.[3] That would be, of course, the foundation for the Dramatic Theology which I have developed. On this point, Rahner and Hans Urs von Balthasar would agree. Their differences are not as great as one might imagine. The central elements in the theology of Rahner or Balthasar can also be found, accentuated a little differently, in the works of Henri de Lubac, SJ, or Bernard Lonergan, SJ. Leo J. O'Donovan, SJ, has noted that both Rahner and Balthasar are sons of Ignatius.[4] Of course, there are differences. I have always worked on the doctrine of redemption and on this level Balthasar was closer to me than Rahner. But Rahner has a well developed "Theology of Death."[5] The question of a violent death had less meaning for him, of course. I am, furthermore, strongly influenced by René Girard.

How do you view the criticism of Fr. Rahner?

Nikolaus Wandinger, one of my assistants, has done research on Rahner and Dramatic Theology.[6] He came to the conclusion that Rahner does not use the terms "transcendental" and "categorical" with enough precision.[7] Those who read Rahner only superficially misunderstand the transcendental method. At any rate, I would say that Rahner's thought is much richer than the abbreviated Transcendental Theology for which he has always been reproached.

Rahner's language was not easy, of course.

Whoever reads and studies Rahner must know something about the history of theology. Rahner attempts to move beyond certain positions. Young people who are not familiar with the history of theology find it difficult to recognize that. By the way, I also found this to be the case with Balthasar. In formulating his systematic thought, Rahner draws upon the work of many writers. If you are not familiar with these authors then you are left hanging in midair. I see that happening with many students. If you have only read five sentences of Gregory of Nyssa or Augustine then you have not really studied them. Then there will be misunderstandings. That is a pervasive problem today; the background knowledge is weak. Rahner does not quote as much as Balthasar, but it is clear that he has a very precise knowledge of neo-scholasticism as well as the main problems of the medieval and patristic periods on which he draws.

The name Rahner is very much associated with Innsbruck. The Karl Rahner archives are here. Do you think that he is still relevant for students today? Does he influence anyone?

Well, doctoral dissertations are still being written on him, especially under the direction of Fr. Neufeld. Rahner is not especially stressed, but he is one of the witnesses on whom we build in Innsbruck.

What do you see as Rahner's legacy?

I would say that he belongs among those who are the great towering figures of theology in the 20th century; those who, on the one hand, prepared the Council and who, on the other, then went beyond and took its message out into the world. He attempted, basically, to interpret the Christian message for today. From this perspective, I think that he remains one of the major figures. His theology, for me, involves the attempt to move away from the theory of human omniscience. Of course, his theory of the general saving will of God and the universality of salvation must be mentioned. Together with others like Balthasar, Lonergan and de Lubac, Rahner took theology beyond neo-scholasticism.

Rahner and Balthasar differed in their assessment of the Council. In the early years following the Council, you had the feeling that things were happening fast and furiously and people were over-reacting. Balthasar was always critical of the Council. When I was in Lyon, Henri de Lubac celebrated his birthday and Balthasar was invited to attend. I asked him to meet with the Swiss Jesuit students. We were full of enthusiasm about the Council. Balthasar was asked what he thought of the Council. He sat there, pretty bitter and, well, one word led to another – against the Council. He was the first one to speak critically of the Council; later Joseph Ratzinger offered a similar critique.

What did you think was especially characteristic of Rahner?

His reaction to Hans Küng's book on infallibility seems to me to be typical: Küng accused him of being, in the final analysis, an ecclesial theologian. Rahner did not agree with Küng.[8] At that time I was still working for *Orientierung*.[9] Küng sent us an article, which was quite brutal in tone, challenging Rahner and Lehmann. We discussed it at an editorial board meeting. I then traveled to see Küng and I told him that he needed to delete all the pejorative remarks. Küng exploded: "There is nothing emotional in it – it is the objective truth." He was not willing to delete a single pejorative statement. So we did not publish his article. Rahner's position, not to support Küng's critique, kept theology from being enmeshed in a totally anti-roman stand.[10] Rahner's authoritative status very much helped to prevent a situation which would suggest a total rupture between Vatican I and Vatican II.

What was Karl Lehmann's position in all of this?

Lehmann contributed an article to a small volume, which Rahner edited, which contained responses to Küng.[11] Rahner felt, in opposition to Küng, that the Church could not abandon certain ideas. We must also expect people to learn ecclesiastical language and to some extent learn to understand subtle distinctions. Theologically, both of them were not that far apart on the question of infallibility. However, Rahner said quite clearly that you cannot just ignore something that has been as definitively stated as the doctrine of infallibility, but we need to work with the language and try to make it more comprehensible for our time. We cannot simply say that it is wrong. It also showed that Rahner had much more sense and respected the historical dimension of the community. Küng, basically, had little historical sensibility.

NOTES

1 Cf. Walter Schmolly, *Eschatologische Hoffnung in Geschichte*. Karl Rahners dogmatisches Grundverständnis der Kirche als theologische Begleitung von deren Selbstvollzug (Innsbruck: Tyrolia, 2001).

2 Willibald Sandler, *Bekehrung des Denkens*. Rahners Anthropologie und Soteriologie als formal-offenes System in triadischer Perspektive (Frankfurt: Peter Lang, 1996).

3 K. Rahner, Theos In The New Testament, in: ibid., *Theological Investigations*, vol. 1, translated by Cornelius Ernst, OP (London: Darton, Longman and Todd, 1961) 79-148, 111: "God's activity in the course of saving history is not a kind of monologue which God conducts by himself; it is a long, dramatic dialogue between God and his creature, in which God confers on man the power to make a genuine answer to his Word, and so makes his own further Word dependent upon the way in which man does in fact freely answer. God's free action never ceases to take new fire in the activity of man. History is not just a play in which God puts himself on the stage and creatures are merely what is performed; the creature is a real co-performer in this human-divine drama of history. And so history has a real and absolute seriousness, an absolute decision, which is not to be relativized as far as the creature is concerned with the remark – at once true and false – that everything rises from God's will and nothing can resist it." Cf. ibid., 116: "And because God's activity is part of a dialogue, his power is not seen as a magnitude continuously and obviously present in the world, something already realized, but as something which is only slowly realized, by a real struggle, in the drama of God and his world, until his βασιλεία is actually present and his δύναμις has really appeared (Mt 24:30; Lk 21:27; cf. Mt 26:64)." Cf. ibid., 117: "With regard to God's personal activity, the New Testament understands that the free, living God can act differently at different times, can enter into different relationships with man. The decisive feature of this understanding is that it involves knowledge of the fact which is precisely *not* a matter of course for the New Testament understanding of God, that the free, incalculable God has spoken his last, *definitive* word in the dramatic dialogue between God and man. God is the Free and Transcendent, whose potentialities could never be exhausted in a finite world, and who in consequence is never really bound by what he has done." – See now in: K. Rahner, *Sämtliche Werke*, vol. 4: Hörer des Wortes. Schriften zur Religionsphilosophie und zur Grundlegung der Theologie. Bearbeitet von Albert Raffelt (Freiburg: Herder, 1997) 346-403.

4 Cf. L. J. O'Donovan, *Two Sons of Ignatius: Drama and Dialectic*, in: *Philosophy & Theology* 11 (1998) 105-124; ibid., *Zwei Söhne des Ignatius – Drama und Dialektik*, in: Albert Raffelt (ed.), *Weg und Weite* (Festschrift Karl Lehmann) (Freiburg: Herder, 2nd edition 2001) 371-385; recently: An-

dreas R. Batlogg, Hans Urs von Balthasar und Karl Rahner: Zwei Schüler des Ignatius, in: Magnus Striet, Jan-Heiner Tück (eds.), *Die Kunst Gottes verstehen*. Hans Urs von Balthasars theologische Provokationen (Freiburg: Herder, 2005) 410-446.

5 Cf. K. Rahner, Zur Theologie des Todes, in: *Zeitschrift für Katholische Theologie* 79 (1957) 1-44; now in: ibid., *Sämtliche Werke*, vol. 9: Maria, Mutter des Herrn. Mariologische Studien. Bearbeitet von Regina Pacis Meyer (Freiburg: Herder, 2004) 395-417.

6 Cf. Nikolaus Wandinger, *Die Sündenlehre als Schlüssel zum Menschen*. Impulse K. Rahner und R. Schwagers zu einer Heuristik theologischer Anthropologie (Münster: LIT, 2003).

7 Cf. Nikolaus Knoepffler, *Der Begriff "transzendental" bei Karl Rahner*. Zur Frage seiner Kantischen Herkunft (Innsbruck: Tyrolia, 1993).

8 Küng praised Karl Rahner effusively in January 1971 in his article "Im Interesse der Sache. Antwort an Karl Rahner," in: *Stimmen der Zeit*: 187 (1971) 43-64, 43: "Tirelessly, relentlessly, he has worked to open many a door for the people of our generation: took up questions which no other Catholic theologian dared to do; revised what appeared to him to be in need of reformulation; set new accents, from the heights of the doctrine on God and Christ all the way to entirely practical matters of parish life and personal spirituality; offered bold, new answers, which were then respectively interpreted as heretical. In all of this he imparted to us young theologians the joy of theology, he gave us the courage to think."

9 *Orientierung* is a Jesuit periodical edited by the Swiss Jesuits. Originally published under the name, *Apologetische Blätter. Mitteilungen des Apologetischen Instituts des Schweizerischen Katholischen Volksvereins*, the periodical was renamed *Orientierung* in 1947, the 11th year of its publication.

10 Cf. K. Rahner, Zum Begriff der Unfehlbarkeit in der Katholischen Theologie. Einige Bemerkungen anlässlich des 100-Jahr-Jubiläums des Unfehlbarkeitsdogmas vom 18. Juli 1870, in: *Stimmen der Zeit* 186 (1970) 18-31; ibid., Kritik an Hans Küng. Zur Frage der Unfehlbarkeit theologischer Sätze, in: *Stimmen der Zeit* 186 (1970) 361-377; ibid., Replik. Bemerkungen zu Hans Küng: Im Interesse der Sache, in: *Stimmen der Zeit* 187 (1971) 145-160.

11 Cf. Karl Rahner (ed.), *Zum Problem Unfehlbarkeit*. Antworten auf die Anfrage von Hans Küng (Quaestiones Disputatae 54) (Freiburg: Herder, 1971) with essays by Karl Rahner, SJ, Luigi Sartori, Joseph Ratzinger, Walter Brandmüller, Rudolf Schnackenburg, Leo Scheffczyk, Yves Congar, OP, Otto Semmelroth, SJ, Heinrich Fries, Heribert Mühlen, Juan Alfaro, SJ, Elmar Klinger, Karl J. Becker, SJ, Herbert Vorgrimler and Karl Lehmann.

7

AN INCREDIBLE FACILITY FOR LANGUAGE

IN CONVERSATION WITH FR. WOLFGANG SEIBEL, SJ, MUNICH

Wolfgang Seibel, SJ, Dr. theol., born 1928, a Jesuit since 1955, 1966-1998 Editor-in-chief and publisher of "Stimmen der Zeit" in Munich, the oldest German Catholic periodical. During the Second Vatican Council he worked as a reporter for the German Catholic News Service in Rome.

What was your relationship with Karl Rahner?

I already knew Fr. Rahner when he was a professor in Innsbruck. When he came to Munich to take the Romano Guardini chair in 1963 he moved into our community and I came into closer contact with him.[1] I met him frequently at the Council where I was a reporter. As editor-in-chief of *Stimmen der Zeit* I saw him more often because he wrote many articles for us and I needed to meet with him because of this.

What stands out most in your recollection of Fr. Rahner?

That's difficult to say. In any event he never was an ivory tower theologian. You could talk to him like any other person. He was always very open, almost somewhat childlike in his openness. He had a certain kind of naiveté. He was very friendly, although he could at times be moody.

Can you recall a time, specifically, when you were surprised by his openness?

I was not really surprised; actually we took it as something to be expected. It would have been more unusual if he had taken on the demeanor of a professor, because among the Jesuits that is seldom the case. This great professor acted in quite an unassuming way. He always ate his meals quickly because he had some candy beforehand in his room. He would weigh himself and when he found that he was overweight he would eat less. Having finished his meal earlier he would become restless at the table and stand up and walk around.

What did you especially value?

What stood out was the simple fact that such an outstanding theologian could be an unassuming person, in his behavior, in how he presented himself! Fr. Rahner was a world class theologian in comparison to other professors, but he did not act in such a way as to call attention to himself, and for us Jesuits there were no special privileges for professors.

When you wanted to have an article from Fr. Rahner, could you choose the topic?

That varied from time to time. Either we spoke with Fr. Rahner as to what topic to treat or about which we thought it important to have a discussion; he always had ideas that interested him. Or he would say, "That's a topic that the periodical should consider," and then we would immediately decide on that; or, and this was often the case, we would use his lecture notes on the topics that we were interested in.

When you edited the texts: could you do that without consulting with Fr. Rahner?

He did not say anything. His manuscripts did not need any editing in terms of content. Sometimes, especially with theological questions, there would be extremely long sentences with many dependent clauses, because he always included his opponents view. Furthermore, he would always dictate his articles and he would add another half sentence to defend against possible objections and that resulted in long sentences. I simply shortened the sentences. I never showed them to him. He did not read the articles again. As long as there were no changes to the content, it did not matter to him.

He was probably grateful for the help – was he not?

In so far as he even noticed it – yes. With other periodicals, strangely enough, he noticed it immediately. He complained once about an editor who, in his opinion, shortened his article too much, but this editor had also changed the content. That is something I never did. I made only grammatical changes; I shortened long sentences and made more paragraphs. Those are formalities that I did not ask him about. That would have inconvenienced him and would have been of no interest to him.

You worked a long time with Fr. Rahner. Was his relationship to the periodical *Geist und Leben*, whose editorial staff was in the same residence, also as close?

It was about the same. Fr. Rahner wrote articles on Theology and Church Politics for *Stimmen der Zeit*. *Geist und Leben* was more interested in articles on spirituality. In addition *Geist und Leben* was published bimonthly and *Stimmen der Zeit* was published monthly.

Did *Geist und Leben* have the same method of editing texts?

That depends on who the editor-in-chief was at the time. Fr. Friedrich Wulf SJ[2] worked in a fashion very similar to mine. He sometimes changed the content which displeased Rahner, but he never dared to say anything to him. Rahner never had the heart to say something about that.

The relationship between daily life and spirituality was very strong in Fr. Rahner's writings. Which of his articles published in *Stimmen der Zeit* would you recommend re-reading?

This close relationship is certainly apparent and has lasting value for Christian life. Fr. Rahner wrote about some core issues for the Church that are still of concern today. I am thinking about his famous article on "Episcopacy and Primacy,"[3] which still has relevance today as the problems have not changed since the Council, but, I believe, have become even more intractable.

It is often said Rahner's writings are too philosophical and people today want a more historical, biblical or liturgical approach to theology. How do you respond to that?

One cannot do everything. Karl Rahner was first and foremost a systematic theologian, a speculative thinker. On the other hand he had an enormous knowledge of history, of Church history and the history of dogma above all. It is clear, looking at his writings on the history of penance, for instance, that he was very well informed. He was definitely grounded in history so it cannot be argued that he was purely a speculative thinker. As far as the bible is concerned, he was certainly not an exegete, but he was very interested in exegesis. That was one of his great strengths; he was incredibly inquisitive about many things. He knew many natural scientists and was passionately interested in the latest results of their research. It was clear that he wished to keep up with all the latest developments in a variety of fields. He had an unquenchable thirst for knowledge, a great desire to know. In his last major public lecture in Freiburg he spoke to that when he noted how little theologians really know.[4] Rahner saw very clearly that it was important not to limit oneself only to the traditional sources of Dogmatic Theology.

In the United States there are many students of Rahner who in turn have their own students. Is Rahner's memory kept alive in Germany?

I do not know the younger generation of theologians well enough to comment on that. Many of Rahner's students became professors themselves and are now retired: Metz, Vorgrimler. Some became bishops like Lehmann, although he had not actually been a student of Rahner's, but a post-doctoral assistant. I don't know how alive his memory is to the younger theologians, but there are doctoral dissertations constantly being written about him, not only in Innsbruck, but also in other places. From that one can conclude that Rahner's theology is still alive.

In your estimation, among his numerous publications, what are the ones of which we should be most conscious? Would it be his more pious works such as _On the Need for and the Blessing of Prayer_ or his

more speculative theological writings such as *Spirit in the World* and *Hearer of the Word?*

In Rahner's "pious" works, his German was excellent. There were no long sentences, no technical expressions. Much of it was formulated masterfully. These works can still be read profitably today. I do not know to what extent he read literature, but his talent for formulation certainly had to come from his brilliance. He had an incredible facility for language. As a rule Fr. Rahner wrote mostly essays and very few books. *Foundations of Christian Faith,* which was his major work, was written under pressure from the Herder Publishing Company. He was put up in a hotel room in Freiburg and a secretary of the publishing house took his dictation.

Fr. Rahner was more a writer of essays. When I began my studies in 1947, his first great essays began to appear. Most were published in *Zeitschrift für Katholische Theologie.* They were a revelation to us compared with the very narrow Neo-scholastic Theology which we had been taught at the Gregorian University in Rome.

Can you say how many of his articles were published in *Stimmen der Zeit* and who edited them?

I cannot answer the question about who edited his articles before I did. From 1966 I was responsible for *Stimmen der Zeit.* Before that I didn't have anything to do with his articles. Also over time the style and manner with which Fr. Rahner worked on his articles changed. He worked much more carefully on them in his early years than he did later,[5] when it became too much of a burden. He dictated the later articles and perhaps read through them once and made some written corrections or additions. It was not an intense reworking of the text. At any rate, the earlier articles are denser and better formulated. Perhaps, he simply had more time when he was in Innsbruck. It also depends on the topic. There are some articles in *Stimmen der Zeit* written during the time of the Council which didn't have to be changed at all, not a single word. It was clear that this was a topic in which he was fully engaged.

At times Rahner had difficulties with Rome: with Cardinal Ottaviani and later with Cardinal Ratzinger ultimately over *Quaestio Dis-*

putata, number 100, which he co-authored together with Heinrich
Fries. Can you speak to this?

The difficulties Karl Rahner had with Rome at that time were not
unusual for theologians who did not simply repeat what was the conventional approach to theology, but presented something new and creative. To that extent, he was in good company with theologians such
as Yves Congar, OP, and Henri de Lubac, SJ. Prior to the Council, Fr.
Rahner had been placed under Roman censorship and everything that
he wrote had to be submitted to the censor. So he said: "I won't write
anything anymore." And then he became a conciliar theologian![6]

What distinguished Fr. Rahner from other theologians?

One of his greatest strengths was that in comparison to many other theologians of that time, he knew Scholastic Theology forwards
and backwards, so in his discussion with the conciliar commissions
he could beat his opponents with their own weapons. He could also
speak fluent Latin. This was not so simple, especially for a German
theologian. The Jesuit theologians knew Latin well because they gave
their lectures in Latin, but it was more difficult for the others. One
time I was in Naples, where Fr. Rahner visited Alfredo Marranzini
SJ,[7] who translated his *Theological Investigations* into Italian, and the
Jesuit student scholastics were awed by the fact that he could answer
all their questions in Latin. Their own professors were not so good.

NOTES

1 In January of 1966, the office of the editorial board of *Stimmen der Zeit*
was moved from the Veterinärstrasse (near the Ludwig-Maximilian-Uni-
versity, near the English Gardens), to Munich-Nymphenburg. The newly
built "Writers House" ("*Schriftstellerhaus*") was named after Fr. Alfred
Delp, SJ, (1907-1945), a former staff member of the editorial board. Delp
was murdered on Feb. 2, 1945, by the National Socialists. In September
2003, the Jesuits had to give up the Alfred-Delp-Haus. The office of the
editorial board is since that time located at the Berchmans College in the
Kaulbachstrasse in Munich.

2 Friedrich Wulf, SJ, (1908-1990), 1947-1979 was the editor-in-chief of
Geist und Leben. During the Second Vatican Council he was an advisor
of the Bishop of Rottenburg-Stuttgart and worked mainly on the Decree

Perfectae Caritatis, the Decree on the Appropriate Renewal of the Religious Life.

3 Cf. K. Rahner, Primat und Episkopat. Einige Überlegungen über Verfassungsprinzipien der Kirche, in: *Stimmen der Zeit* 161 (1957/58) 321-336.

4 Cf. K. Rahner, *Von der Unbegreiflichkeit Gottes*. Erfahrungen eines katholischen Theologen, edited by Albert Raffelt (Freiburg: Herder, 2004) 53; now in: K. Rahner, *Sämtliche Werke*, vol. 25: Erneuerung des Ordenslebens. Zeugnis für Kirche und Welt. Bearbeitet von Andreas R. Batlogg (Freiburg: Herder, 2008) 47-57, 54 f.; English translation: Experiences of a Catholic Theologian, in: *Theological Studies* 61(2000) 3-15, 13: "As a theologian, I maintain that God created the world but, since I know so little about the world, the notion of creation remains strangely empty."

5 Between 1939 and 1984 Karl Rahner published a total of 68 articles in *Stimmen der Zeit*; cf. Andreas R. Batlogg, Karl Rahner als Autor in den "Stimmen der Zeit," in: *Stimmen der Zeit* spezial 1-2004, 16-30; ibid., Von Karl Rahner lernen, in: *Stimmen der Zeit* 222 (2004) 145-146.

6 Karl Rahner was already officially appointed a *peritus* of the Council (by Pope John XXIII) in March of 1962 and thus did not attend the Council only as advisor to the Archbishop of Vienna, Cardinal Franz König. This took place before his preliminary censorship by Rome after his address at the Austrian Katholikentag on June 1, 1962, in Salzburg. It was a decision made single-handedly by then Prefect of the Holy Office, Cardinal Alfredo Ottaviani. Later Pope John XXIII distanced himself from this disciplinary action of Ottaviani after many bishops and Cardinals and several prominent politicians intervened on Rahner's behalf. Cf. Andreas R. Batlogg, Karl Rahners Mitarbeit an den Konzilstexten, in: Franz-Xaver Bischof, Stephan Leimgruber (eds.), *Vierzig Jahre II. Vatikanum*. Zur Wirkungsgeschichte der Konzilstexte (Würzburg: Echter, 2nd edition 2005) 355-376.

7 Cf. Alfredo Marranzini, Impulse nach Italien, in: Paul Imhof, Hubert Biallowons (eds.), *Karl Rahner – Bilder eines Lebens* (Freiburg: Herder, 1985) 101-104.

PART TWO

KARL RAHNER'S ASSISTANTS AND CO-WORKERS

8

NOT A SPECULATIVE ACADEMIC THEOLOGY

IN CONVERSATION WITH ADOLF DARLAP, INNSBRUCK

Adolf Darlap (1924-2007), Dr. theol. was Professor of Church History at the University of Innsbruck and one of the first to work with Karl Rahner.

How did you get to know Karl Rahner?

Before I got to know him personally I knew him as an independent theologian through his publications in *Stimmen der Zeit* and in *Geist und Leben*. After finishing my studies in classical Philology and Philosophy, I began the study of theology in Frankfurt am Main at the Jesuit College Sankt Georgen. I had many conversations there with the Spiritual Director and with professors (among them Fr. Semmelroth[1]) who encouraged me to continue my studies in Innsbruck. That was toward the end of the 1940's. In Innsbruck I very quickly connected with Fr. Rahner. At the time he was lecturing on the tract *De Gratia Christi*. I offered to type the text (which he already had because he had taught the course the first time in 1938/39[2]) onto a stencil so that copies could be made. It was 350 to 450 pages. That's how I came to know him.

I worked very intensely with him in his seminars (beginning with the *Theology of Death*) in the winter semester of 1950/51, because they always opened up new horizons of thought for me. There developed, over time, a group of students who strove to have a closer working relationship with him. There were three or four students: Fr. Kern[3] was among them. Fr. Rahner offered a special colloquium – a kind of advanced seminar – once a week to this group. This fostered a closer relationship with him.

In the middle of the 1950's a proposal was made to publish a new edition of the *Lexikon für Theologie und Kirche*. Herder publishing wanted to have Karl Rahner act as editor. He came to me immediately and asked me to participate in this project. I drafted a plan for the new

edition and edited the first two volumes. I had to leave the editorial
work after I was offered the position of assistant to Bernhard Welte[4]
at the University of Freiburg. Later – this was the time when the intention of Pope John XXIII to convoke a Council was being discussed
– the Publishing House decided to offer an international *Lexikon* for
Pastoral Theology which would be published simultaneously in several languages and later came to be titled *Sacramentum Mundi*. The
planning for this was again entrusted to me. But then the Council
began. Fr. Rahner took me with him to Rome. I was there for the entire Council so as to be in contact with the international publishers
and my co-workers. During this time Karl Rahner received the call to
come to Munich and assume the Romano Guardini chair. He did not
want to remain in Innsbruck. He had difficulties with his superiors
and his colleagues.[5] That already was a big problem for him in 1951.
At that time some of his colleagues reported him to Rome because
of some of his theological positions on Mariology. His publication in
the field of Mariology runs about 400 pages.[6] I collaborated further
with him working on the planning and preparation for the *Theological
Investigations* series.

I continued my work on the *Lexikon* in Munich. Fr. Rahner was
naturally very much in demand. He always received invitations to lecture, to participate in congresses, and received invitations to come to
other countries. More and more work was asked of him. He did not
want to bear the responsibility any longer for continuing the work for
Sacramentum Mundi and so I had to work on that by myself. That was
difficult because of the publication of the text in various languages.
There was a German, Dutch, English, Spanish and Italian edition –
but not a French one – that was prevented by Jean Daniélou, SJ,[7] who
was skeptical of "German Theology," even though he always referred to
it in his writings.

Did Fr. Rahner have enemies?

For a variety of reasons a kind of "hive of intrigue" (*"Intrigenwirtschaft"*)
developed around Rahner. That led to many tensions because of the
presence of various groups with divergent interests at the Institute in
Munich. Personal issues were a part of that. I only want to indicate
that the atmosphere there was not 100 percent positive. Fr. Rahner
was an exceptionally reflective and a very pious man, but his knowl-

edge of human nature was limited. That is my impression. His lectures were not as well received as were those of Romano Guardini. Guardini included in his lectures the works of Dostoevsky, Rilke, Hölderlin and Pascal, authors whose ideas touched the normal student. Rahner basically taught "a diluted" (*"eine verdünnte"*) Dogmatic Theology. At that time the idea for a text, "An Introduction to the Idea of Christianity," came to him which later became *Foundations of Christian Faith*, (1976). It is difficult to judge whether or not he wanted to return to a Theology Faculty, because of this disappointment, but he accepted the call to go to Münster.[8] When he was in Munich later on I worked very hard to get him to return to Innsbruck and above all, to have him move his library and his archives back there. His answer was: "I am not only moving my books to Innsbruck; I'm returning there myself." That was the last phase of his life: from the fall of 1981 to March 1984.

You mentioned that Fr. Rahner was also a pious man.

He was very pious, but also very reflective. He had a very keen analytical mind. He saw connections which were not apparent to others but with the assistance of his philosophical-theological methodology, revealed to them the possibility of new perspectives. That is his great accomplishment! Then there is also the fact that he overcame and corrected the subject-object schema through a transcendentalization of the object. That is expressed in a somewhat complicated manner. Through this transcendental dimension the presence of the divine became visible which previously was not so easily seen.

Was that always present in Rahner's thinking?

He had (along with Martin Heidegger) the opinion that the piety of the philosopher is thinking. Fr. Rahner rose about 4 a.m.; then he took care of his correspondence; then he performed his meditations, prayed the divine office and celebrated Mass. Often because we were working on the *Lexikon* we had to travel to Freiburg. I had to be at the Jesuit residence at 4 a.m. I was the acolyte at the Mass and we took the train at 5 a.m. to Freiburg. Otherwise his week was filled with academic responsibilities; he had to give lectures two to three times a week, hold a seminar two or three times a week and then he also had an evening colloquium.

In addition he received many invitations, which he structured, to a certain extent, thematically. A number of articles resulted from this, "The Christian and His Unbelieving Relatives,"[9] for example. One of his relatives had three or four children and his wife ran off with a French army officer and what can this man do now? The children need a mother. Can he remarry of not? He cannot get married in the Church; he is married ... These were concrete situations, existential circumstances that became the starting point for his reflections.

So there were often pastoral concerns that provided the motivation for his publications?

There is much that he experienced in the articles that he composed. For him, theology was not something that one did in an ivory tower or a speculative process performed at one's desk; rather it was a form of crisis theology (*"Krisentheologie"*) which is not only pious, but also transplants the theological value into life itself.

You referred to Rahner's inadequate knowledge of human nature. Did he sometimes enter too quickly into a relationship?

He was not very discerning in this regard. There were many people in his inner circle who wanted somehow to profit from their relationship with him. I always wondered why he couldn't see through them.

Apparently he had among his colleagues in Innsbruck some critics and he suffered because of that.

Whether you can say that he "suffered" – that I don't know. There were a number of other factors that came into play. To give an example: Fr. Rahner lived in a room which, due to the configuration of the building, included a small adjacent space – so he lived practically in one and one-half rooms. He slept in that small space. There was a water pipe running through that room and he asked the Rector whether he could have a sink installed there. He was told that it was not possible and the reason that he was given was that it went against the spirit of poverty! That is only one small example, but that is how it was at that time. A more significant example was the time when he was criticized by his colleagues in Rome because of his Mariology and a *"visitator"* came to subject him to an examination of his position.[10]

What can you say about Hans Urs von Balthasar's criticism of Karl Rahner?

Von Balthasar was a completely different kind of person than Rahner:[11] strongly extroverted, interested in literature. He had first immersed himself in German studies and wrote *The Apocalypse of the German Soul*, a three volume work which was most interesting. Only after that did he enter the Order. Later he was university chaplain in Basel and he met Adrienne von Speyr,[12] the wife of the historian Werner Kaegi.[13] Adrienne von Speyr experienced visions and von Balthasar wrote books about that. Rahner cast a rather jaundiced eye on these books and visions and commented on them. That created a certain amount of tension between them! That certainly damaged their previously close relationship. Both of them had drafted a plan for a work on Dogmatic Theology which was published in the first volume of *Theological Investigations*.[14] The plan was not able to be realized.

It was not a matter of completely opposite approaches, but differences of opinion. I knew von Balthasar personally. He was a very sympathetic, helpful, caring person, but that, of course, did not eradicate the conflict of interests or the tensions between them. Fr. Rahner once said, rather maliciously – von Balthasar has published a Theological Aesthetic – that in the third millennium the Christian message probably would not be sold under the category of Beauty. That, of course, is a real dig. But it does show that these two held very different positions. This may also be the place to mention the conflict they had about the *theologomenon* of "anonymous Christianity" against which Balthasar wrote an entire book.[15] Incidentally Karl Barth dedicated a wonderful monograph to Balthasar and used, analogously to "anonymous Christians," the term "virtual Christians."

What should Fr. Rahner's legacy be for future generations?

That is not easy to answer. There are so many individual theological positions. I could cite, for example, the relationship of Christology to Anthropology, but that is too general. When you start with what he formulated in one of his early works, *On the Need for and the Blessing of Prayer,* and what he wrote also in *Hearer of the Word,* then you can recognize that for him the human person is not someone submerged into a society bent on amusement or lost in the rat race of daily life or work, but rather the human person has a different purpose. Or he would also say that we should not speak of God as a friend in the sense of a fashionable and one-sided personalism, but we must recognize, as Fr. Rahner proposed, that we are enveloped by a "Mystery" and that ultimately we are introduced into this Mystery. God is not an object among other objects; he is present in us. It is not very easy to say where and how to begin. There are many approaches.

You just referred to Rahner's work *On the Need for and the Blessing of Prayer.*

That is an impressive work. Originally they were homilies which he gave in Munich in 1946 and were published in 1949. They go directly to the heart.

Fr. Rahner valued his relationship with you. Was it a friendship with you or was it more collegial?

It was a friendship. Again and again he would ask me to address him with the informal *"Du"* (Thou). But I did not choose to do so because he represented a father figure for me. I could not address him with the informal or familiar "thou." I have a very intimate relationship with him, even to this very day – I say this with a certain timidity – I speak to him every day. In the last few years I have had five serious operations and I always turned to him and requested his help. I know that there is a connection that will always be there. After Fr. Rahner died, there was a tendency among the Jesuits to think that we have to stop speaking about him so that there would not be any new disputes. We don't want to awaken any great interest in him, but rather allow the dust to settle. That's what a Jesuit from Munich said to me – straight to my face. There were problems with Rome.

I have the impression that Fr. Rahner did not have very many people that he could speak with in the way he did with you.

I can't really judge whether that is so. Fr. Rahner did not need theological conversations or theological inspiration. He had his own means
of access to ideas. It must not be forgotten, a point that has been somewhat neglected, the great influence that the thinking of Martin Heidegger had on him. How the thought process is set in motion, how
problems are to be addressed – that is something Fr. Rahner learned
from Heidegger. They were more methodological, than material influences. Naturally he was a theologian, but he had the "scaffolding" of
philosophy.

To cite another example: Bernhard Welte wrote an essay in 1954
for the large three volume work *The Council of Chalcedon*.[16] In it he
attempted, with the help of Hegel, to reinterpret the classical terminology of the Councils within the context of the terminology of German Idealism and Hegel. Rahner, being the censor of these volumes,
read this essay. From that moment on a new element was introduced
into his Trinitarian Theology and his Christology. That was a very interesting development because you could clearly follow those connections. Welte was from Freiburg, as were Rahner and Heidegger, born
in Messkirch. He was secretary to Archbishop Konrad Gröber, who
allowed Welte to continue to work as a theologian. Welte had written a book on Karl Jasper's philosophy of religion and later held the
Chair for the Philosophy of Religion in Freiburg. I was his assistant
and came to know about his thought more closely.

**During the Council you were with Fr. Rahner in Rome. What did
this ecclesial assembly mean to him?**

The Council was an immense challenge for him and it had begun long
before it officially began. Cardinal Franz König sent the schemata of
the pre-conciliar commissions to him and Fr. Rahner was to write his
evaluations. Because of that process he became very familiar with all
the material. The pre-conciliar schemata were not only pre-conciliar;
they also had their roots theologically in the previous century. That
presented an immense challenge for him.[17] He knew that material and
he knew the various positions; some of the teachings from his former
teachers were represented in those texts. He went really as a *Peritus*
to the Council and he knew what was at stake. Naturally, he spoke up
at the commissions. At this time in Rome there were various Bishops' Conferences with committees formed to support their opinions:

the South Americans, the Europeans, Germans, French and Spanish each formed their own groups. A great deal of work went on behind the scene to provide support for the official Commission. The various Bishops' Conferences cooperated with one another. Each worked on text proposals and presented them. That meant much work. No one had modern technical support in those days. Everything was still in the Stone Age. Everything had to be typed, photocopied and distributed.

And you helped with that? Were you alone?

There were several of us, including Karl Lehmann. I lived in the Germanicum. It was a time of incredible awakening (*"gigantische Aufbruchstimmung"*) and Karl Rahner's theology naturally became a part of this.

Fr. Rahner had an unbelievable ability to work.

He was always intellectually engaged. I recall, for example, the reflections and conversation that took place on the article about Eschatology.[18] I spoke with him for several days in succession and I could see clearly how it all developed, how he would pursue a lead in order to reach an axiomatic level with which to connect Eschatology to Christology. That was a very complicated process, but still clear, which then led to the article. Not one of my teachers had so great an influence on my thinking and on my life as did Fr. Rahner. For that I am eternally grateful.

NOTES

1 Otto Semmelroth, SJ, (1912-1979), became a Jesuit in 1932, Professor for Dogmatic Theology at the College, Sankt Georgen in Frankfurt am Main; a conciliar theologian.

2 Cf. Roman A. Siebenrock, Gnade als Herz der Welt. Der Beitrag Karl Rahners zu einer zeitgemässen Gnadentheologie, in: Mariano Delgado, Matthias Lutz-Bachmann (eds.), *Theologie aus der Erfahrung der Gnade.* Annäherungen an Karl Rahner (Berlin: Morus, 1994) 34-71. Karl Rahner's course on grace will appear in Latin and German in *Sämtliche Werke* as volume 5, probably in 2009.

3 Walter Kern, SJ, (1922-2007), Dr. phil., Dr. theol., Professor for Fundamental Theology at the University of Innsbruck.

4 Bernhard Joseph Welte (1906-1983), 1952 Professor for Questions in Philosophy and Theology, 1958 Professor for Christian Philosophy of Religion at the University of Freiburg, 1955-56 Rector of Albert-Ludwig's-University, Freiburg.

5 See Andreas R. Batlogg, Karl Rahner in Innsbruck. Aus der Wissenschaftsbiographie eines Jesuiten – zugleich ein Stück Fakultätsgeschichte, in: *Zeitschrift für Katholische Theologie* 129 (2007) 397-422.

6 Cf. now: K. Rahner, *Sämtliche Werke*, vol. 9: Maria, Mutter des Herrn. Mariologische Studien. Bearbeitet von Regina Pacis Meyer (Freiburg: Herder, 2004). The editorial comments report thoroughly on the difficulties within the Religious Order, which prevented the publication of the manuscript under the brief title, "Assumptio-Study."

7 Jean Daniélou, SJ, (1905-1974), became a Jesuit in 1929, Professor for Early Christian Literature and History at the Institut Catholique in Paris. With an article in "Études," he set in motion the discussions surrounding Nouvelle Théologie, founder of the series, "Sources Chrétiennes," peritus at the Second Vatican Council, 1969 Cardinal, 1972 named to the Académie Française.

8 Cf. the information provided by Herbert Vorgrimler, *Karl Rahner*. Gotteserfahrung in Leben und Denken (Darmstadt: Primus, 2004) 90-92; Heinrich Fries, Professor in München. 1964-1967, in: Paul Imhof, Hubert Biallowons (eds.), *Karl Rahner – Bilder eines Lebens* (Freiburg: Herder, 1985) 70; Jörg Splett, Auf dem Lehrstuhl Romano Guardinis, in: ibid., 72-73; Eugen Biser, Zu Karl Rahners religionsphilosophischen Konzept, in: ibid., 74-77.

9 Cf. K. Rahner, Der Christ und seine ungläubigen Verwandten, in: ibid., *Schriften zur Theologie*, vol. 3 (Einsiedeln: Benziger, 1956) 419-439. – Now in: ibid., Karl Rahner, *Sämtliche Werke*, vol. 10: Kirche in den Herausforderungen der Zeit. Studien zur Ekklesiologie und zur kirchlichen Existenz. Bearbeitet von Josef Heislbetz und Albert Raffelt (Freiburg: Herder, 2003) 274-289. – See also K. Rahner, The Christian among Unbelieving Relations, in: ibid., *Theological Investigations*, vol. 3, translated by Karl-H. and Boniface Kruger (London: Darton, Longman & Todd, 1967) 355-372.

10 Referred to here is Fr. Felix Malmberg, SJ; cf. also Regina Pacis Meyer's editorial comments in: K. Rahner, *Sämtliche Werke*, vol. 9, XI-LVI, esp. XLIII-XLVII.

11 Cf. Andreas R. Batlogg, Hans Urs von Balthasar und Karl Rahner: zwei Schüler des Ignatius, in: Magnus Striet, Jan-Heiner Tück (eds.), *Die Kunst*

Gottes verstehen. Hans Urs von Balthasars theologische Provokationen (Freiburg: Herder, 2005) 410-436.

12 Adrienne von Speyr (1902-1967), was a medical doctor, mystic and spiritual writer. Married the historian, Emil Dürr († 1934) in 1927, both of whose sons she raised; married Werner Kaegi in 1936, Dürr's successor as Department Chair for History at the University of Basel. In 1940, she converted to Catholicism with Hans Urs von Balthasar's help. Her entire writings, 62 volumes, were published by Johannes-Verlag.

13 Werner Kaegi (1901-1979), 1935-1971, Professor for Medieval and Modern World History at the University of Basel, married Adrienne von Speyr in 1936, translator of the works of the Dutch Historian, Johan Huizinga.

14 K. Rahner, Über den Versuch eines Aufrisses einer Dogmatik, in: ibid., *Schriften zur Theologie,* vol. 1 (Einsiedeln: Benziger, 1954) 9-47. – Now in: ibid., *Sämtliche Werke,* vol. 4: Hörer des Wortes. Schriften zur Religionsphilosophie und zur Grundlegung der Theologie. Bearbeitet von Albert Raffelt (Freiburg: Herder, 1997) 404-448. See, ibid., The Prospects for a Dogmatic Theology and A Scheme for a Treatise of Dogmatic Theology, in: ibid., *Theological Investigations,* vol. 1, translated by Cornelius Ernst, OP (London: Darton, Longman & Todd, 1961) 1-18 and 19-37. Cf. also: Karl H. Neufeld, *Die Brüder Rahner.* Eine Biographie (Freiburg: Herder, 2nd edition 2004) 178-186; Andreas R. Batlogg, *Die Mysterien des Lebens Jesu bei Karl Rahner.* Zugang zum Christusglauben (Innsbruck: Tyrolia, 2nd edition 2003) 385-391.

15 Cf. Hans Urs von Balthasar, *Cordula oder der Ernstfall* (Einsiedeln: Johannes Verlag, 1966, 4th edition 1987); ibid., *The Moment of Christian Witness,* translated by Richard Beckley (Glen Rock, N.J.: Newman Press, 1969).

16 Cf. Bernhard Welte, Homoousios hemin. Gedanken zum Verständnis und zur theologischen Problematik der Kategorien von Chalkedon, in: Alois Grillmeier, Heinrich Bacht (eds.), *Das Konzil von Chalkedon,* vol. 3 (Würzburg: Echter, 5th editon 1979) 51-80. K. Rahner's article "Chalkedon – Ende oder Anfang?" in the same volume (3-49), is a direct reaction to the Welte article and was requested directly by both of the editors; cf. also Andreas R. Batlogg, *Die Mysterien des Lebens Jesu bei Karl Rahner,* 343, footnote 224, with a quote from the correspondence of Alois Grillmeier: "In relation to the discussion regarding Welte's formulations, Pater Rahner developed in a long conversation (with H. Bacht and myself) his hermeneutic of conciliar statements. At the end of the long conversation (…), we invited Pater Rahner to provide us with his comments for an article for Chalcedon, vol. III. This happened and the result is this valuable contribution."

17   A portion of his evaluations for Cardinal König, which were often not
     very complementary towards the Roman authors, was published after
     Rahner's death: "From the conciliar evaluations for Cardinal König," in: K.
     Rahner, *Sehnsucht nach dem geheimnisvollen Gott*. Profil – Texte – Bilder,
     edited by Herbert Vorgrimler (Freiburg: Herder, 1990) 95-165.

18   Cf. Karl Rahner, Theologische Prinzipien der Hermeneutik eschatolo-
     gischer Aussagen, in: *Zeitschrift für Katholische Theologie* 82 (1960) 137-
     158. – See ibid., The Hermeneutics of Eschatological Assertions, in: ibid.,
     Theological Investigations, vol. 4, translated by Kevin Smyth (London: Dar-
     ton, Longman & Todd, 1966) 323-346.

9

HE SIMPLY WAS UNIQUE

IN CONVERSATION WITH KARL CARDINAL LEHMANN, MAINZ

Karl Lehmann, Dr. phil., Dr. theol., born 1936. He first met Karl Rahner at the Second Vatican Council during his studies in Philosophy and Theology at the Gregorian University in Rome. From 1964 to 1967 he served as his assistant at the University of Munich and Münster. In 1968, Lehmann became Professor of Dogmatic Theology in Mainz and in 1973 Professor for Dogmatic and Ecumenical Theology in Freiburg. He has been president of the German Bishops' Conference from 1987 to 2008. In 2001, he was named a Cardinal by Pope John Paul II. Lehmann is also co-editor of Karl Rahner's "Sämtliche Werke" and Chairman of the Karl Rahner Foundation Munich.

On the 10th anniversary of Rahner's death you gave a talk in Freiburg on philosophy in the thought of Karl Rahner.[1] Why did you choose that topic?

During the years 1964-67, when I was Rahner's assistant, Eberhard Simon, Alexander Gerken and Hans Jürgen Verweyen, all wrote books challenging Rahner's philosophical starting point.[2] Their critical concern was whether Karl Rahner's transcendental starting point was sufficiently grounded. Having written a dissertation on Heidegger myself, I had my own questions. Upon reflection, I realized that Rahner is hard to pin down, especially concerning the use of the term transcendental; there are elements of Kant and Maréchal there as well. To respond to these criticisms would require further investigation.

Above all: also at that time, Johann Baptist Metz criticized Rahner's transcendental method for being too individualistic, and failing to include a social starting point. It was my own view that Rahner should address these issues. I realize now in hindsight that Rahner had no interest in replying to his critics. He wanted to move on and develop his thought further, not retrace his intellectual journey. I pressured him, but I came to see that he had made up his mind and had decided differently. He knew that if he concerned himself with these challenges there could be a crisis in the foundation. What was much more important to him was the theological content; that was his main concern. He did not want to be involved in an endless discussion on the foundation of his thought. Still I tried to convince him to take on the challenge. We went to Münster in 1967 and the question was what he was going to teach. I recommended to him that he should focus on the relationship between the general and the particular in salvation history, the categorical and the transcendental: to at least deal with the problem if not philosophically, then theologically.

Hans Urs von Balthasar was another sharp critic of Rahner's approach, publishing his polemic in a small book *Cordula oder der Ernst-fall*.[3] While Rahner felt no compunction to reply, he had to deal with von Balthasar's criticism, because it was presented as a topic by Albert Raffelt in the spring seminar in 1967. But Rahner's reaction was essentially to reject von Balthasar's criticism as "too dumb to be worthy of a response. He has understood nothing." Rahner's position was still very obscure to many people. That's the reason I had one of my students, Nikolaus Schwerdtfeger, now Auxiliary Bishop in Hildesheim, research the topic of the anonymous Christian.[4] He wrote a fantastic dissertation concretizing the categorical element which was always somewhat abstract in Rahner. He brought together those passages about the symbol and the symbolic,[5] the passages about the cross so that it was clear that the transcendental element does not stand by itself, but is always mediated by the categorical and that as a result the historical, the particular of Christianity, plays a greater role for Rahner than might appear.

The problem was that Rahner was a bit one-sided in some of his formulations. It is necessary to read the entire corpus to achieve a balanced perspective of his thought. But neither my concerns nor the criticisms of others affected Rahner. He did not read these criticisms anymore; the objections seemed to him to be too simplistic.

It was now 1967-68, a very controversial time. Having a sharp intuitive sense, it became clear to Rahner that he should not remain on the Philosophy faculty in Munich offering courses to students from all fields of study. He did not want to waste time; he wanted to do theology in the midst of the Church and not sit on the sidelines in the Romano Guardini chair in philosophy. So he made the decision to switch to theology and accept the call to Münster. I discovered later a kind of aphorism by Heidegger: "The older you get the sooner you must take action." In other words: "get going – carry out the plan!"

It is important to remember that at the time of this move to Münster, Rahner was already 63 years old, a time when one might not want to enter into a debate about one's foundations or to contemplate revising them, but nevertheless a time when one can still write a highly intelligent book. Also, Metz, whom Rahner considered his most brilliant student, lived close to Münster. Rahner, often in a quiet and subtle way, did revise his foundational thought, albeit within his basic scheme. The guidelines did not fundamentally change, but it is clear that, for example, from 1966-67 on, he tried to respond to Metz and show that his starting point did not deserve Metz's criticism of being too individualistic.

In the first half of 1967 I was promoted to Doctor of Theology and I received a grant to do post doctoral work. I still did a lot for Rahner, perhaps too much. I directed all the dissertations of those doctoral students who remained in Munich. Practically every two or three weeks I traveled to Munich for one or two days, met with the students, discussed their drafts, wrote evaluations of their work and Fr. Rahner signed them. Then in July of 1968 I received a call to Mainz from Dr. Bernhard Vogel, the Minister of education and cultural affairs.

Fr. Rahner began to strike out in anger. It began with his lecture "Freedom and Manipulation" in Munich in 1970.[6] Can you provide some insight into this turn of events?

Perhaps you know that Josef Pieper in his biography revealed that he chose not to attend this lecture.[7] He maintained that he did not have a proper suit with him, but his decision was made for other reasons and Rahner recognized that. We were at an ecumenical workshop of Lutheran and Catholic theologians, one of the oldest ecumenical study groups in the world, founded in 1946 in Tutzing on Lake Starnberg. Rahner was a member, as were Joseph Ratzinger and Hermann Volk, my predecessor as Bishop of Mainz.

Rahner was to receive the highly prized Romano Guardini Award of the Catholic Academy in Munich (*"Katholische Akademie in Bayern"*) on one of the evenings during our session. My friend, Franz Henrich, the Director, said to me: "Your group is meeting in Tutzing, all of you must come. I will send a bus to pick you up – in 45 minutes you will be in Munich and the bus will bring you back." I asked Fr. Rahner: "What is the title of the lecture you will give after the award is bestowed?" He remained silent and I thought to myself: he has something up his sleeve! It was clear to me that an explosion was about to occur. I asked him two more times and then I realized that it was better not to ask any more. He was somewhat angry and sullen. Still I said to him, "Many people from our meeting are coming. I encouraged them to attend. Don't do anything rash." I surmised that something was up.

Naturally, there was a story behind this. At that time there was an intense discussion regarding celibacy. That was very much in vogue. Rahner was clearly in favor of celibacy and he wrote a letter to a priest friend: 100,000 copies were reprinted and distributed. It was, in part, a passionate endorsement of celibacy.[8] Although he did not make any concrete suggestions regarding this matter, he argued that it should be taken more seriously. He convinced me to draft a memo with him and to gather other signatures and send the results to the bishops. I did so, gathering many signatures from members of the Faith Commission of the German Bishops' Conference, among them Alfons Deissler, Joseph Ratzinger, and Rudolf Schnackenburg. The bishops did what I today often do, out of necessity, namely fail to respond. Fr. Rahner was extremely angry about that. Of the 50 or 60 bishops in the Bishops' Conference, if I remember correctly, only two responded, among them Ernst Tewes.[9]

He was livid at the lack of response.[10] I thought: he is going to do something. He is playing with fire. I said to him once again the day before the ceremony: "Karl, a bus is coming especially for the occasion; Döpfner will be there, Volk will be there." He might very well insult these people. He always gave me the manuscript beforehand, but this time I had nothing in my hands. It was totally clear to me that something was coming. In the lecture, he complained greatly about the undemocratic, unfriendly apparatus of the Bishops' Conference, saying that one could speak to the bishops on an individual basis and find them reasonable, but they were impossible to deal with as a group. Rahner then addressed the issue of Manipulation. But he was not convincing: it actually was not a useful concept. He lost his temper and the bishops became enraged, especially since Hermann Volk and Cardinal Döpfner had gone out of their way to come. Many said: "We came to honor him all the way from Tutzing only to be insulted." Cardinal Döpfner, hearing the reproach asked, "Did you not know what he was

going to do?" Knowing that the lecture was to be published, I told Fr.
Rahner that he should eliminate the harsh invective from the printed
text, but he refused. There was nothing that could be done. In a short
"Afterward" in the publication of the Catholic Academy he sought to
justify himself in response to my distress.[11] He was going to give that
lecture come "hell or high water!" I understood that they should have
responded to the memo on celibacy, but I still found it disrespectful to
use the platform of the award ceremony to berate the bishops.

Our Memorandum was actually not meant for publication; it was
intended for the bishops. It then came into the hands of the Jesuits at
the periodical *Orientierung* (Zurich), who published the text.[12]

**Did you distance yourself from Fr. Rahner because his criticism
was too one-sided?**

It was in that confrontation that I saw the beginning of the development of Karl Rahner into "an angry old man." But I have to admit that
he was often in the right. Two years later, in *Stimmen der Zeit*, he wrote
a brief editorial commentary entitled "March into the Ghetto."[13] It was
an outcry, a real *"dernier cri,"* arguing that the Church was in danger of
denying the Council – going backward, not forward. Kösel Publishing
asked me to compile articles for a book discussing Rahner's editorial
and the responses it evoked.[14] There were several harsh responses to
Rahner's editorial and also several letters to the editor.[15] This book
marked the first time I had publicly distanced myself from Rahner.

While it was true that there was a lack of complete implementation
of liturgical reforms on the part of some bishops, which frustrated
Rahner, still I felt that Rahner had not sufficiently appreciated the difficulty of the task of those whose responsibility it was to carry forward
the work of the Council. To me it represented a certain failure: at the
Council, theologians and bishops worked intensively with one another
in the Commission; prepared schemata together. For the bishops the
Council was a four year long special continuing education program.
One did not need to tell them what they needed to learn. But afterwards, the question arose: how can we maintain this spirit of cooperation? I suggested to Cardinal Döpfner that he should invite Fr. Rahner
over for an evening to drink some wine and to discuss with him his
burdens and concerns so that he would come to know the burdens
a bishop bears. I told him it would be good to meet more often with

Rahner to correct Rahner's misunderstandings. Unfortunately they were able to meet only rarely. Today, I realize that a much-burdened bishop, a moderator of the Bishops' Conference like Döpfner, needs to guard jealously every free evening.

In 1971-75 the Würzburg Synod, the communal synod of the German dioceses, took place. Rahner was very irritable during the synod. There was a difficult vote at the beginning that amounted to a contest between Rahner and Ratzinger which had much to do with a difference in their personalities. They sat next to each other since seating was alphabetical. Karl Rahner was a kind of symbolic figure for the younger members of the synod. Ratzinger, one sensed, had gone in another direction from about the year 1969-70. Fr. Rahner was elected by a very small margin after three or four ballots and Ratzinger was never able entirely to accept this and was hurt by it. This was revealed in his statement in the periodical *Wort und Wahrheit* in which he wrote:[16] "I don't believe in committees, but in prophetic existence."[17] Although he had already shown a certain aversion to commissions and committees in the past, this only served to increase it. Ratzinger left the synod soon afterwards and the synod continued without him.

Fr. Rahner was, above all, antagonistic to Cardinal Joseph Höffner[18] of Cologne.[19] Whenever the Cardinal rose to speak Fr. Rahner was already poised to respond, with his hand raised even before he knew what Höffner was going to say.[20] He was already having trouble with his hearing, but when given permission to speak he always "fired back" immediately. This was not always the most intelligent thing to do.

The proceedings have been published so one can read about this today. There were some famous people who voted for Ratzinger rather than Rahner such as Hans Meier and Ida Friederike Görres. But the young "wild" associate pastors voted for Rahner. It was a curious thing, but Fr. Rahner enjoyed the fact that the young people defended him and had rejected Ratzinger.

Cardinal Volk was in very poor health in those years. He sometimes was aggravated to the point of total frustration at what people were saying in the aula and wanted to respond immediately, but he was prevented from doing so because the order of those who signified that they wanted to speak had to be followed. At one point he was so frustrated he stood behind a column and cried. I went up to him once to try to calm him. That reveals the atmosphere at that time which came to light later in some interviews. Cardinal Döpfner died only one year after the conclusion of the Synod in 1976 which moved Rahner greatly.

Later Karl Rahner became more actively involved with ecumenism. Together with Heinrich Fries he published a book on this issue, *Unity of the Church, Quaestio Disputata*, number 100.[21] Until that time he had done little in Ecumenical Theology. He was neither well acquainted with the situation of the Churches, nor with the theologies of the dialogue partners, but thought about matters from the point of view of his own theological background. But his thought provided a rich bounty from which to draw.

Fr. Rahner apparently had a difficult time dealing not only with some subjects, but also with some people. Did you have occasion to experience that personally?

It's amazing that he never did develop a good relationship with some people. For example, Pope John XXIII always remained a complete mystery to him from the standpoint of personality types. Rahner saw him as an unsophisticated farmer, to be admired for his piety, but somehow not suitable for the time. I remember quite well how I once argued with him. Rahner responded: "Look at him, he is dumb. He is simply dumb!" I disagreed with him and said, "he is clever, but in a different way than Rahner."

But he was being influenced by other people. When he was in Rome, Luise Rinser, who lived in the area, became the focus of much of his attention. It was not a deep personal attachment, but he served as a spiritual companion for her after she asked him for spiritual guidance following her divorce from the famous composer Carl Orff.[22] The relationship became rather burdensome for him as she continued to seek him out all the time. But he felt this was a spiritual and pastoral obligation. He later wrote an article for a Festschrift for Luise Rinser entitled "On the Joy and the Sorrow of the Christian writer."[23]

In connection with his 75th birthday Karl Rahner had an audience with Pope John Paul II. His heart was full of the things he wished to say. He went to the audience, but returned full of sorrow, saying that during the audience he was no longer certain about what he should say to the Pope. He let this all pass, out of a mixture of fatigue and resignation. It was very strange that he had a final opportunity to say something to the Pope and let it slip by. It was probably a sign that his strength was waning.[24]

About Karl Rahner's legacy: you once said or wrote that we still need Karl Rahner. What should be handed on and what is the best way to do this?

That is a very difficult question and cannot be answered so easily, at least I cannot and for the following reason, because his philosophical thought is not so easy. There is no question that Rahner had a genuine talent for philosophy, a very great talent. But to a great extent he was a self-made man, drawing upon himself as his creative source. He did not read very much. He read Kant and Heidegger, with whom he had a seminar on Hegel.[25] He excerpted from Maréchal;[26] he knew the five volumes of Maréchal, *Le point de départ de la métaphysique*. He knew his Aquinas very well. His *Spirit in the World* is filled with quotations from Thomas. But Rahner did not want to be known as a disciple of Heidegger or of Maréchal.[27] It is also difficult to document where Rahner is dependent on someone else's thought. There are only faint clues, not that he wanted to cover that up, but his primary concern was his own independent thinking. Many maintain, for example, that he borrowed much from Pierre Teilhard de Chardin.[28] That's not true. He did not read much Teilhard de Chardin, but he did have a seminar in Innsbruck on him. When others made their presentations during the seminar it stimulated new ideas for Rahner to think about.[29] Considering the type of thinker Rahner was and the originality of his own starting point, however, one might speculate about the influences on his thought by others. In my opinion he would be difficult to duplicate or imitate. There is no Rahner School that has arisen. Karl Rahner simply was unique! It was always clear to me that Rahner's starting point was not monolithic. He cannot and did not want to be limited to the philosophical realm. He was, and knew that he was a brilliant thinker.

I have defended the thesis from the beginning that his spiritual foundations had a stronger and more creative influence on his thinking than did pure philosophy. In my mind philosophy was, for him, always an instrument of interpretation and development. But the root was, I believe, genuinely theological and spiritual. For that reason I recommended to Klaus P. Fischer that he should study Ignatius of Loyola.[30]

It was from Ignatian Spirituality that Rahner drew the fundamental impulses for his life as well as for his thought. These impulses, while deeply hidden, were very active: from them he lived, from them he drew energy. Fischer has done an excellent job of showing that. In my portrait of Rahner I concentrated on this quality and I strongly emphasized the experience of grace.[31]

Experience, often more than any other influence, was paramount for Karl Rahner. I think, for example, of the essay: "The Christian and His Unbelieving Relatives."[32] A revision of the foundations of his thought would have brought some things more clearly to light.

Is Fr. Rahner's theology specifically Ignatian or does it belong more generally to the broader spiritual tradition of the Church?

I believe Fr. Neufeld's book *Die Brüder Rahner* is indispensable because he shows how both brothers were so united with one another throughout their lives, humanly and theologically. I believe that Hugo Rahner's impact on his younger brother Karl was stronger than Karl later was willing to admit. Naturally Karl went his own way. From a human perspective, Hugo was more expansive and more open than Karl, who could be narrow and withdrawn. Hugo never was that. He was always a consummate gentleman; he stood out as the focus of attention at a social gathering, but he did not seek that. Wherever he was, people gravitated to him because of his human qualities. Karl was actually the opposite. In that regard the two brothers were completely different. But they had in common an interest in the theology of the Church Fathers and both of their theological dissertations are closely related thematically. In the last analysis though, I believe, Karl learned much more from Hugo than he commonly admitted.

When Rahner's doctoral dissertation *Spirit in the World* was not accepted in Freiburg, he wrote his theological dissertation "*E Latere Christi*" in just a matter of a few weeks, although it was not published until 1999.[33] Along with philosophy, he continued an intense study of the Fathers of the Church. If one were to analyze this more closely one would discover that, for example, many of his early essays from the 1930's deal with the topic of spiritual experience. Fr. Rahner translated Marcel Viller's book on the spirituality and mysticism of the Church Fathers and completely reworked it for the German edition.

It was published in 1938 and a new edition of it appeared a few years ago under both their names: Viller-Rahner.[34]

In those years Karl Rahner found his own spiritual voice; testimony to this is his most, I believe, widely distributed book *Encounters with Silence*,[35] as well as *The Need and the Blessing of Prayer*.[36] Those are still magnificent works today. Whoever wants to get to know Karl Rahner should begin with these publications. One senses the deep spirituality present in them. No matter how much philosophy one studies or how much history of theology one knows, one already can see in these small books a very independent, profound spirituality which is unique to him – in addition to the tradition and the philosophical thinking. I would add there was also the pastoral component. When he spoke with people and observed how difficult it was for them to understand theologically this or that Church teaching, indulgences, let's say, then he would begin to probe deeply: how can one explain this more clearly?

The strong pastoral element always present in Rahner's thought has been sufficiently appreciated. In the 1920's and especially in the middle of the 1930's in Germany and France, as well as some other countries, there was a protest against what was perceived as sterile Scholastic Theology. The textbooks were all the same whether in French, German or Latin. There was a concern that the average seminarian did not need to be burdened with all the distinctions present in Scholastic Theology. The separation between spirituality and theology was deplored. Balthasar wrote a very famous essay in the 1950's: "Theology and Holiness"[37] in which he argues that the loss of unity between theology and holiness in our time is a major sin of European Theology.[38]

Among the Jesuit faculty in Innsbruck there was an inclination towards what was called Kerygmatic Theology. It is not by chance that Hugo Rahner wrote a book entitled *A Theology of Proclamation*[39] which was not really a book about the "how" of proclamation, but rather a theology of what one proclaims. It is a wonderful book that was re-published by the Scientific Book Society in Darmstadt, but no one speaks about it any more. Because Kerygmatic Theology was presented somewhat in opposition to Speculative Theology it was looked upon in Rome with a critical eye and much suspicion. Johann Baptist Lotz, writing from the perspective of a philosophy of value, attempted to show the legitimacy of such a theology: it is not only about the

"True," but also about the "Good," and, therefore, one has to pay more attention to those to whom it is being addressed.[40]

Karl Rahner wrote an essay about the Theology of Proclamation, which was published, oddly enough, in a Hungarian periodical. It has since been published in the collected works *Sämtliche Werke*.[41] Karl Rahner had developed certain reservations about the Theology of Proclamation; it was a little too naive for him. There were other people, respectable scholastic theologians in Innsbruck, mostly Rahner adversaries like Franz Lakner,[42] who were champions of this Kerygmatic Theology. At that time there were others going in different theological directions such as Thaddäus Soiron and the Benedictine Anselm Stolz. Rahner's concept of theology emerged from this theological milieu. One can read about much of this in Fr. Neufeld's double biography.[43] Karl Rahner did not belong in a narrow sense to the circle which propagated a Theology of Proclamation, but he did receive more inspiration from it than one commonly thinks.

Much of that which shaped him is also found in his smaller spiritual writings. I think, for example, of the small essay, "Everyday Things"[44] which is no more than 30 pages; the 5 minute radio talks. He shows what eating, walking, sitting down, laughing, actually mean for human beings; therein can be found the experience of grace in everyday life. In essence it has to do with anthropology on a small scale.

Rahner was interested in many things. He was able to be enthusiastic. That's the reason it was not a problem for him to write many articles about a variety of themes, which shows that his thinking is universal. In the *Lexikon für Theologie und Kirche*, for example, the question of whether there was human life on other planets arose. And what does he do? He sits down and begins to write. There is an article "Star dwellers"[45] that no one even knows that Rahner wrote, but when one looks for some information on this question it is the best thing one can find.

Of course, one should not underestimate the basic education of a Jesuit prior to the last Council: they studied seven years, three years of philosophy, four of theology and between them there were two years of practical service, mostly as a Latin teacher or a prefect in a boarding school. What they were taught was highly regulated and specific themes had to be treated in Scholastic Theology; there was an immense amount of material which came together in Dogmatic or in Moral Theology. The somewhat briefly treated Scholastic Theology was distasteful for many, but when it came time to take exams with Rahner the students found that he was merciless in requiring that they know about what could be found in Denzinger, the Sacred Scriptures, etc. He did not ask about his own special theories.

The often maligned Scholastic Theology draws from many different theological sources: the writings of the Church Fathers, Sacred Scripture, Augustine, and Thomas Aquinas, exegesis. There are, overall, substantial fragments, constituting, so to speak, a "backpack," of theology. It was, naturally, often boring, because it was frequently far removed from the great texts: a confusing collection of concepts, but despite a certain lack of attractiveness, one could say that whoever went through this program, at the very least, attained a basic understanding. Neo- scholasticism was a reservoir of the tradition. There is much there that belongs to the Church, spiritually and theologically, perhaps, not always sorted out, but simply coming together like a great puzzle.

Fr. Rahner then didn't categorically reject neo-scholasticism?

Absolutely not. That's the reason why many students when taking an oral exam with him were surprised or irritated. Rahner had such a depth of knowledge that when questioned about a subject he could immediately respond.[46] He was also so intelligent that he could integrate that knowledge into his approach so as to allow for corrective elements to his theology, to his philosophical thought. When he found that some ideas could not be so easily integrated he did not force them to fit his approach, but rather asked: What stands behind this? From this questioning came some articles on indulgences, on "good intention"[47] and other topics. Even now, after all this time, I ask myself why he concerned himself with such matters. He would write a *Lexikon* entry, which he did not enjoy doing, but would dictate it in one sitting without any apparent lengthy preparation. In my opinion his best articles appear in *Sacramentum Mundi*;[48] that is a gold mine from which one can see into the workshop of his mind how everything comes together for him. I believe that to learn from Rahner means to inherit all these things, the spiritual starting points, the pastoral experiences which all flow together, the plurality of theological thinking, the function of philosophy, etc.

The plurality of modern philosophy in a certain sense also enriches theology. It is fascinating to say that I can learn from linguistic philosophy that which I cannot find in Thomas. But this enrichment comes about not simply by adding them all together, for this would only produce a hodgepodge, not an integrated vision. Fr. Rahner was, perhaps the last one, who like Hegel, brought together an entire encyclopedia of theological knowledge. Today no one would dare attempt to do that to that degree, to speak about all those things with such a degree of certainty. Whoever alleges that Rahner is not orthodox enough simply does not know him, does not know the sources from which he draws. That is simply a stupid accusation. For years he had problems with the Congregation for the Doctrine of the Faith or with the Holy Office. But at the Second Vatican Council many in the Curia realized how well Rahner knew the tradition; how he respected the tradition and theologized from it. Neo-Scholastic theological data were always a springboard for his own thought; like a master magician, he would find something and suddenly it would take on light and color.

Rahner was so familiar with the foundational ideas in Moral Theology that he could employ them as he willed. That was his genius and even Pietro Parente[49] came to see that. Parente, who always looked down on others as inferior, encountered Rahner in an elevator at the Council one day and said to him "You are really not as bad as I thought." He instinctively recognized that Karl Rahner was more Catholic than many others.

The Second Vatican Council helped improve Rahner's reputation. It was like being in a state of siege for him prior to the Council. The Council provided for a closer look at Rahner – and was an "aha" experience for his attackers –"look, he is actually more reasonable; he knows much more than we thought; he is not a heretic."

That also appears to be true for Rahner. Did he not, during the Council, also give up many prejudices against Rome?

Very definitely. What fascinated me so much was Rahner's selflessness and his willingness to do whatever was necessary to help the Church to understand one or another thing better, and to express it more clearly, as did Yves Congar, OP or Henri de Lubac, SJ, but it never entered his mind to assert himself at any price.[50]

He didn't have any political interest and did not want to "establish" his own theology at the Council?

Definitely not! Of course, when he observed that others were attempting to manipulate the situation he would oppose that; then he would speak quite forcefully. But I would say that was also true of de Lubac, Congar and Ratzinger as well. Ratzinger, however, was not a scholastic theologian; he is more a product of German University Theology. For Rahner, his effort at the Council amounted to a personal offer to the Church; he placed his knowledge at the disposal of the Church. What the Church then decided to do with it, to what extent she wanted to consider it, and how much she would accept – that was up to the Church and he would not fight hard to enforce his agenda. He would passionately defend a position he held, but it was never about having his personal opinion adopted.

I can remember one thing very vividly. It has to do with different passages in *Lumen Gentium* no. 16 and in *Gaudium et Spes* nos. 17-18; about the fact of grace working also outside the Church[51] which indicates that the limits of the Church are not the limits of grace. The entire *theologumenon* of the "Anonymous Christian" would not be possible were that not the case. Rahner occasionally came back to the house and commented that it is astonishing that there are completely new things in the texts that are not taken from the tradition. He noted that Augustine thought entirely differently: that is, that grace is greater the rarer it is. Rahner was of the opinion that much had changed at the Council and theology had somehow changed as well. It was not just things which Rahner had already formulated, but rather it was ideas that, to a certain extent, were in the air. Much of this thought was attributed to Rahner, but it was more that he was in the mainstream of the tradition and others also, like de Lubac, thought in a similar vein. De Lubac's book, *Catholicism* (1938),[52] greatly influenced Rahner and it contributed significantly to his concept of the Anonymous Christian.[53]

What did Hans Küng do at the Council and was he a *peritus*?

He was an official *peritus* of the Bishop of Rottenburg-Stuttgart, who took him to the Council at a later time. During this period he wrote his own ecclesiology. While others were working with mountains of

"*Modi*" (proposed modifications) at the Council – all anonymous, hard work – Hans Küng wrote *The Church*. He did not wish to share in the work.[54]

Allow me to change gears in our conversation: can you say something about the collaboration with Herder Publishing Company?

Yes, Karl Rahner was, as a native of Freiburg, closely associated with the Herder Publishing House, as well as with the Herder family. On the editorial staff level he had a close relationship with the chief of staff, Dr. Robert Scherer, whom Karl Rahner knew from his days as a student. Those on the managerial level, called "Herderians," were not academicians, but highly interested book dealers who had made their way to the top. As book dealers they had an instinct as to whether a book would sell well and knew how to market a book to make it attractive. Franz Johna was one of them with whom Rahner had close contact.[55] He also had a close relationship with the historian, Professor Oskar Köhler, who was the Director of the Lexicographic Institute of Herder Publishing.

Rahner continued to maintain a close relationship with Herder throughout his life, but he was not bound to Herder alone. He also felt a close relationship with Benziger Publishing (Einsiedeln-Zurich); above all with Dr. Oskar Bettschart, who from the very beginning promoted the *Theological Investigations* (from 1954) when Rahner's friend, Robert Scherer at Herder Publishing, could not decide whether to accept the collection of essays for publication.

You have no doubt heard this many times already: Fr. George Sporschill told me that Karl Rahner always emphasized the fact that he considered you to be the best chauffeur.

Thank God that he said not only that, that I am a good driver, but also that I was his best assistant. I don't want to quote any other of Rahner's anecdotes about me. Rahner expressed good wishes to me on the occasion of my ordination as Bishop in our diocesan newspaper, as well as admonitions.[56]

NOTES

1 Karl Lehmann, Philosophisches Denken im Werk Karl Rahners, in: Albert Raffelt (ed.), *Karl Rahner in Erinnerung* (Düsseldorf: Patmos, 1994) 10-27.

2 Eberhard Simons, *Philosophie der Offenbarung in Auseinandersetzung mit "Hörer des Wortes" von Karl Rahner* (Stuttgart: Kohlhammer, 1966); Alexander Gerken, *Offenbarung und Transzendenzerfahrung*. Kritische Thesen zu einer künftigen dialogischen Theologie (Düsseldorf: Patmos, 1969); Hansjürgen Verweyen, *Ontologische Voraussetzungen des Glaubensaktes*. Zur transzendentalen Frage nach der Möglichkeit von Offenbarung (Düsseldorf: Patmos, 1969).

3 Hans Urs von Balthasar, *Cordula oder der Ernstfall* (Einsiedeln: Johannes, 1966); ibid., *The Moment of Christian Witness*, translated by Richard Beckley (Glen Rock, N. J.: Newman, 1969); Andreas R. Batlogg, Hans Urs von Balthasar und Karl Rahner: Zwei Schüler des Ignatius, in: Magnus Striet, Jan-Heiner Tück, (eds.), *Die Kunst Gottes verstehen*. Hans Urs von Balthasars theologische Provokationen (Freiburg: Herder, 2005) 410-446, esp. 439-444.

4 Nikolaus Schwerdtfeger, *Gnade und Welt*. Zum Grundgefüge von Karl Rahners Theorie der "anonymen Christen" (Freiburg: Herder, 1982).

5 K. Rahner, Zur Theologie des Symbols, in: ibid., *Schriften zur Theologie*, vol. 4 (Einsiedeln: Benziger, 1960) 275-311; ibid., The Theology of the Symbol, in: ibid., *Theological Investigations*, vol. 4 (Baltimore, MD: Helicon Press, 1966) 221-252.

6 K. Rahner, *Freiheit und Manipulation in Gesellschaft und Kirche* (Munich: Kösel, 1970); later in ibid., *Toleranz in der Kirche*. Freiheit und Manipulation in Gesellschaft und Kirche. Rückblick auf das Konzil (Freiburg: Herder, 1977) 67-103.

7 Josef Pieper, *Eine Geschichte wie ein Strahl*. Autobiographische Aufzeichnungen seit 1964 (München: Kösel, 1988) 156-158.

8 K. Rahner, Der Zölibat des Weltpriesters im heutigen Gespräch. Ein offener Brief, in: *Geist und Leben* 40 (1967) 122-138; later in: ibid., *Knechte Christi*. Meditationen zum Priestertum (Freiburg: Herder, 1967) 176-207; ibid., *Servants of the Lord*, translated by Richard Stracham (New York: Herder and Herder, 1968); ibid., Der Zölibat des Weltpriesters im Gespräch. Eine Antwort, in: *Geist und Leben* 41 (1968) 285-305; later in: ibid., *Chancen des Glaubens*. Fragmente einer modernen Spiritualität (Freiburg: Herder, 1971) 165-187; ibid., *Opportunities for Faith*: elements of a modern spirituality (New York: Seabury Press, 1975). Later K. Rahner wrote a sequel in response to the incredible amount of mail he received.

9   Ernst Tewes (1908-1998), 1968 Auxiliary Bishop and Vicar General for the vicariates of Munich.

10   Karl Lehmann, Mehr als eine biographische Episode, in: Paul Imhof, Hubert Biallowons (eds.), *Karl Rahner – Bilder eines Lebens* (Freiburg: Herder, 1985) 123-126.

11   K. Rahner, *Freiheit und Manipulation in der Kirche* (Freiburg: 2nd edition, 1970) 56: "On March 18 of this year I gave a lecture at the annual celebration of the Catholic Academy in Bavaria entitled 'Freedom and Manipulation in the Church,' and on March 19, I presented a paper at a College week in Paderborn. Since both of the lectures partly covered the same material and complemented one another I allowed myself to use one text without any essential change for each occasion. If the lecture in Munich appears not to have been entirely appropriate for the occasion of the conferral of the Guardini Award of the Catholic Academy in Bavaria that was because I did not know of their intention to present this award to me at the time I was formulating the paper. There is no reason to think that the subsequent publication of the paper could falsely change the character of this festive event. But I would like to express my heartfelt thanks to the Catholic Academy in Bavaria one again for the bestowal of this award." Münster i. W., 21 March, 1970, Karl Rahner.

12   Memorandum zur Zölibatsdiskussion, in: *Orientierung* 34 (1970) 69-72. According to information from Nikolaus Klein, SJ, (Editorial board of *Orientierung*, Zurich) from September 20, 2005, the former editor-in-chief of the periodical, Ludwig Kaufmann, SJ, had received permission from more than half of the signers of the Memorandum to publish and therefore thought it proper to proceed with the publication of the text.

13   K. Rahner, Marsch ins Getto?, in: *Stimmen der Zeit* 190 (1972) 1-2.

14   Karl Lehmann, Karl Rahner (eds.), *Marsch ins Getto?* Der Weg der deutschen Katholiken in der Bundesrepublik (München: Kösel, 1973).

15   These letters from the readers and a reply by Rahner are re-printed in the published collection by Karl Lehmann and Karl Rahner: 138-143 ("Widerspruch auf *Marsch ins Getto*").

16   Otto Mauer (1907-1973), editor of the periodical, *Wort und Wahrheit*, (Vienna), invited 200 prominent individuals to give their assessment of the state of the Church. See Joseph Ratzinger, in: *Wort und Wahrheit* 27 (1972) 197 f.

17   Ibid., 198: "What are most needed are spiritual initiatives – people who without inhibition, authentically and in an exemplary way live what is the very heart of the gospel. I do not believe in committees but in prophetic existence. That cannot be imposed, (therein lies our helplessness): one can only encourage one to live in this way. The spiritual renewal of Christian-

ity in the individual, the attempt at a possible decisive following of Christ, could be a way of preparing for a new awakening."

18 Joseph Höffner (1906-1987), 1945-1951, Professor for Pastoral Theology and the Social Sciences at the University of Münster, 1962 Bishop of Münster, 1969-1987 Archbishop of Cologne, 1969 Cardinal, 1976-1987, president of the German Bishops' Conference.

19 For background to this, see Karl H. Neufeld, *Die Brüder Rahner*. Eine Biographie (Freiburg: Herder, 2nd edition 2004) 304-311; Sonderberichterstattung Synode (II). Die Konstituierende Sitzung der Gemeinsamen Synode in Würzburg, in: *Herder Korrespondenz* 25 (1971) 92-101, esp. 100f.

20 On the other hand, see the telegram that Karl Rahner received on the occasion of his golden jubilee of ordination to the priesthood (1972) from Cardinal Höffner in the name of the German Bishops' Conference: "Very reverend and dear Father Rahner, on the 50th anniversary of your ordination to the priesthood, I send you personally and in the name of the German Bishops' Conference, from my heart, the blessings of our Lord. Ministry, here and now, to the Gospel, and thus for the unity of the People of God and its completion in the celebration of the Eucharist – these fundamental duties of the priest of the New Testament – are not only the object of your theological writing, but also, and primarily, of your personal priestly ministry for which, with God's help, you have made every endeavor, these past five decades. I thank you for that. May God grant you still many more years of exceptional productivity. Joseph Cardinal Höffner, July 26, 1982." Quoted by K. Rahner, *Im Gespräch*, vol. 1., edited by Paul Imhof, Hubert Biallowons (München: Kösel, 1983) 299, footnote 5.

21 Heinrich Fries, Karl Rahner, *Einigung der Kirchen – reale Möglichkeit* (Quaestiones Disputatae 100) (Freiburg: Herder,1983); now in: K. Rahner, *Sämtliche Werke*, vol. 27: Einheit in Vielheit. Schriften zur ökumenischen Theologie. Bearbeitet von Karl Lehmann und Albert Raffelt (Freiburg: Herder, 2002) 286-396. – See Heinrich Fries, Karl Rahner, *Unity of the Churches*. An Actual Possibility, translated by Ruth C.L. Gritsch, Erik W. Gritsch (New York: Paulist, 1985). Cardinal Ratzinger called the theses by Rahner and Fries a "Parforceritt, a forced argument" and "a trick of theological acrobatics, which unfortunately does not stand up to reality," (quoted according to Heinrich Fries, Karl Rahner, *Einigung der Kirchen – reale Möglichkeit*. Expanded edition [Quaestiones Disputatae 100] (Freiburg: Herder, 1985) 160. See also Bernd Jochen Hilberath, *Karl Rahner*. Gottgeheimnis Mensch (Mainz: Matthias Grünewald, 1995) 183-203; Herbert Vorgrimler, *Karl Rahner*. Gotteserfahrung in Leben und Denken (Darmstadt: Primus, 2004) 128-133; Birgitta Kleinschwärzer-Meister, "Katholisch und deswegen ökumenisch." Karl Rahner und die Ökumene, in: *Una Sancta* 60 (2005) 164-177. Cf. Karl Lehmann, Karl Rahner als Pionier

der Ökumene (Köln: Karl-Rahner-Akademie, 2003); ibid., Karl Rahners Bedeutung für die Kirche, in: *Stimmen der Zeit* spezial 1-2004, 3-15.

22   Luise Rinser was married three times. Her first husband, the father of her two sons, was the composer, Hans Günther Schnell. He died in the march on Russia in 1943. After that, Rinser entered into a simulated marriage with the homosexual, communist, pacifist author, Klaus Hermann. In 1953 she married the composer, Carl Orff. That marriage ended in divorce in 1959.

23   K. Rahner, Von der Grösse und dem Elend des christlichen Schriftstellers, in: *Luise Rinser*. Festschrift zum 60. Geburtstag (Frankfurt: Fischer, 1971) 35-46; later in: K Rahner, *Herausforderung des Christen*. Meditationen – Reflexionen – Interviews (Freiburg: Herder, 1975) 96-108.

24   See: Ich hoffe, dass ich ein Christ bin. Gespräch mit Karl-Heinz Weger und Hildegard Lüning im SDR, I (1979) in: K. Rahner, *Im Gespräch*, vol. 2, edited by Paul Imhof, Hubert Biallowons (München: Kösel, 1983) 87-95, 87 f.: "But, if I may tell this, a couple of days ago I had a private audience with the current pope and I indicated to him that I do not have much time left. He contradicted me at first but when I then said that in any case I was certainly closer to death than those younger than me, he then responded: 'Yes, yes, one once said to me in Poland: one can – the other must.' Thus I belong naturally to the category of those who soon 'must,' but that doesn't really matter." Cf. Christentum an der Schwelle zum dritten Jahrtausend. Gespräch mit Hans Schöpfer, Freiburg/Schweiz (1981), in: ibid., 165-179, 178: "A year ago I had a private audience with Pope John Paul II. I had already met him in Kraukau. He said at the beginning: 'How are you?' I responded in German: 'I am professor emeritus, live in Munich and am waiting for death to come.' He was perhaps a little surprised by that."

25   Cf. (postum) K. Rahner, Protokolle aus den Seminaren Martin Heideggers, in: ibid., *Sämtliche* Werke, vol. 2: Geist in Welt. Philosophische Schriften. Bearbeitet von Albert Raffelt (Freiburg: Herder, 1996) 407-426.

26   Cf. (postum) K. Rahner, Die Grundlagen einer Erkenntnistheorie bei Joseph Maréchal, in: ibid., *Sämtliche* Werke, vol. 2, 373-406.

27   Cf. Ein Lehrer wird befragt. Karl Rahner im Gespräch mit Karl Lehmann. Freiburg 1984, in: Paul Imhof, Hubert Biallowons (eds.), *Glaube in Winterlicher Zeit*. Gespräche mit Karl Rahner aus den letzten Lebensjahren (Düsseldorf: Patmos, 1986) 27-33, 28: "At that time one of my great experiences was reading the books of Joseph Maréchal from Louvain. Maréchal had succeeded in producing a very specific type of modern Thomism. Possibly his fundamental approach "unfortunately" had an affect on me. Later, of course, there was Martin Heidegger. One may not presume that my theology – in terms of content – received much from Heidegger.

That is simply nonsense. I believe there is no single, specific theological subject that Heidegger ever addressed. But, of course, I did learn some things from him: how to interpret a text, to see connections, which at first glance are not immediately apparent, to bring modern day problems to traditional theology, etc. In this, let us say, more formal sense, I am always still grateful to Heidegger." Cf. ibid., *Faith in a Wintry Season*. Conversations and Interviews with Karl Rahner in the last years of his life, edited by Paul Imhof, Hubert Biallowons, translation edited by Harvey D. Egan (New York: Crossroad, 1990).

28   Cf. The Importance of Thomas Aquinas, Interview with Jan van den Eijnden, Innsbruck (May 1982), in: *Faith in a Wintry Season*, 41-58, 53. "A Dutch theologian, whose name now escapes me, once told me that unfortunately not a word about Pierre Teilhard de Chardin, SJ, shows up in my theology, though he clearly inspired all my thought. I could only answer that at least up to that time I had read practically nothing of Teilhard de Chardin. But if you concluded from this that Rahner's theology is independent of Teilhard, I would answer that I don't make any such claim. I would conjecture that in the investigation of someone's thought, that there is obviously an 'atmospheric communication' of a meta-literary kind."

29   See the contributions in: K. Rahner, *Sämtliche Werke*, vol. 15: Verantwortung der Theologie. Im Dialog mit Naturwissenschaften und Gesellschaftstheorie. Bearbeitet von Hans-Dieter Mutschler (Freiburg: Herder, 2002); see Leo J. O'Donovan, Der Dialog mit dem Darwinismus. Zur theologischen Verwendung des evolutiven Weltbilds bei Karl Rahner, in: Herbert Vorgrimler (ed.), *Wagnis Theologie*. Erfahrungen mit der Theologie Karl Rahners (Freiburg: Herder, 1979) 215-229; Hans-Dieter Mutschler, Karl Rahner und die Naturwissenschaft, in: ibid. (ed.), *Gott neu buchstabieren*. Zur Person und Theologie Karl Rahners (Würzburg: Echter, 1994) 97-119.

30   See Klaus Peter Fischer, *Der Mensch als Geheimnis*. Die Anthropologie Karl Rahners (Freiburg: Herder, 2nd edition 1975); ibid., Wo der Mensch an ein Geheimnis grenzt. Die mystagogische Struktur der Theologie Karl Rahners, in: *Zeitschrift für Katholische Theologie* 98 (1976) 159-170; ibid., *Gotteserfahrung*. Mystagogie in der Theologie Karl Rahners und in der Theologie der Befreiung (Mainz: Matthias Grünewald, 1986); ibid., Gott als Geheimnis des Menschen. Karl Rahners theologische Anthropologie – Aspekte und Anfragen, in: *Zeitschrift für Katholische Theologie* 113 (1991) 1-23; ibid., Spiritualität und Theologie. Beobachtungen zum Weg Karl Rahners, in: Mariano Delgado, Matthias Lutz-Bachmann (eds.), *Theologie aus der Erfahrung der Gnade*. Annäherungen an Karl Rahner (Berlin: Morus, 1994) 26-33; ibid., Philosophie und Mystagogie. Karl Rahners "reductio in mysterium" als Prinzip seines Denkens, in: *Zeitschrift für Katholische Theologie* 120 (1998) 34-56.

31   See Karl Lehmann, Karl Rahner. Ein Porträt, in: K. Rahner, *Rechenschaft des Glaubens*. Karl-Rahner-Lesebuch, edited by Karl Lehmann, Albert Raffelt (Freiburg: Herder, 2nd edition 1979) 13*-53,* esp. 36*- 40.* Ibid., English edition, *The Content of Faith*, translation edited by Harvey D. Egan, SJ (New York: Crossrtoad, 1994) 1-42.

32   See the interview with Adolf Darlap in this book.

33   See K. Rahner, *E Latere Christi*. Der Ursprung der Kirche als zweiter Eva aus der Seite Christi des zweiten Adam. Eine Untersuchung über den typologischen Sinn von Joh 19, 34, in: ibid., *Sämtliche Werke*, vol. 3: Spiritualität und Theologie der Kirchenväter. Bearbeitet von Andreas R. Batlogg, Eduard Farrugia, Karl H. Neufeld (Freiburg: Herder, 1999), 1-84 and xvii-xliii (Editionsbericht); see also Andreas R. Batlogg, Karl Rahners theologische Dissertation "E Latere Christi." Zur Genese eines patristischen Projekts (1936), in: *Zeitschrift für Katholische Theologie* 126 (2004) 111-130.

34   See Marcel Viller, *La Spiritualité des priemiers siècles chrétiens* (Paris: Bloud e Gay, 1930); Marcel Viller, Karl Rahner, *Aszese und Mystik in der Väterzeit*. Ein Abriss (Freiburg: Herder, 1939); ibid., *Aszese und Mystik in der Väterzeit*. Ein Abriss der frühkirchlichen Spiritualität. Unveränderte Neuausgabe mit einem Vorwort von Karl H. Neufeld (Herder: Freiburg, 1989); now in: K. Rahner, *Sämtliche Werke*, vol. 3, 123-390.

35   See K. Rahner, *Worte ins Schweigen* (Innsbruck: Felizian Rauch, 1938); ibid., *Encounters with Silence*, translated by James M. Demske, SJ (Westminster, Md.: The Newman Press, 1960). This book is one of the most read and bought of Rahner's works, most recently published in a Jubilee edition, 2004, (*Beten mit Karl Rahner*, 2 vols., Gebete des Lebens und Von der Not und dem Segen des Gebetes.) See Karl H. Neufeld, Worte ins Schweigen. Zum erfahrenem Gottesverständnis Karl Rahners, in: *Zeitschrift für Katholische Theologie* 112 (1990) 427-436; Roman A. Siebenrock, Gezeichnet vom Geheimnis der Gnade. Worte ins Schweigen als ursprüngliche Gottesrede Karl Rahners, in: Christian Kanzian (ed.), *Gott finden in allen Dingen*. Theologie und Spiritualität (Thaur: Kulturverlag, 1998) 199-217.

36   See K. Rahner, *The Need and the Blessing of Prayer* (1946), translated by Bruce W. Gillette (Collegeville, Minn.: Liturgical Press, 1997).

37   See Hans Urs von Balthasar, Theologie und Heiligkeit, in: ibid., *Verbum Caro*. Skizzen zur Theologie I (Einsiedeln: Johannes Verlag, 1960). Originally appeared in: *Wort und Wahrheit* with the subtitle "Zur Revision der Scholastik." See Antonio M. Sicari, *Theologie und Heiligkeit*. Dogmatik und Spiritualität bei Hans Urs von Balthasar, in: Karl Lehmann, Walter Kasper (eds.), *Hans Urs von Balthasar*. Gestalt und Werk (Köln: Commu-

nio, 1989) 191-206; Anton Štrukelj, *Kniende Theologie* (St. Ottilien: Eos, 1999) esp. 7-20.

38   Karl Rahner felt that Hans Urs von Balthasar's much quoted distinction between a "kneeling" and a "sitting theology" was problematic: see the negative comment in the first footnote of *Theological Investigations*, vol. 1 (The Prospects for Dogmatic Theology, 2) (= K. Rahner, *Sämtliche Werke*, vol. 4, 404, footnote no. 1): "And perhaps it has almost always been the case that 'armchair' scientific theology (to make use of an expression, itself problematic, of H.U. von Balthasar's) has learned more from 'praying' (and preaching) non-scientific theology than the reverse."

39   See Hugo Rahner, *Eine Theologie der Verkündigung* (Freiburg: Herder, 2nd edition 1939; Darmstadt: Wissenschaftliche Buchgesellschaft, 3rd edition 1980); ibid., *A Theology of Proclamation*, translated by Richard Dimmler, SJ, William Dych, SJ, Joseph Halpin, SJ, Clement Petrick, SJ, adapted by Joseph Halpin, SJ (New York: Herder and Herder, 1968); see Karl H. Neufeld, Theologiegeschichtliches zur Innsbrucker "Verkündigungstheolgie," in: *Zeitschrift für Katholische Theologie* 115 (1993) 13-26.

40   Johann Baptist Lotz, SJ(1903-1992); see ibid., Wissenschaft und Verkündigung. Ein philosophischer Beitrag zur Eigenständigkeit einer Verkündigungstheologie, in: *Zeitschrift für Katholische Theologie* 62 (1938) 465-501; Gerd Haeffner, Johannes B. Lotz als Mensch und Philosoph. Verwurzelung und Weitung, in: *Stimmen der Zeit* 222 (2004) 171-182.

41   See K. Rahner, Über die Verkündigungstheologie. Eine kritisch-systematische Literaturübersicht, in: *Pazmanita tudósitó* 16 (1941/2) 3-10; now in: K. Rahner, *Sämtliche Werke*, vol. 4: Hörer des Wortes. Schriften zur Religionsphilosophie und zur Grundlegung der Theologie. Bearbeitet von Albert Raffelt (Freiburg: Herder, 1997) 337-345. See also K. Rahner, Kerymatische Theologie, in: *LThK*, vol. 6, 126; now in: ibid., *Sämtliche Werke*, vol. 17: Enzyklopädische Theologie. Die Lexikonbeiträge der Jahre 1956-1973. Bearbeitet von Herbert Vorgrimler (Freiburg: Herder, 2002) 313.

42   Franz S. Lakner, SJ, (1900-1974); see Franz Lakner, Das Zentralobjekt der Theologie. Zur Frage um Existenz und Gestalt einer Seelsorgstheologie, in: *Zeitschrift für Katholische Theologie* 62 (1938) 1-36.

43   See Karl H. Neufeld, *Die Brüder Rahner*, 151 f.

44   See K. Rahner, *Everyday Things*, translated by M. H. Heelan (London: Sheed and Ward, 1965); ibid., Alltägliche Dinge (Einsiedeln: Benziger, 1964); now in: K. Rahner, *Sämtliche Werke*, vol. 23: Glaube im Alltag. Schriften zur Spiritualität und zum christlichen Lebensvollzug. Bearbeitet von Albert Raffelt (Freiburg: Herder 2006) 475-487.

45   See K. Rahner, Sternenbewohner. 2. Theologisch, in: *Lexikon für Theologie und Kirche*, vol. 9, 1061 f; now in: ibid., *Sämtliche Werke*, vol. 17, 414.

46   See Gnade als Mitte menschlicher Existenz. Ein Gespräch mit und über Karl Rahner aus Anlass seines 70. Geburtstages, in: *Herder Korrespondenz* 28 (1974) 77-92, 80: "(My) theology is a thoughtful reflection on the data which is already present in the general awareness of faith and in Scholastic Theology ... I, in a certain sense, attempted to discover the inner virulence and inner dynamism of Scholastic Theology and release it." Now in: ibid., *Sämtliche Werke*, vol. 25, 3-32, 8.

47   See Karl Rahner, Remarks on the Theology of Indulgences, in: ibid., *Theological Investigations*, vol. 2, translated by Karl –H. Kruger, O.F.M. (Baltimore, MD: Helicon Press, 1963) 175-201; ibid., Some Thoughts on 'A Good Intention,' in: *Theological Investigations*, vol. 3, translated by Karl –H. and Boniface Kruger, O.F.M. (Baltimore, MD: Helicon Press, 1967) 105-128; on indulgences see also Karl Rahner, A Brief Theological Study on Indulgence, in: *Theological Investigations*, vol. 10, translated by David Bourke (New York: Seabury Press, 1977), 150-165; ibid., On the Official Teaching of the Church Today On the Subject of Indulgences, in: ibid., 166-198.

48   All of Rahner's articles composed for *Sacramentum Mundi* are now collected in: K. Rahner, *Sämtliche Werke*, vol. 17, 874-1389.

49   Pietro Parente (1891-1986), from 1939 Consultor for the Holy Office and several Roman Congregations, 1955 Archbishop of Perugia, from 1959 Assessor of the Holy Office with headquarters in Rome, 1967 Cardinal. Parente was the quasi right-hand of Cardinal Alfredo Ottaviani, Prefect of the Holy Office; in his "defense" see Günther Wassilowsky, *Universales Heilsakrament Kirche. Karl Rahners Beitrag zur Ekklesiologie des II. Vatikanums.* (Innsbruck: Tyrolia, 2001) 93, footnote 180. Wassilowsky quotes Herbert Vorgrimler: "Alfredo Ottaviani complained to Rahner during a later conversation with him, while driving with him in the car,'his Assessor, P. Parente, placed before him, for his signature, a letter to the Father General of the Jesuits, with instructions for the preliminary censorship of Rahner. Ottaviani was thus blind-sided; P. Parente failed to inform him about this.'"

50   See Andreas R.Batlogg, Karl Rahners Mitarbeit an den Konzilstexten, in: Franz Xaver Bischof, Stephan Leimgruber (eds.), *Vierzig Jahre II. Vatikanum. Zur Wirkungsgeschichte der Konzilstexte.* (Würzburg: Echter, 2nd edition 2005) 355-376, esp. 358-361, "Dienst an der Kirche oder Durchsetzung eigener Lieblingsideen?"

51   *Lumen Gentium* No. 16: "Nor shall divine providence deny the assistance necessary for salvation to those who, without any fault of theirs, have not yet arrived at an explicit knowledge of God, and who, not without

grace, strive to live a good life. Whatever good or truth is found amongst them is considered by the Church to be a preparation for the Gospel and given by him who enlightens all men that they may at length have life."

52   See the review by K. Rahner in: *Zeitschrift für Katholische Theologie* 63 (1939) 443-444; now in: ibid., *Sämtliche Werke*, vol. 4, 384-385.

53   See Nikolaus Schwerdtfeger, *Gnade und Welt*, 4 f., 27 f., 164 f., 190-199, 413-418.

54   See, e.g., Hans Küng, *My Struggle for Freedom*. Memoirs (Grand Rapids, Michigan: William B. Eerdmanns, 2003), ibid., *Erkämpfte Freiheit*. Erinnerungen (Munich: Piper, 2002) 456-473. See already earlier Hans Küng, *Die Kirche*. Vorwort zur Taschenbuchausgabe (München: Piper, 1977) 5 f.

55   See the interview with Elisabeth Cremer and with Albert Raffelt in this book at which Franz Johna was both times present.

56   See K. Rahner, Auch als Bischof ein Theologe der Mitte, in: *Glaube und Leben*. Kirchenzeitung für das Bistum Mainz 39, 1983, Nr. 40, 14. See ibid., *Bekenntnisse*. Rückblick auf 80 Jahre, edited by Georg Sporschill (Vienna: Herold, 1984) 38: "Lehmann is in the best sense of the word balanced and in theology, more in the middle. During the Synod in Würzburg he was very close to Döpfner, so that must have made a good impression in Rome. Apparently, the fact that he was once my assistant did not hurt him, and he never denied or hid that fact. For all of his cautiousness and more conservative approach, Lehmann is certainly a valuable addition to the German episcopacy." – Now in: K. Rahner, *Sämtliche Werke*, vol. 25: Erneuerung des Ordenslebens. Zeugnis für Kirche und Welt. Bearbeitet von Andreas R. Batlogg (Herder, Freiburg 2008) 61-84, 74.

INTELLECTUAL PASSION AND SPIRITUAL COURAGE

IN CONVERSATION WITH JOHANN BAPTIST METZ, MÜNSTER

Johann Baptist Metz, Dr. phil., Dr. theol., born 1928, 1963-1993 Professor of Fundamental Theology at the University of Münster, 1993-1996 Guest Professor of Philosophy of Religion in Vienna. He is a co-editor of the collected works "Sämtliche Werke" of Karl Rahner.

How did you come to know Karl Rahner?

You see before you a representative of the first generation of Fr. Rahner's theology. My relationship with him began very early, around the end of the 1940's. Although at the time I was still quite young, I was studying philosophy and I decided during the course of writing my doctoral dissertation to focus on the theology of Karl Rahner. From the very beginning I had a close, personal relationship with him.

My relationship with Karl Rahner was always characterized by the fact that not only was he a great academic teacher, but he was, what I once, perhaps not very prudently, but honestly called "a father of faith."[1] The blending of theology and spirituality – that was one of the fundamental characteristics of his way of doing theology and in this he distinguished himself from many other theologians in the 20th century. Today, it is more often the case that one either withdraws from the serious scholarly approach to theology to champion a fundamentalist affirmation of Christianity, or attempts to subsume religion into theology or even more radically makes spirituality superfluous by seeking a way to make it comply with the positions put forth in our post-Christian world. Karl Rahner was someone who was able to bring theology, religion and spirituality together in a way that was unique. It is because of my relationship with Rahner that I have come to see and have emphasized this connection: "Theology as a type of Existential Biography."[2]

You revised both *Spirit in the World* and *Hearer of the Word*. Why?

Our relationship was so good that Fr. Rahner entrusted me with working on a new edition or revision of both works.[3] I realize that there
have been some misgivings and questions as to how much I changed
in the revision of *Hearer of the Word*.[4] When I worked on *Spirit in the
World*, I was in the middle of my studies. That was not an ongoing,
but rather a piece-meal revision. What I did, I did always with Karl
Rahner's approval; he was aware of all of that, saw it and agreed to it.
All that is documented in the collected works *Sämtliche Werke*.[5] With
Hearer of the Word, the revision process was such that it was necessary
to print both versions synoptically, in order to show what had been
revised.[6] At that time I lived near Karl Rahner in Munich-Nymphenburg, with the Benedictine Sisters. Mornings I worked on the revision
and in the afternoons he came to see me and looked at the work I had
done. I did not write anything really, nothing at all, that he did not
approve. Today, I regret some of the changes I made and that he accepted: words like "having being" (*"Seinshabe"*),[7] for example. I would
never use today. That was not a term that existed before then. It has
been said that I wanted to go a step farther, from subjectivity to intersubjectivity. You can see that today in the *Sämtliche Werke*, but Rahner
gave me permission for everything: "Do that, do that in the footnotes."

**Is it your opinion that Rahner's view of intersubjectivity received
its due? Or is it neglected?**

That's not something that I can answer exactly. In the 1980's a dissertation was published in America about him for which he wrote the
foreword and he expressed himself regarding my criticism.[8] But between Rahner and me there was never any dispute, as some people
have contended. Naturally, I spoke from a post-transcendental or
post-idealistic paradigm rooted in Political Theology, but the tools of
my criticism I learned from him.

Because I became a soldier when I was a 16 year old boy the question of theodicy was a major issue for me. I had very horrible experiences which probably moved me to study theology and in particular
to try to deal with the question of suffering. What can I say – idealism, a view of a history without interruption, without catastrophe,
without danger, was unimaginable for me. Therefore, I had to speak

to that.[9] In opposition to Rahner, I said that, perhaps, we must use less rigid categories, so that we remain vulnerable to what we experience. If one brings together biography and theology to such an extent, as Rahner did, then we must consequently challenge the adequacy of the transcendental model. The concept of the transcendental model acknowledges subjectivity, but not the subject. It reflects historicity, but not concrete history. Where this deficiency becomes glaringly apparent was revealed in our own German history. I asked Karl: "Why did you never say anything about Auschwitz? Why did that never appear?" I must say with great respect, that he took this question from his student very seriously. He said: "That is something that you must do." I accused him of having an eschatology that dealt too much with the idealistic and too little with apocalyptic. I was a little brusque with him and said: The fact that there is no answer to the human history of suffering – that is apocalyptic – the cry to God that arises out of suffering.

Once when I was with Fr. Rahner at a reception in the 1980's we met Fr. Lotz,[10] who, along with Max Müller and others, had shaped the new philosophy in Catholic thinking. He came up to me and said, and I am paraphrasing: What's wrong? What critical objections do you have against your dear friend and teacher Rahner? I responded: "Fr. Lotz you know when Rahner gets to heaven God will say to him, 'you, dear, great Karl Rahner, what did you do with the apocalyptic of my son Jesus?'" Rahner walked up to us and asked: "What are you talking about?" I told him what I had said to Fr. Lotz and he said that's not something Lotz would have understood. I replied with a question: "and what do you say?" He answered: "That's something you must do." I always said to Karl Rahner that history is interruption not continuity. I emphasize this so that you understand that while we were not always in agreement we had wonderful conversations. That's the reason that I miss him so much. With regard to the fundamental relationship of theology to mysticism (the experience of faith) no one had more of an impact on me and also on my Political Theology. James Matthew Ashley[11] describes that a bit.

There are those who say the expression "Tutiorismus of Risking" is too awkward. Why does Fr. Rahner use this terminology?

You would presumably translate Tutiorismus as "to follow the safer line." Karl Rahner was a courageous man. The formulation of Tutiorism and the expression "Tutiorismus of Risking" goes back, I believe, to a conflict he had with Rome, and with Fr. Bea,[12] specifically in the areas of Mariology and Ecumenism. The term "Fundamentalism" was not in use at that time, but Fr. Rahner was always suspicious that there was a fundamentalist form of certainty of faith. Having recognized the fact of the certitude of faith he said that it was self-evident that one must play it safe, but he believed that there always needed to be an element of risk in faith. This conflict arose during the pre-conciliar period of the 1950's when he had his difficulties with the debates on Mariology.[13] He was, to a certain extent, a Tutiorist in a dialectical sense; certainty of belief is granted only where one risks something for one's salvation. He used this expression in his more pastoral writings, otherwise it is not central,[14] but it was typical and foundational in terms of his mentality.

What influence did Karl Rahner have at Vatican II?

Fr. Rahner was always very reserved. He maintained that he did not have much influence. He was very modest and also a little skeptical about his alleged importance, but it seems irrefutable to me that he belonged to the people who played a role at the Council, influenced bishops and theologians by suggesting new ways of thinking, and opened up new horizons.[15] One can see that in his influence on Cardinals Franz König and Julius Döpfner.

The Würzburg Synod of the dioceses of Germany took place in the first half of the 1970's. The document "Our Hope," ("*Unsere Hoffnung*")[16] which I drafted, was presented for discussion in the commission. Cardinal Döpfner was very grateful for my active participation and asked me one day: "Can I do something for you?" I told him that he could provide an empty parish house in my home region of Bavaria for Fr. Rahner and me so that I could be freed from my "Prussian exile," at least now and then. The Cardinal said: "I will do that gladly. Then I will have paid a debt of gratitude both to you and to your friend and teacher, Karl Rahner." So we went to this priestless parish for our vacation and to be there for the people. From 1973-96 I lived frequently in a small parish in upper Bavaria, Litzldorf, at the foot of the Wendelstein. In the beginning, Fr. Rahner often came there from Munich, but when he returned to Innsbruck in the fall of 1981 I traveled from Rosenheim to Innsbruck, which was only a short distance.

How did Karl Rahner pray? He published some of his prayers. Did he dictate them or simply write them down?

In the early years he wrote everything down. He always wrote with his own hand, but later he used a typewriter. Fr. Rahner was very conservative liturgically and spiritually very alive. By liturgically conservative I mean that he always celebrated Mass devoutly, and preferably celebrated a "silent Mass." I would concelebrate with him or acolyte for him. But he was not comfortable with celebrating Mass as a big liturgical, festive event. This approach to liturgical spirituality is what I meant when I referred to his theology in terms of a "productive example" – his theology was a prayed theology.

There was a conflict between Karl Rahner and Hans Urs von Balthasar, who once wrote an essay on "Theology and Holiness."[17] Balthasar describes the situation of theology in the modern period by contrasting it with the an earlier approach which he contended was a theology done on one's knees, a theology that was the result of prayer; while modern theology has become a theology done at one's desk. I always believed that this judgment of von Balthasar about modern theology did not apply to Karl Rahner because for him theology and spirituality were one. Theological reflection and spiritual experience were deeply rooted and united together in him. Therefore, it is difficult to make a real distinction between the language of prayer and the language of theological reflection in Rahner. Many of his essays flow into a prayer at the end. One should not be surprised that sometimes his prayers sound like theology or that his theology sounds like a prayer.

Did that happen too in his lectures – that one thought: now Fr. Rahner is going to pray?

Please do not forget that for Rahner the First Vatican Council "despite all the antiquated categories," ("*trotz allem Muff*") as he liked to say, was a magnificent Council. And why? "Because it declared that God can be known with certainty through the natural light of human reason." Naturally I cannot enter into a theoretical discussion at this point on reason. But as to what occurred in his lectures: two things happened in them which always had a huge impact on us. In the 1950's Fr. Rahner gave his lectures in Latin – that was required – but then in the middle of the Latin lecture he would stop speaking Latin and continue in German. He would then begin a critical reflection on certain people and their theological positions. The second thing that occurred was that he then began a transition from theology to spirituality. It never was sentimental or pious. Sometimes, it sounded to me, a little Gnostic. In my mind the cry to God is the main feature of prayer. Perhaps, for him it was a "crying out" for more light, more understanding. In the Bible, it is in my opinion a cry for more justice in the face of the history of human suffering.

The most wonderful thing about him was always his questions, which he raised during his lectures. He would often ask questions, childlike hard questions, as I once called them. With Rahner you can see that there are not only childlike easy questions, but also childlike hard questions. I always use the example that the music of Mozart is childlike hard and in the same way Rahner's theology is childlike hard. He always liked and approved of this comparison. The questions that he asked didn't have anything to do with theology, absolutely nothing; rather they could be very simple or often terribly mundane questions. I often wondered how he could even come up with those questions. They came from a profound reconciliation, if you will, between faith and experience, or between theology and spirituality. He described the Christian of the future becoming a mystic, "someone who had experienced something" as he often phrased it.[18] He was that Christian mystic already. Later I spoke of a mysticism with open eyes, not only a mysticism with closed eyes. I said to Rahner: "with you one must always close one's eyes when one says 'God;' I, on the other hand, say that you have to open your eyes." However, I learned from him because he really did open his eyes and he saw much more than I. That was an experience of him that impressed me deeply; everything that he saw and observed about people. I felt myself reminded of the words of Jesus when he tells us that we see, yet we actually do not see[19]. With Rahner, I always thought: He sees! He was not a phenomenologist; he was from head to toe a transcendental philosopher, but he had exceptional eyes. Thus, what I want to say is that I personally learned from him the categories that I later found myself questioning and criticizing. One cannot say more about a teacher than that I still learned from him even when I felt that I must contradict him.

In reference to the controversy that surrounded the publication of the book *Gratwanderung* ("Tightrope") by Luise Rinser, do you think that Karl Rahner was always wise in his choice of friends?

I have known Luise Rinser for a long time, beginning from my time in Munich. She was from Rosenheim and occasionally came to Litzldorf. You bring up her book *Gratwanderung* ("Tightrope").[20] As I see it with its insinuation, it is rather more an exercise in the wishful thinking of the author than the literary account of a *Gratwanderung*. This book ultimately ended my friendship with Luise Rinser. Certainly, she has charm and radiance; that cannot be disputed. I remember very well how we cried and prayed together when Karl Rahner was once seriously ill. In the last years of his life Rahner withdrew into himself. That's something that Luise Rinser did not respect. Rahner was so discreet and a deeply shy person. Perhaps, it was because of that, he was, in the best sense of the word, a dependable friend.

Did you know that Luise Rinser intended to publish her letters to Karl Rahner?

We, on the Board of Trustees of the Karl Rahner Foundation, knew that and tried to prevent it. We knew from the publisher that they wanted to publish them. We could not prevent it, but that's over and done with.

How can one pass on the legacy of Karl Rahner? How can interest in him be kept alive for the next generation?

For me, Karl Rahner is truly one of those who grappled with the connection between faith and experience in what has been called our post-modern world and formulated the connection in a unique way that cannot be copied. But the paradigm can be appropriated: theology as existential biography, the combination of intellectual passion and spiritual courage that issues forth from the spirit of Ignatius of Loyola. The question arises as to whether people will let themselves become part of this. Rahner desired neither to be the only one, nor the first.

Karl Rahner was someone who was the fundamental Churchman; he did not wish to carry on outside the great theological tradition, nor to go before it, nor to uncouple himself from it, but he went ahead only insofar as the Tradition allowed. He had, at times, pushed people along like a donkey. Sometimes he called himself a donkey who had to pull the load. That might also be considered a model for the Church.[21] The Church could learn from him. I did not achieve that: being able to incorporate everything, indulgences, for example. Fr. Rahner criticized neo-scholasticism, but he took it seriously; he attempted to work out of that context, to recognize what was valuable and not simply ignore it.

How do you view Karl Rahner's teaching career in Munich (1964-1967) and in Münster (1967-1971)? Were they happy years?

Munich was not the right place for him, not because of the city, but the Romano Guardini Chair in Philosophy was not right for him He was also probably too speculative, too much of a theologian, though not in the strict sense, not literary enough, nor popular enough. He also was too much of a monk, even though that now sounds a little strange to say.

Münster on the other hand was a good experience. I was Dean when Rahner came to Münster and I was required to welcome him in the name of the faculty on the occasion of his inaugural lecture on January 9, 1968.[22] I quote from my introduction to his lecture. "Today, as a senior member of the faculty and as Dean, I have the privilege of introducing the newest member of the faculty to you, my honored teacher, Karl Rahner. It is an introduction that is incredibly easy to make, for what more can be said about Karl Rahner that has not already been said. I do not want to list any dates or name any of his works, nor refer to the many prizes and honorary doctorates that he has been awarded; I only want to say one thing: today, in many respects, in place of the controversial and ecclesially suspect Rahner, a Rahner who is respected has emerged. His bold *theologumena* come forth now from every mouth. But this should not keep us from remembering that the most amazing awakening and renewal in Catholic Theology that has taken place in the last decade is linked to his name: an awakening from out of the pale and not infrequently rigid formulations of a neo-Scholastic thought pattern and speech, through a decisive confrontation of the scholastic tradition with the line of questioning put forth by contemporary philosophy. Rahner freed his theological starting point from the rock of scholastic objectivism in which Scholastic Theology had appeared to be in all respects embedded. This brought about a series of awakenings: an awakening from the fruitless and unmediated comparison of systematic and historical exegetical theology with the help of the first stage of a developed theological hermeneutic of biblical and theological-historical statements. Challenging the view of the necessity of a distinction between theology and kergyma, he showed in his work, that the most scholarly theology is in the long run also the most kerymatic: an awakening from the official faith of the theologians to a fraternal faith, with the help of a theology of faith which knows about self-seeking, a faith always in peril which understands itself primarily as a *theologia viatorum*, as fraternal service to the hope of all: an awakening from a ghettoized world view of Catholicism to a dialogue with a world that accepts a social pluralism, and this long before the word dialogue became a thoughtless, much laden theological term in popular jargon. Karl Rahner is not simply an interested outsider attempting renewal with his impetuous ideas. He has succeeded in affecting the ecclesial and theological mentality of a number of people. His influence at the Council is evidence of that. Rahner has gone about as far as the great tradition of the Church and theology have allowed, but often with difficulty and in the face of protest. Therefore, his own progress is seen as a recognizable advance in theology and theological consciousness.

Now all that having been said, we should not prematurely erect a monument to him, but we should instead see him as an example of the way to go and as a leader that has begun a never-ending movement. Karl Rahner, himself, has always objected to being characterized in his own life-time as someone whose thought and person should be carved in stone. His work proceeds and involves dealing with new problems and new approaches and we rejoice that he can play a decisive role now on our faculty, at our *alma mater*. Fr. Rahner would have liked to have refused to hold an official inaugural lecture, citing a privilege allowed in Canon Law, i. e. the canonical privilege for the so called *Virgo Superadulta*, for the older bride, who because of advanced age, can be dispensed from the announcement of the banns before the wedding. But that is difficult to apply to university customs. So we settled on a compromise: Fr. Rahner would give his inaugural lecture at the uni-

versity within the framework of the lectures to the faculty this semester on the topic of *Bild – Wort – Symbol* ("Picture – Word – Symbol").
And now I invite him ..."

During his time in Münster we worked together closely, but in the
seminars, the theological-academic conflicts increased. There was a
group of those "true to Rahner" people like Karl Lehmann, who was
an assistant to Rahner, and there were "my people," representatives
of a Political Theology. We offered seminars together and we argued
with each other. Sometimes tense, but unfortunately we were together
only for a brief time. I believe that Rahner felt more comfortable on
the faculty here than he did at the University of Munich. I'm sure he
missed some things, to give a banal example, like being able to go out
during the evening to buy a newspaper for the next day, something
that he could do in Munich. Münster was a small town, much more
provincial. In 1971, he became a Professor emeritus and returned to
Munich. His 70th birthday was celebrated in the Catholic Academy. I
gave the festive keynote address. Cardinal Volk was also present. In my
speech I emphasized that Rahner had become an accepted and well
recognized authority and that even some of the bishops read his work.
Afterwards, Cardinal Volk came up to me and said: "I have read everything that Rahner has written. What are you thinking, Dr. Metz?" He
really scolded me.

During our time together in Münster I was in a serious car accident
and I was in the hospital for a long time and then confined to my home
to recuperate. I could not go to the University and we spent much time
together at my home. Rahner came to visit me very often in the afternoons and evenings at my residence on Kapitel Street. During that
time we spoke about many things together. For me, it was a happy and
enriching time, in spite of, or maybe because of our many theological
disputes about Political Theology: this theology "with its face to the
world" (*"mit dem Gesicht zur Welt"*) and with the "mysticism with open
eyes" (*"Mystik der offenen Augen"*). What's important, though, is that it
was a good time for conversation. The students treasured Rahner and
his lectures were always well attended.

**Do you believe that the *Sämtliche Werke* will be able to further the
legacy of Karl Rahner?**

Originally I made a different proposal, but it was not accepted. I wanted there to be a more popular edition, rather than a complete scholarly edition so that the *Schriften zur Theologie* would remain available for young people, being economically more reasonable so that students might be able to buy them. My idea was to have a collection of 10 volumes; in the German edition of *Schriften zur Theologie* there are 16. I would have preferred a more popular edition as was done in the case of Bloch or Adorno, or a study edition as was done for Nietzsche or Hegel. Thus, the students would be more aware of Rahner's work than they are now, especially younger students. It is really incredible how few young people read Rahner today. Of course, they know his name, but increasingly he is being forgotten; it is a case of the triumph of cultural amnesia today.

At the time decisions about publication were being made difficulties arose between the Board of Trustees and Benziger Publications. Benziger was concerned that they would not be able to sell copies of *Schriften zur Theologie* if the *Sämtliche Werke* were to be published and the Rahner Foundation specifies that its finances are only to be used for a scholarly edition of the *Sämtliche Werke*. That's the reason we have to pay attention when we publish a new volume. But I doubt that our edition of the *Collected Works* will be bought by students. They will not be able to afford the *Sämtliche Werke* and even interested and educated Christians will hardly be able to afford to buy it. The works will be relegated to a place in the libraries. I had wished that Rahner's work could have been made more readily available to young people. So I see certain barriers to his legacy. The tradition will continue through dissertations, but that is not enough.

Rahner, in my opinion, is not the appropriate candidate for a scholarly, complete edition in the manner of the great works of the 19th century. The spirit of theological existence that he represents is, in its conjoining of faith and life-experience, not simply something to be found already codified, in a book, but in a good Ignatian manner, always experienced as a new vision, something to reflect on and practice. That's the reason certain selected texts of Rahner should be read in conjunction with the indispensable *Sämtliche Werke*, for the purpose of acquiring this form of theological and Christian existence.

With this in mind I would suggest that it would be good for the Karl Rahner Society to suggest to Herder Publishing that they make such a reader available to American students. The right people would have to be chosen to select the material. We already have such a Rahner breviary.[23] Every now and then Rahner would relate his theological propositions to everyday life. I think a good example of this is his small essay "Experience of the Spirit"[24] which is a text that acts as a catalyst for thinking about the relationship between reflection and experience, between theology and spirituality which has to be put into practice. I remember that my mother spoke about his essay *On the Need for and the Blessing of Prayer* and his *Encounters with Silence* and she said that I can understand these things much better than your arguments and that shows the need for the publication of Rahner's Practical Theology.

Such publications would not be in competition with our edition, but serve as an important ancillary to it. It would serve as an important aide to the handing on of Rahner's theology. Perhaps, you can promote that idea in the USA. I think it would also be important for the Karl Rahner Society, which is concerned with handing on Rahner's legacy, to be more active in promoting this. We would like to see both things take place – the publication of a great scholarly edition and the publication of something that aides and promotes keeping the work of Karl Rahner fresh in the minds of the young people of today.[25]

NOTES

1 Johann Baptist Metz, Karl Rahner zu vermissen, in: Paul Imhof, Hubert Biallowons (eds.), *Karl Rahner – Bilder eines Lebens* (Freiburg: Herder, 1985) 166-171, 170: "We have lost in K. Rahner not only an outstanding teacher of theology, but also what I dare to call a "father of faith" – in the sense of Paul's distinction in 1 Cor 4, 15:'Even if you should have countless guides to Christ, yet you do not have many fathers.'... As just such a father of faith, we miss K. Rahner." In the homily which Metz preached on the occasion of Karl Rahner's golden jubilee of priesthood on the Feast of Saint Ignatius of Loyola in 1982, in the Jesuit Church in Innsbruck, ibid., *Den Glauben lernen und lehren*. Dank an Karl Rahner (München: Kösel, 1984) there is an explicit reference to Karl Rahner as "father of faith" (see 24-26: "A father of faith and himself without a home.") Cf."Do we miss Karl Rahner?" in: Johann Baptist Metz, *A Passion for God*, The Mystical-Political Dimension of Christianity, translated by J. Matthew Ashley, (New York: Paulist Press, 1998) 92-106.

2 The expression first appeared in the *Laudatio*, which Metz held at the academic event for Karl Rahner's 70th birthday in Munich; see Johann Baptist Metz, Karl Rahner – a theological life. Theologie als mystische Bi-

ographie eines Christenmenschen heute, in: *Stimmen der Zeit* 192 (1974) 305-316, 308: "One can still refer to this body of work as 'Transcendental Theology.'" I prefer to call it by what it attempts to be, a life-story Dogmatic Theology, a kind of Existential Biography, a type of Mystical Biography in dogmatic form at the heart and center of our times." Cf. the revised version in: ibid., *Glaube in Geschichte und Gesellschaft*. Studien zu einer praktischen Fundamentaltheologie (Mainz: Matthias Grünewald, 5th edition 1992) 211-219.

3   Cf. K. Rahner, Vorwort zur zweiten Auflage, in: ibid., *Geist in Welt*. Zur Metaphysik der endlichen Erkenntnis bei Thomas von Aquin (München: Kösel, 2nd edition 1957) 9-10, 9. See also, Preface to the Second German Edition, in: ibid., *Spirit in the World*, translated by William Dych, SJ (New York: Herder and Herder, 1968) xlvii – xlviii, "… my fundamental conception has remained completely unchanged, nor do my duties allow me the time to rework the theme of the book critically as a whole or to carry it further in any fundamental way. So I merely intended to comply with the quite representative wishes for a new edition. For this 1957 edition I am greatly indebted to my student, Dr. John Baptist Metz, to whom I entrusted its preparation. He has gone over the text as a whole, reworking it in some instances (see Part II, Chapter 1) and expanding and supplementing it here and there by small additions to the text. He translated the Latin text upon which the work is based into German, broke most chapters down into smaller sections with subtitles, and above all, in a few sections of the text and especially in the footnotes, confronted the teaching of the book with the most important reviews of the first edition and with other works on the Thomistic metaphysics of knowledge which have appeared since 1939 and treated the theses of this book explicitly. Hence whatever distinguishes the second from the first edition is due to Dr. Metz. Since I am in complete agreement with the results of the generous, intelligent, and penetrating work he has done on my book, it seemed superfluous to single out in particular these additions to and improvements on the text." – See now: K. Rahner, *Sämtliche Werke*, vol. 2: Geist in Welt. Philosophische Schriften. Bearbeitet von Albert Raffelt (Freiburg: Herder, 1996) 6-7. – Cf. K. Rahner, *Hörer des Wortes*. Zur Grundlegung einer Religionsphilosophie. New edition edited by Johann Baptist Metz (München: Kösel, 1963), (3rd edition 1969), (4th edition 1985); now in: K. Rahner, *Sämtliche Werke*, vol. 4: Hörer des Wortes. Schriften zur Religionsphilosophie und zur Grundlegung der Theologie. Bearbeitet von Albert Raffelt (Freiburg: Herder, 1997).

4   Cf. Johann Baptist Metz's letter to Albert Raffelt, the editor of *Sämtliche Werke*, vol. 4, dated Nov. 14, 1996: "I reworked the text page by page and then presented my revisions to Karl Rahner; he discussed with me the revisions page by page and thus all of the additions and revisions (includ-

ing the reworking of chapter 14) as it appears in the new revised edition were all approved by him. The footnotes in the newly revised edition (the first edition had only one footnote) are all to be attributed to me. That was the intention from the very beginning, and I don't want to deny that in the footnotes there are formulations or historical points which were not explicitly critically examined." Quoted according to Albert Raffelt, editor's report, in: K. Rahner, *Sämtliche Werke*, vol. 4, xiii-xxxvii.

5 Cf. K. Rahner, *Sämtliche Werke*, vol. 2, 3-300.

6 Cf. K. Rahner, *Sämtliche Werke*, vol. 4, 1-281. This edition shows both versions in synoptic order: the first (1941) on the left hand side, the second (1963) on the right hand side. Thereby the additions, revisions and deletions are easily seen.

7 Cf. e.g. K. Rahner, *Sämtliche Werke*, vol. 4, 75, 77 and elsewhere.

8 Cf. Karl Rahner, Introduction, in: James J. Bacik, *Apologetics and the eclipse of mystery.* Mystagogy according to Karl Rahner (Notre Dame: University of Notre Dame Press, 1980) ix-x, ix: "Metz's critique of my theology (which he calls transcendental theology) is the only criticism which I can take very seriously. I agree in general with the positive contribution in Metzs [sic!] book. Insofar as the critique by Metz is correct, every concrete mystagogy must obviously from the very beginning consider the societal situation and the Christian praxis to which it addresses itself. If this is not sufficiently done in my theory of mystagogy and in its explanation in this book, then this theory must be filled out. However, it is not therefore false. For it has always been clear in my theology that a 'transcendental experience' (of God and of grace) is always mediated through a categorical experience in history, in interpersonal relationships, and in society. If one not only sees and takes seriously these necessary mediations of transcendental experience but also fills it out in a concrete way, then one already practices in an authentic way, political theology, or, in other words, a practical fundamental theology. On the other hand, such a political theology is, if it truly wishes to concern itself with God, not possible without reflection on those essential characteristics of man, which a transcendental theology discloses. Therefore, I believe, that my theology and that of Metz are not necessarily contradictory. However, I gladly recognize that a concrete mystagogy must, to use Metz's language, be at the same time 'mystical and political.'" – This Introduction by Karl Rahner is dated Advent 1997, Munich.

9 Cf. e.g., Johann Baptist Metz, *Zum Begriff der neuen Politischen Theologie.* 1967-1997 (Mainz: Matthias Grünewald, 1997) 207-211 (= § 12: Ein biographischer Durchblick: "Wie ich mich verändert habe.")

10   Johann Baptist Lotz (1903-1992); cf. Gerd Haeffner, Johannes B. Lotz als Mensch und Philosoph. Verwurzelung und Weitung, in: *Stimmen der Zeit* 222 (2004) 171-182; Otto Muck, Die deutschsprachige Maréchal

Schule – Tranzendentalphilosophie als Metaphysik: Johann Baptist Lotz, Karl Rahner, Walter Brugger, Emerich Coreth u. a., in: Emerich Coreth, Walter M. Neidl, Georg Pfliegersdorffer (eds.), *Christliche Philosophie im katholischen Denken des 19. und 20. Jahrhunderts*, vol. 2: Rückgriff auf scholastische Erbe (Graz: Styria, 1988) 590-622, esp. 594-600.

11   Cf. James Matthew Ashley, Metz's collaboration with Karl Rahner, in: ibid., *Interruptions*. Mysticism, politics, and theology in the work of Johann Baptist Metz (Notre Dame: University of Notre Dame Press, 1998) 73-84.

12   Augustin Bea, SJ, (1881-1968), 1921-1924 Provincial of the Southern German Jesuit province, subsequently teaching activity at the Gregorian University and at the Pontifical Biblical Institute in Rome, 1949 Consultor of the Holy Office, 1959 Cardinal, 1960 President of the Secretariat on Christian Unity.

13   Cf. Regina Pacis Meyer, Editionsbericht, in: K. Rahner, *Sämtliche Werke*, vol. 9: Maria, Mutter des Herrn. Mariologische Studien. Bearbeitet von Regina Pacis Meyer (Freiburg: Herder 2004) xi-lvi; Karl H. Neufeld, Zur Mariologie Karl Rahner – Materialien und Grundlinien, in: *Zeitschrift für Katholische Theologie* (*ZKTh*) 109 (1987) 431-439; ibid., Lehramtliche Missverständnisse. Zu Schwierigkeiten Karl Rahners in Rom, in: (*ZKTh*) 111 (1989) 420-430; ibid., *Die Brüder Rahner*. Eine Biographie (Freiburg: Herder, 2nd edition 2004) 206-214; Herbert Vorgrimler, *Karl Rahner*. Gotteserfahrung in Leben und Denken. (Darmstadt: Primus 2004) 71-74.

14   Cf. K. Rahner, Die Gegenwart der Kirche, in: *Handbuch für Pastoraltheologie*, vol. II/1 (Freiburg: Herder, 1966) 188-233, now in: Karl Rahner, *Sämtliche Werke*, vol. 19: Selbstvollzug der Kirche. Ekklesiologische Grundlegung praktischer Theologie. Bearbeitet von Karl H .Neufeld (Freiburg: Herder, 1995) 255-316, esp. 293, 296, 313, 315f. Cf. Johann Baptist Metz, Fehlt uns Karl Rahner? oder: Wer retten will, muss wagen, in: K. Rahner, *Strukturwandel der Kirche als Aufgabe und Chance* (new edition) (Freiburg: Herder, 1989) 9-24.

15   Cf. Andreas R. Batlogg, Karl Rahners Mitarbeit an den Konzilstexten, in: Franz Xaver Bischof, Stephan Leimgruber (eds.), *Vierzig Jahre II. Vatikanum*. Zur Wirkungsgeschichte der Konzilstexte (Würzburg: Echter, 2nd edition 2005) 355-376; Günther Wassilowsky, *Universales Heilssakrament Kirche*. Karl Rahners Beitrag zur Ekklesiologie des II. Vatikanums (Innsbruck: Tyrolia, 2001).

16   *Unsere Hoffnung*. Ein Bekenntnis zum Glauben in dieser Zeit, in: Gemeinsame Synode der Bistümer in der Bundesrepublik Deutschland. Offizielle Gesamtausgabe, vol. 1 (Freiburg: Herder, 1976) 84-111.

17   Hans Urs von Balthasar, Theologie und Heiligkeit, in: ibid. *Verbum Caro*. Skizzen zur Theologie I (Einsiedeln, Johannes Verlag, 1960) 195-225, 204. The article was originally published in *Wort und Wahrheit* with the subtitle, "Zur Revision der Scholastik;" cf. Elio Guerriero, *Hans Urs von Balthasar*. Eine Monographie (Einsiedeln: Johannes Verlag, 1993) 210-215; Andreas R. Batlogg, Hans Urs von Balthasar und Karl Rahner: zwei Schüler des Ignatius, in: Magnus Striet, Jan-Heiner Tück (eds.), *Die Kunst Gottes verstehen*. Hans Urs von Balthasars theologische Provokationen (Freiburg: Herder, 2005) 410-446, esp. 432f.

18   K. Rahner, Frömmigkeit früher und heute, in: ibid., *Schriften zur Theologie*, vol. 7 (Einsiedeln: Benziger, 1966) 11-31, 22 f. – Now in: ibid., *Sämtliche Werke*, vol. 23: Glaube im Alltag. Schriften zur Spiritualität und zum christlichen Lebensvollzug. Bearbeitet von Albert Raffelt (Freiburg: Herder, 2006) 31-46, 39. See also ibid., Christian Living Formerly And Today, in: ibid., *Theological Investigations*, vol. 7, translated by David Bourke, (New York: Seabury Press, 1971) 3-24, 15, "Simply in order to make it clear what is meant here, and in the consciousness that the concept of 'mysticism' is a loaded one (rightly understood it is not the opposite of belief in the Holy Pneuma but rather identical with it), it could be said: the devout Christian of the future will either be a 'mystic,' one who has 'experienced' something, or he will cease to be anything at all. For devout Christian living as practiced in the future will no longer be sustained and helped by the unanimous, manifest and public convictions and religious customs of all, summoning each one from the outset to a personal experience and a personal decision. For this reason, therefore, the usual religious education as practiced hitherto can only provide a very secondary kind of preparation for the institutional element in the religion of the future."

19   Cf. Mt 13, 13: "I use parables when I speak to them because they look but do not see, they listen but do not hear or understand."

20   Cf. Luise Rinser, *Gratwanderung*. Briefe der Freundschaft an Karl Rahner, 1962-1984, edited by Bogdan Snela (München: Kösel, 1994).

21   Cf. Karl Lehmann, Karl Rahner und die Kirche, in: Albert Raffelt (ed.), *Karl Rahner in Erinnerung* (Düsseldorf: Patmos, 1994) 118-133; Andreas R. Batlogg, Gotteserfahrung und Kirchenkritik bei Karl Rahner, in: Mariano Delgado, Gotthard Fuchs (eds.), *Gotteserfahrung und Kirchenkritik der Mystiker*. Prophetie aus Gotteserfahrung, vol. 3 (Fribourg, Stuttgart: Academic press, Kohlhammer, 2005) 371-401.

22   Cf. K. Rahner, Vom Hören und Sehen. Eine theologische Überlegung, in: Wilhelm Heinen (ed.), *Bild – Wort – Symbol in der Theologie* (Würzburg: Echter, 1969) 139-156; for background, see, Karl H. Neufeld, *Die Brüder Rahner*, 279-284.

23   Cf. Karl Lehmann, Albert Raffelt (eds.), *Rechenschaft des Glaubens*. Karl
      Rahner Lesebuch (Freiburg: Herder, 1979); ibid. (eds.), *Karl Rahner-Lese-
      buch*. Aktualisierte Sonderausgabe von "Rechenschaft des Glaubens" (Frei-
      burg: Herder, 2nd edition 2004). Cf. ibid., *The Content of Faith*, translation
      edited by Harvey D. Egan, SJ (New York: Crossroad, 1994).

24   Cf. K. Rahner, *Erfahrung des Geistes*. Meditation auf Pfingsten. (Frei-
      burg: Herder, 1977); reprinted under the title, "Erfahrung des Heiligen
      Geistes," in: Karl Rahner, *Schriften zur Theologie*, vol. 13 (Zurich: Benziger,
      1978) 226-251, English translation, "Experience of the Holy Spirit" in:
      ibid., *Theological Investigations*, vol. 18, translated by Edward Quinn (New
      York: Crossroad, 1983), 189-210.

25   Cf. the recent publications of Herder Publishing: K. Rahner, *Beten mit
      Karl Rahner* (Freiburg: Herder, 2003); ibid., *Von der Unbegreiflichkeit Got-
      tes*. Erfahrungen eines katholischen Theologen, edited by Albert Raffelt
      (Freiburg: Herder, 2004); now in: K. Rahner, *Sämtliche Werke*, vol. 25: Er-
      neuerung des Ordenslebens. Zeugnis für Kirche und Welt. Bearbeitet von
      Andreas R. Batlogg (Freiburg: Herder, 2008) 47-57; ibid. *Von der Gnade
      des Alltags*. Meditationen in Wort und Bild (Freiburg: Herder, 2006).

II

COLLABORATION WAS NOT EASY!

IN CONVERSATION WITH FR. KARL H. NEUFELD, SJ, INNSBRUCK

Karl H. Neufeld, Dr. theol. habil., Dr. phil., born 1939 in Warendorf/ Nordrhein-Westfalen, a Jesuit since 1960. After serving as an Editor for "Stimmen der Zeit" in Munich, he became the Spiritual Director of the Collegium Germanicum et Hungaricum in Rome in 1976. He was appointed Professor of Dogma at the Gregorian Pontifical University in 1978 and in 1990 became a Professor of Fundamental Theology at the University in Innsbruck, where since 1985 he has been the Director of the "Karl-Rahner-Archiv." 1999-2007 he has been the Editor-in-chief of "Zeitschrift für Katholische Theologie." From 1971-73 he served as Karl Rahner's personal assistant in Munich. In 2004, on the occasion of his 65th birthday, he was presented a Festschrift.[1] Since fall 2007, he has been Spiritual Director of the seminary in Osnabrück (Germany).

Fr. Neufeld, what was your relationship with Karl Rahner?

In the beginning there was no relationship at all. A relationship was established when I was sent by my Provincial to Munich in the summer of 1971 to serve as an assistant to Karl Rahner. This meant that I had to interrupt the work that I was doing for my doctorate in France for two years. I began my work with him in the fall of 1971 in Munich. My task was to prepare volume 10 of *Schriften zur Theologie* and then volume 11 of *Schriften zur Theologie*, on the History of Penance and in addition to that begin preparation for his book, *Foundations of Christian Faith*. That was my official task – being his assistant, a post made possible by the Görres Society because Fr. Rahner, since his retirement, no longer had any academic aides to assist him. So that the work on Fr. Rahner's publications could continue, the Görres Society, specifically Professor Paul Mikat, authorized the appointment of an assistant for Fr. Rahner for two years.

The Provincial then came to me. I was in Frankfurt for a vacation during that summer. I had completed the *"année d'habiliation"* in Paris;

that is the preparation for the doctorate, so that I no longer needed to attend any seminars. I certainly was familiar with Karl Rahner's work from my studies. But no more than any other student would be. I also had attended some of his lectures. During the Council I once heard him speak in Pullach on the collective discovery of Truth.[2] That impressed me a lot. But, other than that I really did not know him and did not have a personal relationship with him. When I arrived in Munich, he knew just what he wanted me to do, but I had absolutely no idea, specifically, what was expected of me. But, in the end, I thought, well, perhaps, it is not so bad if you go there. You will learn a little something besides French Theology.

Did Fr. Rahner speak to you about how your collaboration would work?

No, I had, repeatedly, to tell him that we had to work on some texts together and that I couldn't work on all the texts alone. But, he was always on the go – lecture trips mostly – and I had to accomplish my work relatively independently. I tried again to pin him down. I had, although it was not originally planned, to edit volume 12 of *Schriften zur Theologie* (*Theological Investigations*, vol. 21). He had to be there to answer questions, because they involved older texts and I needed him to provide that information. First of all, I collected and organized the available material. That was something that his assistants in Münster should have done. They didn't get to that. Fr. Rahner had six assistants there and here I was alone. Frido Mann,[3] Elmar Klinger, Heribert Woestmann and Kuno Füssel were his assistants in Münster. In addition he had Annerose Köster who was his secretary and Fr. Roman Bleistein, SJ, as a personal consultant. Fr. Bleistein managed Fr. Rahner's personal calendar: I didn't have to do that. I could work relatively undisturbed. He had another secretary in Munich. Previously, there were six or seven people who had worked on the volumes which I had to work on: Herbert Vorgrimler, Marlies Mügge, Karl-Heinz Weger, SJ, and some others. They worked on those volumes, but nothing came of it. Fr. Rahner then insisted that I be acknowledged specifically in the *Schriften zur Theologie* as an editor.

I had to collect the material for *Foundations of Christian Faith* which was in eight large three ring binders full of documentation. I had begun to work on a publishable version, but my two years had come to

an end. In the meantime I had read and corrected all the publications
which Fr. Rahner had published during this time, for example – *Was
ist ein Sakrament?* which he wrote with Eberhard Jüngel,[4] or the small
book *Experiment Mensch*[5] which was part of the series in the "*Sieben-
stern-Taschenbuch*." This paperback is something that I prepared; Fr.
Rahner really did not concern himself with it, but a foreword had to
be written for it so he said "Make me a draft!" So I wrote three or four
pages for him. He came to me on a Saturday or Sunday morning and
said that the secretary was not there and he needed to submit the text
the next day and could I type that for him? He dictated it to me. Normally that was not my work. Basically, what he dictated was the text
that I had drafted for him and I typed it making two or three slight
corrections. In actual fact, he read to me my own draft.

What other things happened during this time?

I was in Rome with him in April, May 1972. Fr. Rahner held lectures
in Christology at the Gregorian University. I accompanied him frequently to the lectures. Once we were invited to a Catholic student
community at the University of Regensburg. This invitation probably
was meant to cause Joseph Ratzinger embarrassment. Ratzinger was a
Professor there. He sat with Johann Auer in the front row. Afterwards
there was a dispute about hermeneutics. Another time I was in Augs-
burg with Fr. Rahner. We were there because of a discussion begun
with the Communists in the international *Dialog-Zeitschrift*, edited
by Herbert Vorgrimler. Karl Rahner wanted to continue the dialogue
that had been started by the *Paulus Gesellschaft*, but had been broken
off after the Russian march into Czechoslovakia. It was clear that the
dialogue had been broken off because, as someone stated: we are not
going to be able to dialogue with one another because it is a pure dic-
tatorship. Because Vorgrimler did not want to cut all ties he founded
this periodical. It was financed by the German bishops. It provided a
forum for a number of communist writers. That angered some bishops
because they believed that the magazine, in their opinion, was serving to support so-called communist propaganda. There were heated
discussions and the publication of the periodical was finally stopped.[6]

My two years had come to an end and I had not yet finished my
doctorate. Fr. Rahner would have liked to have me continue to work
for him, but he did not bother to request a new stipend so that I would

be able to do so. Then I returned to France, and in 1973-74 I was once again in Chantilly and in Paris. I finished my doctorate and returned to Munich in the Zuccalistrasse. There I finished editing *Schriften zur Theologie*, vol. 12 (*Theological Investigations*, vol. 16): *Experience of the Spirit: Source of Theology*; it is the volume on spiritual experience. In 1976, I came to Rome. Officially I was assigned to work for the periodical, everything else was extra.

Are you referring to the periodical *Stimmen der Zeit*?

Yes, I was in Munich for four years as a member of the editorial staff, although of the four years I actually only worked for two in that capacity, because I was in Rome for the other two years. Fr. Rahner moved out of the Alfred-Delp-Haus. Both of us lived until 1973 in the Zuccalistrasse in Munich-Nymphenburg. When I returned to France, Fr. Rahner moved to the Berchmans College in the Kaulbachstrasse. That's closer to the city center. He thought that he might find some assistants there. He did have one person whom he mentions in the foreword of *Foundations of Christian Faith*, – Harald Schöndorf, SJ

Working with Karl Rahner appears not to have been easy?

It was not easy for anyone to work with Fr. Rahner. Often he would completely monopolize your time; you practically could do nothing else. He always felt that you had to be constantly at his disposal. But sometimes you would not see him for three or four weeks or you might see him and he would have other things on his mind. Then he would leave you in peace.

For example, I had to do the footnotes for his articles. We had a kind of gentlemen's agreement about that. I mean by that: I once asked him how he envisioned that they should look and he said nothing really. I inserted one footnote per page. Of course, there were some things that were in the text itself that I could put in a footnote which would make the text easier to understand. I would take out an interjection which basically interrupted the flow of the text and put it in a footnote. With volume 10 on "The History of Penance," the work was very arduous. There were many citations from the Church Fathers to deal with and Fr. Rahner always worked with "Migne" and quoted the Fathers according to the *Patrologia Latina*. He knew from his brother Hugo that there were academic editions of the writings of the Church Fathers made by both the Viennese and Berliners.[7] He wanted me to use the footnotes and citations from the Christian Fathers of the first three centuries from the Viennese edition. That presented a huge amount of work for me because the academic editions are often organized differently than Migne. Practically speaking that was a very difficult, technical task, very time consuming, which required a great deal of research. I had to work constantly with the Church Fathers, but when I came to *Schriften zur Theologie*, volume 12, and the essay on Origen,[8] it paid off. He had a large number of footnotes which I was able to reduce substantially. That is a question to consider in terms of the *Sämtliche Werke* (the complete works) as to whether we need to refer back to Rahner's original version. At that time, Fr. Rahner wanted the conversion to the newer academic editions, but he did not involve himself in the process for that.

In that connection I recall the following example: Rahner quoted many things from memory – he had an incredible memory. There were, however, many quotations in his works without any citation. There was a quote from Anselm that I could not verify. I looked long and hard and finally I said to Fr. Rahner, I can't find the source. He said that I was too lazy. Then, angrily, he left for the library and searched for the entire afternoon. In the evening he came to me, embarrassed and said that he could not find the reference either. This quote from Anselm was important; it was not simply an illustrative or decorative citation (sometimes I just deleted quotes from the text or put them into indirect address so that they were no longer direct quotations), but this time the flow of the argument depended on this quotation. I let it stand as it was written and added a footnote that stated that: this thought is generally attributed to Anselm, but as it appears here it cannot be authenticated, but it does express what Anselm meant.[9] Fr. Rahner agreed with that.

You often hear that Fr. Rahner knew a great deal, but that he was impatient. Did that seem like a weakness to you?

In general, Fr. Rahner was not unpleasant. Little expressions of impatience can be understood. It depends on the person. Personally, I did not have any difficulties with him in this regard. He never once threw me out.[10] He was capable of doing that when someone appeared at the wrong moment. If he felt that someone was interrupting him, he could be rude and tell them to go away. But there were different situations. For example, there once was a woman who followed him when he travelled, who apparently was mentally unbalanced. She came from Münster and wanted to speak to him at any cost. He did not want to see her. He said to me that I should go and talk to her. This woman knew that Fr. Rahner must be there. She was in the waiting room and she became somewhat hysterical, but I was able to get her to leave. I felt sorry for her, but it wasn't possible to do things differently.

Did you have any further contact with Fr. Rahner after you left Munich?

Fr. Rahner was a member of the board for my doctorate in 1975 in Paris together with Henri Bouillard, SJ, Yves Congar, OP, and Alexandre Dumas. That gave him a little lift. At that time the Rector of the Institute Catholique was Paul Poupard, now a Curia cardinal in the Vatican. He hosted a great banquet. I was not able to attend personally, since I had to prepare my defense. The members of the board came to the defense pretty relaxed by the meal. There were about 100-150 people there, and my defense actually went much better than I imagined it would.

From 1978 on, I was in Rome for the rest of Fr. Rahner's lifetime. I didn't work with him directly any more. I obtained Fr. Rahner's article for René Latourelle's, SJ, and Gerald O'Collins', SJ, book on Fundamental Theology.[11] Fr. Rahner also wrote an article for a book on Dogmatic Theology for which I was the editor.[12] But every time Fr. Rahner was in Rome, he would invite me to go someplace to eat with him. In the last year of his life he invited me to come to the presentation of the French translation of his *Foundations of Christian Faith* in Paris.[13] I traveled to Paris from Rome. Neither Ms. Oeggl, his secretary, nor Fr. Imhof, SJ, was able to accompany him due to other prior commitments, so Fr. Rahner had to fly to Paris alone and arrived in Centre Sèvres on a Sunday evening. The Jesuit reception desk was closed and he stood before the huge iron gate and rang the bell. When a Jesuit came out, he thought that Rahner was a street person (*"clochard"*) who had come to the Centre and wanted a bowl of soup. He began to turn him away because no soup was handed out on Sundays as it was during the week. Thereupon, Fr. Rahner allegedly said: *"Mais, je suis le*

Père Rahner!" Naturally, this Jesuit turned as red as a beet and let him in immediately.

Was that your last encounter with Fr. Rahner?

In Paris he gave a lecture at which Henri de Lubac, SJ and Jean-Marie Lustiger were present – both in the meantime had become cardinals. Fr. Rahner wanted me to read his lecture, just as he would have someone do when he was in the USA, but I told him that when two Cardinals had been invited, he must read the lecture himself. That was difficult for him, although he had learned French in school. After Latin, it was the language in which he could best express himself, but he had not practiced it. Nevertheless, the audience appreciated the fact that he delivered the lecture himself. There were some other receptions at which we saw each other.

Shortly before he died we met in Italy and in Hungary. I was with him for a week in January 1984 in Gallarate near Milan. There was a conference there on his theology for Italian Theology professors and doctoral students. The topic was Theology and Culture – a typical Italian issue.[14] Fr. Rahner spoke in German, but that did not need to be translated. In the discussion that followed I had to do the translating – Italian to German. I think that he enjoyed being there. Afterwards we drove to Lago Maggiore, Isola Bella and the Gran Carlone which is the region from which his patron Saint Charles Borromeo came.

He then invited me to join him in February 1984 for a meeting with atheists in Budapest. This took place at the end of February. The conference interested him very much, but he felt a little abandoned there because all those he had expected to see had abruptly cancelled and didn't attend. Fr. Jean-Yves Calvez, SJ, from Paris, Fr. Karl-Heinz Weger, SJ, Professor Wolfhart Pannenberg and his wife and I were present at a small birthday party for him.

There were a number of birthday celebrations and conferences held in Fr. Rahner's honor when he turned 80 years old. That was apparently strenuous for him.

I was not present at all of them. For example, I was not at the celebration in Freiburg in the middle of February nor in Innsbruck on March 5th. Fr. Rahner, himself, wrote a thank you letter to all who had congratulated him.[15] He then went to the Sanatorium in Hochrum near Innsbruck. Such stays in the hospital were not that unusual for him. He would go to the clinic for treatment for his heart and stay for two or three weeks and then he would be able to continue with his activities. Actually, I was always amazed at how much energy he had for an 80 year old. But this time he did not bounce back.

Some people only want to study Hugo Rahner and do not know anything about Karl Rahner and some are interested only in Karl Rahner and do not know anything about Hugo Rahner. You wrote a book called *Die Brüder Rahner*.[16] Do you think that one day they might rename the "Karl-Rahner-Platz" (Karl Rahner Plaza), in front of the Jesuit Church in Innsbruck and call it the "Brüder-Rahner-Platz" (Rahner Brothers Plaza)?

Well, that is to be seen. There is the fact that Karl Rahner played an important role at the Council and after the Council he played a decisive role in its implementation. Hugo Rahner could not do that. He became ill prior to the Council and died in 1968 of Parkinson's. The Council was pivotal in terms of the significance of both brothers. For Hugo Rahner, the glory years were certainly the 1950's and for Karl Rahner, his glory years, at least in terms of the public perception, involved the time of the Council and the post-conciliar period. When you look at the period of time in which the translations of his writings begin, when the invitations begin, when he begins to receive honorary doctorates then it becomes clear that for Karl Rahner his time of prominence coincides with the Council and the period after the Council – not before. But Hugo Rahner played an immensely significant role in Karl Rahner's life. Without Hugo, Karl Rahner would not have become a professor in Innsbruck, and he would not have been able to do what he then went on to accomplish.

Above and beyond that you can perceive an entire series of parallels in the academic careers of the Rahner brothers. These parallels can be observed in Karl Rahner's approach to dealing with the history of ideas. Accusations that he is not historical fail to appreciate Karl Rahner. He thinks historically, but his focus is on the development of systematic thought. Hugo Rahner's systematic starting point is not as well defined. If you look at, for instance, his *Theology of Proclamation* (1938-39) and compare it with Karl Rahner's *Foundations of Christian*

Faith then you can clearly see that, given the span of 40 years that passed, a similar task was undertaken, that is a summary of the Christian faith at its fundamental level. Hugo Rahner does not speak about the first level of reflection, but his *Theology of Proclamation* is a foundational summary which also motivates. In so far as that is the case, there is a connection.

I believe that in the last analysis, you cannot simply separate one from the other; otherwise you cannot understand either one. If you separate them from each other you confine Karl Rahner only to the area of speculative thought. You can find in Karl Rahner's work reflections on historical issues and on history in the sense that the entire symbolism that plays a role in Hugo's thought also appears in Karl's. That is not the result of the influence of Heidegger, for it appeared long before he had contact with Heidegger and has its roots elsewhere. Here you can see the important influence that Hugo Rahner had on Karl. Hugo Rahner wrote a book entitled *Symbole der Kirche*.[17] It has a very metaphorical quality, but this appreciation for the metaphorical can also be found in Karl Rahner's work. His theological dissertation, *E Latere Christi*,[18] shows that very clearly as he describes the origin of the Church as coming from the pierced side of the crucified. They shared mutual interests; you could say of Hugo Rahner that he completes Karl and of Karl that he completes Hugo.

Do you think it necessary for anyone who wants to study Karl Rahner to return to his early works?

Not necessarily. However, you have to guard against those who try to suggest an alternative to the early essays. When I look at the *Handbook of Pastoral Theology*, for instance, I know that Karl Rahner is a dogmatic theologian, an historian of dogma, but nevertheless, in his book *Sendung und Gnade (Mission and Grace)*[19] or in the *Handbuch der Pastoraltheologie (Handbook of Pastoral Theology)*,[20] he attempts to reflect on the problem of the connection of theory to practice with an eye to its usefulness for the Church. That is also the intention of the Council. The Council published a Pastoral Constitution, and with *Gaudium et Spes*, the Council creates something that never existed before. It must be acknowledged that Karl Rahner worked only on a few of the passages of the Pastoral Constitution. He worked essentially with the pastoral dimension of the theoretical or dogmatic foundation of *Lumen Gentium* and *Dei Verbum*. In both cases, he published, together with Joseph Ratzinger, a *Quaestio Disputata: Episcopacy and Power* and another on *Revelation and Tradition*.

You can see that he did this work in light of his concern for the life of the Church. He wished to offer a pastoral praxis that is theologically anchored and grounded, and to provide a view that has theological value and is not merely a one-dimensional application. But he also wanted to present a Dogmatic Theology which recognizes why it is there, that is not simply a product of historical research which is fine or becomes a product of philosophical research which in itself is very clever. When Fr. Rahner refers to himself as a "dilettante"[21] he means that, in essence, what he was about was not simply producing scholarly research, which would play a lesser role in the Church, but rather what he wanted was to actually serve the Church. Hugo Rahner, too, wanted to serve the Church, but in the context of a new image of the Church; he wanted to offer a new method of examination which sees the truth in its entirety and thus includes its historical aspects. In this, history truly serves the life of the Church. You find these intentions in the work of both Rahner brothers.

These basic perspectives were present in the work of Hugo and Karl Rahner prior to the Council, were they not?

That is the very reason why it is not very easy to convey the importance of the work of Hugo Rahner today. His writings are really in a sense pre-conciliar. They were, for their time, very progressive, but the work of the Council far surpassed what the theologians of Hugo Rahner's time could have imagined. Fr. Jungmann, SJ,[22] for example, who like Karl Rahner was a conciliar theologian, could not even have dreamed that the Canon of the Mass might be prayed in a language other than Latin. He had hoped that the Divine Office could be prayed in German, that the other prayers in the Mass could be said in German – these in the vernacular yes, but please not the Canon! Some were quite amazed at what, all at once, became possible. For today's generation that is something which is now taken for granted because they never experienced anything different. That's the reason why it is difficult to present a work of Hugo Rahner's without having to explain the background. That's also true of the earlier writings of Karl Rahner.

A final question about the *Sämtliche Werke* (Collected Works) of Karl Rahner: why are they important?

First of all, there is the historical background. The materials have been in the "Karl-Rahner-Archiv" in Innsbruck since 1982.[23] Rahner, himself, agreed that the material should be made available to interested and competent scholars. There were always, of course, already people who cited sources from the Rahner Collection that had not been made public. One claimed to know this, another to know that, and everyone wanted, as far as possible, to have access to unpublished texts. That led to more than one disagreement. Fr. Rahner was very free and easy. He gave away many things. We don't know where a good number of manuscripts are. Those are things we are not able to obtain easily. Karl Rahner made decisions based on politics. That's the reason we decided in 1991, that everything that was not by nature clearly a private matter, and that Rahner intended to be made public, would be published! That was a rather radical decision, but it was the only possible solution. No one would be able to say: I saw this and then draw a conclusion based on that, which cannot be verified because the text is not available. That has the following consequence: it has to be recognized that the source for the *Schriften zur Theologie (Theological Investigations)* basically is Rahner's teaching material, which as such cannot be documented in the literature.[24] Students from the Canisianum could document this teaching activity, because they have the Codices. These were sold in the Canisianum; there are hundreds of them, but they are not available to the general public. They are also not truly polished. You can see that in the different editions of the Codex on Penance. When you compare them you can see that there are differences. The same is true of the course on Creation and for the course on Grace. The *Sämtliche Werke* clarify the situation.

NOTES

1 Cf. Andreas R. Batlogg, Mariano Delgado, Roman A. Siebenrock (eds.), *Was den Glauben in Bewegung bringt.* Fundamentaltheologie in der Spur Jesu Christi (Freiburg: Herder: 2004), 541 pages.

2 K. Rahner, Kleines Fragment „Über die kollektive Findung der Wahrheit," in: ibid., *Schriften zur Theologie,* vol. 6 (Einsiedeln: Benziger, 1965) 104-110; cf. ibid., A Small Fragment 'On the Collective Finding of Truth,' in:

ibid., *Theological Investigations*, vol. 6, translated by Hugh M. Riley (New York: Crossroad, 1988) 162-167.

3 Cf. Andreas R. Batlogg, Zwischen Heimatverlust und Weltbürgertum. Der Lebensweg von Frido Mann, in: *Stimmen der Zeit* 226 (2008) 562-564.

4 Karl Rahner, Eberhard Jüngel, *Was ist ein Sakrament?* (Freiburg: Herder, 1971).

5 K. Rahner, *Experiment Mensch*. Vom Umgang zwischen Gott und Mensch (Hamburg: Siebenstern-Taschenbuch-Verlag, 1973).

6 For background to this, see Herbert Vorgrimler, *Karl Rahner*. Gotteserfahrung in Leben und Denken (Darmstadt: Wissenschaftliche Buchgesellschaft, 2004) 105-109.

7 Referred to here is the Berlin Edition of the Church Fathers, "GCS": Die Griechischen christlichen Schriftsteller (Berlin: Akademie Verlag, 1897 ff.), as well as the Viennese Edition of the Latin Gathers, "CSEL": Corpus Scriptorum Ecclesiasticorum Latinorum (Wien: Akademie der Wissenschaften in Wien, 1866 ff.).

8 K. Rahner, Die „geistlichen Sinne" nach Origenes, in: ibid., *Schriften zur Theologie*, Bd. 12 .(Zurich: Benziger, 1975) 111-136; ibid., The 'Spiritual Senses' according to Origen, in: ibid., *Theological Investigations*, vol. 16, translated by David Morland, O. S. B. (New York: Seabury Press, 1979) (New York: Crossroad, 1979) 81-103.

9 Vgl. K. Rahner, Glaube zwischen Rationalität und Emotionalität, in: ibid., *Schriften zur Theologie*, vol. 12, 85-107, 107, Anm. 20; cf. ibid., Faith between Rationality and Emotion, in: ibid., *Theological Investigations*, vol. 16, 60-78, 78, footnote 20: "This term is meant to cover the famous principle of Anselm, 'Fides quaerens intellectum.' The actual word, however, has not as yet been found in Anselm's writing."

10 Cf. the interview with Hans Bernhard Meyer, SJ, in this book.

11 Vgl. K. Rahner, Osservazioni sulla situazione della fede oggi, in: René Latourelle, Gerald O'Collins (eds.), Problemi e prospettive di teologia fondamentale (Brescia: Morcelliana, 1980) 349-358; later under the title "Zur Situation des Glaubens" in: ibid., *Schriften zur Theologie*, vol. 14 (Zurich: Benziger, 1980) 23-47. Cf. K. Rahner, "Observations on the situation of Faith Today," in: Rene Latourelle, Gerald O'Collins (eds.), *Problems and Perspectives of Fundamental Theology* (New York: Paulist Press, 1982) 274-291; later under the title, On the Situation of Faith, in: ibid., *Theological Investigations*, vol. 20, translated by Edward Quinn (New York: Crossroad, 1981) 13-32.

12 Vgl. K. Rahner, L'Europa come partner teologico, in: Problemi e prospettive di teologia dogmatica. A cura di K. H. Neufeld (Brescia: Morcellia-

na, 1983) 375-391; German edition with the title "Aspekte europäischer Theologie" in: Karl H. Neufeld (ed.), *Probleme und Perspektiven dogmatischer Theologie* (Düsseldorf: Patmos, 1986) 383-400; cf. K. Rahner, *Schriften zur Theologie*, vol. 15 (Zurich: Benziger, 1983) 84-103. – English translation: K. Rahner, Aspects of European Theology, in: ibid., *Theological Investigations*, vol. 21, translated by Hugh M. Riley (New York: Crossroad, 1988) 78-98.

13   Cf. Karl H. Neufeld, *Die Brüder Rahner*. Eine Biographie. (Freiburg: Herder, 2nd edition 2004) 389 f.; ibid., Somme d'une théologie – Somme d'une vie. Le Traité fundamental de la foi de Karl Rahner, in: *Nouvelle Révue Theologique* 106 (1984) 817-833; Bernard Sesboüé, Beziehungen zum Nachbarland Frankreich, in: Paul Imhof, Hubert Biallowons (eds.), *Karl Rahner – Bilder eines Lebens* (Freiburg: Herder, 1985) 104-108.

14   Cf. Teologia e Cultura Moderna a confronto: Karl Rahner, in: no. 6 of *Fenomenologia e Societá* (Milan 1985).

15   Cf. the facsimile in: *Karl Rahner – Bilder eines Lebens*, 143.

16   Cf. Karl H. Neufeld, *Die Brüder Rahner*. Eine Biographie (Freiburg: Herder, 1994, 2nd extended edition 2004).

17   Cf. Hugo Rahner, *Symbole der Kirche*. Die Ekklesiologie der Kirchenväter (Salzburg: Otto Müller, 1964).

18   Cf. K. Rahner, *E Latere Christi*. Der Ursprung der Kirche als zweite Eva aus der Seite des zweiten Adam. Eine Untersuchung über den typologischen Sinn von Joh 19, 34, in: ibid., *Sämtliche Werke*, vol. 3, Spiritualität und Theologie der Kirchenväter. Bearbeitet von Andreas R. Batlogg, Eduard Farrugia, Karl H. Neufeld (Freiburg: Herder, 1999) 1-84; cf. also Andreas R. Batlogg, Karl Rahners theologische Dissertation "E latere Christi." Zur Genese eines patristischen Projekts (1936), in: *Zeitschrift für Katholische Theologie* 126 (2004) 111-130.

19   Cf. K. Rahner, *Sendung und Gnade*. Beiträge zur Pastoraltheologie (Innsbruck: Tyrolia, 1959, 5th edition 1988). Cf. also the interview with Walter Strolz in this book.

20   Cf. Franz Xaver Arnold, Karl Rahner, Viktor Schurr, Leonhard M. Weber (eds.), *Handbuch der Pastoraltheologie*, 5 volumes (Freiburg: Herder, 1964-72).

21   Cf. for example, K. Rahner, Gnade als Mitte menschlicher Existenz. Ein Gespräch mit und über Karl Rahner aus Anlass seines 70. Geburtstages, in: *Herder Korrespondenz* 28 (1974) 77-92, 81 f. (= K. Rahner, *Herausforderung des Christen*. Meditationen – Reflexionen. [Freiburg: Herder, 1975] 117-153, 126 f.): "I would even say a little crudely but seriously, I always, in a certain sense, desired to be a dilettante in theology, who only claims a right to his dilettante status in the awareness of the insurmountable

abundance of scientific problems we face today, which cannot be resolved methodologically or in terms of content. Recently I said to colleagues in Munich, who are not theologians: measured by that which a theologian as a scholar, in the ideal case, should actually know, I am, through the 40 years of my theological research, 10 times dumber. Forty years ago the ratio between that which I knew and the presence of problems, insights and methodologies was perhaps 1:4, today it is probably 1:400. That gives me the right to be a dilettante and to confess that I am one and I would accuse my colleagues, to a certain degree, of the fact that they do not do so. They practice their trade in a narrow, very specialized theological discipline; that is admirable: furthermore they are, I would say, good Christians, good priests, who try to come to terms with all the usual theological problems which confront the Christians of today. That is perhaps an unfair criticism, I'll admit that, but it points out what ultimately matters to me: I want to be, in a certain sense, the dilettante who reflects on his dilettante status. I take that dilettante status into account, but do so in regard to the most fundamental questions of theology." Now in: K. Rahner. *Sämtliche Werke*, vol. 25: Erneuerung des Ordenslebens. Zeugnis für Kirche und Welt. Bearbeitet von Andreas R. Batlogg (Freiburg: Herder, 2008) 3-32, 10 f. Or: K. Rahner, Zur Einheit der Kirche der Zukunft, in: Paul Imhof, Hubert Biallowons (eds.), *Glaube in Winterlicher Zeit*. Gespräche mit Karl Rahner aus den letzten Lebensjahren (Düsseldorf: Patmos, 1986) 206-213, 212; cf. K. Rahner, The Unity of the Church to come, in: ibid. Paul Imhof, Hubert Biallowons (eds.), *Faith in a Wintry Season*, translated by Harvey D. Egan (New York: Crossroad, 1991) 168-174, 173 f.: "I am convinced that in my case what predominates are religiously existential concerns. For me, my so-called pious books are just as important, I'd say even more important, than my theological publications. One example would be *The Practice of Faith*. Very soon there will be published a collection of prayers I composed, *Prayers for a Lifetime*. Even earlier I always stressed that in point of fact by profession I never claimed to be a scientific researcher either in philosophy or in theology. I never practiced theology as a sort of art for art's sake. I think I can say that my publications usually grew out of pastoral concern. But in comparison to professional scholars I have remained a theological dilettante." Cf. also Klaus P. Fischer: Als grosser Theologe ein engagierter "Dilletant." Randbemerkungen zum 70. Geburtstag Karl Rahners, in: *Orientierung* 38 (1974) 44-47.

22   Josef Andreas Jungmann, SJ, (1889-1975), Liturgist in Innsbruck, paved the way for *The Constitution of the Sacred Liturgy* at the Second Vatican Council, Conciliar theologian, Editor-in-chief of *Zeitschrift für Katholische Theologie*, 1926-1963.

23   In February 2008, the archives (Karl-Rahner-Archiv) have been moved to Munich (Germany).

24   Cf. K. Rahner, *Schriften zur Theologie*, vol. 1-16 (Einsiedeln/Zurich: Benziger, 1954-1984); the English edition, *Theological Investigations*, comprises 23 volumes.

THEOLOGY FOR THE MIND AND HEART

IN CONVERSATION WITH HERBERT VORGRIMLER, MÜNSTER

Herbert Vorgrimler, Dr. theol, born in 1929, was one of Karl Rahner's closest colleagues. In 1968, he was Professor of Dogma at the University of Lucerne (Switzerland) and from 1972-1994 he served as the successor to Karl Rahner as Professor of Dogma and the History of Dogma at the University of Münster. He is a Co-editor of the "Sämtliche Werke" of Karl Rahner.

How did you get to know Fr. Rahner?

Because my diocese was interested in having well-educated priests, I was given the option of studying either in Rome or in Innsbruck. I chose Innsbruck because I had already heard much about Karl Rahner in Freiburg and I was in contact with his mother there. I also had the opportunity in Freiburg to make the "Spiritual Exercises" with Hugo Rahner, and so in 1950 I went to Innsbruck. Because I was more interested in systematics than in history, I knew that I didn't want to continue to work with Hugo Rahner so I immediately made contact with Karl Rahner. Rahner did not have an assistant or a secretary and I thought that such a productive person needs help. I never was his assistant, but rather a volunteer co-worker and we became friends.

Why was studying with Karl Rahner so important to you?

I studied theology in Freiburg for four semesters. It was purely academic and I found no bridge to spirituality. But in every one of Rahner's lectures and in all his seminars, which were mostly monologues, I found a spiritual depth that not only gripped my intellect, but my heart as well. I was fascinated by him. I also knew that when he asked questions it was never to make us look foolish, but rather to call us to probe further, to enter more deeply into a relationship with God, into a living experience of God.

What do you think of the way that Rahner's work has been received?

I don't think that I have the proper vantage point for a comprehensive evaluation of the reception of Rahner's work. On the one hand, one can find a fairly complete, in depth understanding of Rahner by my student Ralf Miggelbrink[1] and a young group that calls itself the "Innsbruck Rahner Circle" ("*Innsbrucker Rahnerkreis*") which has published a book.[2] On the other hand, I've observed people who use Rahner's work in a very subjective way, quoting him incompletely and maintaining that he was not a theologian, but only a philosopher, or asserting some other such nonsense. In recent times some Bishops' voices can be found among those who are much too theologically limited to understand any of Rahner's statements, but have made up their minds about him.

Fr. Rahner cannot defend himself anymore. Do you think that's the reason that many are now criticizing him?

It is possible to take a single sentence out of context from Rahner, from the *Schriften zur Theologie (Theological Investigations)* and from his interviews that have been published. When you do that, then these statements, as with those of any other person, could be challenged. So you can build a critique that is absolutely unfounded by reading Rahner selectively and basing an interpretation on these selected passages. This can only produce a false interpretation of his work and that is what has occurred. Because Rahner produced such a large body of work, this is unavoidable. When one does not pay attention to the overall argument of a text, but focuses only on individual points, what results is calamitous.

Recently I read a passage in the memoirs of Yves Congar, OP, in which he states that Rahner was courageous, brilliant, creative and generous, but indiscreet.[3] That bothered me, a bit. Was that so?

It would be important to ask exactly what Congar meant by "indiscreet."[4] I observed weaknesses in Rahner at times: he had a propensity for giving monologues, and did not engage in conversation very well, but that may have been because he was practically deaf and heard so poorly. But I never experienced that he was indiscreet. We had many conversations in which the names of colleagues came up. He had his own relationships with Metz, Darlap, and Ms. Rinser, but these were always very appropriate, very focused and never indiscreet.

You wrote the very first biography of Karl Rahner in the 1960's. In 1985, you published, *Karl Rahner verstehen* (*Understanding Karl Rahner*).[5] What was the feedback on these publications?

On the whole, the book reviews were positive. One review appreciated the fact that in my first book, Rahner could be understood within the context of his own time as well as for his uniqueness. His uniqueness can be found in the fact that he not only looked to establish a new language for theology, but that this new language, which had its origin in the work of Guardini and others, had to be confirmed by particular points and themes in Dogmatic Theology. Guardini did not make any additions to the tracts in Dogmatic Theology. His contribution was to show that theology must pay attention to literature, to poetry, to the works of Hölderlin, Rilke, and Dostoevsky. But where was the impact of this new language, for example, for the sacraments or the theology of creation? Rahner tried to adopt this new thinking, which departs from neo-scholasticism, and integrate it in such a way as to be faithful to the tradition.

To come back to your question about the repercussions of my biographies: of course, I took various things from my conversations with Rahner and I believed what he told me. One story that he recounted was about his doctorate in Philosophy in Freiburg. I probably had misjudged the neo-scholasticism as it was taught in Freiburg because Rahner told me that a German Cardinal said to him: "What Vorgrimler writes about Martin Honecker in Freiburg will set his academic career back five years."[6] Individual points in my books were attacked.

In your latest biography of Rahner you say that your opinion of the situation in Freiburg, described in your first book, derived from a conversation with Karl Rahner. Is that so?[7]

I did indeed take these things for a fact in 1961, when I wrote the first small book. At that time Rahner was very bitter about the situation in Freiburg.

Your book, *Karl Rahner verstehen* (*Understanding Karl Rahner*), published in 1985, has an appendix which contains many of Karl Rahner's letters from the time of the Council.[8] These letters contain, at times, coarse observations and harsh words directed against some Jesuit colleagues, some Bishops and Cardinals. Do you think it was appropriate to include this inside view of Karl Rahner?

That decision must be viewed within a definite context. Fr. Rahner wrote me a letter almost every day. Because of our working together on *Lexikon für Theologie und Kirche* and on the series *Quaestiones Disputatae*, it was almost unavoidable that we corresponded so much. It was a time of reconstruction in Germany and Austria and it was very difficult to communicate by phone effectively. As to the issue of the appropriateness of the publication of these letters – at the time I paid attention above all to the question: What is beneficial for a chronicle and what would provide insight into the Council and its commissions that would allow one to be able justly to determine the contributions of individual theologians? My main focus was on the institution of the Permanent Diaconate, but everything that was personally defamatory, I left out. Private things and private judgments are in parentheses. I tried to be very careful and I don't believe that I made a slip in that regard. Rahner's general judgments about the Roman Curia I allowed to stand. They were not very positive, because of what he had experienced. He was especially disappointed by the fact that the then Superior General of the Society of Jesus, Janssens, did so little to protect him and his colleagues. Of course, I allowed Rahner's comment that, "a superior General is not a delivery boy for the Holy Office" to stand.[9]

If such reflections had not have been published do you think that anything essential would have been left out?

From my point of view many dumb things were written about the Council afterwards. I remember, for example, the title of a book: *The Rhine flows into the Tiber*[10] and similar things. That made it appear as if a cabal of middle European theologians had come to dominate the Council. Rahner was often characterized by the press as the leading figure of the Council. A young theologian, Günther Wassilowsky, has written a monograph on the proceedings of the Council and the proceedings of the commissions. Meticulously, in detail, he shows how Rahner worked as part of a team. Wassilowsky writes in his dissertation, that my edition of the Rahner letters from the time of the Council has an indispensable documentary value because Rahner did not want to keep a journal and because they make it possible to assign particular issues to specific Commissions.[11]

In your book, *Karl Rahner – Sehnsucht nach dem geheimnisvollen Gott* (1991), you quoted extensively from the evaluations of the drafts of the Council that Karl Rahner did for Vienna's Cardinal Franz König.[12] This book also contains some of Rahner's harsh judgments. Did it not hurt his reputation for you to publish evaluations that were meant only for Cardinal König?

There are people, naturally, who were upset with some of Rahner's comments. But there were others who said: Finally, someone has the courage to speak clearly and write plainly. We are living in a time when those who oppose Rahner have come together and expressed themselves strongly. From the beginning it was not to be feared that with the publication of these writings a new evil would arise. The opposing fronts, Rahner's supporters and Rahner's detractors, can now be seen clearly. Cardinal Giuseppi Siri,[13] of Genoa, contributed greatly to the defamation of Rahner with his Gethsemani book and gathered a group of supporters both in Italy and Germany. There is no dialogue possible with these people; they live from their prejudices. So far, I don't believe that we stirred up any new controversies with the book. The Rahner polarization was always there.

From my personal friendship with Cardinal König, I am convinced that he was a very reflective and very intelligent person. When I worked with him in his office on Atheism[14] he often said that: "Speech is silver, silence is gold." He was a very cautious man, but he wanted me to publish Rahner's judgments. His article for the Jesuit periodical *Entschluss* contained the first texts that provided the impetus for my publishing Rahner's work. I think that König had such perspective

and insight into ecclesial relations that if there was something to fear
he would not have wanted the material to be published.

A question about the Rahner jubilee year in 2004: How beneficial was that?

First of all, in that jubilee year we held many symposia. I gave thirteen
lectures in the German speaking region on Karl Rahner. I visited the
smaller schools and important people such as Karl Lehmann spoke
in Freiburg and Munich. It was clear that there was a lively interest in
Rahner. I also worked with videos in order to convey a living impression of him and they were well received. From that experience I can
say that the memorial year was fruitful and positive. The publishing
companies did their best and I am very satisfied with the response
to my new Rahner book[15] and the publisher is, of course, pleased as
well.

However, a religion teacher in the Rhineland, David Berger, published
a book containing malicious, defamatory statements about Rahner's
work. He made up a list of statements which were designed to challenge Rahner which he called *Quaestiones Non Disputatae*.[16] But the
public soon came to recognize that this was only subjective polemic
which presented no possibility of a reasonable dialogue and the best
response was to ignore it. I believe that, on the whole, the results of
the Rahner year were quite positive. There was, however, some silli-
ness attached to it – there was a Rahner wine, although he drank beer
and did not know much about wine and some similar things.[17] There
also were some exaggerated statements by some thoughtless people
who, fascinated by Rahner's spiritual side, wrote essays arguing that
he should be canonized a saint or should be declared a teacher of the
Church. That actually produced more harm than good.

You have already referred to the Innsbruck Rahner Circle; which of the new generation of Rahner scholars, in your opinion, deserves recognition?

What I especially appreciate is that the Innsbruck group has, very intentionally, chosen an evolutionary approach to their study of Rahner
and is consistent in pursuing that. Significant insights into Rahner's
thought can only take place by returning to explore the starting points

in the 1930's and the time of his exile in Vienna. Whoever does not know and pay attention to this can come too easily to the conclusion that Rahner became more radical as he got older. That would be a misjudgment that cannot be proved. What I see as most characteristic of Rahner's theology is that of perceiving theology as at the service of proclamation and in the service of individual piety. That has always fascinated me greatly.

Each member of the group has their own central focus of concern, their own particular work, which is important to the progress of the group, so each member of the group must be named. What Fr. Batlogg has achieved regarding the mysteries of Jesus' life, *desiderata* in Dogmatic Theology, or what Günther Wassilowsky learned about Rahner's contribution to the Council, or Roman A. Siebenrock about the Theology of Grace and the self-communication of God – these are all valuable contributions, in and of themselves, and are worthy of individual recognition. I mentioned earlier the work of Klaus P. Fischer citing the importance of the Ignatian roots of Rahner's theology. Arno Zahlauer went even further in investigating that. Certainly, as can be seen, each member of the group deserves to be mentioned.[18]

There are also those who do not explicitly belong to this group, all of whom have written dissertations on Rahner: my students Ralf Miggelbrink, Bernhard Grümme and Andrea Taffener, as well as Nikolaus Schwerdtfeger, Auxiliary Bishop of Hildesheim.[19]

You received a good response to your book, *Karl Rahner – Gotteserfahrung in Leben und Denken*. On page 31 of this book you write about a "living lie" referring to every ideological elevation of the priesthood: "Rahner concerned himself with the subject of 'priestly existence' in several publications. Every ideological elevation of the priesthood (a second Christ, a representation of Jesus Christ as juxtaposed to the community, acting in the person of Jesus Christ, an impersonal presence, etc.) was something he found deeply distasteful due to the underlying 'living lie.'" I ask this question having myself written a dissertation on "*essentia et non gradu tantum*" in *Lumen Gentium* No. 10.[20] Can you clarify your comment?

I see the increasing emphasis of this ideology as an attempt on the part of Church authority to increase vocations to the priesthood by trying to elevate the image of the priest. Gisbert Greshake's book,[21]

Priestersein (*The Meaning of Christian Priesthood*), whose publication was financed by a Church group, spells this out at length. When Rahner presented his understanding of priesthood it was a much more sensible interpretation. In his view the priest is not only a partner of Jesus, as in the Jesuit model, a companion or associate of Jesus, but the servant of Jesus Christ as well.[22]

This view is much more faithful to the Council's understanding of the ministerial character of the hierarchy as service to the Church, although in the typical compromise language of the Council expressions such as *in persona Christi* can still be found.[23] But if one takes seriously the humble, modest, ministerial character of Church Office expressed in the documents then it becomes clear that to behave in an exalted manner deviates from the Council's intention.

In actual life situations today, with their challenges to the office of the priest, it is clear that it doesn't help at all to adopt the elevated ideology of priesthood. It does not profit a priest in the middle of a life crisis when he says to himself time and again, "You are a second Christ" or "You are the representative of Jesus Christ in this community" or something similar.

What then in your opinion does help really and truly?

At this time, there is much that must be said about the meaning of Church Office, but I believe that we have not yet taken a good look at what is at its core and center. Fr. Rahner was very concerned about the future formation of the priest. He saw the inner strength of the priest coming from the life of the community, with his community members at his side. The priest has to be the kind of person who, on the one hand, is gifted in the art of accompanying others, to be what has been called a "director of souls:"[24] helping others in their faith journey, step by step to deepen their faith, to glean insights into the faith and to develop a faith consciousness in the sense cited in *Lumen Gentium* No. 12.[25] On the other hand, he should be competent to impart theological information.

For example, the priest when confronted directly with such questions as: "Why must we die?" should not respond by attributing death to the sin of Adam in paradise[26] and teach that the death of all people was the penalty imposed for something which people have not themselves committed. In those situations Rahner did not ask for less the-

ology or a watered down version in the sense of a Theology of Proclamation, but rather demanded a deeply grounded knowledge of the
faith and the possibility of a hermeneutic of dogma and knowledge of
biblical passages. This has to occur in conversations, in homilies, and
in the classroom. Rahner insisted that training for this must be part
of the formation of the priest. If we followed Rahner today we would
not experience what is now all too common, namely: that unqualified
people want to be ordained priests; that they come to the seminary
with the opinion that they know everything already. They then look
upon the program as just a burdensome passage to priestly ordination.
Such people then take their stupidity out into the community.

**The *theologumenon* of the universal saving will of God is, for the
time being, a generally accepted truth of theology. You write that it
is central to the theology of Karl Rahner. Others contend that the
Theology of Grace is at the core of his theology. How important
then is the concept of the "Anonymous Christian"?**

One has to be aware of the background of this question. It comes from
a traditional question which was very much an issue in my youth:
How can non-believers, people who have serious doubts about the
faith, achieve salvation with God? To begin with there were those who
took a strong stand against the salvation of non-believers on the basis
of Mk 16:16: "Who does not believe will be condemned." The scholastics mitigated this with their suggestion of "*fides implicita.*" Rahner
approached this issue from a strong pneumatological perspective, arguing that God's Spirit is given to everyone because God loves every
person and because God takes so seriously the chance everyone has to
come to Him in freedom. No one in the entire history of the world,
beginning with Adam and Eve, has been without God's Spirit. It has
to do with Rahner's central, personal view of grace; that grace is not
about an actual help with this or that decision in life, but rather about
the very indwelling of God in the human person in the form of the
Holy Spirit Himself, Who speaks within the person, gives inspiration, is active and who finally helps the person to say yes to God. This
belief to me is so central to Rahner that I would not recognize Rahner
without it – this optimistic perspective of world history and human
history.

That is precisely, in my opinion, what is new in Rahner's Theology
of Grace. When I was in school, I remember that the tract on grace began with a list of how many different types of grace there actually were.
The living God did not appear at all as the one who gives Himself to
human persons and makes them His own. Rather there are all these
specific aids: sanctifying grace, habitual grace, actual grace. There was
all this discussion about created and none about uncreated grace.[27]
Rahner allowed his thinking in this area to become productive for all
Dogmatic Theology. Think, for example, of ecclesiology, where he has
the courage to speak of the "catechism of the heart," namely the light
of faith, of the *sensus fidei*, which God awakens in the heart of each
person, a singular, individual illumination. He says explicitly that what
the Church verbalizes in its dogmas and in the catechism is a secondary reflection on this light produced by the Holy Spirit that leads to
the inner hierarchy of truths of the faith, a "catechism of the heart,"[28]
which can be distinguished from the official catechism.

Are you thinking of something specifically?

In the later writings of Rahner, there are admonitions to the magisterium to respect the "catechism of the heart." It is a constant concern
of Rahner that the official authoritative warnings of the magisterium,
with their claim to genuine obedience, should be combined with regard for the "catechism of the heart," so that authentic teaching is not
seen as something foreign, as imposed from without like a yoke.[29]

**About Karl Rahner's work on lexicons: you were his closest col-
league and in the course of the publication of his *Sämtliche Werke*
(*Collected Works*), you edited many of his lexicon articles.[30] How
did he produce these articles and how did he have the time and energy to do this? How was he able to address so many diverse topics?**

Let me say this: Fr. Rahner was under some illusions about this. He
was under the impression that he would be able to reach all the clergy
with a lexicon and that they would be using the lexicon to prepare a
homily or a religious education class. At the time of the second edition
of the *Lexikon für Theologie und Kirche*, which he prepared, there were
no good lay theologians. One can see from his introductions that he
thought he was addressing himself primarily to the clergy in pasto-

ral ministry. He could not see that the lexicon would become merely something to decorate the book shelf and that the homilies would still not be carefully prepared. It was his heartfelt concern to enrich the clergy with a more serious, but Spiritual Theology. That's the reason he did not shy away from any effort, nor spare any of his strength.[31] I also have to say that he was an incredibly disciplined person. He went to bed early and he didn't do any work in the evening. He rose early, around 4 or 4:30 a.m. He celebrated Mass and after having quickly eaten his breakfast, he sat down at the typewriter. He worked the entire morning allowing for no visitors. He occasionally had visitors in the afternoon and also heard confessions and did other things. He also did not have any time consuming hobbies.

Apparently he only had time for theology. Fr, Rahner is said to have stated that: "One can't chase all the rabbits."

Apart from theology, he enjoyed reading modern literature, Graham Greene for example, because he believed that was a way in which he got to know a world in which he did not live.

Did he go to the theater or to any concerts?

No, he was not interested in either theater or concerts. At that time, there was no television. Fr. Rahner also did not listen to the radio. Once he responded to an interviewer's question about what hobbies he cultivated and he simply responded: "Reading."[32]

In your last Rahner biography you quote Rahner's opinion on "God is dead Theology" which was aired on Italian television: "I cannot do otherwise than to explain that I simply and clearly reject this theology."[33] Fr. Rahner defends a negative theology or a *theologia negativa*. I have the impression that you esteem Karl Rahner very much, but that did not keep you from expressing your own opinion and supplementing or correcting Rahner now and then. Does that have to do with the fact that one cannot simply reiterate, in the sense of parroting what he says?

In this regard, if I can be presumptuous and describe my own position, I would say, as to the very core questions I am indebted to the

Dogmatic Theology of Rahner. I would not know how anyone could do it or express it better. This has nothing to do with simply parroting Rahner. That would also be impossible because of his frequent use of "if" and "but" and his many dependent clauses, by means of which he tried to make himself understood by those theologians trained in neo-scholasticism. René Laurentin observed during the Council that he was amazed that Rahner, when he spoke Latin, was understood and accepted by the Roman commission members because they were acquainted with the line of argumentation.[34] I do not have such students. I am obliged to use simpler, less traditional terms than those which Rahner used in order to convey his thought. That does not prevent me from having my own opinion on certain matters and being able to distance myself from Rahner.[35] But I do not have the feeling that when I criticize Rahner I make myself more important. Many students of Rahner have this desire, to, as they say, commit patricide; that is something that does not even enter my mind.

But, when Rahner, for instance, defines the Church as the victorious mercy of God, or as the vanguard which embodies the grace of God in history, that is too much for me. In a review of his *Foundations of Christian Faith*, I wrote that was a regrettable triumphalism. In a later essay in *Schriften zur Theologie (Theological Investigations)*, he accepted that criticism and said that, perhaps, he was somewhat excessive in this affirmation of the Church.[36] I also differed with his view of eschatology in so far as he maintained that the human person, after death, in the presence of God, no longer changes, but has reached the fullness of his history in so far as basically nothing new can happen. For me, that is too static a view of fulfillment in God. There are examples in the Tradition, as in the Greek Fathers, like Gregory of Nyssa, of a much more dynamic perspective, of always new encounters with God[37] – distance from God and encounter with God – as can be found in the Canticle of Canticles where the bridegroom and the bride find each other, lose each other and find each other again. That is much more plausible to me than the static perspective that Rahner defends. But I do not feel the need to promulgate that with a lot of fuss.

Did you ever speak with Fr. Rahner about these differences?

That never occurred to me. We discussed different theological topics naturally. At that time I planned to write a book on the question as to whether God suffers, whether God can feel pain. We discussed that a great deal because the God of the tradition appears to be so unfeeling, so little moved by what creatures suffer. That discussion went back and forth, pro and con and I had the impression that Rahner, even in his old age, could still learn something.

You have in your book, *Karl Rahner – Gotteserfahrung in Leben und Denken*, a section with the title: "Friends, Friends?" You name Johann Baptist Metz, Hans Urs von Balthasar and Joseph Ratzinger. Would you expand on that? What were you implying?

Rahner was a very irenic, peace-loving person. He did not defend himself against attacks. He truly had the desire to have many friends in theology and so was somehow defenseless and unprotected. He thought that he would be understood and that his line of reasoning would be accepted. In this regard he experienced a number of great disappointments.[38]

One disappointment was the ever-growing distance between him and Metz which was made worse by the use of images that were totally off the mark. Rahner cannot be defined solely by the concept of Transcendental Theology.[39] His was a theology of seeking and questioning, the ever new act of questioning. Metz used the fairy tale of the poor rabbit and the two hedgehogs to critique Rahner's theological approach: the rabbit runs and runs, but because the hedgehogs sit at two separate locations, they can say "I'm already here!" For Metz, the rabbit represents Political Theology and the two hedgehogs embody Transcendental Theology. I refuted that in an essay.[40] That pleased Rahner. Metz made other comments that suggested opposition to Rahner, for example, his accusation that Rahner did not take history seriously; that he represents an a-historical idealism. That does not mean that there was not a lasting fundamental consensus between Rahner and Metz, especially with regard to the issue of the suffering of God or on the Trinity. In my biography I mention these experiences to show how Rahner was hurt by these attacks and how he suffered for his theology.

With Balthasar, the turning point in their relationship came with the publication *Cordula oder der Ernstfall* in 1966.[41] In 1964, he wrote an essay for Rahner's sixtieth birthday and sang his praises.[42] From 1966 on, Balthasar spoke of Rahner as the embodiment of all heresies, a theologian who could lead one to atheism. As far as Ratzinger is concerned, he expressed himself in his autobiographical comments, so summarily, so crudely, ignorantly and so carelessly, and I have to say this directly, because of his high position as the Prefect of the Congregation for the Doctrine of the Faith.[43] I do not know if the "sun" of the pontificate will now bring about a more moderate tone to his views. What has come to light is truly more than regrettable and I said that in all candor. These were three people whom Rahner viewed as friends, whom he believed were theologically very close to him, and would support him. Then he had to experience and suffer their repudiation of him.

You stress that the goal for Karl Rahner and Heinrich Fries was "concrete ways of agreement, not unity of the Protestant (Lutheran and Reformed) Churches and the Roman Catholic Church."[44] Why do you stress that so?

The book by Rahner-Fries appeared in 1983.[45] Since that time much progress has been made in ecumenical dialogues. There was the Agreement on Justification in the German speaking world. I don't know how the ecumenical dialogue is going in the USA and in other countries, but I know from Cardinal Kasper that he favors the formulation "a reconciled difference" for the ecumenical dialogue.[46] Rahner already laid the ground work for this with his admonition that we shouldn't dream of a union, an institutional union of all Churches with and under the Pope – this is something we should not anticipate. The Pope should, in Rahner's opinion, reduce his role, withdraw his claim to primacy of jurisdiction in everything and instead play the part of the referee when there are disagreements. He thought that we could recognize Protestant ordination purely and simply by signing an agreement to do so since it would be achieved through the intercession of the Holy Spirit and through trusting in the Spirit of God. It is important that we not demand Protestant communities give up their unique lives and traditions and become more Marian, for example. Even before the Rahner-Fries book, Rahner had already predicted, in his book about Church Office, what is now coming to light ecumenically, as can be seen in the positions held by people like Kasper.[47] Of course, there will always be movements to the contrary. I believe that there is a strong movement within the Catholic Church that still continues to think in terms of an institutional union.

Evidently Rahner wished to get something going in the dialogue, not so much in terms of offering instructions, or suggesting an "ecumenism of return," but rather by influencing the mentality of rapprochement between the Christian Confessions.

On this point I am in complete agreement with Ratzinger and admire his courage in putting this in writing. When we reach consensus, ecumenically, for example, with the Eastern Churches, we may only demand from them the common beliefs which were in place prior to the separation in the year 1054, so that all dogmatic declarations enacted subsequently are non-binding.[48] Objectively, then, this is not an institutional union, but rather a reconciled difference.

The newer Marian dogmas and the dogma of Papal Infallibility and other statements of belief produced by the Council of Trent would not be binding on the Eastern Churches. Ratzinger includes this essay in his collection of articles published in 1982 and he did not revise it as he did many other articles that he had written when he was young.[49]

What do you miss the most when you think of Karl Rahner?

Some considered him an angry old man and many were upset by his harsh statements in the later years of his life. But I must say that it is this side of him that I miss the most. There were so many new developments and changes in the Church following the Council which could be expected to cause loud outbursts, warnings and admonishments – and what do we see? Practically our entire theology has run aground – theologians have dived for cover. People close their mouths, ears and eyes and act as though nothing has happened. Rahner was brave and had the kind of courage necessary to challenge authority and risk facing disapproval when he thought something needed to be said. Today no one dares to do this anymore. We live in a climate either of complacency or fear.

Where do you think Rahner's courage to challenge authority came from? Where authors were silent he had the courage to say something. That is remarkable.

I do not think that it came from a desire to gain attention. He did not want to create a public disturbance. Rather it came from the depth of his conscience. He felt a personal responsibility for the Church and beyond that, because the Church is only an instrument responsible for the Christian faith. When he saw that certain ecclesial authorities endangered the Church by their thinking, he felt the need to respond: "Here I have to speak, as long as I have breath within me."

He even put his position at risk. He said: "If I am condemned to be silent, then I will remain silent. If I am forbidden to write, then I will no longer write, but the responsibility will be on their side, not mine." He did not say, as some younger theologians did in the past and do today, that he would leave the Church or resign the priesthood, but he said instead, "that I will become a Carthusian or a Trappist and I will worship and reverence God in silence and I will at least have done my duty." He also did not want to criticize the magisterium unfairly. He had differences with his Cardinal friends Döpfner and Volk, both of whom responded to him by saying that if he were in their position for a year he would see things differently and would be more prudent. He also had used the term "Official Church" when criticizing the magisterium, which was not well received by the Bishops, but these impulses came from his conscience. Rahner had truly experienced the Spirit of the Council, as opposed to what was merely the letter of the Council. For him the "Letter" was a compromise, the "Spirit" was much broader and wider.[50] For example, we can see that in the area of ecumenism the Council demanded that Catholics should emphasize that which unites us over that which divides us. But can we keep silent, when we see that the Council's admonition is ignored and we find an increase in that which divides us: increased Marianism, an incredible amount of canonizations and beatifications, the public promotion of the papacy? That is how I would explain the older Rahner and his outbursts.[51]

Do you fear that the significance of Fr. Rahner and his theology somehow gets lost in our theologically deficient atmosphere? Or to put it another way – is it worth-while today to read Karl Rahner?

I think, at this moment there is no alternative to Rahner. At this time we are celebrating the 100th birthday of Hans Urs von Balthasar, whose theology is so greatly dominated by a masochism of suffering, a masochistic tendency toward pain, by reflections on the crucifixion and the dark night of the soul, that it presents an impossible approach for many. It also does not reflect the lifestyle of the hierarchy, who now sing his praises from the rooftops, while they, themselves, do not live in this manner and do not practice such spirituality. "Patchwork Religion" has become the alternative to Rahner – "cafeteria religion." People are religious; they are searching, but when they read Rahner, they find such a blunt, direct yes to the Church,[52] such an unconditional assent to the institutional Church that they are put off and immediately turn away and do not come to recognize Rahner's genuine theological and spiritual depth.

They then begin to construct with a little bit of esoterica here and a little Buddhism there, a religion that cannot possibly provide support to deal with the storms of life and the catastrophes of sickness and death. Rahner could be of help here and his approach could continue to have great meaning. Of course, in the current situation in Catholicism there have been too many concessions made to this cafeteria religiosity. The number of self-help books reaches into the hundreds of thousands by contrast with the small number of books dealing with serious theology. People experience from these self-help books that faith is fine, and God is your best friend, and Jesus is your comrade, your "buddy." Everything is surrounded by angels, angels of gentleness, angels of sadness, and angels of patience – all there for people to find – that's it.

As we come to the end of this interview do you have any advice? Why, for instance, should young people read Karl Rahner? What would they gain by this?

I think that people, including young people, often experience loneliness. When that occurs they begin to feel that everything in them is empty and barren. What they would find by reading Rahner is how to deal with such a situation and begin to experience what Ignatius of Loyola called "consolation without prior cause."[53] They would receive from the spiritual insights of Rahner's theology the realization that in our innermost selves we are not alone, but that God's Spirit dwells within us and is with us on our journey and gives us strength. Thus the spiritual side of Rahner's theology can have a future and not be just a relic of the past. I have had young people in my courses ask me: "How can I get closer to Rahner?" I always respond: "For God's sake, don't begin with *Foundations of Christian Faith* or something similar, but with *The Need and the Blessing of Prayer*, or *Encounters with Silence*, which is also part of the new collection *Prayers for a Lifetime*.[54] At first it might seem that the language is too melodramatic for today, but after a while, as one suddenly grows still, the realization will come: "That's it, what I have been searching for!"

A theology with heart and soul, so to say?

Yes indeed, indeed. Karl Rahner had his human weaknesses. He made no concessions to ameliorate the difficulty of his language. He knew that he was difficult, and he said then plainly: "Yes, one must then read it again and again when one has not understood it."

NOTES

1 See Ralf Miggelbrink, *Ekstatische Gottesliebe im tätigen Weltbezug*. Der Beitrag Karl Rahners zur zeitgenössischen Gotteslehre (Altenberge: Oros, 1989); ibid., Latens Deitas. Das Gottesdenken in der Theologie Karl Rahners, in: Roman A. Siebenrock (ed.), *Karl Rahner in der Diskussion*. Erstes und zweites Karl-Rahner- Symposion. Themen – Referate – Ergebnisse (Innsbruck: Tyrolia, 2001) 99-129.

2 See Andreas R. Batlogg, Paul Rulands, Walter Schmolly, Roman A. Siebenrock, Günther Wassilowsky, Arno Zahlauer. *Der Denkweg Karl Rahners*. Quellen – Entwicklungen – Perspektiven (Mainz: Matthias Grüne-wald, 2003, 2nd edition 2004).

3 See the entry of May 28, 1963, in: Yves Congar, *Mon Journal du Concile*, vol. 1 (Paris 2002) 382: "Le P. Rahner monopolise la parole une fois de plus. Il est magnifique, il est courageux, il est persicace et profound, mais finalement indiscret. On ne peut plus parler, on en perd l'occasion et même le goût."

4 Actually, here "indiscreet" should be translated by the term "insistent." In an earlier recollection Congar reports that Rahner appeared "to have co-opted the microphone." He sprang to the microphone very quickly, more quickly than the others. "If I recall correctly, there were three microphones; one Msgr. G. Philips took for himself – as he was the facilitator. The other two, which were placed at either end of the table, were for the use of the approximately ten *periti*. They were to hand the microphone to each other if they wished to speak, and if the President, Cardinal Ottaviani, gave his permission. Rahner, however, seemed to commandeer the microphone for he entered into the debate more passionately and more often than did the others, thereby taking control of the proceedings from them. That is not

to say that he imparted nothing of consequence. When Rahner spoke, he did so with body and soul:" Yves Congar, Erinnerungen an Karl Rahner auf dem Zweiten Vatikanum, in: Paul Imhof, Hubert Billowons (eds.), *Karl Rahner – Bilder eines Lebens* (Freiburg: Herder, 1985) 65-68, 65.

5 See Herbert Vorgrimler, *Karl Rahner.* Leben – Denken – Werke (Munich: Manz, 1963) (the original Flemish edition was published under the title *Karl Rahner – Denkers over God en Wereld*, (Tielt: Lannoo, 1962); ibid., *Understanding Karl Rahner.* An Introduction to his Life and Thought (New York: Crossroad, 1986).

6 Cf. Herbert Vorgrimler, *Karl Rahner*, 19; "Martin Heidegger came to Freiburg in 1928 and though he had been rooted in Neo-Kantianism, from 1927 on he went his own radical way. Martin Honecker also taught philosophy in Freiburg and held the Concordat Chair of Philosophy. He was an average and somewhat limited representative of rational neo-scholasticism which had as little to do with Thomas Aquinas as the bearded characters of Montmartre have to do with Existentialism. Karl Rahner was assigned to do his doctoral dissertation under the direction of Martin Honecker." Ibid., 23; "If what I have written here is a diatribe against Honecker and those like him (the dumb ones never die out and in some corners a pseudo-scientific approach still flourishes), Karl Rahner never once defended himself against Honecker. It would not have been difficult – he only would have needed to publish Honecker's silly evaluation somewhere at the end of the dissertation."

7 See Herbert Vorgrimler, *Karl Rahner.* Gotteserfahrung in Leben und Denken (Darmstadt: Primus, 2004) 35, footnote 94: "I regret my unfair judgment of Martin Honecker that appeared in my small Rahner-biography of 1963, 19. It resulted from the fact that I was not able to really know Honecker, influenced as I was by Rahner's bitter and polemical opinion of him."

8 Cf. K. Rahner, A Brief Correspondence from the Time of the Council, in: Herbert Vorgrimler, Understanding Karl Rahner, 141-184.

9 See: Erlebtes von Karl Rahner. Zuschrift zu "Schützen die Orden ihre Theologen?," in: *Orientierung* 39 (1975) 3-4, 4: "The superiors of religious orders are required more and more be too much the messengers of high Roman congregations and must so act as though the measures taken come from themselves." Now in: K. Rahner, *Sämtliche Werke*, vol. 25: Erneuerung des Ordenslebens. Zeugnis für Kirche und Welt (Freiburg: Herder, 2008) 287-288, 287. – See, in addition: K. Rahner, *Bekenntnisse.* Rückblick auf 80 Jahre, edited by Georg Sporschill (Wien: Herold, 1984) 25: "The superiors of religious orders more and more were expected to implement the dictates of the top Roman Congregations and act as though those measures came from themselves ... In the prevailing atmosphere it

was impossible for a superior of a religious order to defend the accused and oppose the Holy Office, even if he opposed the measures taken. Today one would expect that kind of courage. P. Janssens did not have that, at least not in my case. He was not angry with me; he even once said to me: 'look, lightning bolts are coming from the Holy Office, one cannot know whom they will strike or why.' He was a decent and pious man but he was not a great model. He simply accepted such measures of the Holy Office with obedience and passed them on. The religious superior also had to report to the Holy Office as to how the delinquent person reacted to the restrictions placed on him; whether he responded with the proper degree of humility and modesty. That was the Roman mentality at that time, which today one rightly finds to be terrible." Referred to here is Fr. Johannes B. Janssens, SJ (1889-1964), from 1946 to 1964 Father General of the Society of Jesus. – See now in: K. Rahner, *Sämtliche Werke*, vol. 25, 59-84, 66 f.

10   Cf. Ralp M. Wiltgen, *The Rhine flows into the Tiber*. A History of Vatican II (Chumleigh: Augustine, 1967).

11   Cf. Günther Wassilowsky, *Universales Heilssakrament Kirche*. Karl Rahners Beitrag zur Ekklesiologie des II. Vatikanums (Innsbruck: Tyrolia, 2001) 41.

12   Cf. Aus den Konzilsgutachten für Kardinal König, in: K. Rahner, *Sehnsucht nach dem geheimmisvollen Gott*. Profil – Texte – Bilder, edited by Herbert Vorgrimler (Freiburg: Herder, 1990) 95-165.

13   Giuseppe Siri (1906-1989), 1946 Archbishop of Genoa, 1953 Cardinal; cf. Giuseppe Siri, *Getsemani*. Riflessioni sur movimento teologico comtempraneo (Roma: Fraternita della Santissima Vergine Maria, 1980).

14   Cf. Franz König, *Glaube ist Freiheit*. Erinnerungen und Gedanken eines Mannes der Kirche. Gespräche mit Yves Chauffin (Wien: XXX, 1981) 177- 179, as well as the friendly recollection of cooperative effort: Franz König, Zum Geleit, in: Herbert Vorgrimler, *Wegsuche*. Kleine Schriften zur Theologie, vol. 1 (Altenberge: Oros, 1997) V-VII, esp. VI; Herbert Vorgrimler, Dialog mit Nichtglaubenden. Ein Kommentar, in: ibid., 555-575.

15   Cf. Herbert Vorgrimler, *Karl Rahner* (see footnote 7.)

16   Cf. David Berger, (ed.), *Karl Rahner*. Kritische Annäherungen (Quaestiones Non Disputatae 8) (Siegburg: Schmitt, 2004).

17   Cf. Personally. Karl Rahner in conversation with Paul Muigg and Johann A. Mair, Innsbruck 1984, in: Paul Imhof, Hubert Biallowons (eds.), *Glaube in Winterlicher Zeit*. Gespräche mit Karl Rahner aus den letzten Lebensjahren (Düsseldorf: Patmos, 1986) 39-43, 42: "I do not drink much. When I go to a restaurant, I order a small beer. I have to honestly say, I don't care that much for wine."

18   Cf. Andreas R. Batlogg, *Die Mysterien des Lebens Jesu bei Karl Rahner.*
Zugang zum Christusglauben (Innsbruck: Tyrolia, 2nd edition 2003); Roman A. Siebenrock, Gnade als Herz der Welt. Der Beitrag Karl Rahners
zu einer zeitgemässen Gnadentheologie, in: Mariano Delgado, Matthias
Lutz-Bachmann (eds.), *Theologie aus der Erfahrung der Gnade.* Annäherungen an Karl Rahner (Berlin: Morus, 1994) 34-71; Klaus P. Fischer, *Der
Mensch als Geheimnis.* Die Anthropologie Karl Rahners (Freiburg, Herder,
2nd edition 1975); ibid., "Wo der Mensch an ein Geheimnis grenzt." Die
mystagogische Struktur der Theologie Karl Rahners, in: *Zeitschrift für Katholische Theologie* (= *ZKTh*) 98 (1976) 159-170; ibid., *Gotteserfahrung.*
Mystagogie in der Theologie Karl Rahners und in der Theologie der Befreiung (Mainz: Matthias Grünewald, 1986); ibid., Gott als das Geheimnis des Menschen. Karl Rahners theologische Anthropologie – Aspekte
und Anfragen, in: *ZKTh* 113 (1991) 1-23; Spiritualität und Theologie.
Beobachtungen zum Weg Karl Rahners, in: Mariano Delgado, Matthias
Lutz-Bachmann (eds.), *Theologie aus der Erfahrung der Gnade*, 26-33; ibid.,
Philosophie und Mystagogie. Karl Rahners "reductio in Mysterium" als
Prinzip seines Denkens, in: *ZKTh* 120 (1998) 34-56.

19   Cf. Bernhard Grümme, *"Noch ist die Träne nicht weggewischt von jegli-
chem Angesicht."* Überlegungen zur Rede von Erlösung bei Karl Rahner
und Franz Rosenzweig (Altenberge: Oros, 1966); Ralf Miggelbrink, * Ekstatische Gottesliebe im tätigen Weltbezug.* Der Beitrag Karl Rahners zu einer
zeitgenössischen Gotteslehre (Altenberge: Oros, 1989); Andrea Tafferner,
*Gottes-und Nächstenliebe in der deutschsprachigen Theologie des 20. Jahrhun-
derts* (Innsbruck: Tyrolia, 1992); Nikolaus Schwerdtfeger, *Gnade und Welt.*
Zum Grundgefüge von Karl Rahners Theorie der "anonymen Christen."
(Freiburg: Herder, 1982).

20   Cf. Lumen Gentium, No. 10: "Though they differ from one another in
essence and not only in degree, the common priesthood of the faithful and
the ministerial or hierarchical priesthood are nonetheless interrelated." Cf.
Melvin E. Michalski, *The Relationship between the Universal Priesthood of
the Baptized and the Ministerial Priesthood of the Ordained in Vatican II and
in Subsequent Theology.* Understanding Essentia et non Gradu tantum. Lumen Gentium No. 10 (Lewiston, N. Y.: Mellen University Press, 1996).

21   Cf. Gisbert Greshake, *Priester sein in dieser Zeit.* Theologie – Pasto-
rale Praxis – Spiritualität (Freiburg: Herder, 2000); ibid., *The Meaning of
Christian Priesthood* (Christian Classics, Westminster, Maryland: 1989).

22   K. Rahner, *Knechte Christi.* Meditationen zum Priestertum (Freiburg:
Herder, 1967); ibid., *Servants of the Lord*, translated by Richard Strachan
(New York: Herder and Herder, 1968).

23   For example, *Lumen Gentium*, No. 10 "[The ministerial priest] [a]ct-
ing in the person of Christ, [...] brings about the Eucharistic Sacrifice,...";

further: *Lumen Gentium*, Nos. 21, 25, 28; *Prebyterorum Ordninis*, No. 2:
"... the sacerdotal office of priests is conferred by that special sacrament
through which priests, by the anointing of the Holy Spirit, are marked
with a special character and are so configured to Christ the Priest that they
can act in the person of Christ the Head."; further, *Prebyterorum Ordinis*,
Nos. 12, 13, 19, 21.

24   Cf. Gnade als Mitte menschlicher Existenz. Ein Gespräch mit und über
Karl Rahner aus Anlaß seines 70. Geburtstages, in: *Herder Korrespondenz*
28 (1974) 77-92, 89: "Could not one imagine a program for the development of a young seminarian, a program that would not involve the study
of one or two years of academic theology which would lead to becoming
an expert in some obscure point, but rather would consist in being under
the guidance of a true 'Master' who would act as both a theologian and
spiritual guru. This person would hand on to the young seminarian an understanding of what Christianity, the spiritual life, prayer, and theological
reflection are all about. Perhaps, there is one or another blessed spiritual
director who is such a master. In the past young seminarians who wanted
to be priests, pious and Christian, came from and remained in a Christian
milieu and then were drilled in this Christian life in seminaries in a praise-
worthy way. But one did not have to teach them any theology other than
a decent theology divided into a variety of disciplines. But today people
come into theology who are still seeking what Christianity truly means,
who perhaps still harbor serious reservations about whether one can actually really pray, what it really means to have a special relationship to Jesus.
They take for granted that there are certain social norms and attitudes and
critical attitudes and practice these, but nothing else. How will Christianity be passed on to these young seminarians, for that is actually the self
evident reason for theological studies? I don't deny that this takes place
through the grace of God and a certain basic human instinct in the one to
be ordained. But one should not rely only on the grace of God and basic
human instinct alone." – See now in: K. Rahner, *Sämtliche Werke*, vol. 25,
3-32, 25 f.

25   *Lumen Gentium*, No. 12: "The holy People of God shares also in Christ's
prophetic office. It spreads abroad a living witness to Him, ... The body of
the faithful as a whole, anointed as they are by the Holy One (cf. Jn 2:20,
27), cannot err in matters of belief."

26   K. Rahner, Die Sünde Adams, in: ibid., *Schriften zur Theologie*, vol. 9
(Einsiedeln: Benziger, 1970) 259-275; see ibid., The Sin of Adam, in: ibid.,
Theological Investigations, vol. 11 (New York: Seabury Press, 1974) 247-
262.

27   Ludwig Ott, *Grundriss der katholischen Dogmatik* (Freiburg: Herder,
10th edition 1981), esp. 266-235; see ibid., *Fundamentals of Catholic Dog-*

ma, edited in English by James Canon Bastible. Translated from the German by Patrick Lynch (St. Louis, Mo.: B. Herder Book Co., 1954).

28 Earlier references to this term can be found in: K. Rahner, Bemerkungen zum dogmatischen Traktat "De Trinitate" (1960), in: ibid., *Schriften zur Theologie*, vol. 4 (Einsiedeln: Benziger, 1960) 103-133, 105; see ibid., Remarks On The Dogmatic Treatise "De Trinitate" in: ibid., *Theological Investigations*, vol. 4 (London: Darton, Longman & Todd, 1966) 77-102, 79: "One could suspect that as regards the catechism of the head and the heart, in contrast to the catechism in books, the Christian idea of the Incarnation would not have to change at all, if there were no Trinity." – Or K. Rahner, "Abgestiegen ins Totenreich" from 1957, in: ibid., *Schriften zur Theologie*, vol. 7 (Einsiedeln, Benziger, 1957) 145-149, 145; see ibid., "He Descended Into Hell," in: ibid., *Theological Investigations*, vol. 7 (New York: Herder and Herder, 1971) 145-150, "But the day which falls between these two, namely Holy Saturday, is overlooked by us. It carries no significance in our religious life, in the catechism of our heart." – Similarly, see K. Rahner, Offizielle Glaubenslehre der Kirche und faktische Gläubigkeit des Volkes (1981), in: ibid., *Schriften zur Theologie*, vol. 16 (Zurich: Benziger, 1984) 217-230; see ibid., What the Church Officially Teaches and What the People Actually Believe," in: ibid., *Theological Investigations*, vol. 22 (New York: Crossroad, 1991) 165-175.

29 Cf. Herbert Vorgrimler, Der "Katechismus der Katholischen Kirche" in der Perspektive systematischer Theologie, in: *Theologische Revue* 91 (1995) 3-8.

30 Cf. K. Rahner, *Sämtliche Werke*, vol. 17: Enzyklopädische Theologie. Die Lexikonbeiträge der Jahre 1956-1973. Bearbeitet von Herbert Vorgrimler (Freiburg: Herder, 2002) (1474 pages!).

31 Cf. K. Rahner, Einführung: Das neue "Lexikon für Theologie und Kirche," (1957), in: ibid., *Sämtliche Werke*, vol. 17, 81-85, esp. 85: "One frequently assumes that the clergy read too little or purchase too few books or purchase only those that do not challenge the mind or spirit. The older clerics are out to pasture and the younger ones are preoccupied with travel. The publisher of *LTHK* proceeds confidently from the opposite opinion of those whom the publisher expects to buy the work. The publisher naturally expects purchasers throughout the entire catholic world, above all, however, purchasers among the German-speaking clergy, whom they especially wish to serve." Cf., ibid., Josef Höfer, Vorwort (Lexikon für Theologie und Kirche, Volume I [1957], in: K. Rahner, *Sämtliche Werke*, vol. 17:, 86.

32 Cf. Personally. Karl Rahner in conversation with Paul Muigg and Johann A. Mair, Innsbruck 1984, in: *Glaube in Winterlicher Zeit*, 39: "I am not a sports enthusiast, I do not have an actual hobby as others have. My hobby was always my career as a theologian. And I found that enriching."

33   Quoted according to Herbert Vorgrimler, *Karl Rahner*. Gotteserfahrung in Leben und Denken, 99.

34   Cf. René Laurentin, Ein Eindruck vom Konzil, in: Elmar Klinger, Klaus Wittstadt (eds.), *Glaube im Prozess*. Christsein nach dem II. Vatikanum (Festschrift Karl Rahner) (Freiburg: Herder, 1984) 65.

35   Cf. e.g., the comment in: Herbert Vorgrimler, *Gott*. Vater, Sohn und Heiliger Geist (Aschaffenburg: Aschendorff, 3rd edition 2005) 9: "The following pages thus are written for people who want *to understand* what they believe and who are willing to have questions posed regarding their faith. That being stated – Karl Rahner is a trustworthy and honest companion – not in all things but in many."

36   Cf. Herbert Vorgrimler, Nachdenken über Jesus und seine kirchlichen Nachfolger, In: *Deutsches Allgemeines Sonntagsblatt*, Nr. 38 (19. 9. 1976); also: K. Rahner, Grundkurs des Glaubens, in: ibid., *Schriften zur Theologie*, vol. 14 (Zürich: Benziger, 1980) 48-62, 60 f.; now in: ibid., *Sämtliche Werke*, vol. 26: Grundkurs des Glaubens. Studien zum Begriff des Christentums. Bearbeitet von Nikolaus Schwerdtfeger und Albert Raffelt (Freiburg: Herder, 1999) 449-459, 458; see ibid., Foundations of Christian Faith, in: ibid., *Theological Investigations*, vol. 19 (New York: Crossroad, 1983) 3-15, 14: "My friend Herbert Vorgrimler has rightly drawn my attention to the omission in the chapter on ecclesiology of a topic on which I have written elsewhere relatively recently and forcefully – the topic of the Church of sinners, of the sinful Church, An impartial consideration of this topic could be of great importance, particularly at the present time to enable people to adopt a critical attitude towards the Church. As I said, Vorgrimler is right in this respect. The ecclesiology of this book has turned out to be perhaps too innocuous, even somewhat triumphalistic."

37   Cf. Herbert Vorgrimler, *Hoffnung auf Vollendung*. Aufriss der Eschatologie (Quaestiones Disputatae 90). (Freiburg: Herder, 2nd edition 1980).

38   Cf. K. Rahner, *Bekenntnisse*, 37: "Metz has made it a priority to develop a free standing Political Theology. He interprets *it* in general as being far removed from my theology. Naturally Metz has always and everywhere admitted that he was my student and owes a great deal to me, but he has emphasized even more firmly that he has a critical relationship to my theology. We have never actually discussed this. He has upset me because he has with some frequency mentioned in his lectures the comparison between the hedgehog and the hare. A hedgehog and a hare make a bet about who can run faster. They run next to each other in two potato sacks and can only see each other when they reach the goal. The hare runs like crazy but the hedgehog places his wife at the other end and as the hare charges toward the finish line the hedgehog's wife cries out: 'I'm already here!' Then Metz explains, I am the hedgehog, who allegedly, with his transcendental

apriori theology has always already reached the theological results, while Metz with his Political Theology must labor terribly. In the Festschrift for my 75th birthday Vorgrimler asked where then the second hedgehog might be. A Transcendental Theology, which always reflects back on itself, labors perhaps much more than the Political Theology, which happily and nonchalantly skips its way into the dawn of the future – so to speak. Personally that cannot be construed to suggest anything further. Metz praised me also to the point of exaggeration on the occasion of my 60th anniversary of religious profession. I am in a close personal friendship with him, and with Vorgrimler." – See now in: ibid., *Sämtliche Werke*, vol. 25, 59-84, 73 f.

39 Cf. Johann Baptist Metz, *Glaube in Geschichte und Gesellschaft*. Studien zu einer praktischen Fundamentaltheologie (Mainz: 3rd edition 1980) 143-145: "Ein Märchen – gegen den Strich gelesen."

40 Cf. Herbert Vorgrimler. Der Begriff der Selbsttranszendenz in der Theologie Karl Rahners, In: ibid. (ed.), *Wagnis Theologie*. Erfahrungen mit der Theologie Karl Rahners (Freiburg: Herder, 1979) 242-258, esp. 258: "Since there is not space here for a thorough rebuttal, I limit myself here to the tale favored by Metz of the hare of Political Theology and the hedgehog of Transcendental Theology. To apply the fairy tale to the two theologies is precisely faulty in that it presupposes there are two hedgehogs whereas Transcendental Theology is simply and only one. To accuse Rahner of some cunning trickery is terrible since the metaphor is not at all applicable."

41 Cf. Andreas R. Batlogg, Hans Urs von Balthasar und Karl Rahner: zwei Schüler des Ignatius, in: Magnus Striet, Jan-Heiner Tück (eds.), *Die Kunst Gottes verstehen*. Hans Urs von Balthasars theologische Provokationen (Freiburg: Herder, 2005) 410-446, esp. 439-444.

42 Cf. Hans Urs von Balthasar, Karl Rahner zum 60. Geburtstag am 5. März 1964, in: *Neue Zürcher Nachrichten*, 29. 2. 1964, Beilage Christliche Kultur Nr. 8.

43 Cf. Joseph Ratzinger, *Aus meinem Leben*. Erinnerungen (1927-1977) (Stuttgart: dva, 1998) esp. 82, 89, 130 f., 157; cf. the book review with a critique of the Rahner presentation in: *Zeitschrift für Katholische Theologie* 120 (1998) 465 f. (Andreas R. Batlogg).

44 Herbert Vorgrimler, *Karl Rahner*. Gotteserfahrung in Leben und Denken, 130.

45 Cf. Heinrich Fries, Karl Rahner, *Einigung der Kirchen – reale Möglichkeit* (Quaestiones Disputate 100) (Freiburg: Herder, 1983); now in: K. Rahner, *Sämtliche Werke*, vol. 27: Einheit in Vielheit: Schriften zur ökumenischen Theologie. Bearbeitet von Karl Lehmann und Albert Raffelt (Freiburg im Breisgau: Herder 2002) 286-396. – See Heinrich Fries, Karl

Rahner, *Unity of the Churches. An Actual Possibility*, translated by Ruth C. L. Gritsch and Erik W. Gritsch (New York: Paulist 1985).

46   Cf. zum Begriff: Christoph Böttigheimer, "Differenzierter Konsens" und "versöhnte Verschiedenheit." Über die Tradition der Konzentration christlicher Glaubensaussagen, in: *Catholica* 59 (2005) 51-66.

47   Cf. K. Rahner, *Vorfragen zu einem ökumenischen Amtsverständnis* (Quaestiones Disputatae 65) (Freiburg: Herder, 1974); now in: K. Rahner, *Sämtliche Werke*, vol. 27, 223-285.

48   Joseph Ratzinger, Prognosen für die Zukunft des Ökumenismus in: *Ökumenisches Forum*. Grazer Hefte für konkrete Ökumene 1 (1977) 31-41, 36: "Rome must not demand of the East any more allegiance to the teaching of papal primacy than was formulated and lived in the first millennium." Cf. Walter Kasper, *Wege der Einheit*. Perspektiven für Ökumene (Freiburg: Herder, 2005) 193f. Cf., ibid., *That they may all be one: the call to unity* (New York: Burns & Oates, 2004).

49   Cf. Joseph Ratzinger, *Theologische Prinzipienlehre*. Bausteine zur Fundamentaltheologie (München: Erich Wewel 1982) esp. 209: "With regard to Papal primacy. Rome should not demand of the East any more than that which was formulated and lived in the first millennium." Cf. further, ibid., 214-239 ("Rom und die Kirchen des Ostens nach der Aufhebung der Exkommunikation von 1054").

50   Cf. Herbert Vorgrimler, Vom "Geist des Konzils," in: ibid., *Wegsuche*. Kleine Schriften zur Theologie, vol. 2 (Altenberge: Oros,1998) 139-169.

51   Cf. Andreas R. Batlogg, Gotteserfahrung und Kirchenkritik bei Karl Rahner, in: Mariano Delgado, Gotthard Fuchs (eds.), *Die Kirchlichkeit der Mystiker*. Prophetie aus Gotteserfahrung, vol. 3 (Fribourg: Academic Press, Stuttgart: Kohlhammer, 2005) 371-401.

52   Cf. e.g., K. Rahner, Über das Ja zur konkreten Kirche (1969), in: ibid., *Schriften zur Theologie*, vol. 9 (Zurich: Benziger, 1970) 479-497; ibid., Vom Mut zum kirchlichen Christentum (1979), in: ibid., *Schriften zur Theologie*, vol. 14 (Zurich: Benziger, 1980) 11-22; see also ibid., Concerning Our Assent to the Church as she exists in the concrete, in: ibid., *Theological Investigations*, vol. 12 (New York: Crossroad 1974) 142-160; ibid., Courage For An Ecclesial Christianity, in: ibid., *Theological Investigations*, vol. 20 (New York: Crossroad, 1981) 3-12.

53   Cf. *Spiritual Exercises*, No. 330.

54   Cf. K. Rahner, *Von der Not und dem Segen des Gebetes* (1949) (Freiburg: Herder, 2004); ibid., *Gebete des Lebens* (Freiburg: Herder, 2004) (therein: *Worte ins Schweigen* from 1938). Both volumes have been newly released in the Jubilee year 2004, *Beten mit Karl Rahner* (2 vols.). – See ibid., *The Need and the Blessing of Prayer*, translated by Bruce W. Gillette (Collegeville,

Minn.: Liturgical Press, 1997); ibid., *Encounters with Silence*, translated by James M. Demske, SJ (Westminster, Md.: The Newman Press, 1960).

PART THREE

KARL RAHNER AS A JESUIT COLLEAGUE

13

THEOLOGY IN THE SERVICE OF
CHRISTIAN LIFE

IN CONVERSATION WITH FR. EMERICH CORETH, SJ, INNSBRUCK

Emerich Coreth, SJ, (1919-2006), Dr. phil., Dr. theol., a Jesuit since 1937, 1957-1958 and 1968-1969 Dean of the Theology Faculty University of Innsbruck, 1961-1967 Rector of the Jesuit Residence, 1969-1971 Rector of the University of Innsbruck, 1973-1977 Provincial of the Austrian Jesuit Province.

What is your opinion of Karl Rahner?

Fr. Rahner was a really brilliant person, extraordinarily gifted. If I ever met a true genius in my life, then it was he: his imaginative approach to problems, his way of working them out – it was incredible, breathtaking.

I first met Fr. Rahner in 1939, when I was finishing my novitiate. I had not yet begun my studies, but I had already heard about Fr. Rahner who was respected by the students for his depth and vitality. That was a time of new beginnings in theological thinking. Above all what one should remember about him is his existentially engaged thinking. Theology was not only an abstract science for him, but truly his life: theology at the service of Christian Life, in the service of proclamation! Theology was for him truly a matter of concern, a means to answer the problems of the time. At heart Karl Rahner was a deeply religious person.

Did that come from his family?

I believe so. I once met his mother briefly when she was already past ninety. I don't really know much about the family, but still – two sons became Jesuits! Hugo Rahner[1] was not less talented than his younger brother and he was, in terms of personality, much nicer and friendlier.

Hugo was quick-witted and an outstanding speaker. You cannot dismiss Karl Rahner's older brother. With him every class was a pleasure; he had a profound knowledge of patristics and Church history and at the same time was humorous and brilliantly witty, completely different from Karl Rahner. Karl had more of a somber, penetrating style; he was a problem solver. At any rate: from this family came these two Jesuit priests. There must have been a lively faith present in the family, a Christian upbringing, a very solid background in the faith: that's beyond question.

How did you get to know Fr. Rahner?

The first time I encountered Fr. Rahner was when I was finishing my novitiate in St. Andrä im Lavanttal (*Kärnten*), and he was telling us novices about his work. Of course, we did not understand much about what he was teaching. I got to know him better later on, and I was quite strongly influenced by him. I completed my doctoral studies in theology in 1948 and went to Rome while Fr. Rahner returned again to Innsbruck.

In 1950 I came to Innsbruck as a young teacher and in my early years there, I discussed things with him often. I think that played a role in my taking a transcendental approach to Metaphysics. I had already studied Joseph Maréchal[2] and Johann Baptist Lotz[3] had been my teacher in Pullach. The transcendental approach appealed to me, but I had not yet come to embracing it fully. In the meantime I also studied idealism: especially the work of Hegel. Then I began –strongly inspired by Karl Rahner – to write my book *Metaphysics*.[4] Fr. Rahner, by the way, was one of the censors and, I learned afterwards, did not criticize or offer any objections to what I had written.

Is your principal work influenced more by *Spirit in the World* or by *Hearer of the Word*?

I think that to really understand Karl Rahner's philosophical position *Hearer of the Word* is more important than *Spirit in the World*. The latter was his first work on the Metaphysics of finite knowledge in Thomas Aquinas and was strongly influenced by the thought of Heidegger. But he developed his own intellectual position in *Hearer of the Word*, an a priori established, transcendentally grounded metaphysics which posits first and foremost a transcendental openness to a relationship with God, an orientation to the Absolute. Thus, *Hearer of the Word* is a listening for an encounter with the Absolute in the world and in history – in the Word of God as it encounters us. It is precisely in that point that I see revealed the fundamental problem with the theology of that time: the transfer of a transcendental a priori from philosophy to theology.

You can find this fundamental assertion again in his late work, *Foundations of Christian Faith* (1976). There he begins with the same starting point, essentially unchanged, and comes to a Christological a priori, or a transcendental Christology. Fr. Rahner struggled for years to find an a priori for all theology, a starting point, a principle, so to speak, from which you could not unconditionally deduce everything, but which would still make everything intelligible. That for him is Christ. Now Christ is, however, never a pure a priori, nor is faith in him, but rather it is undeducible; it is a free saving act of God. Strictly speaking, a transcendental a priori is philosophically unprovable. That is faith. Certainly it changes, in a way, my world, my value system, in so far as Christ has become incarnate, suffered and rose for the salvation of the whole world and all of humanity. That is the key point for Karl Rahner: all of creation is different, since the Son of God has become human. You can also find this a priori difference in Karl Rahner's *theologumenon* of the anonymous Christian. Somehow, everyone is already in the order of salvation, whether one knows it or not, whether one believes it or not. Fr. Rahner calls this the "supernatural existential;" existential in the strict sense meant by Martin Heidegger. Existential is an ontological determination of existence. Existence is the manner of being of the human person. Heidegger calls a constitutive, ontological determination of human existence an "existential;" an ontological determination of human existence is simply the act of redemption: life in Christ. I believe that is an idea that deserves great consideration.

But is that not something only a believer can understand or accept?

Naturally. In the first place that is only discernible for a believer. It can only be realized and recognized in faith. One can never prove this by means of a pure transcendental reflection on human existence.

Fr. Rahner wrote an article on "The Unity of Love of God and Love of Neighbor" (1965). Would you say that there are moments where this, what you have described as a purely philosophical perspective, is transformed into a more theological one?

Completely, and indeed truly in an existential – theological sense. Karl Rahner never wanted to be a philosopher. I heard him say that repeatedly; he wanted to be a theologian. It almost seemed that he regretted that I was a philosopher, because philosophy never attains the fullness of reality. Theology, in faith, is the full reality. Philosophy, brutally stated, is an abstraction.

There has been criticism of Fr. Rahner that he moves too quickly from the concept of Being to God. Do you see that as a problem?

I believe that I could be accused of doing the same thing: that already included in Being is the idea of the unconditioned, an absolute. Neither human nor angel in heaven can deny that. I have always emphasized the absoluteness of Being in my *Metaphysics* and my later writings. I have spoken of the horizon of Being, an horizon of absolute validity. In the final analysis that is already to speak of God. Therefore, being is, metaphysically speaking, understood already as a participation in absolute Being. I do not know that Fr. Rahner would say anything different. I do not believe in *"esse commune."* That is an abstraction, a concept. There is no *"esse commune"* in reality. Reality is always to be found only in concrete beings, in individual being. It is a principle, a metaphysical principle, a real principle, that through Being every being comes to be.

You said previously that Fr. Rahner was a deeply religious person.

That is what I believe to be so. That can be seen clearly in his writings such as *On Prayer* (1949). You also experienced the depth of his religious faith when you heard him preach or when you spoke to him. His homilies were truly spirit-filled, committed to the salvation of the world, and to the concerns of the Church. But he preferred to hide his personal piety. He rose very early in the morning, about 4:30 a.m. or even earlier, and celebrated Mass by himself. He did not draw at-

tention to that, but his dedication – he preached every Sunday in the
Jesuit Church in the 1950's and 1960's[5] – was self-evident.

For some people the Second Vatican Council (1962-1965) was a
big disappointment. I have the impression that for Karl Rahner it
was a breakthrough. He was able to prevail, both personally and
theologically, in terms of influencing the outcome of the Dogmatic
Constitution on Revelation (*Dei Verbum*).

You could say that. He was not only Cardinal Franz König's theological advisor, but also was named an official *peritus* by Pope John XXIII.
It is very clear that Fr., Rahner invested himself enormously in the
work of the Council. He gave lectures before different Bishops' Conferences at the Council and theologians came to him to seek his advice.
He had a strong influence; he was almost the leading theologian of the
Council. He never called attention to his role, but you felt it and could
see that it was so. The others deferred to him! That experience was a
great confirmation for him of his theology and his entire work.

What did your friendship with Karl Rahner mean to you?

I would hardly call it a "friendship." You really cannot get that close to
Karl Rahner. As I have already said, in the early years, at the beginning
of the 1950's, I spoke with him often and we had many discussions
about various things. He was comfortable with me as a conversation
partner. But as time went on, we gradually spoke less and less. First of
all, I was busy and secondly he was overworked. Whenever I tried to
approach him I would find him busy writing, either by hand or using
his "two finger" system on the typewriter. Increasingly, he had less and
less time to talk. Also, by that time, he had his own secretary, and you
could not simply go to see him without making a prior appointment
through her. And it was rare that there was an opportunity for that.

In December 1981 Fr. Rahner returned to Innsbruck.

Yes, the Jesuit residence had been renovated at that time. Unfortunately, in those last years, I didn't have much contact with him. It was
difficult; he withdrew more and more and physically he was not very
well. He felt himself at home here, more than he did in Munich. But

I cannot say that I had much contact with him. He had his own office, with his own secretary. He worked on organizing all his archives and was busy with a great deal of correspondence. I didn't feel that it was right to disturb him. In addition to the enormous amount of correspondence, he still had lectures to give. He was intellectually very stimulating.

It was very clear how much he revered his father in the Order, Ignatius of Loyola.

Yes, he revered him and lived and worked in the spirit of our Order's founder. He saw himself totally as a disciple of Ignatius. In the final analysis, you could see that his theology was inspired by the *Spiritual Exercises*. Both Rahner brothers were very interested in Ignatius. Hugo Rahner wanted to write a biography of him. Unfortunately, due to illness, he was not able to realize this goal, but he was able to write some things about Ignatius.

What would be your response to someone who asked if one should bother studying Rahner since his language is so difficult?

There is so much that I could say about that! Understanding Karl Rahner is not limited to understanding only his philosophical starting point. He grappled with almost all of the problems raised in theology and took a position with regard to them. His theology is very diverse and, therefore, can provide a stimulus to go in a variety of directions in order to deal with many different theological questions. It does serve to provide direction, but not in so restrictive a fashion as to preclude going another way. Fr. Rahner also changed his mind on some things. For example, in one of his early articles he tried to prove monogenism, the descent of man, metaphysically.[6] He did not continue to do that later in his life. But he did grapple with every problem in all its complexity.

It was said that Fr. Rahner's sister, Elisabeth, picked up Professor Martin Honecker's preliminary evaluation of Fr. Rahner's dissertation on Thomas Aquinas in which he wrote that Rahner's approach to Thomas was misleading. Fr. Rahner refused to do a rewrite and

decided not to continue to pursue a doctorate in that area. Did this bother him?

Perhaps, initially, but later it did not bother him at all. He viewed it rather as strange that his dissertation was not accepted. But he very quickly gained a doctorate in theology here in Innsbruck[7] and qualified as a university lecturer six months later. He seemed, for the most part, to be pleased with the switch to theology,[8] but he also held that philosophy was important. I wrote an article about that once.[9]

I was unhappy with his constant criticism of the Church. Sometimes his complaints about the Church would begin as early as breakfast. Hugo Rahner was often concerned about its ramifications for Karl.[10] But he was able to find a way to bring Karl to Rome and he was well received there. Karl seemed to feel better about this. Up until the 1950's he liked to see himself in the martyr role: as a martyr to Rome. Naturally he caused some tensions with Rome, but it was not so bad. Yes, some people took offense. But he did not know influential people well. Hugo and I plotted to change that. At that time I was Rector of the Jesuit Residence and we found a way to have Karl invited to give lectures at the Gregorian University. That went very well and he was received by Cardinal Ottaviani in a cordial manner. Karl Rahner blossomed and came back in a very good mood. He was very satisfied with how it went and we talked about that; it felt as if a huge weight was lifted from my heart. At times Hugo would come to me and ask: "How are you doing with Karl?" He had his worries about him, just as I did.

NOTES

1   Hugo Rahner, SJ, (1900-1968) taught Church history and Patrology from 1937-1964 at the University of Innsbruck. 1945-1946, and from 1953 to 1954, he was Dean of the Theology Faculty, and 1949-1950 Rector of the University of Innsbruck. Cf. Andreas R. Batlogg, Hugo Rahner als Mensch und Theologe, in: Stimmen der Zeit 213 (2000) 517-530.

2   Joseph Maréchal, SJ, (1878-1944) taught as Professor of Philosophy in Louvain (Belgium) and influenced with his main work, Le Point de départ de la métaphysique, (1923 ff.), numerous so-called transcendental theologians and philosophers.

3   Johann Baptist Lotz, SJ, (1903-1992), Professor for the History of Philosophy in Pullach near Munich, (Berchmannskolleg).

4 Cf. Emerich Coreth, *Metaphysik*, (Innsbruck: Tyrolia, 1961) (3rd edition 1980). English translation by Joseph Donceel with a Critique by Bernard Lonergan, „Metaphysics as Horizon," in: Emerich Coreth, *Metaphysics* (New York: Seabury Press, 1973).

5 Cf. K. Rahner, *Biblische Predigten*, (Freiburg: Herder, 1965).

6 Cf. Karl Rahner, Paul Overhage, *Das Problem der Hominisation* (Quaestiones Disputatae 12/13) (Freiburg: Herder, 1961).

7 This doctoral dissertation was first published in 1999. Cf. K. Rahner, *E Latere Christi. Der Ursprung der Kirche als zweiter Eva aus der Seite Christi des zweiten Adam. Eine Untersuchung über den typologischen Sinn von Joh 19, 34*, in: K. Rahner, *Sämtliche Werke*, vol. 3: Spiritualität und Theologie der Kirchenväter (Freiburg: Herder, 1999) 1-84; cf. Andreas R. Batlogg, Karl Rahners theologische Dissertation *E Latere Christi. Zur Genese eines theologischen Projekts* (1936), in: *Zeitschrift für Katholische Theologie* 126 (2004) 111-130.

8 Cf. K. Rahner, *Zur Rezeption des Thomas von Aquin*, in: Paul Imhof, Hubert Biallowons (eds.), *Glaube in Winterlicher Zeit. Gespräche mit Karl Rahner aus den letzten Lebensjahren* (Düsseldorf: Patmos, 1986) 49-71, 53. – English translation: *Faith in a Wintry Season*, 44: "In view of what happened, however, the frequently repeated claim that I was transferred to Innsbruck and into dogmatic theology because of that rejection is false. I had submitted my work toward the end of the summer term in 1936. I then had to go to Innsbruck, since my superiors had changed my assignment and I was to earn a further degree in dogmatic theology. Innsbruck needed a professor after the retirement of Johann Stufler and Joseph Müller, the predecessors of Franz Mitzka and me. These reasons led to my reassignment. And only after I had begun to prepare my doctorate in theology did I receive the letter from Honecker, telling me that he did not accept my dissertation. So even if he had accepted it, I'd have become a dogmatic theologian in Innsbruck, and quite gladly. (…) And, to be frank, I myself had no great attraction to the history of philosophy. Certainly, I would have been a quite respectable historian of philosophy, but my heart didn't bleed when I was reassigned by my superiors."

9 Cf. Emerich Coreth, Philosophische Grundlagen der Theologie Karl Rahners, in: *Stimmen der Zeit* 119 (1994) 525-536.

10   Cf. the letter of Hugo Rahner to Karl Rahner in the appendix of this book ("Von Bruder zu Bruder," 1955).

14
POSSESSED BY THEOLOGY

IN CONVERSATION WITH FR. ALBERT KELLER, SJ, MUNICH

Albert Keller, SJ, Dr. phil., lic. theol., born 1932, a Jesuit since 1952; Professor of Epistemology and Philosophy at the Jesuit College of Philosophy in Munich and Rector from 1970-1976; from 1976-1980 Director of the Institute for Communication and Media at the College; Professor emeritus since 2002.

What was your experience of Fr. Rahner here at Berchmans College?

When Rahner left Münster as Professor emeritus, he returned to Munich and lived in the "Writer's House" in the Zuccalistrasse. Then he came to Berchmans College and lived here for several years. He had a room and an office. When he was not traveling, he would dictate every day. He had secretaries who had to be very patient. In the morning he would begin his dictation at 9:00 a.m. and go until about noon, with a break of about 30-45 minutes for coffee. His work was published just as he dictated it. He did not edit or rewrite it. You could tell that many articles were dictated: often there were very long sentences. He had an aversion to being interrupted in the morning and would react angrily if this occurred while he was dictating.

Did he have a "Do not disturb" sign on his door?

No. We all knew that in the morning you were not to disturb Fr. Rahner. Unless it was the Father General or someone else in very high position who called, the phone call would not be put through.

What was your relationship to Fr. Rahner?

At the time, I was Rector of the College. When he took a break he would come to the college, so we often met during the coffee break. During that time he would be completely relaxed. When he was invited out and he was to be picked up, he would be ready 20 minutes in advance, and then would always ask impatiently: "Where are they already?" If someone was to pick him up at 10 o'clock, then he would be ready at 9:30. When we were invited to visit a family, after about an hour he would say that it was time to leave. This impatience was simply a part of him.

Apparently he rose early.

That was well known. When he held the Guardini Teaching Chair (*"Romano-Guardini-Lehrstuhl"*) in Munich, he scheduled his lectures to begin at the earliest possible time in the morning. I believe that he began the class at 7:15 a.m. He only wanted students to come who were really interested. That's the reason he scheduled his class at the earliest possible time; no one else began classes that early.[1]

Fr. Rahner was a professor in Innsbruck, Munich and Münster. Did he ever say he should have stayed in Innsbruck the entire time, where he spent the last years of his life?

When he left Münster in 1971 he came directly back to Munich. What he regretted was that he had not been as successful in Munich as his predecessor Romano Guardini. Guardini was a brilliant rhetorician, not a "Show-Man," but an aesthete who spoke excellent German and was a master of literature. That was not Fr. Rahner. He also could speak very eloquently, but he was much more interested in the ideas, than in their formulation. With Guardini, it was exactly the opposite. If you were inclined to be somewhat harsh and critical you could say that it is pleasing to read Guardini, but it is not exciting. Everything is beautiful and balanced and not rubbish, but it doesn't compare with Fr. Rahner, who had his own ideas and insights. On the other hand, Guardini had full lecture halls; lectured in the largest auditorium and attracted people from all the faculties – not only philosophers, theologians. You could say that Guardini was a cult figure: you felt it. Rahner did not fill the lecture hall and that rankled him. He was somewhat hurt that he was not appreciated as much as Guardini. That's the reason he accepted the invitation to go to Münster in 1967.

What are the memories of Fr. Rahner that stay with you?

The first thing, certainly, is his lack of patience! But I can also remember, very vividly, his discussing something with someone, and thinking that he was not conceited. He didn't speak only to other professors. He never said, that's only a – let's say a businessman: I'm not going to bother to talk to him. He spoke to anyone. Only when someone would be obstinate and would not listen to his line of argumentation would he say, very politely, this priceless sentence: "Keep to your opinion, for you it is good enough!" That's something I heard him say often, and I enjoyed it: it's a great sentence.

He also knew, very well, how to get others to help him. Karl Lehmann, Herbert Vorgrimler, Johann Baptist Metz, Roman Bleistein and others; they all worked very hard for him. Fr. Rahner could importune; otherwise he would not have been able to produce so much and been able to communicate his ideas. Perhaps, he also expected that Luise Rinser would be able to help him in this way: that she would review his writings and improve his style. She was a well-known author.

Was Fr. Rahner communicative during coffee breaks?

During coffee breaks, yes. But "small talk" was not his thing. We often told jokes. If they were theologically interesting and he liked them, he would remember them. For example, he liked the joke which a lawyer told him. The lawyer said: "Some people were having an argument about whether or not God exists. Some people said there is a God. Others said: there is no God. I've come to this conclusion: the truth probably lies somewhere in-between." That one he liked.

Elisabeth Cremer, Fr. Rahner's sister and Franz Johna of Herder Publishing told me that Fr. Rahner answered all the letters which he received. Was that actually possible? Did his secretary help him with this?

Some letters were answered by a secretary or by an assistant, if they were not too personal. Here in the house, Fr. Karl-Heinz Weger, SJ, and Fr. Roman Bleistein, SJ, both of whom have since died, helped him a great deal.[2] When Fr. Rahner held the Guardini Teaching Chair, Jörg Splett was his assistant.[3] He is now a professor in Frankfurt. His assistants worked very hard for him. He used the morning to work on his theological ideas and no one was allowed, as I have said, to disturb him. In the afternoon he wrote letters or did some reading.

Did he have the time to do much reading?

He certainly did not have much time. In addition to his work he was active in Church politics, for instance he worked with the General Synod of the German dioceses in Würzburg from 1971 to 1975. He invested a great deal of time in that and before that, of course, he was at the Council where he worked extremely hard reading and editing texts. But it was in Innsbruck that he devoted himself intensively to studying the Church Fathers and everything else. In his old age he only read about current ecclesiastical matters and didn't bother to study other theologians any more.

Fr. Rahner had a good relationship with Cardinal Julius Döpfner, the Archbishop of Munich and Freising.

They understood one another very well, but he also had a good relationship with Cardinal Hermann Volk from Mainz. Fr. Rahner liked a sure, solid sense of authority. He once said in reference to the Order that he had encountered mostly followers and only a few leaders. He did not mean that in an angry way. He spoke about a Jesuit who was a famous Provincial: Fr. Hayler.[4] Fr. Hayler was Fr. Rahner's Provincial sometime in the 1920's. Hayler was once ordered to come to Rome to see the Superior General who wanted to reprimand him for being so independent. Hayler made the trip to Rome, seeing this as a kind of "Culpa," a type of disciplinary measure because of his actions. He was made to wait in the Superior General's waiting room. After waiting an hour he said to Fr. General's secretary: "If Fr. General has so much time – I don't," and he took the train back to Germany without meeting with the Superior General. Fr. Rahner liked that. He said: Fr. Hayler was a leader, a man who knew what he wanted and who stood up for it.

He liked Cardinal Döpfner for the same reason.[5] Döpfner was the same type, energetic and originally somewhat conservative, but he admitted that he was not always right, but when he thought he was, he stood his ground.

Döpfner's successor as Archbishop was Joseph Ratzinger, who prevented Johann Baptist Metz from coming to the University in Munich.

Fr. Rahner desperately wanted Metz to succeed Heinrich Fries, but Cardinal Ratzinger and the Minister of Culture, Hans Maier, refused to allow it. Fr. Rahner spared no effort to try to gain that position for his friend and student, Metz. He wrote a long newspaper article, which he entitled, reminiscent of the Dreyfus affair,[6] "I protest."[7] Fr. Rahner quite vociferously challenged Ratzinger and Maier; it was not at all peaceful. But in the last analysis his intervention failed.

What can young theologians learn from Karl Rahner? I read that Hans Küng, during the course of the debate on his book, *Infallibility*, said to Fr. Rahner, who had defended that dogma: "You have had your turn, now it's our turn." Is Fr. Rahner passé and not only because of the difficulty of his language?

Hans Küng's work does not possess nearly the same theological quality as that of Karl Rahner. He has his ideas, there is no disputing that, but as to theological substance – there Fr. Rahner is unsurpassed. For example – and this is in strong contrast to Küng – when he challenged the traditional use of the term "person" in regard to the Trinity in an article,[8] he also noted that he was not attempting to impose his ideas on the magisterium of the Church. He did not maintain that the Church had to change its language. Küng would say that the dogma must be revised. That would be completely foreign to Rahner. He understood that a concept like that of person, which has had a definite meaning for centuries of theology, cannot simply be discarded. Although, de facto, he seriously questioned the concept, he did not want to challenge the magisterium. That is something that young theologians can learn from Fr. Rahner – the style and manner which he employed when he entered into a theological discussion that involved the traditional teaching of the Church. Still it is almost shocking to realize how innovative his ideas were and still are today.

Were you, yourself a student of Rahner?

No. I studied my theology in Rome at the Gregorian University from 1962 to 1966 during the Council. I met Fr. Rahner, now and then at small conferences, which he held for the Germans. I learned my theology, however, by studying his books. I attended lectures at the Gregorian University, but I thought that there was more to be gleaned from Fr. Rahner's books than that which I heard at the University.

Karl Rahner's spiritual writings, such as *On Prayer* or *Encounters with Silence* appear to me to be somehow timeless. The most important, to me, of his spiritual writings was his commentary on the *Spiritual Exercises*, the *Meditations on the Ignatian Exercises* (1965). There he is not splitting theological hairs, but is very pastoral and spiritual. His own piety shines through and he reveals that when he says: "I am standing before God." It is not as common in Germany, as it is in some other places, to acknowledge your religious feelings. We are more reserved, but Fr. Rahner does it! The personal piety out of which he lived and constructed his theology can be clearly seen in his books. In the introduction to his book, *Foundations of Christian Faith*, he writes "[a Christian] knows that he has not thought enough, has not loved enough, and has not suffered enough."[9] He does not broadcast his personal experiences, but he does not conceal them either. That made an impression on me.

For what are you most grateful?

If you judge Fr. Rahner in terms of his being a model human being, then your response has to be negative. He was a man possessed by his work – that was his life: no vacation, no theater, etc. He only was interested in theology, but theology not just as an academic discipline, but concerned with people. His involvement with theology was determined by the question: How can I understand the faith and present it in such a way that people today will find it relevant? I have found this professional ethos only in a few other seekers after knowledge, theologians or physicists, who have no other interest than in their discipline, who forego family and live only for their research. Karl Rahner was such a person.

NOTES

1 Cf. Jörg Splett, Auf dem Lehrstuhl Romano Guardinis, in: Paul Imhof, Hubert Biallowons (eds.), *Karl Rahner – Bilder eines Lebens* (Freiburg: Herder, 1985), 72-73.

2 Karl-Heinz Weger, SJ, (1932-1998), Dr. theol., was Professor for the Foundations of Theology and Philosophical Anthropology at the College of Philosophy in Munich and Director of the Institute for Questions of Religious Criticism; Roman Bleistein, SJ, (1928-2000), Dr. phil., Professor for Pedagogy for Adults at the College of Philosophy and co-worker for *Stimmen der Zeit.*

3 Jörg Splett, Dr. phil., born in 1936, Professor emeritus for Philosophy at the College Sankt Georgen in Frankfurt am Main (1971-1995), and Instructor at the College of Philosophy in Munich. Cf. Jörg Splett, Im Dienst der Wahrheit. Abschiedsvorlesung, in: *Theologie und Philosophie 80* (2005) 321-333.

4 Franz Xaver Hayler, SJ, (1876-1965), 1928-1935 Provincial of the Upper German Jesuit Province with headquarters in Munich.

5 Julius Döpfner (1913-1976), at 35 years of age named Bishop of Würzburg, later of Berlin. Since 1961, Archbishop of Munich and Freising and President of the German Bishops' Conference. He was one of the leading German Bishops at the Second Vatican Council and, together with Cardinals Gregorio Pietro Agagianian (Vatican), Giacomo Lercaro (Bologna), and Léon Joseph Suenens (Brussels), one of the four moderators of the Council selected by Pope Paul VI.

6 Alfred Dreyfus (1859-1935), a Jew from the region of Alsace, a Staff Officer in the French Army, who was found guilty (of alleged acts of treason, selling military secrets to the German Reich) and in 1894 sentenced to life-long banishment on the island of Cheyenne, (French-Guinea). The Dreyfus-Affair developed into the greatest inner-political crisis of the Third French Republic. In an open letter to the French president ("J' accuse"), Émile Zola called for the rehabilitation of Dreyfus, who was the victim of an anti-Semitic conspiracy.

7 Cf. further information about this in the interview with Alfons Klein, SJ, in this book.

8 Cf. K. Rahner, Der dreifaltige Gott als transzendenter Ursprung der Heilsgeschichte, in: *Mysterium Salutis*, vol. 2 (1965) 317-347.

9 Cf. K. Rahner, *Grundkurs des Glaubens*. Einführung in den Begriff des Christentums (Freiburg: Herder, 1976), 14; now in: K. Rahner, *Sämtliche*

Werke, vol. 26: Grundkurs des Glaubens. Studien zum Begriff des Christentums (Freiburg: Herder, 1999) 9.

15

A TRUE JESUIT

IN CONVERSATION WITH FR. ALFONS KLEIN, SJ, MUNICH

Alfons Klein, SJ, Dr. theol., born 1929, a Jesuit since 1948, 1978-1984 Provincial of the Upper German Province of the Jesuits with headquarters in Munich. Since then a Pastoral Minister at the Jesuit Church, St. Michael, in the capital of Bavaria.

How did you get to know Fr. Rahner?

I first met him in Innsbruck where, as a young Jesuit, I studied philosophy then theology and after my tertianship, I did doctoral studies, which I completed in 1965.

You, as Provincial, gave the homily at Fr. Rahner's funeral. Who decided that the Provincial should preach and not one of the numerous bishops or a cardinal who were present for his funeral?

I discussed that at length with a number of my Jesuit colleagues at the time. Karl Rahner was, first and foremost, a Jesuit. That's why we finally decided that a Jesuit should preach. The Society of Jesus was his life; it was his home. Just as Nathaniel was a true Israelite so Rahner was a true Jesuit – with a daily workload, with all the advantages, with all the hardships and with all the suffering which is associated with that. We thought that there would be many other occasions where it would be appropriate for him to be honored for his theological expertise, but not at his funeral. And so the difficult question of who should be asked to preach at his funeral was decided. Many of his eminent students attended, for example, Johann Baptist Metz; many bishops were there – Karl Lehmann, Hermann Volk, Friedrich Wetter, Ernst Tewes, Egon Kapellari and Reinhold Stecher. For us Jesuits it was important to show how Fr. Rahner lived as a human being, what he was like as a person, a priest and as a Jesuit. We believed that, at his funeral, his theological accomplishments should not be made the most prominent aspect of who he was.

Why are there short Latin phrases in the homily?

It is a common practice among us Jesuits to recall some of the key guiding principles of the Order, which are Latin phrases: *Deus semper maior, adiuvare animas, sentire cum ecclesia, discretio spirituum*, for example. These are "key phrases" in Ignatian Spirituality. I preached as a Jesuit colleague and not as an academician. The *Spiritual Exercises* left their mark on Fr. Rahner. He rooted his life in them and I tried to show that in my homily.[1]

At the end of your homily you note that Fr. Rahner said: "If I have been able to help anyone in my life, just a little, to find the courage to speak to God, to think of God, to believe in God, to hope and to love; then I think that it has been worth it to have lived." Then you say: "It was worth the effort, dear Karl Rahner and we all thank God and thank you with all our hearts."

I was very close to Fr. Rahner and so I was able to pass on not only what he had written, but what he had said to me in private.

I bring this up because I read somewhere that Fr. Alfred Delp, SJ, said something similar.

I was about to mention that. You always have to be careful with quotes. Some say that it was Delp that said that: "A person's life has meaning if they have been able to bring more love and more hope into the world." Of course, more than one person has voiced similar sentiments.

Did you live together with Fr. Rahner?

When I was studying in Innsbruck we lived in the same house, in the Jesuit residence. He often came to my room and would ask if he could stay with me for awhile. Sometimes, he simply was looking for a quiet place to stay. He would look out the window for about 20 minutes; say thank you and then leave. He hated being asked constantly – how are you? Apparently he came to me because I could sense what he needed

at that moment. He did not want constantly to be involved in theological conversations. Fr. Rahner sometimes simply wanted to have
some peace. One time I came to his room and found him in tears. I
asked him what was wrong. He said: "Herder Publishing is constantly
making demands on me to write something for them. I feel under such
pressure. I have written five pages and tore all of them up and threw
them into the waste paper basket. Don't force me always to produce
something!" With me he did not have to produce anything or answer
any questions. He needed that; it was good for him.

We were together not only in Innsbruck, but also on the Philosophy
faculty of the Jesuits in Munich, in the Kaulbachstrasse, where he lived
in the 1970's. He didn't teach at that time anymore, but he lived there,
had people to work with, an assistant, and I was his Rector.

Why did Herder publishing put such pressure on him?

Because it wanted to make money! The publishers knew that anything
new by Rahner would be sold even before it was written. Rahner always lived with this pressure. That's the burden he was under when
he cried out: "I am only human. I can't always produce." Unhappy and
irritated he said: "I do not write because I want to write or because I
have something that I want to say. I write because this stupid Herder
demands that I deliver something that it can publish and sell."

**Later on Fr. Rahner had a secretary to whom he dictated his
thoughts. At the beginning, he apparently wrote everything himself.**

Not everything. But at the beginning, when he was working on something, he typed it himself, with the "two finger" system. On Wednesday evenings in Innsbruck, he always held a Colloquium for all the
faculties. On occasion he would say: "That went well tonight. If I had
recorded it, then I would have had another article." I replied: "I will do
it so that no one even notices it." I had a tape recorder that you could
carry in your pocket. You could not see the microphone – it was as
small as a pin. The recorder ran for five hours so you did not constantly have to change the tape. I arranged to get one for him and told him
to tell Herder to pay for it since they earn so much money from his
work. Fr. Rahner did that. He spoke spontaneously, without prepara-

tion; because he did not know in advance what questions would be asked. If he decided that what was recorded was worthwhile, then he had a secretary type it for an article.

Before he used the recorder for the first time, Fr. Rahner was as curious as a child as to how it worked and was at the same time tense and impatient. An hour before the Colloquium was to begin, he called me and asked: "When are you going to come so that we can prepare everything?" I advised him not to keep looking at the pocket of his sport coat during the Colloquium to see if the recorder was working because his listeners might think he was having heart problems.

He was incredibly creative?

Yes, that is correct – in both content and form. When lecturing, Fr. Rahner often spoke in a complicated way. The reason for that was that he took into consideration every possible objection to his argumentation in order to show that he was aware of them. So sometimes he went on at unbelievable length, inserting dependent clauses, to clarify and explain his arguments. He had all that in his head and every sentence that he spoke was of publishable quality. Something else that was unique to him was that his manner of expression could suddenly change and Fr. Rahner would pray then, in the course of the lecture, like a child, very simply – the same person who had been speaking abstractly and in a complicated way! That was very moving: he was transformed – simple words coming from his heart. We experienced that often.

If you look at *Encounters with Silence* (1938) or *On Prayer* (1949) then you find a profound, but also a simple spirituality.

Yes, Karl Rahner was that as well – a spiritual person – not only a highly talented academician. When I made my priesthood retreat with him, often he could not continue to speak because he was fighting back tears; so deeply was he touched by the passion of his beloved Lord Jesus Christ.

But Fr. Rahner felt the burden he was under?

He always felt the pressure to produce something. He experienced it as an affliction and he felt helpless.

But when he returned to Innsbruck, at a relatively advanced age, he worked pretty intensively.

I seldom found that he simply wasted time lying around doing nothing. He almost always was working. But he enjoyed being with others, with those with whom he was comfortable. Then he would suggest that they go out to eat a pizza or just go somewhere. He liked ice cream very much. It had to be with people whom he knew would leave him alone and not feel that they had to engage him in a complicated, theoretical conversation.

I assume that Fr. Rahner led a very ordered, disciplined life. He went to bed early and rose very early. What struck you about his daily routine?

Only the fact that he had a very clear routine – that meant that he normally rose at a specific time and not according to his mood or desire. I assume that he did his meditation, as it is prescribed for a Jesuit, celebrated Mass and prayed the Divine Office. What other things he did during the course of the day I do not know. But he actually was always preoccupied with God, with revelation, with the mystery of God.

Do you have a special memory of Fr. Rahner, perhaps a conversation that impressed you deeply?

Fr. Rahner suffered due to the Church. Immediately, prior to the Council, he was forbidden to publish. He didn't say that it did not bother him. It did wound him! What impressed me was that there was a Jesuit who worked on behalf of children of guest workers, who were not Christian. They were born in Germany and this Jesuit said these are people who live here and we must take care of their needs! He came, repeatedly, into conflict with the Church because these children did not follow Catholic teachings. This Jesuit responded by saying: "That's crazy; they are Muslims, must the Church then always place burdens on other's shoulders?" What did Karl Rahner do? He defended this Jesuit! He was someone who not only suffered because of the Church; he also had the courage to stand up publicly and support someone who challenged the Church.

Once Fr. Rahner wrote an article against Cardinal Ratzinger. It occurred during a time in which the Society of Jesus was being treated very badly by the Pope and the Vatican. Fr. Rahner suffered because of that.[2] Ratzinger, the Archbishop of Munich and Freising (together with the Bavarian Minister of Culture, Hans Maier) wanted to prevent the call of Johann Baptist Metz, one of Rahner's most eminent students, to Munich to succeed theologian Heinrich Fries. Ratzinger succeeded in preventing Metz's appointment. Rahner wrote a long article: "I Protest" in response.[3] He knew that, as the Provincial, I would have to tell him that he shouldn't do that; that he needed to inform me in advance. He then said to me: "I did not inform you because you would have had to say no. I did not want to create problems for you. You are always so generous and you always defend me."[4] By "going it alone," Fr. Rahner acted to protect me, so that no one could hold me responsible for his action. But I had to disapprove of his manner of acting, although I recognized that Fr. Rahner had, personally, a good motive for his public protest. I summoned him to my office. The rumor then spread that I had actually attacked him, without any regard for his age or the importance of his person.[5]

Karl Rahner always spoke out when he believed that the Church was doing something that was not right. Toward the end of his life, he was often criticized by those who did not agree with his theological positions. On one occasion, a mail carrier in Munich insulted him, calling him an unbeliever or a heretic. By this example, it is clear that people who understood nothing of theology, who had never read anything he wrote, recognized that the leadership of the Church was against him and felt free to insult him. Rahner received unimaginably terrible letters and cards from different people. They felt supported by the hierarchical Church in their actions. Fr. Rahner did not simply tear up this mail and throw it away, but rather showed some of it to me. He had three files filled with these stupid and terribly negative letters that contained such terms as "traitor," "heretic," etc. He could not say: "Throw it out." Fr. Rahner told me that he always wanted to be a man of the Church and to defend the true faith. And now there are people who insult him and maintain that he is destroying their faith. That hurt him very deeply.

Do you know why, towards the end of his life, he returned to Innsbruck?

I have only my suspicions. Rahner was always somewhat of a restless person; he could not stay in one place for long. The move to Innsbruck was an example of this. When he left Innsbruck at the end of 1963 he said: "One cannot live there!" Then he went to Munich and after a time he said of Munich: "No one comes to see me! I don't feel at home here. I don't feel comfortable." He didn't blame anyone, but he was restless and wanted to switch communities.

Fr. Rahner was apparently temperamental. What did you particularly appreciate about him?

His intellectual honesty. Fr. Rahner never allowed himself to be rigid. He was flexible and took questions seriously. He entered into genuine discussions with those who thought differently. He also tried, in my opinion, perhaps a little naively, to remain faithful to the Catholic faith and to dogma. He wanted to look at the faith tradition with an eye to making it relevant for today so as to hand it on. He never wanted to change what was essential to the faith, but to free it from time bound formulations. But Fr. Rahner always asserted that what is essential is the dogma! Of course, that will be expressed in each age in the language of the time, and with the images of the age. He was someone who broke through barriers, which someone else would have seen as impenetrable. Fr. Rahner often said: "That is only the packaging; those are only words; what counts are the reality and the truthfulness which cannot be locked up in letters." That reminds me of the saying of Jesus about the fulfillment of the Law.[6] Jesus wanted to free us from all that which makes us suffer.

Fr. Rahner apparently was not accepted by every fellow Jesuit.

Yes, that was so. You have to understand that when you are a professor in Innsbruck and there are ten other professors on the faculty with you, and only one is being lauded; they would not be human if they were never jealous. It was certainly not always easy to be a professor on the same faculty as Fr. Rahner.

Are there any examples of Fr. Rahner's sense of humor, where he would really laugh or make others laugh?

I already noted that he was always curious, like a child. He was always interested in the latest thing. He always reacted completely naturally. Once when someone was made a cardinal, Fr. Rahner commented: "Now he has finally reached his goal, the ambitious one." Fr. Rahner was no prisoner of theology or of academics; he was also a human being who cared about those in need. Whenever he was in Vienna, he always lived in a Caritas House with Father Georg Sporschill, SJ, and a group of young people, all of whom had been in jail. In spite of that, he wanted to live there. He did not go to live with the Jesuits. He would stay overnight with these former convicts and young people who were hard to educate.[7] He was completely happy there. He was interested in them and they felt that. They did not address him as "Professor," but simply as "Karl" and that pleased him no end. These former convicts were invited to his 80th birthday in Innsbruck and spoke about his relationship with them. He was not ashamed of that. It was clear that they viewed him as a father. He did not judge them. These are things that are not well-known, but that was Karl Rahner, the man. When a fellow Jesuit or any other person was in dire straits and needed help, he was there for them. Sometimes, of course, he was too trusting and naïve.

Was this the situation with regard to Fr. Rahner and Luise Rinser? Was he too naïve?

I believe you could say that. I cannot deny that he had a relationship with her: that is a fact. But she was the initiator, the one who wanted to gain something from this relationship by claiming that she was a close friend of his. Personally, I am 100 percent convinced that there never was any sexual aspect to this relationship. Fr. Rahner told me, however, that I must be prepared for what Luise Rinser would say after his death. He did not want their exchange of letters to be published, since he believed them to be an entirely personal matter. But he also said to me: "You have to reckon with the fact that she will do it; she is fixated on that and insists on that!" They both used pet names for each other. Why shouldn't Fr. Rahner have done that? He was a completely normal human being, with feelings, not just an academician.

What would you say if someone asks if they should invest themselves in him as a theologian and a human being? And what we can still learn today from Fr. Rahner?

I would say: Yes, devote yourself to Karl Rahner. He modeled what it looks like when one seeks God, when one truly and honestly has respect for the mystery of God. That was important to him – the mystery, the incomprehensible mystery that we call God. In the exact same way reverence was important to him, honest searching which moves the heart, but does not dispense with reason, but fully uses it. He saw the need to encounter the mystery of life – to ask the questions: Who am I? Where do I come from? – To think in an intellectually honest way from the perspective of one's faith to show that one is a seeker and not a fanatical "know-it-all." That is something that is missing today and that is more important than choosing to be in the camp on the right or the camp on the left. To seek honestly, study hard, to find one's way to the heart of the matter – that is what you can learn from Karl Rahner. Fr. Rahner was theologically more sophisticated than most people who listened to him. He truly examined reality. He did not want to establish a fan club or create "groupies" in the Church. He wanted to make the dogmas more intelligible and free them from their time-conditioned expressions. He wanted to be an entirely traditional, genuine, believing human being.

NOTES

1 Cf. Karl Rahner's Funeral Homily, translated by Melvin E. Michalski, in: *Philosophy & Theology* 8 (1993) 93-96.

2 Cf. K. Rahner, Zur Situation des Jesuitenordens nach den Schwierigkeiten mit dem Vatikan, in: ibid., *Schriften zur Theologie*, vol. 15 (Zürich: Benziger, 1983) 355-372; now in: K. Rahner, *Sämtliche Werke:* Erneuerung des Ordenslebens. Zeugnis für Kirche und Welt. Bearbeitet von Andreas R. Batlogg (Freiburg: Herder, 2008) 335-350.

3 Cf. K. Rahner, Ich protestiere, in: *Publik-Forum* 8 (1979) Nr. 23, 15-19; cf. ibid., Ich protestiere, in: *Süddeutsche Zeitung*, 14.11.1979, 9.

4 Cf. K. Rahner's explanation in Publik-Forum, 16: "I belong to a Religious Order and I am protesting a decision of a high-ranking official in the Church. After lengthy deliberation I have decided to publish this complaint without observing the requirement that I request permission from my superior prior to doing so. He would probably not have granted permission,

nor would he have been able to do so for reasons that have nothing at all to do with the matter. I believe that in this conflict situation I could not act otherwise. I can only hope that Church officials take no punitive action against my provincial or my Religious Order because of my actions. I do not want to make any unwarranted comparisons, but Friedrich von Spee once published his famous Cautio Criminalis without receiving prior approval from the Order."

5   Cf. Alfons Klein, Protest und Ordensgehorsam, in: Paul Imhof, Hubert Biallowons (eds.), *Karl Rahner – Bilder eines Lebens* (Freiburg: Herder 1985) 126-127, 127: "What then occurred, would have caused a person, who at that moment had been waiting outside my office to see me, to allege, and with good reason, that Jesuit Religious Superiors to this day still practice corporal punishment without regard for who the member of the community is. Namely, when Fr. Rahner entered the office of the provincial for his scheduled appointment, he said with a loud voice: 'Father Provincial, now you can strike me.' At that moment one could hear a loud cry of pain and wailing. – Fr. Rahner had let himself fall into the seat of the sofa so forcefully that he hit his head against the wainscoting. The conversation itself was much less painful."

6   Cf. Mt 5, 17: "Do not think that I have come to abolish the law or the prophets. I have come not to abolish, but to fulfill."

7   Cf. the interview with Georg Sporschill, SJ, in this book.

16

GENIUS, BUT ALSO HUMAN

IN CONVERSATION WITH FR. HANS ROTTER, SJ, INNSBRUCK

Hans Rotter, SJ, Dr. theol, lic. phil., born 1932, a Jesuit since 1953, Professor of Moral Theology at the University of Innsbruck, 1974-1975 Dean of the Theology Faculty Innsbruck. On becoming Professor emeritus he began work as a Hospital Chaplain and Pastoral Minister to Religious Sisters in Zams/Tirol.

How did you come to know Karl Rahner?

I first came to know him as a student, listening to his lectures and participating in his famous evening Colloquia where you could ask him questions, but he didn't want to take questions that arose from his classes. Rather he wanted novel questions, questions about things that one could not read about in the texts. He would take three questions and as a rule would speak for about an hour and a half responding to them.

Could he always answer all three questions?

Generally, he would begin by answering the first question if it was good and would devote the most time to answering it. Because of that he spoke more briefly in response to the second and third questions. It was a very novel and creative way to deal with theology. Fr. Rahner allowed himself to be challenged. That was my first impression of him. But, of course, I also heard things about him from others. I came to Innsbruck in 1961 and at that time he was at the Council. Fr. Rahner was in Rome and only came occasionally to the Jesuit Residence. But he always took advantage of the opportunity to talk to the young students about the Council and about the plans he had at that time. These conversations were always very impressive and lively. He was, in my opinion, very excited about the Council, his encounters and with all that was going on in the discussions.

He also told us about the projects he was working on for Herder Publishing. Then he left Innsbruck. He told us that we had good teachers in Dogmatic Theology and that he was not needed. That, of course, was his explanation. Fr. Rahner wanted a change and I believe that he wanted it because he simply did not want to teach traditional Scholastic Theology. He was looking for a different challenge. It very much appealed to him to have the chance to succeed Romano Guardini in Munich, but unfortunately that proved, to a certain extent, to be a disappointment. He did not have the same measure of success that Guardini had when he offered a lecture series to all the members of the different faculties. Although he worked very hard and strained to make the discussion lively and intellectual, it just was too theological. He also experienced some difficulties with the Theology Faculty, which did not grant him the right (although it had been previously agreed upon) to have doctoral students. So he went to Münster. After a while he retired from there and went to Munich. At the time I was Academic Dean in Innsbruck and we were going through a crisis involving Fr. Schupp.[1]

What was that about?

Fr. Schupp was denounced. An investigation by two evaluators resulted in a judgment that his teaching did not sufficiently agree with the teaching of the Catholic Church. The Provincial was of the opinion that Fr. Schupp should defend himself and state his position. He refused to do this. He said that when someone writes such stupid evaluations as these two did, then it was hopeless to discuss anything with them. He then resigned immediately and left. He left both the faculty and the Society of Jesus. Suddenly we did not have a dogmatic theologian. Dogmatic Theology was always the most important discipline in the curriculum and it was naturally intolerable to begin a semester without a professor of dogma. It would be very difficult to find someone at that point, but Fr. Rahner was willing to step in and help out. He lived in Munich at the time and every two weeks he came for a double class period or for smaller blocks of time.

At that time Fr. Rahner came to my room, took out a cigarette and wanted to talk. That was very nice and it was typical of him to do this;

he liked to talk with young people. Such informal conversations were more comfortable for him; he was accepted and there was no rivalry. He didn't need to convince anyone of his viewpoint nor did he have to justify it. He could speak in a less complicated way and that was something he appeared to treasure very much. At that time I had a very good, friendly relationship with him. He was very willing to step in and help out our faculty and students. We, of course, tried to find new professors. That became possible and Fr. Rahner then left us.

But did he not leave Munich in the fall of 1981 and move to Innsbruck? He once wrote that he wanted to die in Innsbruck and be buried there.[2]

He spoke frequently about dying. It always impressed me when he would speak about that. For example he would say: "It is enough! It is enough!" He meant that he did what he could do and he was ready to leave the stage, as we say.

What would you say is the most important thing about Karl Rahner, the person? What did you treasure the most about him?

I experienced him as a person with an enormous curiosity. It was very amusing to see that even in many small things. He wanted to use our large Italian coffee machine, for example. He wanted to see how it worked. Or, lost in thought, he would take something out of someone's hand, for example a cigarette lighter, and play with it until he figured out how it worked and then he would give it back. Once he said to me when I was driving with him in a car and listening to the radio: "That is so strange. Now I have spoken often in Studio Tirol, but I still do not understand how that works with the electrical wires and antennas." He continually asked questions about everything. Thus it stimulated him to be working on a book with Fr. Sporschill that dealt with questions that young people asked.[3] He liked to be confronted with things and people that challenged him, which forced him to reflect on how something is to be understood, where it was not a matter of giving some banal answer. This pensiveness was something I saw consistently in him.

What was your experience of Rahner as a Moral Theologian?

Rahner was naturally interested in anything in theology. I found that I profited most from reading the first four volumes of *Theological Investigations* and the accompanying *Quaestiones Disputatae*, which were published prior to the Council. Then came the difficulties and the opposition from Rome. After that he became involved in the Council and was reconciled with Cardinal Ottaviani. I almost want to say they became friends.[4] Ottaviani really respected him and Fr. Rahner no longer had any problems with Rome.

Oddly enough, Fr. Rahner at that time toyed with the idea that he would like to qualify as a university lecturer in Moral Theology. The Provincial did not want that. Most likely the professors here and Fr. Rector were opposed to that because they thought: If Fr. Rahner is having difficulties in dogmatic issues then he will only have greater problems in Moral Theology. But Fr. Rahner wanted new challenges; he wanted to tackle something new. In the end he stayed with dogma, but there was a sharp change in direction in his development as a teacher. He no longer, as was earlier the case, wrote articles with speculative, deeply penetrating fundamental questions but, rather, it became more important to him to focus on and discuss Church structures. This again caused some difficulties because it inevitably involved a certain confrontation with the Church system.

This phase began after the Council?

Yes. After he retired as professor in Münster (1971) he came to Munich. There was always talk that the Order had placed certain restrictions on him in terms of what he could say. I do not know if this indeed was the case, but he developed a completely different way of articulating his ideas. It was also the time when Joseph Ratzinger was Archbishop of Munich and Freising[5] and Fr. Rahner felt himself pushed aside.

Johann Baptist Metz, at that time, wanted to succeed Heinrich Fries in Munich?

Yes, but Cardinal Ratzinger prevented that.[6] There were also strong disagreements among the Theology Faculty with regard to that appointment. There were members of the faculty who were strongly opposed to Metz. He was viewed as a restless spirit and many wanted "smoother sailing" and so chose Leo Scheffczyk.[7] Metz also was attracted to Munich because he ministered part-time in a small parish in Upper Bavaria. He wanted to leave Münster and later he was, as a Professor emeritus, appointed to a multiyear Guest Professorship for Philosophy of Religion and Worldview at the Interdisciplinary faculty in Vienna.

Fr. Rahner then became more interested in contemporary social issues?

Yes. A very turbulent time followed beginning in 1968. There were many changes. Fr. Rahner was very interested in these things. He told a young Jesuit once that he wanted to go to Schwabing[8] to see how marijuana was smoked and he let himself be taken there. He was simply fascinated by the young people who moved in this circle.

Let me come back to the impression that the *Theological Investigations* had on you.

The first three volumes had a concept that proved a great success for Fr. Rahner and for Benziger Publishing.[9] Gradually more volumes were published. That it would finally come to be 16 volumes (in German) – that could not have been foreseen in 1954 when the first volume appeared. The first three volumes were, in my opinion, theologically revolutionary. They had a great effect.

Fr. Rahner also had some remarkable volumes in the series that he and Heinrich Schlier published – *Quaestiones Disputatae*?

Yes. "Inspiration in the Bible" (1961), for example, and "The Dynamic Element in the Church" (1964), "On the Theology of Death" (1961), "The Church and the Sacraments" (1963). Then came "The Episcopate and the Primacy" (1962), and "Revelation and Tradition" (1966),[10] both of which he wrote with Joseph Ratzinger by the way. Those were true *Quaestiones Disputatae*: they forced you to struggle with new theological concepts. In the later volumes Rahner's theology was more fully developed, but what was more interesting was the ap-

plication of his theological approach to different issues. The genuine
surprises for the theological world were, however, to be found in the
first volumes.

What should we receive from Fr. Rahner?

I was a student in a course, taught by both Fr. Schupp and Fr. Rahner.[11] It proceeded this way: at each session Fr. Schupp delivered a
long lecture about something which played a role in Rahner's theology. Then Fr. Rahner would respond. I recall once that Fr. Schupp
confronted Fr. Rahner with the allegation that he did not really think
historically; that he spoke of historicity rather than history; that he
did not understand salvation history in the sense of concrete history
with variations and changes. I felt sorry for Fr. Rahner, although I tend
to agree with Fr. Schupp. Fr. Rahner seemed unable to reply to this
charge. He stated again and again that he meant real history, but one
had the impression, that, perhaps, he really did not truly understand
Fr. Schupp's objection.

I know from Fr. Rahner, himself, that he was very hurt by the criticism of his students, and sometimes he almost appeared to be wounded. All the famous Rahner disciples, beginning with Metz, had at
some point felt the need to distance themselves from their teacher. In
that sense, I would say, that I believe that the legacy of Fr. Rahner cannot consist simply in taking specific, concrete positions and making
of them a theology for all times, but rather it is a matter of following
his direction and developing his ideas further. One must reexamine
his ideas and the direction of his thought in terms of Karl Rahner's
mentality from its premises and in the light of new experiences. Fr.
Rahner is not the endpoint.

Once he spoke about a conversation that he had with Heinrich
Schlier. Schlier was an exegete, a Protestant who converted to Catholicism.[12] Fr. Rahner told me that Schlier once said to him that he was
greatly interested in the development of exegesis, in the development
of new methods and new perspectives. But he no longer felt himself to
be in a position to fully integrate all that new information because he
was too old and intellectually was no longer so flexible. Certainly it's
possible to take what one has learned and develop it somewhat with
new information, but you cannot always begin again from ground
zero. Fr. Rahner agreed with that and acknowledged that he experi-

enced something similar. Yet, although he recognized that the criticism of his students might in many ways be correct, still he could not jettison his own position so as to be able to begin where Metz began or where Küng or others began. He simply accepted that there were limitations. Perhaps, that is why, following the Council, he did not continue the constant probing that he had done earlier, the asking of foundational questions of Dogmatic Theology, but instead turned to other approaches.

Fr. Raymund Schwager, SJ, and Fr. George Vass, SJ, who taught Dogmatic Theology in Innsbruck, had similar concerns about Fr. Rahner and the importance of history.

Fr. Rahner began his career with Heidegger and with transcendental philosophy as his specific philosophical starting point. Even when he was able to move beyond it; it still remained his starting point. This starting point had its limitations and his students recognized them from the beginning. Metz, for instance, when he published the revised edition of Rahner's book *Spirit in the World* recognized this. Rahner's students quickly saw the limits of transcendental philosophy, but Fr. Rahner could not do that himself any more.

Do you think that a student of theology today would be able to make sense of Fr. Rahner's work since the theological historical context has changed radically?

I think the manner and the way in which Fr. Rahner engaged the tradition presupposes that one knows the tradition well in order to recognize what he achieved. Naturally that was something that had a much stronger impact at that time than is the case today. What made a great impression at that time was the spirit of freedom in theology. During the period of Pope Pius XII both theology and philosophy were strictly regimented. When I was a student in philosophy it was actually forbidden to read Pierre Teilhard de Chardin, SJ. Fr. Rahner managed – and that was his great achievement – while staying connected to Church tradition, to take a giant leap forward. That was viewed as a monumental release from very restrictive chains. I recall, for instance, his article on the Eucharist.[13] It sounds banal, but Fr. Rahner freed many things from casuistry, from dogmatic shackles, which we, at the time, found to be very confining.

Did Fr. Rahner ever speak of Pierre Teilhard de Chardin or was he personally influenced by his example?

That I do not know, but there were certain affinities. Fr. Rahner was very interested in the question of monogenism as well as in questions regarding evolution.[14] Considering that and Fr. Rahner's mystical background, it would not be surprising if he had come upon Teilhard de Chardin. I do not know to what extent he read him. For us students such things were under lock and key.

In the year 1982 Fr. Rahner was invited to the Canisianum to say something on the topic of priesthood – you were Rector at the time. He had only a small piece of paper with written notes and he began to speak. That impressed me greatly. It appeared that he wanted the students from all parts of the world to take something with them to their homelands, to think about his reflections further and not merely repeat what he had said.

Fr. Rahner's openness was incredible. He was interested in people, interested in dialogue, and he was interested in seeing that people work creatively, independently in the Church.

He could also be impatient and complain about the Church, could he not?

Fr. Rahner was extremely engaged. With regard to his love for the Church – that was something that interested me greatly. His discussions on television with Hans Küng, for example, show that. The issue they discussed had to do with the question of infallibility of dogma. Küng defended the position that dogmas must in the end be given a new context and formulated anew. And Fr. Rahner responded that dogmas do need to be interpreted anew for each generation, but that nothing can change in terms of the wording. He simply did not want to abandon the Church and her teaching.

This fidelity to the Church and her tradition is somehow surprising. Küng was seen at that time as the up and coming great Catholic
theologian. On the other hand Henri de Lubac, SJ, Yves Congar,
OP, and Hans Urs von Balthasar became cardinals, but Rahner
didn't.

That was something that Rahner was aware of and it was something
that hurt him a bit – the lack of recognition by Rome. He made jokes
about it: about the idea that, perhaps, he might once have a little stripe
of red on his cassock or some such thing, but his theology was a bit too
aggressive and confrontational. De Lubac wrote magnificent things,
but he was much more concerned with Patristics and not so immediately involved with concrete, hot button issues, or Hans Urs von
Balthasar whom Rahner called "The Stroker." Fr. Rahner felt all these
things deeply. I once came upon a small book which Rahner had just
received at that time from Hans Urs von Balthasar.

Do you mean *Cordula oder der Ernstfall* (1966)?

Exactly. Balthasar sent it to Fr. Rahner with the dedication: "With a
plea for a true theology of the cross." That, of course, was meant by
Hans Urs to be a criticism of Karl. Fr. Rahner was always very sensitive. He also believed that there was a genuine request in this, but his
theology was not as aesthetic as that of Hans Urs von Balthasar, who
involved himself with beautiful, spiritual literature and with his rich
wisdom of the Fathers. Fr. Rahner concerned himself with the burning questions of the moment, and that brought him constantly into
the line of fire.

**Fr. Rahner was editor-in-chief of a periodical for Sisters for many
years. You then followed him as editor-in-chief.**

That was a time of intensive collaboration with Fr. Rahner. *Jetzt* began in 1968 as a periodical of the Confederation of Women's Orders
and Congregations in Austria. But it already lost many subscribers in
its first years because of its audacious "letters to the editor" and the
departure of some of the editorial board members who left their religious orders. However, due to the generosity of the Superiors of the
religious orders, the periodical did not shut down, but it was no longer

run by the Sisters who, by then, had withdrawn from the project. From 1970 on *Jetzt* appeared as an independent publication. Karl Rahner succeeded Hildegard Waach as editor-in-chief. The actual work of editing was done by Hildegard Waach. Fr. Rahner diligently came to the editorial board meetings and would ask from time to time: "What should I write for you?" He was really concerned about the periodical, perhaps, because of the strong opposition it encountered from various people. After Karl Rahner died, the task of editor-in-chief fell to me. In spite of all the efforts of the editorial staff, the sharp decline in the number of religious sisters and many changes, eventually led to the shutting down of the periodical in 1998.

What was his relationship to Herlinde Pissarek-Hudelist?[15] She was always present for the evening colloquia.

Ms. Pissarek-Hudelist was someone who was close to him. She had been his teaching assistant in the past. He supported her career because he absolutely believed that women should play a part in the Church.

How would you describe the dark side of Karl Rahner?

Certainly, Fr. Rahner suffered much in his life. He suffered when he was a professor in Innsbruck, although he was to blame for that. If he went away for a lecture engagement, when he returned he would proceed to lecture for an hour and then was known to say that: "Since we have lost much time while I was gone, let's continue for another hour." The result of this was that the professor who was to lecture after him was left standing at the door of the lecture hall and was not able to have his assigned hour. Of course, that was not a good thing to do. Every professor on the faculty knew that Fr. Rahner was a genius, but in terms of life in the community that was something else. One cannot continually genuflect before Fr. Rahner. Fr. Rahner felt a constant sense of rejection and a refusal to recognize him. It was a custom in the Jesuit community to celebrate a new publication from a member of the community with a glass of schnapps. So when Fr. Rahner had a new publication it was celebrated. One of the Jesuits remarked – half jokingly: "So Fr. Rahner did you incubate an egg again?" Fr. Rahner, obviously insulted said: "All right, if you don't want to celebrate – then forget it." And he left! He was easily offended.

Then came the controversy with Rome. Obviously it is irritating not to be recognized when you believe that you have earned that right. Then there were differences of opinion with some of his colleagues such as Professor Schmaus in Munich and other influential theologians. There was also the criticism he suffered on the part of his disciples. Wherever one looks, I must say that as much as he had his admirers, the admiration from his professional colleagues was always somewhat restrained and mixed with criticism and reservations. From that perspective, he often felt isolated and lonely. I believe that that was also one of the reasons why he sought, again and again, to have contact with young people, because he felt that they were non-judgmental and he also experienced greater recognition.

NOTES

1   Franz Schupp, born 1936, Dr. theol., Dr. phil., a Jesuit from 1960-1976, Professor for Dogmatic Theology at the University of Innsbruck; since 1979 Professor for Philosophy at the University in Paderborn.

2   Cf. Karl Rahner's last statement. Interview with Wolfgang Pfaundler, in: *das fenster*. Tiroler Kulturzeitschrift 18 (1984) Heft 34/35, 3418-3422, 3419: "And because I am so old and because the world will remain as it is, I will experience my final hour here and will be buried in Tirol, and I can say, that's completely fine with me"; now in: K. Rahner, *Sämtliche Werke*, vol. 31: Im Gespräch über Kirche und Gesellschaft. Interviews und Stellungnahmen. Bearbeitet von Albert Raffelt (Freiburg: Herder, 2007) 442-451. – Cf. also Andreas R. Batlogg, Wo, bitte, geht's hier zum Karl-Rahner Platz? Die Innsbrucker Jahre Karl Rahners SJ, in: *das fenster*. Tiroler Kulturzeitschrift 28 (1994) Heft 57, 5508-5510.

3   Cf. *Mein Problem*. Karl Rahner antwortet jungen Menschen (Freiburg: Herder, 1982). Ibid., K. Rahner, *Is Chrisitan Life Possible Today?* English translation by Salvator Attanasio (New Jersey: Dimension Books,1984).

4   Cf. K. Rahner, *I Remember*. An Autobiographical Interview with Meinhold Krauss, translated by Harvey D. Egan, SJ (Crossroad: New York, 1985) 64-65: "Ottavaviani was a Roman canonist, a church lawyer. At that time he directed the Holy Office now called the Congregation for the Doctrine of the Faith. He styled himself a watchdog of the Holy See. Naturally, he had a somewhat old-fashioned theology, which he regarded as self-evident. Hence, he objected to this and that in my theology. But personally he was actually a splendid fellow. He founded or directed an orphanage on his own initiative. He was personally very nice. He once took me in his

Mercedes from Innsbruck to Munich for a Eucharistic Congress. We said the rosary in Latin together and didn't discuss church politics at all. During the Council, when he was the head of the theological commission for the Council, to which I belonged as a *peritus,* he once said to me: 'Well, we have absolutely nothing against you. You see, this extraordinary Roman censor is a special privilege by which we wish to protect you from misunderstandings of dumb friends.' Then I said: 'Your Eminence, I renounce privileges.' And since then, there hasn't actually been anything more. They even invited me to visit the old, retired prefect of the Congregation, but I didn't go. In the old days one experienced and interpreted these things differently, even in the Congregation itself. Perhaps at the time they considered me a rash and wild theologian who needed his knuckles rapped. But that had nothing at all to do with personal animosity or the like. To be sure, certain things did happen that absolutely shouldn't have."

5   Joseph Ratzinger, born 1927, Professor of Dogmatic Theology and one of the young *periti* of the Council, was named Archbishop of Munich and Freising in 1977 and in the same year was made a Cardinal. In the fall of 1981, Pope John Paul II named him Prefect of the Congregation for the Doctrine of the Faith in Rome, a function he held for 24 years. On April 16, 2005, Ratzinger was elected pope and took the name Benedict XVI.

6   Cf. K. Rahner, *Bekenntnisse.* Rückblick auf 80 Jahre (Wien: Herold, 1984) 42 f.: "Metz was the number one choice of the theology faculty in Munich to succeed Heinrich Fries. The Cardinal in conjunction with Hans Maier, who also was not in favor of Metz, saw to it that Metz was bypassed by the Ministerium in the selection process. That was juridically correct, but the question is whether the Ministerium is qualified to decide which theology is better. With regard to the Cardinal, as a private theologian, he has the right to like or not like the Political Theology of Metz. But in this case, in my opinion, he exceeded the competency which a bishop has in this matter of the selection of a candidate to a professorship to a public university. The bishop has the right to test the orthodoxy and the quality of the person's moral life when a theologian is being considered for a faculty position. In both of these matters, he could not be opposed to Metz. I wrote Ratzinger an 'Open Letter' regarding the proposed choice of Metz for the faculty in Munich. It appeared in *Publik-Forum* and Ratzinger, in all fairness, rejected my opinion. He did not agree with it, of course, but he invited me once to have dinner with him and then arranged for a chauffer to take me home. Before dinner we spoke about this matter for about an hour but nothing came of it."

7   Leo Scheffczyk (1920-2005), Professor of Dogmatic Theology in Tübingen, from 1965 in Munich, became a Cardinal in 2001.

8   Schwabing is a neighborhood of Munich in which many students live.

9   Cf. Oscar Bettschart, Schriften zur Theologie – Rückbesinnung eines Verlegers, in: Paul Imhof, Hubert Biallowons (eds.), *Karl Rahner – Bilder eines Lebens* (Freiburg: Herder, 1985) 54-56.

10   K. Rahner, *Bekenntnisse*, 41 f.: "During the Council Ratzinger was a young, progressive theological advisor to Cardinal Frings. In order to defeat a preconciliar schema, we cooperated on drafting a document, which was presented to the German, Belgian and the French Bishops' Conferences. They promoted our proposal in order to demonstrate to the Council that one could be a good Catholic despite not speaking in preconciliar terminology. Our common proposal soon found its way into the recycling bin, but that is not to say that the loss was a great misfortune. Nonetheless it did have the benefit of bringing about the disappearance of the schemas produced by the Roman theologians. The Council produced its declarations, decrees and constitutions itself in the various commissions. That was perhaps the critical issue at the beginning of the Council and on that point Ratzinger and I were of one heart and one spirit. Whether he would still think so today, I don't know. Perhaps he would say we were caught up in the euphoria of the Council and moved in a direction which proved to be a dead end. Outside of this we did not have a great deal to do with one another at the Council for the simple reason that I was in the Theological Commission and Ratzinger was in a different commission."

11   This event was subsequently documented in: Walter Rahberger, Hanjo Sauer (eds.), *Vermittlung im Fragment*. Franz Schupp als Lehrer der Theologien (Regensburg: Pustet, 2003) 211-279: Zum Begriff "Offenbarung." Gemeinsame Vorlesung von Franz Schupp und Karl Rahner im Wintersemester 1972/73.

12   Heinrich Schlier (1900-1978).

13   Cf. K. Rahner, The Presence of Christ in the Sacrament of the Lord's Supper, in: K. Rahner, *Theological Investigations*, vol. 4, translated by Kevin Smyth (London: Darton, Longman & Todd, 1966) 287-311, esp. 296-306.

14   Cf. e.g., K. Rahner, Theologisches zum Monogenismus, in: *Zeitschrift für Katholische Theologie* 76 (1954) 1-18, 187-223; ibid., Erbsünde und Monogenismus, in: Karl-Heinz Weger (ed.), *Theologie der Erbsünde* (Quaestiones Disputatae 44) (Freiburg: Herder, 1970) 176-223; cf. also K. Rahner, *Sämtliche Werke*, vol. 15: Verantwortung der Theologie. Im Dialog mit Naturwissenschaften und Gesellschaftstheorie. Bearbeitet von Hans-Dieter Mutschler (Freiburg: Herder, 2002).

15   Herlinde Pissarek-Hudelist, (1932-1994), since 1984 Professor for Catechetics and Religious Education at the University of Innsbruck, was worldwide the first Academic Dean of a Catholic Theology Faculty (1989-

1993). Cf. Günther Bader, Martha Heizer (eds.), *Theologie erden*. Erinnerungen an Herlinde Pissarek-Hudelist (Thaur: Kulturverlag, 1996).

PART FOUR

KARL RAHNER'S PERSONALITY

17

ONLY THE LITTLE SISTER WITH WHOM ONE COULD NOT CARRY ON AN INTELLIGENT CONVERSATION?

IN CONVERSATION WITH ELISABETH CREMER AND FRANZ JOHNA, MERZHAUSEN

Elisabeth Cremer (1909-2004, nee Rahner, Dr. phil., was Karl Rahner's younger sister. She lived the final years of her life with her son in Merzhausen near Freiburg.

Franz Johna, born 1929, Translator and Editor of spiritual books, was an Editor at Herder Publishing, Freiburg, until 1994.

Ms. Cremer, when you think about your brother Karl, what comes to your mind?

We were a family of seven children. Karl was five years older than I. My father was a secondary school teacher and my mother took in boarders, whom my father would tutor to help supplement the family income. At the time a difference of five years in age was substantial. Karl certainly perceived me as a little sister with whom he could not carry on an intelligent conversation. Once he even called me a simpleton. I was not someone with whom he discussed things. But it was not in his personality to speak much. He was very reserved: of all the siblings he said the least.

(*Franz Johna:*) But still, I recall that later on your brother Karl developed the closest relationship with you of all the siblings. When he came to the publishing house in Freiburg, before he continued on his way, he seldom said that he wanted to pay a brief visit to his sister Ms. Deppe, in Herdern,[1] but rather he almost always said: "Let's drive quickly to Merzhausen."

(*Elisabeth Cremer:*) But he was always in a hurry. He liked to play with the children. I have four boys, but he could not be demonstrably affectionate. My mother lived in an old age home in her later years and she always regretted that Karl seldom had conversations of a spiritual nature with her. I had the impression that he could do that with other people much more easily than he could with his own family. My mother was very interested in these things and she would have liked to have spoken to him about spirituality, but Karl was always very, very reserved. He was extraordinarily willing to be of service. When my brother Hugo died, Karl was there immediately for the funeral. He was also there for my husband's funeral and at the time took an active part in responding to the needs of the family. One of my sons, Thomas, broke through Karl's cool reserve. Thomas always had many problems and wanted to speak about them with his uncle Karl. He found in Karl someone truly compassionate.

(*Franz Johna:*) I recall vividly how once, Fr. Rahner, after a visit with Ms. Cremer, proudly stated that Thomas is a medical doctor in Heidelberg. He was very happy about that.

(*Elisabeth Cremer:*) That's something I really want to stress again: Karl was always there, but he did not say very much.

Was that generally the case when Fr. Rahner came for a visit? Was he also so reserved with the other siblings?

(*Elisabeth Cremer:*) Yes, it's true that within the family he was reluctant to carry on a conversation. I had the impression that he was much more open with strangers. Once he held a lecture here in Freiburg. Many of his female fans came and one of them said that she would write to him. Because I knew that he always complained about the stack of letters he received with their many questions, I said: "I don't know if you are going to have any luck. Karl always has many letters to reply to." After some time I met this woman again and she told me that he answered her immediately.

(*Franz Johna:*) Yes, that was his way. As far as I know he left no letter unanswered. There were always letters sent to the publisher with the request, "please forward to Fr. Rahner." In spite of the many obligations to the many publishers or to Catholic academic conferences who besieged him; despite many questions from journalists; from radio or television broadcasters seeking an interview, an article and many other things; he did not neglect the personal side. I remember a time when my wife and I were visiting Colmar and the Albert Schweitzer house

in Kayserberg with Fr. Rahner. It was not our first trip with Fr. Rahner. He was always drawn to Alsace when he was in Freiburg. Our first
stop was the Unterlinden Museum in Colmar. My wife was buying
the tickets and he had already hastened into the museum to view the
Isenheimer Altar in the rear. After about five minutes he came to us
and said that we should continue our tour and take our time; he would
make himself comfortable in the foyer. We somewhat rapidly ended
our visit and returned to the entrance. Fr. Rahner was sitting, relaxed
in a chair, observing the comings and goings of the visitors and next to
him were two or three postcards on which he had written a greeting
to good friends.

(*Elisabeth Cremer:*) He sent postcards often, mostly with a short
"Greeting!" But when you wrote to him about some serious concern,
then he formulated his position in his letters with great precision,
clearly having given it serious thought. He also officiated at my wedding.

**Why did Karl officiate and not your brother Hugo who was also a
Jesuit and a priest?**

That happened in the middle of the Second World War. Hugo was
not able to come. The Theology Faculty in Innsbruck was seized by
the Nazis and the Jesuits received an invitation from the Bishop of
Sitten (Sion) in Wallis to come there. All the international students in
theology went there. At that time Jesuits were forbidden in Switzerland, so Pope Pius XI released all the Jesuits from their vows so that
they could remain in Switzerland as secular priests. At that time Karl
was with another part of the faculty in Vienna. He was there more
in the capacity of a pastoral minister and he was able to come to our
wedding.[2]

**Did Hugo's being a Jesuit influence Karl's decision to enter the
same Order?**

Karl has always said that our brother's decision to become a Jesuit had
nothing to do with his choice.[3] That was typical of him. My parents
heard about his desire to join the Jesuits from his religion teacher.[4]
The teacher visited my parents and told them that he actually was not
in favor of Karl's entering the Jesuits, but Karl presented his decision

to our parents as an accomplished fact.[5] Three weeks after his graduation from high school he entered the novitiate in Feldkirch (Austria).

What did you mean by saying that the way he came to decide and announce his decision to enter the Jesuits was "typical" for Karl?

It was not part of Karl's personality to be open and forthcoming. He could be very critical.

(*Franz Johna:*) Fr. Rahner had a certain dry, sober charm, I would say. He was not effusive or wildly enthusiastic, but very, very correct and straight forward, but still completely charming and cordial.

Apparently your brother had great energy and will power and could work with great concentration. Were you sometimes surprised that he was so diligent?

One of my sons once went with Karl and a few other Jesuits to my sister-in law's vacation house in Spain. Karl had wanted to go away for a vacation, but he adhered to a very strict, self-imposed discipline that required him to work a certain number of hours with full concentration before he would relax. When he fulfilled his self-imposed quota then he could relax and be on vacation.

(*Franz Johna:*) I can testify to his work discipline. Even in his later years when he was working on his manuscript for *Foundations of Christian Faith* and wanted to finish it, he came to Freiburg and stayed at a hotel near the publishing house. Every day, punctually at 9:30 a.m., a secretary, as had been previously arranged by the publisher, was at his place and he dictated his work, walking back and forth, nearly without taking a break until 12: 30 p.m. It demanded great concentration and strict discipline in order to formulate the often difficult theological arguments and simultaneously to dictate them in such a way that they were ready to be published. During this time he would periodically ask the secretary: "How many pages are there now?" or "How long have we been at the dictation – two hours?" When he finished his work quota then he felt relieved and content.

In 1936, when Professor Martin Honecker would not accept Karl Rahner's philosophical doctoral dissertation,[6] did the family en-

courage Karl to change some things so that Honecker would accept it?

(*Elisabeth Cremer*:) The family did not say anything about that. Even if they did, Karl would still have stubbornly gone his own way; he would not be swayed by what others said. It was not even an issue for him that he should oblige Professor Honecker by changing anything in order to finish his doctoral work, but it turned out that it was not even necessary.[7] Karl had finished his doctoral thesis in theology in Innsbruck and became a university lecturer in Dogmatic Theology. Soon after the Nazi's came to power, Hugo, who had been professor of Church History since 1937, left for Switzerland in the fall of 1938 and Karl went to Vienna one year later.

Am I wrong in my impression that he got along very well with Hugo and was not only his "little brother?"

(*Elisabeth Cremer*:) The two of them appreciated one another and had a good relationship.[8] In the course of time the stature of each naturally shifted. At first, Hugo was the more famous, the more important and the more recognized of the two. Hugo and Karl published a few things together. When our father turned 60, they presented him with their first scholarly publication in a *Festschrift*. Unfortunately, I have never seen it. There is only one copy of it and it has been entrusted to the Karl Rahner archives in Innsbruck.[9] Later on, both of them amused themselves about the first "children" of their intellectual activity.[10]

So there was no competition between Hugo and Karl?

No. At the beginning there was a kind of a joke, "Let's see who of us has published more at the end of the year." But Hugo became sick relatively early in life. He suffered with Parkinson's and had to give up teaching earlier than planned because his mobility was very limited due to the illness. He died shortly before Christmas in 1968. For his 100th birthday there was a wonderful article about him in *Stimmen der Zeit*.[11]

What concerns did Karl Rahner have? Did he ever mention that theology or the Church caused him to be concerned?

Naturally, he was critical of the Church just as one can be critical of one's own mother, but he never called her existence into question. He was unshakable in his fidelity to her and he knew: "I can express myself critically, but I cannot shake her foundations."

(*Franz Johna:*) Fr. Rahner could, it appeared to me, be upset about this or that curial matter or about typical Roman procedures, but as to the Church itself, she was for him something certain and unshakable: that one can say with certainty. To my knowledge, even when Pope Paul VI was the target of sharp and heated criticism, Karl Rahner would not participate in that. Of course, it ate away at him when, for example, he was told, in connection with the granting of an Imprimatur or in some other matter, that there were doubts about his loyalty to the Church or even about his orthodoxy. All that notwithstanding, it did not change anything with regard to his ultimate loyalty and fidelity to the Church.

But some of his publications were met with criticism on the part of Church leaders at the end of his life, such as those regarding "Quaestio Disputata, number 100," (1983) which he wrote with Heinrich Fries: *Unity in the Church."*

(*Franz Johna:*) Yes, there was some heated criticism about that, but that began much earlier in 1949 and 1951 with the article from *Theological Investigations* – "The Many Masses and the one Sacrifice."[12] Today one can wonder about those themes that were once considered so controversial.

(*Elisabeth Cremer:*) My grandmother went to the Cathedral every day at 9 a.m. and always came home very excited: "Five holy Masses I had today." At that time there were certain priests from the Archdiocesan Offices who celebrated their Mass at the side altars. She apparently went from one altar to the next where a priest was saying Mass. In those days Masses were, so to speak, "collected."

In Basel (Switzerland), a friend of mine told me that she once heard Karl Rahner lecture there and he was very well received. It may be

true that his writing was difficult to understand, but hearing him speak apparently made a deep impression on many people.

Karl once received some kind of prize for his literary skills.[13]

(*Franz Johna:*) That was in Tübingen. Fr. Rahner could present his ideas in a very creative fashion. It is important to distinguish between scholarly theological reflection and religious existential meditation. He possessed a special gift which gave him the ability to be articulate in both genres, and a way of formulating ideas that did not fear challenging the reader.[14] In the last twenty years of his life he received pressure from many sides to write more books and articles and he seldom found that he could refuse. So he paid less and less attention to the editing and his written work became more complicated and difficult to understand.

I have already mentioned how in his last years he, after much thought and concentration, would dictate a manuscript. The final, formal and reader-friendly version Fr. Rahner gladly left to others to produce. Many people always wanted something from him, which they often got, sometimes with some grumbling. I say that from personal experience. Fr. Rahner was open to suggestions. When I, for example, presented him with the idea of a "small theological meditation series" whose uniqueness consisted in the relationship between theological reflection and religious meditation on the central themes of faith, for an audience of spiritually interested readers, he not only welcomed this idea, but made a little notation for himself and it was not long before a manuscript arrived from him, *Was heisst Jesus lieben?*, (1982) or *Was heisst Auferstehung?*[15] But as much as he was able to turn the idea of a series into a concrete reality, still the editor had to contend with page long paragraphs and long sentences.

(*Elisabeth Cremer:*) That comes from the Latin. He had to teach his classes in Latin in Innsbruck.

(*Franz Johna:*) That comes from the Latin, certainly, and from the fact that in simultaneously reflecting and dictating, he could not pay very much attention to form. He expected help from the editor, which we gladly provided. Fr. Rahner always said to me: "Please look at that critically and shape that a little." So we carefully examined his manuscripts, provided them with subtitles and insertions, subdivided them into meaningful units and most significantly broke down the long sentences to make them more understandable, however without any

changes as to their content. He always received the final version before
it went to press and sometimes he made additions. Fr. Rahner was
grateful for this help.

(*Elisabeth Cremer:*) Hugo once allegedly said that when he retired,
he would translate Karl into decent German. Karl did not take offense
at that.

**Did Fr. Rahner ever express the wish to have a secretary or an as-
sistant who would help him with the editing of the text?**

(*Franz Johna:*) He always had very good assistants. I can recall the time
when Karl Lehmann was with him. His broad knowledge of literature
and his meticulous precision stood Fr. Rahner in good stead at the
time of his greatest productivity. He provided the finishing touches to
many of Fr. Rahner's manuscripts. This is not to diminish the importance of the work of his other assistants, Fr. Roman Bleistein and Fr.
Paul Imhof.

**When I, in the fall of 1981, came to Innsbruck for doctoral studies,
I heard that Karl Rahner might possibly move from Munich back
to Innsbruck. Apparently he came with a tape measure to measure
the rooms to see whether there was enough room for his books.
Why did he return to Tirol?**

(*Franz Johna:*) I believe that in the last analysis he was no longer comfortable in Munich. Once I visited Fr. Rahner late in the morning in
Munich, in the Kaulbachstrasse, and he took me to the refectory for
the noon meal, where all the Jesuits were already gathered. It was like
a cafeteria. I was not familiar with the concept of self-service – getting
one's tray, plate and silverware, standing in line for soup, getting one's
meal from the kitchen staff, finally finding a place to eat and at the end
bringing one's dishes to the counter as Fr. Rahner had instructed me.
The atmosphere was somber; everyone knew everyone else, but did
not pay particular attention to one another. It was clear to me why Fr.
Rahner gladly took advantage of the opportunity of having a visitor
in order to go out somewhere else for a leisurely meal. On another
occasion I visited him on a late Friday afternoon. He was at his desk,
but finished quickly as it was time to leave for the restaurant to which
I had invited him for dinner. He noticed that he had a button missing

on his pants and disconcertedly said to me: "On Friday afternoon one may not accidentally lose a button," and he went to change his pants. On the weekend everything was shut down. He was somewhat bemused by that and felt somewhat helpless.

(*Elisabeth Cremer:*) But one can sew on a button oneself!

(*Franz Johna:*) Naturally, but that's what he couldn't do. I had the feeling that he did not like that feeling of isolation; that no one seemed to take much notice of another; that each person buried himself in his work. It may be that he experienced Innsbruck differently and saw himself more at home there; that there was more togetherness. The older he became the more poignantly he experienced the feeling of being on one's own, left to fend for oneself, at least on the weekend. It limited his activity.

Mr. Johna, did you also have the opportunities to experience Fr. Rahner's spiritual side?

(*Franz Johna:*) He was a pious man, but very reserved about that.

(*Elisabeth Cremer:*) Karl always said that the pious person of tomorrow must be a mystic.[16] I believe, that was a reference to his form of piety.

(*Franz Johna:*) Yes, a deep inner piety. That's why he was so critical of certain prominent pious practices – for example, the growing cult of apparitions.

(*Elisabeth Cremer:*) I still recall that he once stated that if one were to critically examine everything that the Mother of God allegedly said in those apparitions in terms of their theological correctness, one would find many heresies.

(*Franz Johna:*) But he was completely open to religious customs. My wife and I were visiting a church with Fr. Rahner in the late afternoon. The empty church was almost completely dark; the only light came from a few votive candles burning at the Marian altar. Fr. Rahner was the first to finish the walk around the church and stood before the Marian altar to light a candle. My wife reached for her purse and wanted to do the same, but Fr. Rahner restrained her hand and said "Let it be, one is enough ...!" It is one of my memories of Fr. Rahner which I will never forget.[17]

Mr. Johna, did you also have contact with Fr. Rahner of a more private nature?

He often came, and I think gladly, to our house. It did him good to be included in a family circle in the evening or at noon; to sit with us at our table. Then he would suddenly say to our son, who was 12 or 14 years old at the time: "Robert, show me your room!" And soon he lay stretched out on the bed, his jacket and shoes off, our son nearby at his desk. When our son was studying Latin in school, he asked him once impishly: "What is this?" Then he wrote a Latin sentence on a napkin that can be loosely translated as "Through the rosy cheeks of a woman great evil comes into the world."[18]

Another time he asked our son and daughter after supper: "Do you know of a sentence in which not a single vowel is present?" We all said, there is not a German sentence without a vowel. Thereupon he wrote on a napkin: "Wnn d nch Frbg ghst, dnn bst d dhm – Wenn Du nach Freiburg gehst, dann bist du daheim" ("When you go to Freiburg, then you are home.") Here is the napkin. Fr. Rahner liked children; he himself possessed a kind of childlike curiosity.

I once heard that he, when he had a visit from an African or from an American, would immediately take out an atlas and ask his visitor to show him on the map where he came from. Apparently he always had an atlas at hand.

(*Elisabeth Cremer:*) Karl truly had this genuine, childlike curiosity. Once he went into a department store with a fellow Jesuit priest and seeing the perfume bottles, he began to open them, one after another to smell them. One had to restrain him from opening them all.

(*Franz Johna:*) When he sat in the car, he would question whether we should have made a turn because he always followed the route on the map he was holding. Once he told me, as we were taking a trip by car, that if he were to come into the world a second time, there were two things that he had missed that he would do – learn to drive a car and learn to speak fluent English.

(*Elisabeth Cremer:*) He probably could understand English better than he could speak it. Academic language and colloquial language are two different things.

(*Franz Johna:*) He was able to read and understand an English text, but because of the increasing internationalization of theology, German began to take a back seat to English. Fr. Rahner felt a need to become more proficient in English because of that.

Fr. Rahner always answered letters very conscientiously. What do you want to say about the published letters of Luise Rinser?

(*Elisabeth Cremer:*) My God, what should I say about that? First of all, in my opinion, he had an absolute right to a friendship, also to a friendship with a woman. But Luise Rinser shamelessly exploited that. When I deeply befriend someone then I don't do something like that.

(*Franz Johna:*) In the meantime the discussion about that has died down. Whoever knew Fr. Rahner personally realized that too much was being read into his relationship with Luise Rinser. Fr. Rahner was a trusting person and kept up his friendships. I, myself, saw how he would address a postcard: "Heartfelt greetings." For him that was a matter of politeness and regard. One needs to put these things in perspective. He would send me a card even when it was only from Feldberg in the Black Forest. He wanted to give others a little joy. Friendships meant a great deal to him and this is how he kept them up.

(*Elisabeth Cremer:*) Luise Rinser always needed to have a relationship with important people. Before Karl, there was the Dalai Lama. She would even stand at the reception desk of the Jesuit residence in Innsbruck and ask for Karl Rahner. Maybe she took it as a sign of love if he came.

Luise Rinser was a married woman and her husband was a famous composer.[19] She always tried to be connected in some way to an important and successful man. Karl might have seen that coming, that situation with the letters. The letters that were published were only her letters to him. Not his to her.

(*Franz Johna:*) The Jesuits had the right of publication and they would not allow his letters to be published.

Mr. Johna, do you have any mementos of Karl Rahner?

I have photocopies of some of his high school essays which I received for the preparation of the volume, *Bilder eines Leben* ("Images of a Life") which are very interesting. Among them one finds thoughts about the time in which they were written. One essay comes from the year 1919: "Last Sunday we celebrated the anniversary of the German November Revolution. Some were happy that the princes were deposed. That was the main theme of the speeches on that day and that higher salaries would be paid. Still others remembered with quiet sadness the olden days, when postal service and trains still functioned and when one could still buy coal." They are very touching essays.

(*Elisabeth Cremer:*) In the past it was common to give essays as homework assignments. My youngest brother would let Hugo, in Innsbruck, know the topic when he had to write an essay for homework.

(*Franz Johna:*) The title on the cover of the notebook of Karl Rahner's essays reads: "*Realgymnasium mit Oberrealschule*, Freiburg i. Br., School year 1919-1920." Karl Rahner was 15 at the time.

I also have a manuscript of a lecture that Fr. Rahner gave in Mainz: "Followers of the Crucified."[20] I thought to use that as a small volume in the series that I have already referred to as "Small Theological Meditations." Fr. Rahner sent the manuscript with a note saying: "Enclosed, as previously agreed, I am sending you a copy of my lecture given in Mainz. If it meets with your approval and you think it fits with the other lectures in the series and would make a significant volume, then I would be pleased." This text also needed much editing work; it was hardly divided into sections or subheadings and one sentence ran into the next. Fr. Rahner assumed we would be doing the necessary editing work which we were glad to do as every manuscript of his was valuable to the publishing house. I think he was confident that he was entrusting his manuscripts into capable hands. That was the wonderful part of our collaboration with Fr. Rahner: much of value and lasting merit came about because of close, trusted teamwork. It was a great joy for all involved, the publishing house and for me, not least of all, and it pleased Fr. Rahner.

NOTES

1 Referred to is Karl Rahner's older sister, Anna Maria Charlotte Deppe (1897-1987), nee Rahner.

2 For background see Hugo Rahner, Die Geschichte eines Jahrhunderts. Ein Jubiläum der Theologischen Fakultät der Universität Innsbruck 1857-1957, in: *Zeitschrift für Katholische Theologie* 80 (1958) 1-65; Karl H. Neufeld, *Die Brüder Rahner. Eine Biographie* (Freiburg: Herder, 2nd edition

2004); ibid., "Aufhebung" und Weiterleben der Theologischen Fakultät Innsbruck (1938-1945). Fakten, Reaktionen und Hintergründe während des Zweiten Weltkriegs, in: *Zeitschrift für Katholische Theologie* 119 (1997) 27-50; Andreas R. Batlogg, Die Theologische Fakultät Innsbruck zwischen "Anschluss" und Aufhebung (1938), in: *Zeitschrift für Katholische Theologie* 120 (1998) 164-183; ibid., In die Pflicht genommen: Im Wiener Seelsorgeamt, in: ibid., Paul Rulands, Walter Schmolly, Roman A. Siebenrock, Günther Wassilowsky, Arno Zahlauer, *Der Denkweg Karl Rahners*. Quellen – Entwicklungen – Perspektiven (Mainz: Matthias Grünewald, 2nd edition 2004) 144-157.

3 Cf. K. Rahner, Erinnerungen im Gespräch mit Meinold Krauss (Freiburg: Herder 1984) 36 f. – See also K. Rahner, I Remember: An autobiographical interview with Meinold Krauss, translated by Harvey D. Egan (New York: Crossroad, 1985), 36: "Alemannian Germans do not speak much about such things, even with brothers they especially like. He became a Jesuit. I would say that certainly made my decision easier somehow. But I don't attribute great significance to my brother's example for my decision. I remember now trembling as I informed him – by letter, since he was already in the Order, having entered three years ahead of me – that I also wanted to be a Jesuit. I saw him once, I believe, when he was in the novitiate, and also in Valkenburg, Holland, where he studied philosophy. But I would still maintain that this didn't play a direct, decisive role." – Now in: K. Rahner, *Sämtliche* Werke, vol. 25: Erneuerung des Ordenslebens. Zeugnis für Kirche und Welt. Bearbeitet von Andreas R. Batlogg (Freiburg: Herder, 2008) 85-143, 100.

4 The religion teacher was Meinrad Vogelbacher (1879-1965). Hugo, like Karl, remained in close contact with him throughout his life. Vogelbacher had studied in Rome and lived in the "Collegium Germanicum et Hungaricum," under the direction of the Jesuits.

5 K. Rahner, *I Remember*, 26: "At first I told my parents nothing about my plans to become a Jesuit. The Alemannian Germans of my region are rather reserved in this regard. They don't speak easily about things like that. As it happened, my parents learned of my intention from my religion teacher. He said: 'No, Karl isn't suited for that. He should become something else.' Well, by God, it happened all the same, and has lasted for sixty years." See also K. Rahner, *Sämtliche Werke*, vol. 25, 93 f.

6 A Jesuit since 1922, Karl Rahner was destined for a teaching career as a professor for the History of Philosophy by his superiors in the Society of Jesus. He was to teach at the Jesuit College in Pullach near Munich. For that role he needed a doctorate in philosophy. After his four years of theology, he was ordained to the priesthood (1932), and after a further year of formation ("tertiship") in Austria, he studied philosophy from 1934-

1936 in his native city of Freiburg. Among his professors there was Martin Heidegger. His thesis director was Martin Honecker.

7   Karl Rahner submitted his thesis, "The Metaphysics of finite knowledge in Thomas Aquinas," for preliminary evaluation to Professor Honecker in June of 1936 and traveled to Innsbruck, Austria, where he was promoted to Doctor of Theology, shortly before Christmas, 1936. In July 1937 he received a teaching position as instructor of Dogmatic Theology and the History of Dogma. Only in August of 1937, 14 months after he had left Freiburg, did he learn from Professor Honecker that he would accept his philosophical dissertation only if Rahner were to undertake certain revisions which Rahner, however, was not ready to do. Furthermore, he no longer needed the doctorate in philosophy since in the interim he had a teaching position on the theology faculty in Innsbruck. For the historical background see Karl H. Neufeld, *Die Brüder Rahner*, as well as Albert Raffelt, Editionsbericht, in: K. Rahner, *Sämtliche* Werke, vol. 2: Geist in Welt. Philosophische Schriften. Bearbeitet von Albert Raffelt (Freiburg: Herder, 1996) XIII-XXXVII, esp. XXIV-XXIX.

8   Cf. Abraham P Kustermann, Karl H. Neufeld (eds.), "Gemeinsame Arbeit in brüderlicher Liebe." Hugo und Karl Rahner. Dokumente und Würdigung ihrer Weggemeinschaft (Stuttgart: Akademie der Diözese Rottenburg-Stuttgart, 1993).

9   This commemorative volume comprising 375 pages, of which there is only one copy, is entitled *Sacra Historia*: "dedicated to our dear father for his 60th birthday, 1868-1928." It contains six essays by Hugo and five by Karl Rahner. It has to do with texts that were probably written during their early student days in the Society of Jesus; cf. Karl H. Neufeld, *Die Brüder Rahner*, 39-41.

10   Cf. Hugo Rahner, Eucharisticon fraternitatis, in: Johann Baptist Metz, Walter Kern, Adolf Darlap, Herbert Vorgrimler (eds.), *Gott in Welt* (Festschrift Karl Rahner), vol. 2 (Freiburg: Herder, 1964) 895-899.

11   Cf. Andreas R. Batlogg, Hugo Rahner als Mensch und Theologe, in: *Stimmen der Zeit* 213 (2000) 517-530.

12   A through evaluation of this article and the history of its reception in papal speeches and writings are found in the work of Georg Rheinbay, *Das ordentliche Lehramt in der Kirche. Die Konzeption Papst Pius XII. und das Modell Karl Rahners im Vergleich* (Trier: Paulinus, 1988).

13   On October 20, 1973, Karl Rahner was awarded the "Sigmund Freud prize for Academic Prose" by the German Academy for language and literature. Cf. Paul Imhof, Hubert Biallowons (eds.), *Karl Rahner – Bilder eines Lebens.* (Freiburg: Herder, 1985), 98. Cf. also Herbert Vorgrimler, *Karl Rahner, Gotteserfahrung im Leben und Denken.* (Darmstadt: Primus, 2004) 12. – The German Nobel prize winner for literature in 1972, Hein-

rich Böll, admired Rahner's powerful eloquence: cf. Heinrich Böll, Auf der Suche nach einer neuen Sprache, in: *Karl Rahner – Bilder eines Lebens*, 97-98.

14   Cf. also Franz K. Mayr, Vermutungen zu Karl Rahners Sprachstil, in: Herbert Vorgrimler (ed.), *Wagnis Theologie*. Erfahrungen mit der Theologie Karl Rahners (Freiburg: Herder, 1979) 143-159.

15   This text has been published posthumously; cf. Karl Rahner, *Was heisst Auferstehung?* Meditationen zu Karfreitag und Ostern, edited by Albert Raffelt (Freiburg: Herder, 1985).

16   Cf. K. Rahner, Frömmigkeit früher und heute, in: ibid., *Schriften zur Theologie*, vol. 7 (Einsiedeln: Benziger, 1966) 11-31, 22 f. – See also, ibid., "Christian Living formerly and today," in: ibid., *Theological Investigations*, vol. 7, translated by David Burke (New York: Herder and Herder, 1971) 3-24, 15: "Simply in order to make it clear what is meant here, and in the consciousness that the concept of 'mysticism' is a loaded one (rightly understood it is not the opposite of belief in the Holy Pneuma but rather identical with it) it could be said: the devout Christian of the future will either be a 'mystic,' one who has 'experienced' something, or he will cease to be anything at all. For devout Christian living as practiced in the future will no longer be sustained and helped by the unanimous, manifest and public convictions and religious customs of all, summoning each one from the outset to a personal experience and a personal decision. For this reason, therefore, the usual religious education as practiced hitherto can only provide a very secondary kind of formation or preparation for the institutional element in the religion of the future. The mystical approach of which we are speaking must impart the correct 'image of God,' based upon the accepted experience of man's basic orientation to God, the experience that the basis of man's existence is the abyss: that God is essentially the inconceivable; that his inconceivability grows, and yet does not detract from the fact that the more rightly God is understood the more nearly does his self-bestowing love touch us; the experience that in mapping the course of one's life one can never confine God to specific points in it without being brought up against the fact that when one does so, the sum fails to come out right; the experience that he becomes our 'happiness' only when we pray to him and love him unconditionally; ..."

17   Cf. Franz Johna, Eine reicht ... Persönliche Erinnerung an Karl Rahner, in: *Christ in der Gegenwart* 56 (2004) 95. – A story very similar to this is reported by a former doctoral student and friend of Rahner. It happened during the last weeks of Rahner's life: "When I wanted to do the same, he brushed my hand aside and said: 'One candle is enough.'" (Leo J. O'Donovan, Licht für das Geheimnis, in: *Karl Rahner – Bilder eines Lebens*, 132-135, 135).

18 "Mala mali malo mala maxima peperit mundo."

19 Luise Rinser was married to composer, Carl Orff, from 1953-1959. The marriage ended in divorce.

20 Cf. K. Rahner, Nachfolge des Gekreuzigten, in: ibid., *Schriften zur Theologie*, vol. 13 (Zürich: Benziger, 1978) 188-203; now in: ibid., *Sämtliche Werke*, vol. 29: Geistliche Schriften. Bearbeitet von Herbert Vorgrimler (Freiburg: Herder, 2007) 243-254; see ibid., Following the Crucified, in: ibid., *Theological Investigations*, vol. 18, translated by Edward Quinn (New York: Crossroad, 1983) 157-170.

18

PRIEST AND PIOUS CHRISTIAN

IN CONVERSATION WITH FR. KLAUS EGGER, INNSBRUCK

Klaus Egger, Dr. theol., born 1934, 1969-1979 Rector of the Diocesan Seminary in Innsbruck, 1979-1989 Professor of Religious Pedagogy at the Pedagogical Academy and Honorary Professor on the Theology Faculty of Innsbruck, 1989-1998 Vicar General of the Diocese of Innsbruck. From 1998-2009 he was the Bishop's Vicar for Religious Orders. He is still active as a Retreat Director.

How did you come to know Karl Rahner?

I first came to know him when I was a server at Mass in the Jesuit Church. I knew him as a priest who was very withdrawn, but celebrated Mass very piously. But he was also known as someone who, it was said, would one day be a very famous professor – this was the beginning of the 1950's. Hugo Rahner[1] was already a well know professor and it was said that his brother would also one day become very famous.

The next time I encountered Karl Rahner was at a lecture. He walked back and forth in front of the lecture hall, as was his custom, and when he saw me, he recognized me as a former altar boy and said to me: "How are you?" I told him that I had just come back from Belgium where I had studied Fundamental Theology for a year in Louvain. He responded by saying: "Ah, then you may be able to help me. I have an article on 'Ätiologie' in the new *Lexikon für Theologie und Kirche*. Not much has been written on this by us in German. Do you know of anything that has come from the French speaking world of theology?" It just so happened that I had a professor in Louvain who worked in that area, Fr. Gustave Lambert, SJ,[2] and I told Fr. Rahner about this and he referenced that article in the *Lexikon*.[3] That impressed me no end. Fr. Rahner had trusted me with a task even though he had only known

258 ENCOUNTERS WITH KARL RAHNER

me as a Mass server who was a novice in the area of theology. From that point on I began a personal relationship with him.

What did that entail specifically?

For about three or four years, I went with him every week to the sauna, which was in the diocesan seminary. Fr. Rahner wanted someone who would pick him up, go with him up the hill to the seminary, reserve a room for him where he could rest following the sauna and then would accompany him back to the Jesuit residence. That would take place, I believe on Tuesdays, which I called the "Rahner day." It sometimes took an hour for us to go from the Jesuit residence to the seminary because he would always stop along the way to gaze in amazement at everything he saw. We did not talk much about theology; he simply took in the world about him – the traffic, the lampposts – such things like that. What was especially nice was that every time he came he would bring a reprint of some article that he had published for the seminarian whose room he would use to rest in after the sauna and wrote in it: "With thanks, the author." That was my first experience of him of a more personal nature.

Then, as the Rector of the Diocesan Seminary, I invited him two or three times to lecture at the Rector's conferences. He always was very accommodating.

I can think of another incident: I was preparing for my doctorate and I still had to do the *rigorosum* (an oral comprehensive exam) in Dogma.[4] I had already completed the oral exams in Scripture and in Moral Theology. At that time there was a rule that whoever has a *rigorosum* does not need to take exams every semester, because the exam requirement is counted in the *rigorosum* as completed. I was missing one exam with Fr. Rahner, because he was in Rome at the time and I couldn't reach him. Finally, I was able to reach him – this was about 1963-64, but he was very busy at the Council. I knocked on his door and asked whether I could disturb him for a moment. I told him that the Academic Dean, Engelbert Gutwenger, SJ, insisted that I take the test. Fr. Rahner protested that that was nonsense since I would be taking the *rigorosum*. I agreed, but told him that Fr. Gutwenger insisted on it. Then Fr. Rahner asked me: "Do you have the test certificate here?" I didn't have one with me; thereupon he left the room, knocked on the doors of several young Jesuit students and asked them for a test certificate. Then he asked me if I had studied and I answered yes. Then he wrote on the certificate: *valde bene* ("very good"). He added: Have a good *rigorosum*.

Then, there was another time that showed me how he valued me as a person. I was with him in his office and Walter Strolz, who worked for Tyrolia publishing in Innsbruck and who later switched to Herder publishing in Freiburg, telephoned him. At that time his work *Christian in the Market Place* had been published. Strolz needed some information. Fr. Rahner said rather curtly: "Keep it short, I have a visitor here with me." That, of course, made me feel very good.

Later, I had less contact with him, but I still would meet him occasionally. Then in the fall of 1981, I heard that he was planning to come back to Innsbruck. He was looking for a secretary and I knew Elfriede Oeggl from before. She asked me, at the time, for a letter of recommendation. She was finally chosen and was exceedingly happy about that. Fr. Rahner said to me: "First of all, I must say that she is the best secretary that I ever had. She can type as fast as I speak and I only took her because you recommended her."[5]

How did you experience Karl Rahner's piety?

In the last years of his life, every six or eight weeks, I would take a trip with him. During those times I got to know him simply as a human being. Occasionally, we would talk a little about theology, but he also spoke about his family, about his fellow Jesuits and the Council. Fr. Georg Sporschill, SJ, once told me that he was happy that he was able to talk to me about everyday things. I once went with him for three days to South Tirol for a vacation. We stayed overnight with a pastor friend who had a house chapel. Fr. Rahner said to me then: "You be the main celebrant; I can't do that so well anymore." He was always very human. What struck me during those trips – I always tried to choose a place to travel to where there would be an interesting church from an art-history perspective, or a work of art or something similar to view. We saw a great deal that was new to him. It impressed me that whenever we went into a church for the first ten minutes, he would kneel and pray as though absolutely no one else was there. Then he stood up and began to look at the church. It was always the same.

One time we went to see a church in South Tirol. In the back of the church was a statue of Mary, a Fatima Madonna, with a votive light stand. Fr. Rahner looked at it from top to bottom and then he began to search his pockets. I thought, at first, that he was looking for a handkerchief. Suddenly, he took out a coin, put it in the coin box and lit two candles. That impressed me very much: a world famous theologian lights candles before a Fatima Madonna. That experience was something precious to me, because I realized that I was experiencing him both as a priest and as a simple pious Christian.

You once published a story about a visit you made with Fr. Rahner to a Benedictine monastery in South Tirol.[6]

I knew the abbot of the Benedictine monastery, Marienberg in Vinschgau, and we wanted to go there. The night before our trip Fr. Rahner asked me if he could bring along a fellow Jesuit from America. That Jesuit was Fr. Walchers[7] who had shared the same dining room table with Pierre Teilhard de Chardin, SJ, for five years in Peking. The three of us drove to Marienberg. The abbot gave us a guided tour of the famous Angel crypt which was built in the 12th century and is certainly one of the most treasured in all of central Europe because of its paintings. The abbot showed us the back wall on which the heavenly Jerusalem is depicted with angels holding a banner upon which no words are written. The abbot asked Fr. Rahner whether he could imagine what possible words could have been written on the banner. Those who restored the frescos believed that there never were any words inscribed there. Fr. Rahner did not say anything. A little later the abbot asked him again because he thought that, perhaps, Fr. Rahner had not heard him the first time. But Fr. Rahner again did not respond. The next time I visited Marienberg, the abbot told me that two days after our visit he received a letter from Karl Rahner in which he wrote, and I am paraphrasing: "Dear Abbot, I would like to thank you very much for the guided tour of the crypt. Twice you asked me a question. I was so tired from the trip that at that time I could not answer. But your question stayed with me all the way back to Innsbruck: 'Why are there no words on the banner which the angels hold?' Then it came to me: those who, like the angels, behold the face of God, no longer have anything more to say."

I had a unique, personal relationship with him at this time. It was the end of March 1984, as he lay resting in the sanatorium in Hochrum near Innsbruck that I asked him whether he would preach at the 25th anniversary of my ordination at Easter. He said yes immediately. I then went to a conference of religious education teachers in Salzburg, but I was feeling apprehensive. I did not know that, in the meantime, Fr. Rahner had been transferred to the university hospital in Innsbruck. On a Saturday morning, at breakfast, one of the participants at the conference said that he heard on the radio that Karl Rahner had died. That news upset me so much that I couldn't even speak one word until that afternoon. I was simply rendered speechless. I then drove back home and immediately called Ms. Oeggl, who told me how Fr. Rahner had died.[8]

Fr. Rahner was buried in the crypt of the Jesuit Church. For two or three days the rosary for the departed was prayed in the evening. Almost all those present were Jesuits, but I also went to pray with them. Never before in my life had I experienced so poignantly how the act of the communal praying of the rosary could aide in saying farewell to someone who had died. By the time of the Requiem Mass held for Fr. Rahner, I found myself completely at peace.

I remembered that Fr. Rahner was once asked at a theological colloquium what he thought of the rosary. I was in the seminary from 1953-59; that was a time when it was taken for granted that you prayed the rosary daily. But also at that time we believed that we learned the fundamental liturgical forms from Fr. Josef Andreas Jungmann, SJ:[9] the other liturgical practices were peripheral. Perhaps, Fr. Rahner was asked what he thought of the rosary by someone, because he hoped he would say it was outdated. But Fr. Rahner said, surprisingly: "One can have various opinions about that. I only want to say, I pray the rosary daily!" That memory came back to me as we prayed the rosary for the departed, as a way of dealing with our grief.

What affected you the most, and has remained in your memory in Rahner's theology?

That was his understanding of the doctrine of Grace. In 1955-56 Fr. Rahner lectured on the tract, *De Gratia Christi*, and that opened up a whole world to me He also noted in his lecture in Freiburg on the occasion of his 80th birthday that, for him, the doctrine of grace retained the importance that it had in Greek Theology, where it was regarded as foundational.[10] People today must know that the first word of God is: I love you! It does not matter who you are, you have my support!

ENCOUNTERS WITH KARL RAHNER

It was only much later that I was made fully aware of the import of Rahner's teaching on grace, when I was making a thirty day retreat with a Swiss Jesuit in Freiburg. I had been making week long retreats for over ten years, but now it finally dawned on me – there is a super abundance of grace. I felt it and I said to myself: "Yes, that's it!" That's what I had not understood properly in those lectures.

To come back to my days as a student: I wrote my dissertation under the direction of Fr. Franz Lakner, SJ. Fr. Rahner once asked me whether I wanted to write a dissertation, but at that time it would take two or three years to do so and I was already an assistant pastor. I had already taken seminars with Fr. Lakner and I had written a paper about being a child of God and the indwelling of the Holy Spirit in the writings of Louis Thomasin. This paper was meant to be an example of the Latin or Western Theology of the new construction of the doctrine of grace as it was conceived of by Fr. Rahner among others. On the thirty day retreat it struck me that those elements of this dissertation on the indwelling of the Holy Spirit, on God's self-communication, on uncreated grace, suddenly came together once more. I then realized how deeply all this had left its mark on me.

How did Fr. Rahner interact with others?

There were people whom he simply liked: for example Fr. Georg Sporschill, who worked with youth who had been released from jail. Whenever Rahner was in Vienna, he stayed with them. They called him "Rahner-father" ("*Rahner-Vater*"). There were also other persons with whom he was close. They came to Innsbruck for three days and asked him questions about religion.[11]

Fr. Rahner did not only have contact with Jesuits. He accepted invitations to the diocesan seminary and several of his co-workers and assistants were not Jesuits, for example, Adolf Darlap, Herbert Vorgrimler, Johann Baptist Metz and Karl Lehmann.

Fr. Rahner had a lot of contact with non-Jesuits. Think, for example of Paul Michael Zulehner or Paul Wess, who was more of a critic of Rahner, to name only two. Fr. Rahner was very open in this regard – what he liked about Zulehner was that he was a little impertinent. He liked his lively way.

I enjoyed attending Fr. Rahner's Wednesday evening *colloquia* in the last two years of his life. What impressed me the most was how he spoke about God's self-communication. As I heard him speak about it, I thought, this is uniquely Karl Rahner! There is truly something of substance here, something truly meaningful. Grace as the self-communication of God – that was Rahner's contribution! In your opinion: What is his ultimate legacy? What have we, perhaps, not even yet begun to draw on?

It is very difficult for students of theology today to fully appreciate Karl Rahner's theology of grace. It is expressed in neo-Scholastic language. The terminology which he uses in the theology of grace has indeed been broken open, but it remains tied to scholastic categories. Who today begins to discuss the theology of grace with the terms such as "created" and "uncreated grace," "actual" and "sanctifying grace?" All these distinctions, which derive from Neo-scholastic Theology, are only made, with great difficulty, comprehensible if you have already had the foundation of at least two years of scholastic philosophy which we had at the time. Sometimes this is passed over.

In the series *Innsbrucker Theologische Studien*, interesting books have been published by the Protestant theologian Ralf Stolina and by the Freiburg student, Arno Zahlauer, who have pointed out that Karl Rahner discovered in Ignatius an "exemplary model."[12] In a few weeks a dissertation by the Jesuit Andreas R. Batlogg will be published in this series which shows how deeply Fr. Rahner was influenced by the *Spiritual Exercises*; it will clarify some things.[13] The short sentence with which Fr. Rahner once ended a heated discussion with Karl-Heinz Weger, SJ, on Rahner's "proof" for the existence of God, speaks volumes: "I believe, because I pray."[14] Note well, that he does not say that he prays because he believes, but rather that he believes, because he prays!

This Theology of Grace, which has at its innermost core the self-communication of God to us, and comes to us at a time which does not know how to cope with a personal "Thou" relationship with God, is really monumental. That has to do with the *Spiritual Exercises* where Ignatius points out that there is a genuine and direct contact between the Creator and his creature:[15] ultimately a self-communication of God.

In connection with the theodicy question – I recently came across a statement of Paul Claudel's which proved to be enormously helpful. He says, and I paraphrase: Jesus did not come to take away our suffering. He did not come to explain it. He came in order to fill suffering with the presence of God. That is precisely what is found in the 11th chapter of the Gospel of Luke – after the Lord's Prayer – "If you then, who are wicked, know how to give good gifts to your children, how much more the Father in Heaven will give the Holy Spirit to those who ask him." (Lk 11:13)

I have been the Spiritual Director for a long time for a woman who lives in a village near Innsbruck whose husband and oldest son both died on the same day in a mountain climbing accident. For her, of course, that was a personal catastrophe, but it also caused her to question: Why? In my conversations with her I tried to help her cope with this and show her that God's good Spirit would be with her, would accompany her. God does not send this or that help, but rather God gives God's self to enable you to come to terms with what happened. This woman is much esteemed in the community. It is now eleven years since her husband and son died and when someone in the village experiences an unexpected catastrophe they call upon her to bring them comfort. This "consolation in despair" or "consolation without prior cause" as it is called in the *Spiritual Exercises*,[16] has to do with uncreated grace. That would require a good deal of explanation, but in the last analysis it means that the quiet voice of the good Spirit is within me, in my heart, a Spirit who leads me to make better choices that have to do with the riches of God (that's how I translate "The Kingdom of God") and that allows us to enrich this world with a little heaven!

Those are the asymptotic approximations to the thesis of the self-communication of God. When I address such topics in retreat conferences, I find that people react very positively. You cannot talk to them in the language of theological terminology.

Would you agree that we have not yet fully explored and understood the doctrine of grace as Fr. Rahner developed it?

I maintain that unfortunately in reference to ordinary pastoral ministry and preaching there is still much that we have to do to catch up to him. As I stated, the problem for many younger people is with the language Rahner uses. You have to become accustomed to reading Karl Rahner. Ultimately what you have to do is what he clearly expresses with the term "productive model." He used this term for the first time in 1956 in reference to Ignatius being as he termed it, a "productive model," that is, Ignatius functions as a living icon that acts in an efficacious manner to produce a change in me. I believe that he first used this expression in the 1960's in reference to Jesus Christ. When I open myself to an encounter with Jesus he then triggers something within me. That is the function of meditating on the mysteries connected with the life of Jesus in the *Spiritual Exercises*: when I commit myself, with all my senses attuned, something begins to be changed within me. I think to myself, sometimes, Fr. Rahner must also be a "productive model" for us. We should not simply repeat what he has said, but rather let his spark ignite something within us so that we can speak meaningfully to our own time in our own language.

At the conclusion of a lecture "Marian Devotion Today," Fr. Rahner took questions that were posed to him. There was a small disagreement between one of the evening's participants and Fr. Rahner. As his final word of the evening, Fr. Rahner said: "One should pray a 'Hail Mary'. That would be more important than all the theological talk about Mary."[17] I thought I also would like to say that, but Fr. Rahner says it because he believes it. He does not say it to sound pious, but he truly believes it. We should find our way from thinking to believing. That's what "productive model" means; that in me a product emerges, something is brought into being.

NOTES

1 Hugo Rahner, SJ, (1900-1968), was Karl Rahner's brother, older by four years. Beginning in 1935, he was Professor of Patristics and Church History on the Theology Faculty at the University of Innsbruck. He was a recognized scholar in Ignatian studies. In 1945-46 and 1953-54 he was Dean of the Theology Faculty, 1949-50 Rector of the University, from 1950 to 1956 Rector of the Canisianum. Due to illness he ceased his teaching career in the early 1960's.

2 Cf. Gustave Lambert, Le drame du jardin d'Eden, in: *Nouvelle revue théologique* 76 (1954) 917-948, 1044-1072.

3 Cf. K. Rahner, Ätiologie, in: *Lexikon für Theologie und Kirche*, vol. 1, 1011-1012; now in: ibid., *Sämtliche Werke*, vol. 17: Enzyklopädische Theologie. Die Lexikonbeiträge der Jahre 1956-1963. Bearbeitet von Herbert Vorgrimler (Freiburg: Herder, 2002) 130-140.

4 The degree requirements of the Theology Faculty of the University of Innsbruck stated that in addition to the written work (dissertation), the candidate needed to take three, two hour oral exams in various theological disciplines every four weeks within a three month period. These grades counted as much toward the final grade as did the dissertation. The grades of these examinations are recorded in the *Liber Suffragorum examinum rigorosum ab anno 1901-1968* and are preserved in the archive of the Catholic Theology Faculty of the University of Innsbruck. What can be seen there is a typewritten page with the addition of hand written comments, "The Theological *Rigorosa*," which gives the decision of the professors meeting on January 7, 1910, with the different classifications. The vote *cum applausa* would be given if all the individual exam results were "eminenter;" "unanima cum laude" was given if at least two of the examinations were "eminenter," the other grades had to be at least "bene."

5 See the interview with Elfriede Oeggl in this book.

6 Cf. Klaus Egger, Im Kloster Marienberg, in: Paul Imhof, Hubert Biallowons (eds.), *Karl Rahner – Bilder eines Lebens* (Freiburg: Herder, 1985) 134-135.

7 Johannes Walchers, SJ, (1912-1922), 1938-1946 Missionary in China; 1948-1975 taught French and German at Cranwell Preparatory School in Lenox, Massachusetts.

8 Cf. Elfriede Oeggl, Das Sterben, in: *Karl Rahner – Bilder eines Lebens*, 162-163.

9 Josef Andreas Jungmann, SJ, (1889-1975), Professor of Liturgy at the University of Innsbruck. Prepared the way for the Constitution on the Sacred Liturgy of the Second Vatican Council, conciliar theologian, 1926-1963 editor-in-chief of the periodical, *Zeitschrift für Katholische Theologie*.

10 Cf. K. Rahner, *Von der Unbegreiflichkeit Gottes*. Erfahrungen eines katholischen Theologen, edited by Albert Raffelt (Freiburg: Herder, 2004) 38 f. – Cf. ibid., Experiences Of A Catholic Theologian, translated by Declan Marmion, S. M., Gesa Thiessen, in: *Theological Studies* 61 (2000) 3-15, 9: "My contention, moreover, is that a Christian theologian is not prevented from thinking that the theme of human sinfulness and forgiveness of guilt through pure grace is, in a certain sense, somewhat secondary compared to the theme of God's radical *self*-communication. It is not as if we do not get caught up time and again in our egoism because we are sinners. It is not as if we are not in need of God's forgiving grace, something we need to accept as pure grace – without our thinking we have any personal claim on God. It is not as if God's self-communication does not always take place in fact by way of forgiveness. It is not as if our fundamental experience of sinfulness – a despairing experience as far as we are concerned, but one in which we initially experience our freedom in a concrete way – does

not correspond to the actual situation in which a person truly begins to reach out for God. Christian experience had given concrete witness to this fact down through the ages. But today we see how difficult it is for people to accept justification simply as forgiveness of sin. Moreover, for a Catholic theologian, God and God's promise of self to humanity (in whatever way this is understood in greater detail) already exists as pure grace prior to sin, a completely unexpected miracle of God. God bestows God's self and turns such a love into the adventure that is God's own history. If we accept this, then I think we can easily hold that God's self-communication to the creature is more pivotal than sin and the forgiveness of sin."

11   Cf. *"Denn du kommst unserem Tun mit Deiner Gnade zuvor..."* Zur Theologie der Seelsorge heute. Paul M. Zulehner im Gespräch mit Karl Rahner (Düsseldorf: Patmos, 3rd edition 1987).

12   Cf. Ralf Stolina, *Die Theologie Karl Rahners: Inkarnatorische Spiritualität.* Menschwerdung Gottes und Gebet. (Innsbruck: Tyrolia ,1996); Arno Zahlauer, *Karl Rahner und sein "produktives Vorbild" Ignatius von Loyola.* (Innsbruck: Tyrolia, 1996).

13   Cf. Andreas R.Batlogg, *Die Mysterien des Lebens Jesu bei Karl Rahner.* Zugang zum Christusglauben (Innsbruck: Tyrolia, 2001, 2nd edition 2003).

14   Cf. Karl-Heinz Weger, "Ich glaube, weil ich bete." Für Karl Rahner zum 80. Geburtstag, in: *Geist und Leben* 57 (1984) 48-52, 51: "Once I fiercely debated with him the 'adequacy' of his transcendental proof for the existence of God. For every one of Rahner's replies I had another question and another objection (and I was serious in raising them.) As the discussion became hopeless, Rahner ended the conversation with the words: 'I believe, because I pray.' I have not forgotten these words; I will never forget them."

15   Cf. Ignatius of Loyola, *Spiritual Exercises*, number 15.

16   Cf. Ibid., number 330; see: Hans Zollner, Trost – Zunahme an Hoffnung, Glaube und Liebe. Zum theologischen Fundament der ignatianischen "Unterscheidung der Geister" (Innsbruck: Tyrolia, 2004) esp. 147-154.

17   Cf. Marienverehrung heute? Karl Rahner im Gespräch mit den Teilnehmern eines Kolloquiums über Marienverehrung, Innsbruck 1983, in: Paul Imhof, Hubert Biallowons (eds.), *Glaube in Winterlicher Zeit.* Gespräche mit Karl Rahner aus den letzten Lebensjahren (Düsseldorf: Patmos, 1986) 105-113, 113. – Cf. Ibid., Marian Devotion Today, in: *Faith in a Wintry Season.* Conversations and Interviews with Karl Rahner in the last years of his life, edited by Paul Imhof, Hubert Biallowons, translation edited by Harvey D. Egan (New York: Crossroad, 1991) 84-91, 91: "I would like to say one final thing. When any one of us prays a Hail Mary and does it truly from the heart, then that is certainly much more significant than

all our learned talk about it, much more significant than all the theological language that we have used in this conversation."

19

WE ARE MODERN!

IN CONVERSATION WITH MS. ELFRIEDE OEGGL, INNSBRUCK

Elfriede Oeggl, born in 1939, is married and the mother of a daughter. From 1981-1984 she was the last secretary of Karl Rahner.

How did you happen to become Karl Rahner's secretary?

That is not so easy to say in a few words. Many of my recollections of Fr. Rahner are unforgettable and in a way left their mark on me. In his small book *Who is your brother?*[1] he wrote this dedication to me: "For Ms. Oeggl with all good wishes for a good collaboration, Karl Rahner, SJ." Our working together began with my answering an advertisement, which read: "secretarial help, hourly, sought for the Jesuit residence." I applied for the job and was told that I had little chance as I was the 40th applicant for the position. But I received a call and was told to come for an interview. I only knew Fr. Rahner by name and was really anxious.

I waited at the receptionist's desk of the Jesuit residence. Then he came, a small, old man, descending the staircase unsteadily, almost tripping over his shoelaces. I bent down to tie his shoes. This spontaneous gesture embarrassed the both of us a little. Fr. Rahner asked me a few trivial questions and finally said: "Do you have a driver's license? Can you drive and do you have a car at your disposal?" When I answered: "Yes," his disposition grew brighter and he invited me into his office. I asked him if he wanted me to type something. "No," he said: "That will not be necessary." He then asked if I would sit at the typewriter so that he could see how that looked – that pleased him. I sat and typed some short sentences on a completely outdated manual typewriter which seemed to come from the Middle Ages, which required all my strength to operate. Yet I could not prevent a dollar sign appearing after almost every word. In despair, I removed the page from the typewriter, folded it carefully and put it in my pocket and said: "I cannot show this to you, I actually can type much better than this." Fr. Rahner looked at me with a somewhat baffled expression on his face; mumbled something about my hearing from him later and two days later he telephoned and said: "You are number one!"

What was your work schedule like?

We agreed on working three hours in the morning. In the beginning it was very difficult for me. First of all, there was the struggle with the typewriter, then the content, which was totally foreign to me. Furthermore, it was Fr. Rahner's custom to dictate a text for me to type while he walked back and forth, so that when he was walking away from me I could hardly understand a word he was saying. After a period of time I gave up and asked him to repeat his last word. I should not have done that. Fr. Rahner quickly turned and threw his key ring – with which he was continually playing as he dictated – at me and growled: "Do not interrupt me!" In shock, I immediately started to cry. He seemed to be surprised at my reaction and our first morning at work ended abruptly. I went home heartbroken and decided that I would have to discontinue my working for him. But the next morning I found a stack of 15 chocolate bars on my desk; so the situation was resolved.

We soon purchased a super, modern electric typewriter and the relationship between Fr. Rahner and me, his secretary, was apparently now all right; everything proceeded smoothly. We also purchased a copy machine because it was so laborious to work with carbon copies and because every correction was so noticeable. Fr. Rahner said: "We will make copies! We are modern!"

After the shock of your first day at working with Fr. Rahner, what was a typical workday like?

I was always fascinated by how Fr. Rahner approached a topic. First of all he would repeat the title a few times – not without some grumbling: "Ah! It is very difficult always to know what they want!" Then he would dictate, word for word; it was like seeing giant gears meshing with one another, slowly gripping each other until the "machine" runs, as we Tirolean's say. Thus it followed – thought upon thought, sentence after sentence. Fr. Rahner always dictated rapidly with each sentence always coming out in a finished form: each sentence growing

longer and longer. He would manage to work like this for about an
hour.

**Originally you were supposed to work with Fr. Rahner for three
hours in the morning. Apparently you didn't do that.**

No. Karl Rahner loved riding in the car. He enjoyed nothing more
than going for ride in a car on a beautiful day. He would get in the car
and off we would go – south over the Brenner Pass. The trip to the autobahn took a toll on our nerves: for Fr. Rahner, because there were so
many obstacles – red lights that forced us to stop; trucks, which drove
too slowly and in the "no passing" zones – and for me because I had to
be deaf to all that and hold out until we were finally on the autobahn.
Then he sighed every time, relieved: "So – and now we'll let the stal-
lion run." For Fr. Rahner that meant speeds of 140-160 km per hour;
anything slower than that was for him "creeping along." Once when I
was driving slower, he reached, impetuously, for the gear shifter and
grumbled: "Is there something broken?" He wanted to push it himself.
I became so irritated, as well as terrified, that I pushed his hand aside
and snapped at him: "No, Professor! Perhaps, you want to get to God
in heaven as fast as possible, but I want to get home to my family
again."

Your assistance was not limited to office management?

I quickly realized that some activities were too difficult for Fr. Rahner.
With permission of the Rector of the community I was allowed to
help straighten up his room. He thanked me for my help profusely,
with joy and gratitude. He was rather awkward in practical matters.
On the other hand, he was, despite his advanced age and increasing
tiredness and weakness, incredibly persistent. He finished every task
conscientiously and punctually. Even when he was in the sanatorium
in Hochrum near Innsbruck, in the last week of his life, he dictated
some prayers and work he had promised on the topic of suffering. Fr.
Rahner was an indefatigable, sensitive person and an attentive spiritual advisor. He did not make distinctions: everyone who came to him
found him a fatherly friend and advisor. In these ways he showed that
his thoughts, what he said, what he wrote and how he lived, all came
from his heart.

The years that I worked for him, allowed me to share with him in a new incomprehensibly, exciting way, experiences which have penetrated to the depths of my being, experiences like the grace to be with him in his hour of death, the sharing in a peaceful farewell.[2]

NOTES

1 Cf. K. Rahner, Wer ist Dein Bruder? (Freiburg: Herder, 1981, 2nd edition, 1982). The small volume carries the dedication: "To Dr. Egon Kapellari and the Catholic College Community of Graz." Kapellari, born in 1936, was from 1964 to 1981 the chaplain and the Director of the Afro-Asiatic Institute in Graz. In 1981 he became the Bishop of Gurk-Klagenfurt (Carinthia); in 2001 the Bishop of Graz-Sekau (Styria).

2 Cf. Elfriede Oeggl, Das Sterben, in: Paul Imhof, Hubert Biallowons (eds.), Karl Rahner – Bilder eines Lebens (Freiburg: Herder, 1985) 162-163.

20

THE WOMAN OF THE
ANONYMOUS CHRISTIAN

IN CONVERSATION WITH FR. FRIEDRICH AND
FR. HARALD RÖPER, BINGEN

Friedrich Franz Röper, Dr. phil., born 1941 in Hamburg, is a priest in the Liebfrauen parish of the Diocese of Mainz, Diocesan Director of the Catholic Worker Movement and the President of an association for helping youth as well as the head of the Father Röper Foundation. Harald Christian Röper, also a priest, is his twin brother and a Pastor in Eppertshausen and two additional parishes. He was head of the Deanery of Dieburg, and since 1994, has been the Diocesan Director of the Kolping Society and the Acting Director of the Father Röper Foundation.

How did your mother come to know Karl Rahner?

(*Friedrich Röper:*) She once read something of his and wrote to Fr. Rahner about it. He wrote back and asked her to tell him about her situation in greater detail. Our mother was in a mixed marriage[1] and she described the difficulties she experienced in her life because of that. Fr. Rahner thought about what she had told him and wrote an essay with his reflections and sent it to her.[2] He said to her that actually what he had written was really her essay. Then both of them corresponded with one another for a long time and at some point she visited him in Innsbruck.

When was that?

In 1953 my brother and I were still very young. We were always with my mother and so we met Rahner. Luise Rinser mentions my mother twice in her book, referring to her as the "woman of the Anonymous Christian."[3] Somewhere she is referred to as "Ms. A" (for Anita). Fr.

Rahner encouraged our mother to write a book about her experiences, which she did, under the pseudonym Schäfer.[4] The book, *Es ist Licht genug,* was published by Tyrolia Publishing. The whole family is described there. The second book was *The Anonymous Christian.*[5]

After the death of your father you moved from Hamburg to Bingen am Rhein.

(*Harald Röper:*) Fr. Rahner visited us there and even spent the night. My brother and I were about 16 years old at the time and naturally were in awe of this great theologian. In the beginning Fr. Rahner was not so well known. I have all his books, complete with dedication and date.

Can you remember back to the very first meeting in Innsbruck?

At that time he lived very modestly in a room in the Jesuit residence in the Sillgasse, to which he returned in the last years of his life. We often met him in Mainz and later in Bingen. Our mother traveled to hear many of his speeches. She also gave a little gift of money to Fr. Rahner.

Did you know at that time that you would one day study theology?

(*Friedrich Röper:*) Of course not. My brother, Harald, on the other hand, was "called from on high" as we say in German, called very early on. He knew when he was sixteen what he wanted to be. My brother knew people who were intelligent and also pious. Normally the saying here is always: "The pious are the dummies." So it was good to know that not all the pious people are dumb.

How was Rahner's piety revealed to you?

(*Harald Röper:*) Once I concelebrated with him after I was ordained. Fr. Rahner always said a private Mass early in the morning, quite quickly and then ate his breakfast.

Did Father Rahner show an interest in your studies?

You could say that. My mother wrote often that her two sons were studying theology. Fr. Rahner also wrote a letter of recommendation for me to the seminary. He wrote to congratulate my brother and me on our ordination. We did not ask him for personal favors, however, although he did preach at the 150th anniversary of my Parish Church in Eppertshausen. He also officiated at our older brother's wedding in Berlin; he is an attorney.

What do you remember most about Fr. Rahner?

(Friedrich Röper:) He was a pious, modest man. He was friendly and interested in everything. We also got to know his mother who lived in a home for the elderly in Freiburg. She went there when she was 65 years old because she thought she would die soon; she lived to be 101. When I went to see her with my mother and brother, she made fruit salad for us.

Did you have further encounters with Karl Rahner?

(Harald Röper:) He once paid a visit to my mother's brother who was a businessman in Hamburg. Fr. Rahner was "passed around," so to speak, a lot in the family. He came for a visit twice a year. I would say that we were friends with him.

Both of you are priests of the Diocese of Mainz, whose Bishop is Karl Lehmann. Had you ever met him while he was an assistant to Fr. Rahner?

Yes, naturally we met Karl Lehmann, but we were not in close contact with him. We knew, of course, that Fr. Rahner found him to be a very diligent and a very intelligent assistant. He was always concerned as to how he was going to be able to cope with his work when Lehmann would leave for a position somewhere else. When Karl Lehmann became Bishop of Mainz in 1983, Fr. Rahner wondered how he would fare as a bishop.[6] In his *Rede des Ignatius von Loyola an einen Jesuiten von heute*, he warned his colleagues about becoming bishops[7] – but Lehmann is not a Jesuit.

Did Fr. Rahner appreciate you because both of you were theologians and wanted to become priests? Did he ever suggest that you should become Jesuits?

(*Friedrich Röper:*) Fr. Rahner never said to either of us that we should become priests. I did not have many theological conversations with him. Our meetings actually had more to do with private matters. He was interested in many things. For example, we have established an agency to do social work here. That's why I do not have a parish, because I am a director of a social agency that cares for 80 children. We have three houses here in Mainz and three more in Ingenheim. We also have 50 co-workers. Fr. Rahner took an active interest in these things; he was very concerned about how things were going. He also always asked about our mother's foster children. He was always incredibly interested in what was happening. He did not simply ask perfunctorily how it was all going; he truly was concerned.

Your mother was not an academic theologian. Was Fr. Rahner then not concerned with the fact that he was engaged in discussions with an average, even if reflective, "stay-at-home" mother?

(*Harald Röper:*) Our mother was not an academician, that's true, but she was intensively involved with theological questions and read a great deal. She was, so to speak, Fr. Rahner's private pupil. Over the course of time a very close relationship developed. In the beginning Fr. Rahner was not as well known as he is now. Because of that we also related to him in a different way then, than we did later.

In the beginning he sent his letters to a cover address, not directly to my mother, because our father would not approve. It was a difficult situation: our father was Lutheran. We lived in Hamburg in a good middle class Protestant milieu. At that time that presented a problem for a marriage. Those who were brought up in a Catholic household cannot imagine the problems an interfaith marriage presented. Our father did not want our mother and Fr. Rahner to be discussing the situation. In order not to create any discord, Fr. Rahner would send his letters to an acquaintance who would then pass them on to my mother. In the beginning we did not know about any of this. Our father first became aware of this when the book *Es ist Licht genug* appeared; but then he was proud of this.

How large was your family?

We were ten children from two marriages. The first set was Lutheran, and the second – that's us, the twins, plus a brother and a little sister who died – was Catholic. My father's first wife, who died, had six children. Practically speaking, our mother raised the children. She had married a widowed psychiatrist who had six children, although the oldest boy had already moved out. What made our family situation even more difficult was the fact that our father was half-Jewish, so our mother's marital status fell under the Nürnberg Laws.[8] You can imagine that created a very difficult situation at that time.

What were your mother's visits with Fr. Rahner like?

(Friedrich Röper:) We would take her to – let's say – Munich and she would visit with Fr. Rahner for two hours, the two of them speaking to each other. After two hours we would come back and then all of us would go someplace to eat. During the meal we would talk about everyday things. What are the children doing? How is the little dog? In Innsbruck, Fr. Rahner once caught our dog in the door. He felt so guilty about that that he would ask about the dog every time. Our mother did not like to talk to other people about these visits. She did not want any rumors to start. Sometimes we took trips together: to South Tirol or to the Baltic Sea. I could show you photos of these excursions, where Fr. Rahner is talking to me and my brother as we are walking together and our mother is walking a few steps behind us not wanting to be noticed. She was considerate of Fr. Rahner. She did not push herself into the foreground: she is not Luise Rinser. Perhaps, in the end Rinser was a little disappointed. Fr. Rahner did not continue to mention her any longer. We met her once in Salzburg in the *Paulus-Gesellschaft*.[9] I believe her book *Gratwanderung* is the result of this disappointment. She also writes about a Benedictine abbot there.[10]

Shortly after Fr. Rahner's 80th birthday he died. What was your mother's reaction to that?

The three of us, my brother, my mother and I, were at the great birthday celebration held at the *Katholische Akademie* in Freiburg. For my mother, Fr. Rahner was the elixir of life. It was very difficult for her when he died. She was in a hospital in Hamburg at the time. She was at the point of death and she missed his phone calls. Both of them telephoned each other often. They had planned to write a book together. When Fr. Rahner died, our mother missed her conversation partner. Before it became popular to call, they wrote many letters that are now in the Karl Rahner archives.

Did you have the impression that your mother was worried when Fr. Rahner was critical or when he had difficulties with Rome?

(*Harald Röper:*) That was something that was always brought up, naturally. I would say, theology was our mother's interest and when all of us were together he did not always want to discuss theology – it was time to relax. So we spoke about the family or other matters. Of course, he also spoke at times about his colleagues or fellow Jesuits. But it would not have been appropriate for us to blab about who he thought to be smart or not, and what he thought about this one or that. At home we did not constantly discuss academic theology. It would have been completely out of place, if we, preparing for the priesthood, had asked Fr. Rahner to give a lecture, so to speak.

NOTES

1 Rather than speaking of a "mixed marriage" (the literal translation of the Latin canonical term, "*matrimonium mixtum*"), it would be better to speak of a "confessionally diverse" or of a "denominationally diverse" marriage: a marriage between two baptized persons, one of whom is Catholic, the other of whom is of a different denomination: cf. canon 1124 CIC/1983.

2 Cf. K. Rahner, Über Konversionen, in: *Hochland* 46 (1953/54) 119-126: later in: ibid., *Schriften zur Theologie*, vol. 3 (Einsiedeln: Benziger 1956) 441-453. – Cf. ibid., *Theological Investigations*, vol. 3, translated by Karl-H. and Boniface Kruger (New York: Crossroad, 1982) 373-384 ("On Conversions to the Church").

3 Cf. Luise Rinser, *Gratwanderung*. Briefe der Freundschaft an Karl Rahner 1962-1984, edited by Bogdan Snela (Munich: Kösel, 1994) 248: "However, about the 'Anonymous Christians' you (you and A.) have already said enough." Cf. also, ibid., 398: "You always promoted and supported that woman – what is her name (*The Anonymous Christian*) and me, me?"

4 F. M. Schäfer, *Es ist Licht genug*. Gespräche über den Glauben und seine vergessene Tiefe (Innsbruck: Tyrolia, 1959).

5 Anita Röper, *Die anonymen Christen* (Mainz: Matthias Grünewald, 1963),
   American edition: *The Anonymous Christian* (New York 1966); Argentin-
   ean edition: *El hombre, cristiano implicito* (Buenos Aires 1968). See also,
   ibid. *Sind die Christen Heiden?* (Kevelaer: Butzon & Bercker, 1964); ibid.,
   Karl Rahner als Seelsorger (Innsbruck: Tyrolia, 1987).

6 Cf. K. Rahner, Auch als Bischof ein Theologe der Mitte, in: *Glaube und Leben*. Kirchenzeitung für das Bistum Mainz 39 (1983) Nr. 40, 14: "While it
   may often be appropriate to take a middle position – a stance of objectivity
   – at times one is also required to have the courage to defend a position that
   appears one-sided, that does not please everyone, a position that opposes
   others whom one respects, who perhaps occupy a more elevated position
   than oneself. May I, an old friend, wish him, in his office as bishop and
   for his future as an episcopal theologian, not only, but also especially, this
   virtue?"

7 Cf. K. Rahner, Rede des Ignatius von Loyola an einen Jesuiten von heute,
   in: ibid., *Schriften zur Theologie*, vol. 15 (Zürich: Benziger, 1983) 378-405,
   388 f.. – See ibid., *Ignatius of Loyola*. With an historical introduction by
   Paul Imhof (London, Collins, 1979), 11-38, 23: "If a Jesuit becomes a bishop or a cardinal today, you see nothing odd in it; it would seem to you to be
   basically quite normal that there should be and indeed were, times when a
   Jesuit cardinal was almost a permanent fixture in the curia ... You may indeed with an untroubled mind become a bishop like Hélder Câmara, who
   risks life and limb for the poor. But consider carefully where those 'episcopal chairs' are today: how they, perhaps, point to something completely
   different, which you should not occupy, even though someone might assume to prove to you that they are indispensable to the church." – Now in:
   ibid., *Sämtliche Werke*, vol. 25: Erneuerung des Ordenslebens. Zeugnis für
   Kirche und Welt. Bearbeitet von Andreas R. Batlogg (Freiburg: Herder,
   2008) 299-329.

8 The expression "The Nürnberg laws" is a collective term for the two laws
   of the nationalist socialist government concerning race which were passed
   in Nürnberg on September 15, 1935, at the assembly of the *Nationalsozial-
   istischen Arbeiterpartei Deutschlands* (NSDAP), the Nationalist Socialist
   Workers Party. The two laws have to do with the protection of German
   blood and with German honor, as well as with citizenship in the German
   Reich. Marriages and sexual intercourse between "those with German
   blood" and Jews were forbidden in the so-called *Blutschutzgesetz* ("*Ras-
   senschande*"). For so-called Arians the status of 'Citizen of the Reich" was
   established; cf. Alisa Schapira, "Nürnberger Gesetze," in: Christian Zent-
   ner, Friedemann Bedürftig (eds.), *Das Grosse Lexikon des Dritten Reiches*
   (München: Südwest Verlag, 1985) 423 f.

9 The so-called "Paulus-Gesellschaft" was founded in 1955 by the charismatic priest, Erich Kellner. He sought a thorough renewal of the Church.

The Society strove for, among other things, a promotion of the dialogue with those who were very reserved in their views of the Church: for example, atheists and Marxists. Numerous symposia with natural scientists and with reformers in the Marxist camp, such as Ernst Bloch or Roger Garaudy, took place. These dialogues are a piece of Church History and of Cultural History. Cf. K. Rahner, *Sämtliche Werke*, vol. 15: Verantwortung der Theologie. Im Dialog mit Naturwissenschaften und Gesellschaftstheorie. Bearbeitet von Hans-Dieter Mutschler (Freiburg: Herder, 2002).

10 Alluded to here is Johannes Maria Hoeck, OSB, (1902-1995), from 1951-1961 abbot of Ettal, from 1961-1972 abbot of the Benedictine cloister in Scheyern in Upper Bavaria. As the chairperson of the Bavarian Benedictines (1961-1968), he participated in the Second Vatican Council. Cf. also Luise Rinser, *Saturn auf der Sonne* (Frankfurt: Fischer, 1994) 138-165, 208-238.

A MASTER OF GOOD QUESTIONS – A LITTLE LIKE SOCRATES

IN CONVERSATION WITH FR. GEORG SPORSCHILL, SJ, VIENNA

Georg Sporschill, SJ, Dr. phil., Mag. theol., Dr. theol. h. c., born 1946, is a Jesuit since 1976 and was ordained in 1978. He was Editor-in-chief of the Jesuit periodical "Entschluss," and a Chaplain and youth minister. Since autumn 1991, he worked for more than ten years in Romania where he built houses and villages for homeless children. Since 2004 he works also in the Republic of Moldova and Bulgaria.[1] In the last years of Karl Rahner's life Sporschill spent much time with him. He also published a small volume of Rahner's memoirs.[2]

How did you come to know Fr. Rahner?

I was the Editor-in-chief of the periodical *Entschluss*[3] and Fr. Rahner would help me by contributing an article almost every month. For that I had to chauffeur him in his car, go out to eat with him, and be available to help him: that was a blessing. He would personally counsel me on important questions. For example, I was supposed to become a Professor of Pastoral Theology in Innsbruck; that was what the Provincial wanted. But I am not the Professor type. I just can't do it. Fr. Rahner then wrote a three page letter to the Provincial explaining why I would not be the right choice. He saved me from a career that would not have been right for me.[4]

In Vienna you brought Fr. Rahner into contact with the homeless. How did that come about?

I was commissioned by Caritas in the 1980's to found a homeless shelter for youth just out of jail. When Fr. Rahner came to Vienna, he decided to spend the night in the homeless shelter, rather than in a hotel or a Jesuit residence. He was a person who was filled with curiosity, interested in anything that was unfamiliar to him and he asked many questions about my work. I believe that it impressed him, that because of me, in my social work, he would discover many unusual or at least unfamiliar things. He was someone who liked to experience new things.

You also undertook a book project with Fr. Rahner?

Yes. It is called *Is Christian Life Possible Today?* (*Mein Problem*)[5] and it has been translated into many languages. The book consists of a compilation of letters that these young people wrote, which I brought to him to read and he dictated his responses to me.[6] These young people were friends of mine. Actually I forced him into this project, that is, I lovingly put pressure on him. But it is a fine book.

Do you miss Fr. Rahner?

After he died, I was very sad. I was not in Austria when he died, but in Israel. At the time, I thought, perhaps, if I had been there he would not have died. But, with the passage of time one learns to live with everything. I still feel that I am very, very close to him. I meet him also in prayer. In the last years there were few people that I was as close to as I was to him. Fr. Rahner always helped me. He was someone who gladly helped others, although he was a famous professor. He was someone who enjoyed being socially engaged. That's why I involved him with my young people or called him when I needed him.

What fascinated you so about him?

Fr. Rahner was very curious even about the smallest things. He was interested in everything and asked many questions. I once wanted to have an edition of *Entschluss* that focused on the theme of happiness and he rejected the idea. Later I asked him to write something about happiness for the periodical and he refused again. One day he confronted me with the question: "Must one then always be happy?" But by his questions he also prodded you to look for answers! Whether one must always be happy – that is a question for further reflection. On another occasion when we were at the main train station in Munich where there always are a large number of people, he, reacting to the crush of the crowd, exclaimed: "Must there be so many immortal souls?" He always asked questions that stimulated the imagination. He was a master of good questions; a little like Socrates.

Did you know from the beginning that a deep relationship would develop between you?

No, absolutely not. In the beginning I naturally was very reserved in his presence. He was, after all, a famous professor. But, somehow, a very personal relationship quickly developed. I joined the Jesuits when I was thirty years old. Before that I had worked as an educational consultant for the county government of Vorarlberg (Austria). Fr. Rahner was supposed to preach at my First Mass, but he was ill. Later, through me he gained access to different social experiences; we were often out and about together.

How and where did you meet?

Twice a month I came to Innsbruck. In the morning, if his secretary Ms. Oeggl permitted it, we would work.[7] She was very good for him, but she was the boss. If you wanted something from him, you had to go through her. I always said to him that I would not be able to tolerate that, always being told what to do. But he said: "I understand that, but for such an old fool like me that's best." She did a great deal for him and he trusted her completely. He always bought sweets for her and also groceries. He said to me: "She doesn't earn very much money and in this way I can indirectly help a little with her income." So he went shopping for her and everyday he would place something for her on her desk.

Were you in Innsbruck on March 5, 1984, for his 80th birthday?

Yes, together with 10 or 12 of the young people from my group, all of whom had been in jail, all former criminals. He was very pleased that we came. Naturally there was a great academic celebration at the University. All of us were with him in his room and each one of them presented him with a cake. All the young people knew that he liked to eat sweets. Before I left for Israel I visited him in the hospital and I telephoned him from the airport. He said to me: "Georg, I have an oxygen mask over my nose;" somehow that pleased him. A couple of days later, he died. The various celebrations for his birthday were simply too much for him.

Karl Rahner received his letters back from a woman who did not want the letters to fall into the wrong hands after her death. On the other hand, the author, Luise Rinser, (1911-2002) kept the letters she had received from Rahner and then in 1994 published the book, *Gratwanderung*,[8] that caused quite a stir.

After a while Luise Rinser got on his nerves, but she pursued him doggedly. She wrote him many letters and that was disconcerting to him. He already had the feeling that she was becoming too possessive of him. He wanted to be free of her, but I believe that there was nothing behind this relationship as was later speculated. There was certainly not a sexual relationship. That both of them had given each other pet names is one thing, but to publish this is indiscreet and stupid.

What was Fr. Rahner's method of working?

He wrote a good deal and sometimes I had the impression that it was very stressful for him to write so much. He said to me: "Yes, I have to, I simply do it, I write. I must write, I dictate." He always dictated, but what he dictated was already good enough to be published. When he was to do something for me I would give him a topic and then he would think about it for a few days and then he would say: "Now you can come." Then he dictated everything, including the punctuation. I would transcribe it and then he would correct it once more. In writing, he was like a machine. He even once said to me: "If I had had two secretaries, I could have written twice as much."

Did he have much correspondence?

He wrote an incredible number of letters and cards. He always called the letters "business mail," but he also wrote many very personal letters. He looked after a woman in Bavaria, for instance, for a number of years. I believe, he wrote or called her everyday. She was certainly the woman he had known the best. He was a companion to her for thirty or forty years. I believe that I was the only person he allowed to meet

her personally. Others who drove him to Chiemsee were only permit-
ted to drive to the house, drop him off and pick him up an hour later.
She was a handicapped, elderly woman, very modest and very discreet.
She was a friend to him, a friend in the noblest sense.

**In the USA I am often asked: Why should we concern ourselves
with the theology of Karl Rahner? How would you answer that
question?**

Karl Rahner dealt with all the contemporary questions in a radical
and honest way. You always had the impression that he took the human person seriously. The last Council benefited from this perspective
and it would affect the renewal of all theology as well. Many questions
were raised, but he never said – that's stupid. Rather he simply asked
questions and thereby pushed theological inquiry further and further.
He was very rooted in the tradition. I said to him: "Do you still know
much Latin?" He answered: "No. I have forgotten everything, but
Augustine: I could still read him in my sleep." It sounds a little paradoxical, but his rootedness in the tradition helped him to deal with
modern questions. And so, I believe, he brought hope to many people
and opened up theology to new ideas. Certainly, he thought about
nothing but God his entire life. I am theologically not so competent. I
was more a friend, like a son to him. Fr. Rahner wrote some beautiful
things. His prayers are almost lyrical texts.

**You mean the early publications like *Worte ins Schweigen* (1938,
Encounters with Silence), *Von der Not und dem Segen des Gebetes*
(1949, *The Need and the Blessing of Prayer*), *Heilige Stunde und Passionsandacht* (1949, *Watch and Pray with Me. The Seven Last Words
of Jesus Christ*), *Kleines Kirchenjahr* (1954, *The Eternal Year*) and
Biblische Predigten (1965, *Biblical Homilies*)?**

These speak to everyone, not only to theologians.

**What remains in your memory of Karl Rahner as the most impor-
tant?**

His unbelievable breadth of spirit. I could speak to him about everything. And I was never afraid that I could not ask this or that question.

He was not narrow-minded or rigid, absolutely not! He was open to everything. I never lived with him in a community. I met Karl Rahner personally through my friend Wolfgang Feneberg, who was a Jesuit at the time, but who has since married. When Rahner had dictated the article that he had promised me, he would often say afterwards: "Could we go out to eat or go somewhere for a ride?" So, in the morning we worked an hour or two and in the afternoon we drove most often to South Tirol (*Südtirol*). Once we even drove to Venice, simply to have coffee.

Did Fr. Rahner talk much while you were driving?

He loved to be chauffeured. Often, he was very still, sometimes he did not say a word, but only looked out the window. It was like a meditation. But even in those times of silence, he blessed me with an awesome nearness and gave me much courage. Once, for example, I told him some very personal things. I could tell him everything and then at night when we returned home, it was in Innsbruck, under one of the bridges, he stopped and asked me: "Georg, should I give you absolution?" He was under the impression that for all practical purposes I had gone to confession. I said only: "Please." I always used the formal address when speaking to him; he always addressed me informally. He was truly like a father. Yet when we were together he could also be like a child. I gave him a gift of a camera; then he took photos all the time and was happy as a child. Such things gave him great pleasure.

Of those who were not Jesuits, who was closest to him?

Johann Baptist Metz played a great role; he thought highly of him and Rahner was impressed with him. But certainly he was closest, as I said, to this woman in Bavaria. Their letters show him as he truly was. When he moved from Munich to Innsbruck in the fall of 1981 he made a sketch of how his room looked: recliner, bed, bookcases, waiting room. He then took pictures and sent them to her.

NOTES

1 Cf. Andreas R. Batlogg, Die zweite Meile. Georg Sporschills Leben mit rumänischen Straßenkindern, in: *Stimmen der Zeit* 225 (2007) 352-355.

2 See K. Rahner, *Bekenntnisse*. Rückblick auf 80 Jahre, edited by Georg Sporschill (Vienna: Herold, 1984); now in: K. Rahner, *Sämtliche Werke*, vol. 25: Erneuerung des Ordenslebens. Zeugnis für Kirche und Welt. Bearbeitet von Andreas R. Batlogg (Freiburg: Herder 2008) 61-84.

3 *Entschluss*. Jesuiten – Gesellschaft – Spiritualität, founded (by Austrian Jesuits) in 1946 ("Der große Entschluss. Monatsschrift für aktives Christentum"), permanently discontinued with issue number 12 in the 54th volume (1999).

4 See the interview with Hans B. Meyer, SJ, in this book.

5 *Mein Problem*. Karl Rahner antwortet jungen Menschen (Freiburg: Herder, 1983) (many editions with several translations in European languages). English translation, K. Rahner, *Is Christian Life Possible Today?* Translated by Salvator Attanasio (New Jersey: Dimension Books, 1984).

6 Cf. ibid., 5: "This is how this book came to be: A priest, a youth minister in a big city, asked young people to write these letters to me. In doing so, he perhaps, without knowing it, praised me and promised these young people more than I can deliver. With mild pressure he convinced me to answer these letters or at least to try. The letters are therefore genuine. What these young people had written pertained to what moves them. These letters are presented here in their original form and only here and there something is left out in order to show respect towards the authors of the letters. Therefore the names of those addressed have been changed."

7 See the interview with Elfriede Oeggl in this book.

8 See Luise Rinser, *Gratwanderung*. Briefe der Freundschaft an Karl Rahner 1962-1984, edited by Bogdan Snela (München: Kösel, 1994).

PART FIVE

KARL RAHNER AS TEACHER AND AUTHOR

INTERPRETER OF IGNATIUS OF LOYOLA

IN CONVERSATION WITH FR. ANDREAS BATLOGG, SJ, MUNICH

Andreas R. Batlogg, SJ, Mag. theol., Dr. theol., born 1962, a Jesuit since 1985. Since December 2000, he has been working as the Deputy Editor of the Jesuit periodical, "Stimmen der Zeit" in Munich. Since the fall of 2005, he has been the Co-editor of the "Sämtliche Werke" of Karl Rahner. A member of the board of trustees of the Karl-Rahner-Stiftung München (Karl Rahner Foundation Munich) since 2007, he was elected to be the Vice-chairman. Since 2008 he is also Director of the Karl-Rahner-Archiv, which has been moved from Innsbruck (Austria) to Munich (Germany).

You wrote your doctoral dissertation on Karl Rahner. What did you learn from this?

In the foreword to the dissertation that I submitted to the university, (but not in the published version), I wrote: "I have not finished my study of Karl Rahner, not by a long shot." I have co-authored a lengthy study of Rahner, but that does not mean that I know all about Rahner. I know a good deal about a small portion of Rahner, but I still want to know more. Even after many years of study I realize that there are things which I have not yet adequately grasped. For example, there are passages in his study of Thomas Aquinas, in *Spirit in the World*, which I do not fully comprehend because I was not educated in the neo-Scholastic system.

Did you know Fr. Rahner personally?

Not as a fellow Jesuit. I became a Jesuit in 1985; by then he was already dead. But I began my studies in Innsbruck in the fall of 1981; that was when Fr. Rahner came to the capital of Tirol. I met him a few times: on the street, at the Theology Faculty, at the Wednesday evening colloquia. A couple of times Fr. Rahner came to the seminary – at the time I was studying for the Diocese of Feldkirch – and he lectured to us. Instinctively I felt: there is something about this man! Fr. Walter Kern, SJ,[1] was my first Theology Professor. He always encouraged us students to read Karl Rahner for ourselves and not only books or articles about him.

In the summer of 1984, I was spending a semester in Israel. While there I read the small book by Karl Rahner, *Was heisst Jesus lieben?* (What does it mean to love Jesus?) It left a deep impression on me and formed me. Later I wrote my Master's paper on that topic which I later summarized and published as a short article for Rahner's 90th birthday and the 10th anniversary of his death.[2] I was astonished that a theologian could write a publication of almost 100 pages practically without any footnotes. The literary style of a theological meditation to express theology without complicated footnotes fascinated me.

Where were you when Fr. Rahner died?

I flew to Tel Aviv in the middle of March, a few days after Karl Rahner's 80th birthday. On March 31, 1984, I was sitting in a hotel in Jerusalem. Fr. Georg Sporschill, SJ, a close friend of Fr. Rahner, was sitting next to me. We heard on the radio the report: "Yesterday in Innsbruck, Austria, the theologian and Jesuit Karl Rahner died." Fr. Sporschill began to cry. At first I found that embarrassing, but then I was very moved. I thought to myself: A Jesuit, a social worker who works with criminals and youth released from jail becomes so emotional when he hears this death notice. What kind of person must Karl Rahner have been to cause such a response?

How did you later come to deepen your knowledge of Karl Rahner's theology?

After my semester in Israel, I worked for a time with Fr. Sporschill. He was editor-in-chief of the periodical *Entschluss* in Vienna.[3] I did not receive any money for doing so, but he gave me the first seven volumes of Karl Rahner's *Schriften zur Theologie* which he had received as part of the personal effects of a German Jesuit, who had died quite young from a brain tumor. When you have studied two or three years and then receive seven volumes with the same book jacket, that fits handsomely on a bookshelf. I simply began to read and I say, with some emotion, I am still reading! I have simply not stopped reading Karl Rahner!

What did you discover about Fr. Rahner when you, yourself, became a Jesuit?

I did not know when I was in Israel that a year later I would join the Jesuits. The decision has certain logic to it, because I had made the Ignatian Exercises several times and got to know Jesuits on the Theology Faculty and held them in high esteem. Then I had the good fortune during the course of my formation, to get to know a whole series of Jesuits a little better who, in one way or another, worked closely with Fr. Rahner or lived with him.

Fr. Kern, in a certain sense, laid the foundation. Then came Fr. Sporschill. After my novitiate, I lived for more than a year in Munich where I did a practicum at the periodical *Geist und Leben*. Paul Imhof, who had edited and published the last four volumes of *Schriften zur Theologie* as well as some collections of interviews with Karl Rahner, was Editor-in-chief at the time. Friedrich Wulf, SJ, who for decades had been the Director of *Geist und Leben*, also lived in the German Jesuits' "Writers' House." He, together with Karl Rahner, was at the Council. Moreover, Fr. Rahner, from 1964 to the beginning of the 1970's, belonged to the community of writers in Munich.[4] Fr. Josef Sudbrack, SJ, who succeeded Wulf as editor-in-chief and Fr. Wolfgang Seibel, SJ, who had been responsible for the fate of *Stimmen der Zeit* for thirty-two years, also were there. Fr. Rahner wrote many articles for both periodicals. A young Jesuit, in this atmosphere, experiences a plethora of things! I felt that I was becoming very close to Fr. Rahner through all of that. I not only read his work, but, in a roundabout way, so to speak, got to know him personally.

I returned to Innsbruck at the beginning of 1989 and met Fr. Karl H. Neufeld, SJ, who came from the Gregorian University in Rome to Innsbruck when he received a call. He was Fr. Rahner's assistant in Munich in the early 1970's. I wrote my Master's thesis under his tutelage and I was his assistant for two years. After my ordination to priesthood (1993) and after working for one year in the formation of future priests, I was given permission to pursue doctoral studies. At that time, together with Roman A. Siebenrock, the secretary of the Karl Rahner Archives, I began to read the works of Karl Rahner.

The Innsbruck Circle of Rahner Scholars came into being, to which doctoral students came on a rotating basis. The idea for a book was born from this which would contain our different perspectives on Karl Rahner.[5]

Is Karl Rahner still relevant for the students of theology today?

Theology students today, 18, 19 or 20 years old, who begin their study of theology, will hear about Karl Rahner sporadically. But for most students, he is a figure from the past about whom they will hear little or, at best, as a figure in the history of theology. Granted, in Innsbruck the students will walk over the Karl Rahner Platz in front of the Jesuit Church, but who of them even asks who the man was, and who of them knows what his connection was to the Theology Faculty? Most students are illiterate about theological history. Students today look to other sources for their spiritual formation. Karl Rahner – never heard of him; Hans Urs von Balthasar – never heard of him; Henri de Lubac, Yves Congar, Hans Küng – never heard of them! I think it is an opportunity to point to Karl Rahner as an example of how to study theology; when one asks existential questions; when one probes deeply into things and asks again and again. That, to me, is to buck the trend. Today the "party line" is to say rather: "Look in the Catechism; that's where you will find all the answers!" I find that Karl Rahner's method is very maieutic; for me, he is like a midwife who assists me to do theology myself.

Have you ever found Karl Rahner's theology to be too difficult?

Naturally, there is also the so-called "difficult Rahner." *Spirit in the World* and *Hearer of the Word* make demands on you. But as a Jesuit I must add to that the experience I had of my first reading of Rahner in which I began to discover and understand some things about my Order's founder, Ignatius of Loyola – to wit – he is not only a saint who stood on the threshold between the Middle Ages and the Modern era; he was also a theologian. His Exercises are not only spiritual practices, but are theological instructions for an encounter with God. The Exercises serve not only for one's private, pious life: they also communicate knowledge. That is what I learned from Fr. Rahner.

When Fr. Rahner became a Jesuit in 1922, he had the good fortune to enter the Order during a period in which there were great breakthroughs. The Jesuits discovered their founder, so to speak, anew. In 1894, more than 350 years after the founding of the Order, the edition of the *Monumenta Historica Societatis Iesu* was begun. Karl Rahner had immersed himself in some of the original texts. Only a few insiders knew of Ignatius' autobiography. The *Spiritual Exercises* were passed on in a theologically attenuated version. It is still a goal in our own time to become aware of Ignatius not only hagiographically, but also theologically. A Hugo Rahner, a Karl Rahner, a Hans Urs von Balthasar, a Gaston Fessard and others have sought to promote that.

The way Karl Rahner was shaped by the Exercises is, therefore, important to you?

The *Spiritual Exercises* are a magnificent instruction by means of meditation on different stages in the life of Jesus to discover this Jesus of Nazareth as the Christ, the Messiah, who stands in a unique relationship to God. Only by looking at Jesus the Christ is it possible to make a life-choice. The question in the Ignatian Exercises is really: How do I come to an absolute decision? Karl Rahner reflected on that in a remarkable article.[6] He had – as had his brother Hugo, or, perhaps, Erich Przywara, SJ,[7] tried to draw on the knowledge gained from the Exercises and sought to translate that into theology.

The tragedy regarding the mysteries of the life of Jesus was that they were only used as a model for moral teaching or moralizing, but they are more than that. For Karl Rahner there was more substance to them. But he also claimed more than he was able to develop. In his *Scheme for a Treatise of Dogmatic Theology,*[8] which he drafted shortly before the beginning of the Second World War together with Hans Urs von Balthasar, you can find once more a reference to the mysteries of the life of Jesus. That could not be found in any other treatise on Dogmatic Theology. In 1939, Karl Rahner had already earned a PhD; had written a post-doctoral thesis ("*Habilitation*"); was a lecturer for Dogma and the History of Dogma on the Theology Faculty of Innsbruck, and had to deal with a strenuous program of courses and seminars. The question can be raised: How did he happen to come up with the idea to develop a plan for a Dogmatic Theology in which an element of spirituality appears that is not to be found anywhere else? When he published this outline in 1954, this component was still present. Balthasar brings up this particular point in his review. Behind this is the question of concurrence: how can a past event have an impact on salvation in the here and now? Rahner's first reflections on this issue of concurrence can be found in the last chapter of his theological dissertation *E Latere Christi* (1936). That issue continued to haunt him his entire life.

The approach to the study of Rahner in the 1960's and 70's was ruled by a fixation on the transcendental philosophical and transcendental theological starting points of his work and simply ignored his Ignatian roots. There are, however, underlying issues that need to be seen more clearly. Thus, one need not polemically argue that there should be a "Rahner teaching office" in Innsbruck which should seek to relate everything in Rahner back to that basic "*semper idem*" foundational Ignatian experience, or reduce everything to that. I believe that Fr. Rahner was also formed theologically by the normal activities of his daily life; his faithful practice over a period of decades as a priest and a Jesuit formed him much more strongly than many want to or can accept. That would comprise about a third of what contributed to his way of thinking, the second third certainly involved the influence of neoscholasticism, which is completely foreign to my generation, and the final third involved certainly something of his own creation with the help of the method of thinking he learned from Marin Heidegger.

How did you come to choose the topic of your doctoral dissertation?

The suggestion came, on the one hand, from Fr. Neufeld and, on the other; the impetus came from the fact that it was the logical continuation of my Master's thesis of 1991. *Was heisst Jesus lieben?* is something of a popular version of the difficult challenge as to how one can make orthodox Christological statements without using the terminology of the Councils of Nicaea and Chalcedon. My starting point was the fundamental theological approach: the mysteries of the life of Jesus as an entry to the faith in Jesus as the Christ. Studies on the search for the historical Jesus had been long underway since Albert Schweitzer and were already passé when Karl Rahner wanted to propose that the mysteries of the life of Jesus be brought into a dogmatic schema. My question was about the possible entryway to faith. The motif of the mysteries of the life of Jesus can serve as an entryway, as it were, that allows one to enter the theological building. In the Exercises it is not theology that is the most prominent aspect, but rather an experience. You must first have the experience before you can reflect on it. For Karl Rahner the life of Jesus is a *"locus theologicus."* He is trying to recover for Dogmatic Theology what was in the High Middle Ages forced into spirituality and stagnated there, as it were, in exile. He was, by the way, not the only one with his personal interest. Alois Grillmeier also sought to do that and most recently, so did Alex Stock in his *Poetische Dogmatik.*[9]

Could you determine whether Fr. Rahner also developed an existential relationship to Jesus? Did his identification with Jesus proceed more from the head or more from the heart?

Who can look into the heart of a Jesuit? That is something profoundly personal: One does not meddle with that. From his youth, Karl Rahner was rather reserved. He was not talkative, and certainly not when it came to personal matters. In 1978, he wrote his *Speech of Ignatius to a Jesuit today.*[10] There are some autobiographical things in it, reserved, of course, but Fr. Rahner did, in some sense, bare his soul in this speech. He summed up his whole life as a member of the Society of Jesus and I quote the 70 year old Rahner directly: "I would never have been able to live my life as a Jesuit if I had not found an inner relationship in unconditional faith in Jesus Christ the crucified and risen one."[11]

Is your doctoral dissertation a contribution which gives us further insight into Karl Rahner? Did you discover an entry into his thought that, perhaps, has been overlooked until now?

One of the standard criticisms of Karl Rahner is that he does not know history, but rather only speaks of historicity. That is, perhaps, a very German distinction. To that I must say in terms of theological history: at the time Karl Rahner spoke of the mysteries of the life of Jesus both the term "life of Jesus" was tainted (by the failure of the search for the historical Jesus) as well as the term, "mysteries," (by the "Theology of Mystery" of the Benedictines promulgated by the Benedictine Odo Casel, O. S. B.). Neither of them had anything to do with what Karl Rahner meant by the term. But he did not move, so to speak, in a spiritual no man's land. Karl Rahner did not want to write a "Jesuology," but, at the same time, he pointed out the danger of acting as so many theologians did. For them, if Jesus had never lived, their theology would still get on quite well.

Fr. Rahner had, for example, absolutely no hesitation in bringing the life of Jesus to young people when he recommended that they pray the rosary, which, for him, was a Jesus prayer. One can easily imagine that for an average young man, who has had frustrating prayer experiences, the suggestion that he try a form of prayer which does not enjoy great popularity in his generation, can seem somewhat strange. But Fr. Rahner suggested in one of his fictional letters precisely that.[12] One's own life can, as it were, be a continuation of the life of Jesus – through baptism. There are close connections here with Sacramental Theology.

Regarding the topic *Sämtliche Werke* (Collected Works): Why does there need to be such a complete edition of Rahner's work?

Many people ask this question. First I realize that there are quite a few people who say, pointing to the 16 volumes of *Schriften zur Theologie* (and also to the 23 volumes of *Theological Investigations*) that a complete edition is not necessary. To put this in perspective, I would note that these 16 volumes encompass only about one third of the entire corpus. There are always writings that are not recoverable or that are accessible only in libraries. The question is: How does one keep someone's work alive in a comprehensive way? That justifies the publication of a complete edition. I am convinced that Karl Rahner is still to be discovered and I say with Karl Lehmann: Karl Rahner is possibly a man for the future.[13] Perhaps, given the political orientation of the current Church, he is not a man for today or for tomorrow, but for the future.

Looking towards Karl Rahner's 100th birthday and the 20th anniversary of his death in 2004: what do you see happening then?

I assume that there will be various conferences: articles and books will be published. I hope that not only the name Karl Rahner will be acknowledged and revered.[14] It doesn't amount to much when former colleagues, assistants or friends, for the umpteenth time burn incense, give themselves over to impassioned speeches and treat Karl Rahner as an icon on one's domestic altar.

When someone has written as much as Karl Rahner has, there is always the danger of being cited as the source of ideal catch phrases for topics with which one has never been involved. An authority is always looked for, to be used either in a negative or a positive sense. Karl Rahner did not, unlike Hans Us von Balthasar, Henri de Lubac, SJ, or Yves Congar, OP, become a cardinal. Therefore, one must also be careful because of ecclesiastical politics. But, I think it is not about, as Roman Siebenrock likes to say, putting Karl Rahner in storage (*"ein-motten"*), as if to relegate him to a museum. Rather, it is about asking the question: where are the topics about which one can say when one studies theology today, when one reflects today about the faith: "Can this theology be of help?" For me, that is the positive benefit towards which one must continue to work. It is all about finding out – what truly is of worth; what truly will be gained?

To speak from a theological-historical perspective, I believe that the problem of neo-scholasticism can be seen in its systematic bypassing of the canon of life's questions. It became sterile. Today the problem is exactly the reverse; we start with life and its issues, not with a theory. Everyone uses the same concepts, but everyone understands them somewhat differently. For Karl Rahner theology always had to do with life and vice-versa: life with theology in so far as life wants to come into contact with God. I am very strongly opposed to the idea that any separation can be made between a "pious" and an "academic" Rahner. There are, of course, different *genera* in his writings. But for him both were always important. I observed that Karl Rahner was always wrestling with issues, asking questions, quarrelling with someone. That is an important reason for readers to get a taste of Karl Rahner. A conference can analyze, but what is crucial does not take place in analysis, but rather when people deal with texts which stir something within them.

One final question: What recent studies about Rahner are worth-while?

The series *Innsbrucker theologische Studien*, begun initially by Fr. Kern, has truly developed into a series that has continued to publish serious research on Rahner. I can think of Arno Zahlauer, Paul Rulands,

Franz Gmainer-Pranzl, Nikolaus Knoepffler, Engelbert Guggenberger, Franz Gruber, Johannes Herzgsell, and Walter Schmolly. They have all done worthwhile work which should not be overlooked by Rahner research scholars. But there are also meaningful studies to be found elsewhere.

The huge amount of work of Rahner is always ideal as a quarry for topics which often were not his topics at all. Or, they are used for facile possibilities: a person has a topic and tries desperately to connect it with something Karl Rahner wrote. They take a contemporary issue and then simply try to support it by citing quotations from Rahner. That I do not accept as an adequate method of reception. It is not acceptable to take words out of context – that's manipulation! Reading Rahner contextually, you can quickly see that many findings are not as spectacular as one sometimes would like.

A complete edition can present Karl Rahner in a comprehensive way. I agree totally with Roman Siebenrock that many of the interpretations of Rahner's work will be shown to be obsolete when one challenges them by asking: Where is that in the text? Many assertions will be seen as pointless. Karl Rahner, himself, often pointed out how easily you can come up with inconsistencies in his work,[15] as when doctoral students said: Here you said this and there that. He did not want to be placed in a box. There are ruptures in his work and you do not have to harmonize everything and, so to speak, protect Rahner from himself. That is so typically German: that everything always has to be so systematic!

During the course of my dissertation I had to take leave of many preconceived ideas that I had when I began. Karl Rahner thinks about many things in a very traditional way. It is not fitting to confine one's judgment about Rahner to what is revealed in the interviews that he gave in the last years of his life in which often an "angry old man" speaks, who is disappointed with many things which are proceeding so haltingly in the Church, or are even being pushed back to the preconciliar period.

Karl Rahner responded to many things simply in a traditional way without being trapped by the tradition. His creative responses to tradition are fascinating. He criticized some things because he knew what was right and did not simply just repeat the past formulas. The allegation that he destroyed the neo-Scholastic system is absurd. He criticized its one-sidedness and he defended the tradition against those who distorted it. That takes no small measure of intelligence.

NOTES

1 Walter Kern, SJ (1922-2007), Dr. phil., Dr. theol., was Professor of Fundamental Theology at the University of Innsbruck from 1969-1989. Prior to that he taught the History of Philosophy at the Jesuit College in Pullach near Munich. The internationally recognized Hegel scholar was the first Director of the Karl-Rahner-Archiv in Innsbruck.

2 Cf. Andreas R. Batlogg, Karl Rahner: Jesus lieben? Zum Schicksal einer Veröffentlichung aus den 80er Jahren, in: Geist und Leben 67 (1994) 90-101.

3 The monthly periodical of the Austrian Jesuits first appeared in April 1946 as Der grosse Entschluss. Monthly periodical for active Christians. In 1969 (25th anniversary) the periodical was renamed Entschluss. With the December issue of 1999 (54th volume), production was halted. Editors-in-chief were Ferdinand Platzer, SJ and Georg Strangfeld, SJ (1946-1954); Dominik Thalhammer, SJ (1955-1962); Michael Horatczuk, SJ (1963-1973); Werner Reiss, SJ (1974-1977); Georg Sporschill, SJ (1978-1989); Gustav Schörghofer, SJ (1990-1997); and Thomas Neulinger, SJ (1998-1999).

4 The Writers' House was located in the Veterinärstrasse until January of 1966, in the immediate neighborhood of the Ludwig-Maximilians-University. In January 1966 the newly built Writers' House was opened in the Zuccalistrasse in Munich-Nymphenburg, the Alfred-Delp-Haus, named after Alfred Delp (1907-1945) a former co-worker of Stimmen der Zeit who was murdered by the National Socialists. In the fall of 2003 the German Jesuits had to close the Alfred-Delp-Haus.

5 Cf. Andreas R. Batlogg, Paul Rulands, Walter Schmolly, Roman A. Siebenrock, Günther Wassilowsky, Arno Zahlauer, Der Denkweg Karl Rahners. Quellen – Entwicklungen – Perspektiven (Mainz: Grünewald, 2003, 2nd edition 2004).

6 Cf. K. Rahner, Einige Bemerkungen zu einer neuen Aufgabe der Fundamentaltheologie, in: ibid., Schriften zur Theologie, vol. 12 (Einsiedeln: Benziger, 1975) 198-211; ibid., Reflections on a Task for Fundamental Theology, in: ibid., Theological Investigations, vol. 16, translated by David Morland, O. S. B. (New York: Seabury Press, 1979) 156-166.

7 Erich Przywara, SJ (1889-1972), co-worker at Stimmen der Zeit in Munich, wrote the three volume work Deus semper maior. Theologie der Exerzitien. (1938-1940). He was one of the formative figures of Catholic spiritual life in the first half of the 20th century.

8 Cf. K. Rahner, Versuch eines Aufrisses einer Dogmatik, in: ibid., *Schriften zur Theologie*, vol. 1 (Einsiedeln: Benziger, 1954) 9-47; now in: ibid., *Sämtliche Werke*, vol. 4: *Hörer des Wortes*. Schriften zur Religionsphilosophie und zur Grundlegung der Theologie. Bearbeitet von Albert Raffelt (Freiburg: Herder, 1997) 414-443; ibid., A Scheme for a Treatise of Dogmatic Theology, in: *Theological Investigations*, vol. 1, translated by Cornelius Ernst, OP (London: Darton, Longman & Todd, 1961) 19-37, and The Prospects for Dogmatic Theology, 1- 18; cf. Andreas R. Batlogg, *Die Mysterien des Lebens Jesu bei Karl Rahner*. Zugang zum Christusglauben (Innsbruck: Tyrolia, 2nd edition 2003); ibid., Karl Rahners Projekt einer Theologie der Mysterien des Lebens Jesu. Systematisches Denken als Ausdruck ignatianischer Spiritualität, in: Thomas Gertler, Stephan Ch. Kessler, Willi Lambert (eds.), *Zur grösseren Ehre Gottes: Ignatius von Loyola neu entdeckt für die Theologie der Gegenwart* (Freiburg: Herder, 2006) 349-367.

9 Cf. Alois Grillmeier, Geschichtlicher Überblick über die Mysterien Jesu im allgemeinen, in: *Mysterium Salutis*, vol. 3/2 (1969) 3-22; ibid., Mit ihm und in ihm. Das Mysterium und die Mysterien Christi, in: ibid., *Mit ihm und in ihm*. Christologische Forschungen und Perspektiven (Freiburg: Herder, 1975) 716-735; Alex Stock, *Poetische Dogmatik: Christologie*, vol. 3: Leib und Leben (Paderborn: F. Schöningh, 1998).

10 Cf. K. Rahner, Rede des Ignatius von Loyola an einen Jesuiten von heute, in: ibid., *Schriften zur Theologie*, vol. 15 (Zurich: Benziger, 1983) 373-408; now in: ibid., *Sämtliche Werke*, vol. 25: Erneuerung des Ordenslebens. Zeugnis für Kirche und Welt. Bearbeitet von Andreas R. Batlogg (Freiburg: Herder, 2008) 299-329; cf. ibid., *Ignatius of Loyola*. With an historical introduction by Paul Imhof (London: Collins, 1979), 11-38.

11 K. Rahner, Wie kann ein Mensch von heute noch Jesuit sein und bleiben? In: *Jesuiten*. Wohin steuert der Orden? (Freiburg: Herder, 1974) 142-145, 145; now in: K. Rahner, *Sämtliche Werke*, vol. 25, 283-285.

12 *Mein Problem*. Karl Rahner antwortet jungen Menschen (Freiburg: Herder, sixth edition 1984) 40; ibid., *Is Christian Life Possible Today?* Translated by Salvator Attanasio (Denville, New Jersey: Dimension Books, 1984) 37-38: "As crazy as this may sound in our day, I would nevertheless recommend that for once you try to pray the rosary for yourself alone. The restful, relaxed, spoken succession of the same words and a glimpse into the mysteries of the life of Jesus invoked in it can, if one in so doing does not become impatient but tries to slowly train oneself properly, call forth that particular stillness in one which brings a person to God."

13 Karl Lehmann, Karl Rahner zum Gedächtnis. Neunzigster Geburtstag – zehnter Todestag, in: *Stimmen der Zeit* 212 (1994) 147-150.

14 Cf. M. Striet, Ein bleibendes Vermächtnis. Was die Theologie heute von Karl Rahner lernen kann, in: *Herder Korrespondenz* 58 (2004) 559-

564; Albert Raffelt, Nach wie vor starke Resonanz. Ein Rückblick auf das "Rahnerjahr" 2004, in: ibid., 564-568.

15   Certainly without cynicism, but with an awareness of gaps and inconsistencies in his own work Karl Rahner said at the end of his life: "I recently told someone who is writing a doctoral dissertation on me and my theology: Reckon, of course, with the fact that you will find things where I contradict myself and fail to notice that. Everyone always begins anew at a certain place and then develops something from that point on, which perhaps, in the first attempt does not fit that well with what has preceded it thus far;" quoted according to Paul Zulehner *Denn du kommst unserem Tun mit deiner Gnade zuvor... Zur Theologie der Seelsorge heute. Paul M. Zulehner im Gespräch mit Karl Rahner* (Düsseldorf: Patmos, third edition 1987) 30.

23

READING RAHNER — AN ASSET

IN CONVERSATION WITH IRMGARD BSTEH, MUNICH

Irmgard Bsteh, born 1930 in Vienna (Austria), a member of the International Movement of Christian Women, "Grail," worked in the office of the Secretariat of Pax Christi in Vienna, and since 1964, in Munich. Since the beginning of the 1970's she has focused on being a strict observer of the media and on working with authors and editors.

How did you become acquainted with Karl Rahner?

Normally, you find out about someone by personal encounter, but you can also come to know them through reading their work. At any rate, that's how my contact with Karl Rahner came about. I had to remain in bed from 1944-45, due to tuberculosis and the lack of medicine to treat my illness, and so I began to read the classics, biographies, historical works and theology. During my next stay at the hospital I read Hugo Rahner's book, *Griechische Mythen in Christlicher Deutung,* (Greek Myths in Christian Interpretation)[1] – a splendid volume to read aloud.

My first real experience of Karl Rahner came in the form of reading small booklets, a typical format after the war. When I saw his name, I thought: that must be Hugo Rahner's brother. My first impression was: here is someone who is addressing real contemporary issues; issues that are of concern to us here and now; questions about our faith; questions with which I could identify. Where else could you find anyone doing that at that time?

During that time I shared a bedroom in a boarding school with girls, from Nazi families, who had nothing good to say about Christianity and most definitely not about the Church. This was, for me, more stimulating than having conversations with people who thought as I did. Years later, because of this view I turned down Prelate Karl Rudolf's[2] offer to work in the Pastoral Ministry Office in Vienna; I would always be with others who thought as I did.

At the time, I asked myself what religion I would choose if I had to choose now as if for the first time. If *one* is truly right and takes me completely and thoroughly seriously, allows for critical questions instead of "shoving them into the closet," as I call it, then I do not have to get to know all the rest. I decided to remain what I was, which was a very important, freeing experience for me. What then did I find in Karl Rahner? – The very same observations that I had been making! Almost incredulous I observed that this Jesuit not only asked the same kind of questions that I had struggled with in my innermost being, but also voiced his objections to things alleged to be self-evident and the "conventional wisdom." That, of course, could not continue to bode well. I became addicted. Whatever I could get my hands on by Karl Rahner, I bought; later that was all published in large volumes. Bit by bit, I made it part of me, going over and over it until it made sense. Not being an academically trained theologian, the inevitable odds and ends that remained did not bother me.

Did you want to meet Fr. Rahner personally as a result of these aha experiences?

My first encounter with Karl Rahner occurred while I was vacationing in Innsbruck in the beginning of the 1950's, but it was not a personal meeting. It was Sunday, the Spitalskirche, the Hospital Church, the Church of the Holy Spirit on Maria-Theresien Strasse, the main street in Innsbruck, was full to over flowing.[3] I had to stand. Fr. Rahner delivered the homily in a monotone and because of the poor acoustics it was hard to understand, at times. But the people must have known why they had come. That close proximity was, of course, also important to me. But his written work had already become so significant to me that I had high expectations of this immediate encounter. It was not to be the last.

In 1964, as a result of my joining the International Movement of Christian Women, I moved from the Grail community in Vienna to a small center, sharing an apartment with a small *Wohngemeinschaft*, (house-community), in Munich; there were monthly gatherings of like-minded people. In 1965 I traveled to Innsbruck for the conferral of the doctorate on my brother, Andreas.[4] Afterwards, at the banquet table, I found myself next to Karl Rahner. He wanted to know what I did in Munich. We exchanged only a few words.

Was this encounter a prelude to more intensive encounters?

From then on, Fr. Rahner was no longer a stranger to me. In the same year I worked up my courage and went to the Writers' House in the Zuccalistrasse, where he lived after assuming the Romano Guardini chair in Munich, and asked him whether he would speak to our house community about the new understanding of mission inspired by the Second Vatican Council and the dialogue with non-Christians. Some of the women in our group had returned from their ministries in Africa and were very interested in that topic. Fr. Rahner agreed to do it. That afternoon left a lasting positive impression! I asked his research assistant, Adolf Darlap,[5] about his stipend. Darlap responded: "Ah, Fr. Rahner is worth his weight in gold!" He then, however, quoted an amount and I sent it to Darlap. Not long after that he drove over to us and brought greetings from Fr. Rahner along with six volumes of *Theological Investigations* that had been published so far.

Now there was no holding me back. One time I packed one of the volumes to read on a train ride from Munich to Duisburg. I could scarcely imagine how important what I had read and absorbed would become for my later work. I would be, in a sense, equipped for my conversations with "those who thought differently."

At the end of the 1960's I had another operation with painful consequences that lasted for years. At times infections would put me out of commission. Going to Church was out of the question. Once Fr. Rahner had heard of this, (though not from me), he called up unexpectedly and said that he would come to celebrate the Eucharist. I was speechless. He responded to my silence: "Na – it should not be a compulsory blessing!" And it was not. The humble celebration with a fellow Jesuit from America in our living room I shall never forget. There is a small photo of that somewhere.

The reading that you did from the writings of Karl Rahner influenced you greatly. How did that affect your future work?

Over time something happened that I had never anticipated; I began to compare the wishes, the ideas, and the problems my young housemates experienced, especially with regard to partnership, with the way that was handled in the mass media. Some assertions were accurate, but others, although they made a claim to being universally valid, were only infrequently correct and yet others were totally invalid. I wrote to some editors and, much to my amazement, found that they were interested in my ideas. This was followed by invitations to the interested offices and finally by my personal invitations for Viennese coffee at my table. It was the most diverse of women conversation partners, all more or less curious as to how I came to propose this: From where did this come? Nevertheless they believed me when I said that it arose out of my own personal initiative and did not come from another source. It was important to me that it should come from me without ecclesial sponsorship. My motivation – something to do with the Church? This last assumption came about, perhaps, because I made no secret of my position on certain topics involving the image of humanity and also no secret of my "world view," particularly my faith conviction and my critical, loyal critical, view of the Church. First of all, stereotypes were put aside as well as what I call "assumptions." Only thus could a Church of today, a form of Christianity proposed by the Council, come into view with, for example, an acceptance of freedom of conscience and religious freedom. The concept of a "hierarchy of truths"[6] and other such similar ideas, they had never heard of, let alone trusted the Church to consider. Sometimes the skepticism seemed to be almost physically tangible, ("the Church will not be happy with you!") because they thought that I was only representing my private opinion. But, I could make reference to influential conciliar theologians, particularly to one. Their faces revealed to me again and again that they believed that what I was saying was "credible." What I owe to the reading of Rahner proved to be and continues to be an asset. It seems to be inexhaustible. Time and again I would tell Karl Rahner of such conversations. He was always very interested and sometimes he would smile and always counseled me saying: "Only say it in your own words!"

I remember, for example, Feuerbach's "conception of competition," ("*Konkurrenzvorstellung*"); God competes with human beings. I stated: the more the human person becomes dependent on God, the more he becomes human; he becomes what he is. Jesus did not only draw close to God like no other, he, so to speak, became one with God. That's the reason he is the model of what it is to be human. I could always turn to Fr. Rahner with questions and my uncertainties. He responded in very simple terms – there is no other way of expressing it. At any rate, I received confirmation of my actions. There was no prior model to follow for my undertaking and I needed help with practical and financial issues. But as a customer of the newspapers, radio and television – there I was king. Employment was out of the question, especially with the Church: "whose bread you eat, that is whose song you sing." All of that was very clear to Fr. Rahner. In the middle of a conversation, Fr. Rahner asked me how much money I needed. Until it could be figured out how my expenses would be paid, he wanted to help out. He kept his promise, month after month, in sickness and in health, with incredible dependability. The receipts for the payments he made remain a guarded treasure for me.

Is there an area of Fr. Rahner's theology that is particularly beneficial?

Yes, there is one point which I personally have found to be more significant than others: the importance of the evangelical counsels. Long after I had decided in favor of a celibate lifestyle I read Fr. Rahner's words on this.

In this way I learned to theologically substantiate this way of life for myself and for others, and not only with – as one could find in many prominent statements heard and read – the argument of greater availability, greater love, etc. Both of these virtues I had witnessed convincingly and observed in faith-filled married spouses. Fr. Rahner had explored that topic in new ways in his essays and expressed the strongest objections to the pious arguments. Indeed, he boldly asked whether one might dispense with marriage totally. He came to the conclusion – which seemed to me to be irrefutable and still seems so, which is found in volume 3 of his *Theological Investigations*.[7] In addition he created a parable with the brilliant image of the sparrows and the dove.[8]

I was privileged to experience just how appropriate this parable was by an incident that took place in the house community house where I lived. A young nurse told me about her dating experience and her futile search for a partner. She had seen that I was also "without a man" and that I was still happy with my life and she found this odd. Sometimes I referred to myself as an "unmanned spaceship," but this time I sat down with her and began to explain that this was not accidental, but intentional. I could not imagine any better way to explain my decision than the parable of the sparrows and the dove. As to the consequences of my decision to release the sparrows from my hand and let them fly free, I then explained, being deliberately dramatic: if it is not true, what we as Christians await as the "dove on the roof," then we have had the worst luck and we are the biggest fools of all to let the valuable sparrow, marriage, out of our hand even before we have the dove that has been promised – that is still being awaited. I will never forget Elisabeth's sudden exclamation: "So, if I do not believe *what* you believe, still I must believe *that* you believe."

Fr. Rahner simply had to hear of this and he was very pleased when he heard it. He said: "Yes, only say it in your own words!" He was very spirited. Later he asked me, in the middle of a conversation, as if it were the most natural thing in the world: "Can you write something about your life in the midst of the dissenters? That could help to overcome today's religious ignorance." My reaction was almost one of shock and where could I go in order to write under the present circumstances? So, I declined, somewhat embarrassed, and Rahner accepted my response. Sometime later, perhaps a year or so, he came to me a second time with that request. Now I saw that this was someone to whom I owed so much and he made a request of me. So my reaction this time was: I will try to do it immediately. I worked on this for about a year because there were so many experiences from which to choose and I never was able to find large blocks of time in which to think and write. The only thing I knew immediately was that the most important point to reflect on was: a lifestyle for the sake of the kingdom of heaven. I accepted the awkward wording. For me, as someone living in the world, it is more appropriate than "evangelical counsels" a term which I associate with those in religious life. Fr. Rahner had a different point of view, as can been seen from his exchange with Hans Urs von Balthasar.[9] For me it was a matter of my own experiences and the experiences of others with me! For a long time this way of life had proved to be a surprisingly important foundation in terms of my commitment, in more ways than one.

What was the reaction to your research?

I personally got to know married priests. In my conversations with them they came to discover, sometimes very poignantly, how important Fr. Rahner's reflections are to both vocations. You could see that

for some of those priests, as well as those still in office, that this was
the first time that they had encountered such a view. I wrote about
insights that came naturally to me from observations of daily life, for
instance, that celibacy (my for-the-sake-of-the-Kingdom of heaven)
was, so to speak, like a medal whose second side (not the back side)
practically went unnoticed. Instead of experiencing the lack of a family
of one's own, there existed a new relationship – namely the favorites
of Jesus, the weak, the poor the disadvantaged! How many priests are
there who live out their lives in faithfulness to celibacy, but who do
not get to see the other side of the medal! (They do not turn it over!)
To my good fortune I also encountered those who do. From a small
clipping which I received from Fr. Rahner, I know; he listened to one.
I was convinced. It was conclusive; yes, he must have had great relationships.

At last I could, following his wish, send the manuscript to Innsbruck, where Fr. Rahner spent the last stage of life. I came to his office in the Jesuit residence at the previously scheduled time. We talked
briefly; he recommended a revision, which was easy for me to make.
And he then said: "Make this available to priests!" I had never before
seen him so tired. I packed up my things; he accompanied me to the
door; he touched my arm and said insistently – "Pray for me!" That
was the last personal, farewell.

I saw Fr. Rahner only one more time at the *Festakademie* in Freiburg
for his 80th birthday. In his address Rahner spoke about God, the
incomprehensible, unnamable, unfathomable mystery of whom we
can only stutter in analogies and despite that, may not remain silent![10]
Soon after that Bishop Reinhold Stecher presided over the funeral
Mass of the Resurrection in the Jesuit Church in Innsbruck. In the
cold rain we held Fr. Rahner's final commendation. I can still picture
the freezing Bishop Karl Lehmann in front of the coffin at the entrance to the crypt. My small book was published after his death and
it seems strangely to be a kind of testament, for without Fr. Rahner, it
never would have come into being.[11] With every new encounter I had
as a result of this book I heard once again his request: the first and the
second.

NOTES

1 Cf. Hugo Rahner, *Griechische Mythen in Christlichen Deutung.* Gesammelte
Aufsätze (Zurich: Rhein-Verlag, 1945, 2nd edition 1957), (Lizenzausga-

be Darmstadt 1957; New edition: Freiburg: Herder Spektrum, 1992); cf. ibid., *Greek Myths and Christian Mystery*, translated by Brian Battershaw (New York: Harper & Row, 1963).

2 Karl Rudolf (1886-1964), pastoral theologian and pastor, renewed pastoral praxis and prepared the way toward the Second Vatican Council; cf. ibid., *Aufbau im Widerstand*. Ein Seelsorge-Bericht aus Österreich 1938-1945 (Salzburg: Pustet, 1947); Andreas R. Batlogg, In die Pflicht genommen: Im Wiener Seelsorgeamt, in: ibid., Paul Rulands, Walter Schmolly, Roman A. Siebenrock, Günther Wassilowsky, Arno Zahlauer, *Der Denkweg Karl Rahners*. Quellen – Entwicklungen – Perspektiven (Mainz: Grünewald, 2nd edition 2004) 144-157.

3 For many years after World War II, Karl Rahner preached regularly, every Sunday, in the Hospital Church (Spitalskirche) in Innsbruck. He preached there because shortly before Christmas 1943, the Jesuit Church was severely damaged in a bombing and could not be opened until 1953. Cf. K. Rahner, *Kleines Kirchenjahr* (Munich: Ars sacra, 1954); a selection of the homilies held in the mid 1950's in the Jesuit or the University Church can be found in: ibid., *Biblische Predigten* (Freiburg: Herder, 1965, second edition 1966), with an introduction by Herbert Vorgrimler (5-6); ibid., *Biblical Homilies*, translated by Desmond Forristal and Richard Strachan (New York: Herder and Herder, 1966).

4 Andreas Bsteh, S. V. D., Dr. theol., was born in 1933, since 1954 a member of the Society of the Divine Word (Styler Missionaries), Professor of Fundamental Theology and Religious Studies at the Theological College St. Gabriel in Mödling (Lower Austria), Director of the Institute for Religious Studies. Cf. K. Rahner, Welt in Gott. Zum christlichen Schöpfungsbegriff, in: Andreas Bsteh (ed.), *Sein als Offenbarung in Christentum und Hinduismus* (Mödling: St. Gabriel, 1984) 69-82. This volume, a collection of essays, is dedicated to Karl Rahner on the occasion of his 80th birthday; cf. Andreas Bsteh, Introduction, in: ibid., 9-12, 12: "*Professor Karl Rahner SJ* not only took a personal interest in the initiative of these conferences on Theology of Religion from their very inception, but also participated in all of them, taking up important questions. The editor of the 'Essays on the Theology of Religion' and the contributors to this 4th volume in this series are pleased to dedicate this book to him on the occasion of his 80th birthday as an expression of their high regard and sincere wishes for God's blessings."

5 Cf. the interview with Adolf Darlap in this book.

6 Cf. K. Rahner, Hierarchie der Wahrheiten, in: ibid., *Schriften zur Theologie*, vol. 15 (Zurich: Benziger, 1983) 163-168; ibid., A Hierarchy of Truths, in: *Theological Investigations*, vol. 21, translated by Hugh M. Riley (New York: Crossroad, 1988) 162-167.

7 Cf. K. Rahner, Zur Theologie der Entsagung, in: ibid., *Schriften zur Theologie*, vol. 3 (Einsiedeln: Benziger, 1956) 61-72: originally this contribution
   appeared (under the same title) in: *Orientierung* 17 (1953) 252-255, or
   (in Dutch translation) in: *Tijdschrift voor geestlijk Leven* 9 (1953) 480-497
   ("Theologische zin van de Onthechting door Praktijk van de evangelische
   Raden"); ibid., Reflections on the Theology of Renunciation, in: *Theologi-
   cal Investigations*, vol.3, translated by Karl-H. and Boniface Kruger (New
   York: Crossroad, 1967) 47-57; K. Rahner, Passion und Aszese. Zur phi-
   losophisch-theologischen Grundlegung der christlichen Aszese, in: ibid.,
   Schriften zur Theologie, vol. 3, 73-104; ibid., The Passion and Asceticism.
   Thoughts on the philosophic-theological basis of Christian asceticism, in:
   Theological Investigations, vol. 3, 38-85.

8 Cf. K. Rahner, Über die evangelischen Räte, in: *Geist und Leben* 37 (1954)
   17-37; later in: ibid., *Schriften zur Theologie*, vol. 7 (Einsiedeln: Benziger,
   1966) 404-434; ibid., On the Evangelical Counsels, in: *Theological Investigations*, vol.8, translated by David Bourke (London: Darton, Longman
   & Todd, 1971) 133-167, 154-155: "Of course the obedient acceptance of
   'passion' as an inevitable factor in human existence does constitute such an
   actualization of this faith, permeating and dominating the whole of human
   life. Indeed it is the only possible absolute, for only in the *prolixitas mortis*
   which dominates the whole of life can man be he who surrenders the whole
   of himself, since in 'passion' he becomes wholly drawn out of himself. And
   it is in this process that there takes place that exercise of faith and love in
   which man gives himself *wholly* over to that which is no longer his own and
   no longer under his control. But precisely this passion can, nevertheless,
   only be the highest and ultimate act and so the act of faith and hope in
   which man gives himself over to God over whom he has no control if man
   freely goes to meet this event of 'passion' in the absolute by renouncing a
   positive 'this-worldly' good, one that he can experience, possess and enjoy.
   Otherwise this faith remains at the level of mere 'theory' formulated in a
   state of withdrawal from the world, or of ideological consolation which is
   only entertained when the world is no longer able to console. The 'bird in
   the bush' is only believed in when one in deed and in truth lets the 'bird in
   the hand' fly away, and that too before it is taken away from one, and before
   the 'bird in the bush' has yet been laid hold of."

9 Cf. K. Rahner, Laie und Ordensleben. Überlegungen zur Theologie der
   Säkularinstitute, in: *Sendung und Gnade*. Beiträge zur Pastoraltheologie
   (Innsbruck: Tyrolia, 5th edition 1989) 353-391; ibid., "The Layman and
   the Religious Life, On the theology of secular institutes," in: *Mission and
   Grace*, vol. 2, translated by Cecily Hastings and Richard Strachan (New
   York: Sheed and Ward, 1964) 182-228; now in: K. Rahner, *Sämtliche
   Werke*, vol. 16: Kirchliche Erneuerung. Studien zur Pastoraltheologie und
   Struktur der Kirche. Bearbeitet von Albert Raffelt (Freiburg: Herder,

2005) 86-107. – With this essay which originally appeared in *Orientierung* (1956), Rahner is reacting directly to an essay by Hans Urs von Balthasar (Wesen und Tragweite der Säkularinsitute, in: *Civitas* 11, 1955-1956, 196-210): "Hans Urs von Balthasar believes in an essay in *Civitas* that it must be maintained that the Papal Theology of the secular institutes,'also by the best of the Church's theologians of our time' has not yet been surpassed and that in particular the serious objection cannot be spared (205), that my understanding of the essence of the lay state robs the relation between the religious life and the lay state of every basis" (*Sämtliche Werke*, vol. 16, 86). Balthasar was referring to: K. Rahner, Über das Laienapostolat, in: *Der grosse Entschluss* 9 (1954) 245-250, 282-285, 318-324; later in: ibid., *Schriften zur Theologie*, vol. 2 (Einsiedeln, Benziger, 1955) 339-373 (now in: *Sämtliche Werke*, vol. 16, 51-76); ibid., Notes on the Lay Apostolate, in: ibid., *Theological Investigations*, vol. 2, translated by Karl-H. Kruger (London: Darton, Longman & Todd, 1963) 319-352;, or, referring to K. Rahner, Nochmals: das eigentliche Apostolat der Laien, in: *Der grosse Entschluss* 10 (1955) 217-221 (now in: *Sämtliche Werke*, vol. 26, 77-85).

10 Cf. K. Rahner, Erfahrungen eines katholischen Theologen, in: Karl Lehmann (ed.), *Vor dem Geheimnis Gottes den Menschen verstehen*. Karl Rahner zum 80. Geburtstag (Munich: Schnell & Steiner, 1984) 105-119; cf. K. Rahner, *Von der Unbegreiflichkeit Gottes*. Erfahrungen eines katholischen Theologen, edited by Albert Raffelt (Freiburg: Herder, 2nd edition, 2005); K. Rahner, Experiences of a Catholic Theologian, translated by Declan Marmion and Gesa Thiessen, in: *Theological Studies* 61 (2000) 3-15.

11 Cf. Irmgard Bsteh, *Perlen brauchen Körperwärme*. Wie Glaube im Alltag lebendig wird. Ein Zeugnis (Mainz: Matthias Grünewald, 1985).

24

HELPFUL SUGGESTIONS

IN CONVERSATION WITH FR. PETER KNAUER, SJ,
FRANKFURT AM MAIN

Peter Knauer, SJ, lic. phil., Dr. theol., born 1935, a Jesuit since 1953, a Professor of Fundamental Theology at the College, Sankt Georgen, in Frankfurt am Main. Since becoming Professor emeritus (2003), he works in the "Foyer Catholique Européen" and in OCIPE (Office Catholique d'Information et d'Initative pour l'Europe) in Brussels.

When did you first become aware of Fr. Rahner and what influence did he have on your theological thinking?

I remember that I already had heard of Fr. Rahner while I was still a novice. That was the time when the first volumes of *Theological Investigations* appeared. You had the impression that he answered questions that you always had within you in some way, but that he was able to clearly formulate them. That was my first impression. When I look at all of Rahner's work, what I think is key is his concept of Christian revelation as the self-communication of God: communication not as information, but rather as God giving Himself.[1] Equally important is his teaching about the "supernatural existential"[2] – that we are created in Christ; that we, from the very beginning, are already completely immersed in God's grace and so can understand and accept the proclamation of the grace of God in the correct way. Those are the main ideas that I owe to him.

About the term "supernatural existential" – some people question whether that is an appropriate term. They contend that if it is supernatural, then it cannot be an existential, or if an existential – then it cannot be supernatural.

That is a completely false way of posing the issue. To put it simply, when we speak of "nature," we understand what is created as such and when we refer to "grace" we understand that indeed this created world is created in the love of the Father and the Son. Of course, this cannot be open to observation. Misunderstandings regarding the language of "natural" and "supernatural" occur when these terms are understood as if they were two elements of created reality – one on top of the other. "Natural" is everything that comes from God. "Supernatural" refers to all natural reality as it is taken up and assumed into communion with God.

Do you not find that to be too abstract – the self-communication of God on the one hand and the supernatural existential on the other?

They are both the same, only the self-communication of God is hidden and it is recognized and named the "supernatural existential" from the perspective of faith. It is within the context of the proclamation of faith that it becomes apparent to us that we are assumed into the love of God for God, of the Father for the Son. That is the manifestation of the self-communication of God. The Christian message faces us with the claim to be the Word of God. To the question of who God really is, the Christian message answers by pointing to the world as God's creation. Nothing can be without God. This can also be known by the light of reason; it is not a statement of faith. This is called the "natural knowledge of God," but no created reality can be a sufficient basis for communion with God. God dwells in unapproachable light. Moreover, the Christian message says that beyond the fact of our being created we are taken up into the love of the Father for the Son. We are, indeed, from the very beginning, created in this love. That can be found in the creed: to be created in Christ – "through him everything is made." That means that, in the Christian perspective, plain and simple, the world is a world loved by God. It is, from all eternity, taken up into the love of the Father for the Son. The supernatural existential means exactly the same thing as when I say that we are created in Christ, but that cannot be understood apart from faith. It comes to light only through the Christian message. But the condition for the possibility of believing in the promised communion with God consists in the fact that, from the very beginning, it is the true reality of the human person. That is what Karl Rahner means, by the supernatural existential.[3]

Do you have any personal memories of Karl Rahner?

Very early on I wrote to him when I was a philosophy student in Pullach about his article on the logic of an existential decision in the *Festschrift* for the Jubilee of Ignatius of Loyola in 1956.[4] I sensed that he had the right idea, but that he based it on the wrong Ignatian text. At that time, I was working on a translation of the diary of Ignatius;[5] I had just begun to translate Ignatius from the Spanish. I had the impression that Fr. Rahner's theory about the "consolación sin causa,"[6] ("consolation without prior cause,") was not accurate in that Rahner held that this consolation was "without an object;" that contradicts the Ignatian texts.

Did Rahner respond to your letter?

He sent me a short, typewritten letter, which I still have, about a half page in length, single-spaced, without margins and with all kinds of typos and typed over letters. It was an interesting letter. He said: "You know, you could be right, I would have to examine this carefully once again."[7]

Did you take that as somewhat of a confirmation?

That wasn't the issue. Later, I was doing my doctoral studies in Münster, and Fr. Rahner was a professor in Münster[8] for a number of years. Before he was appointed to the faculty, he had been invited to give a guest lecture there[9] by the Dean at the time, Erwin Iserloh.[10] At the beginning of his lecture he wanted to thank the Dean for the invitation, but he could not remember the Dean's name; that was truly amusing. He repeated himself several times: "I would like to thank the Dean …," but he simply could not recall the name.

Another recollection: I participated in a seminar he held. At the time Karl Lehmann was his assistant; he is the one who signed my grade sheet. It was a huge seminar with sixty participants. Everyone had to write a seminar paper and a few were selected to read aloud what they had written, usually a sentence or two. Perhaps I'm exaggerating, but

I seem to recall that Fr. Rahner would then begin to speak. He would walk through the entire lecture hall and always when he came to the blackboard, he would pick up a piece of chalk and draw a circle on the board which had nothing to do with what he said. When he came to the light switch he would shut it on and off again. It seemed that he simply spoke to himself.

I was able to interest him in being a reader for my doctoral thesis.[11] I showed him a letter from Gerhard Ebeling,[12] who had written me about my research. Rahner agreed to become my second reader. In his evaluation he wrote, and I'm paraphrasing, that he didn't exactly know if all of it was Catholic. I had written on the famous Protestant author and great Martin Luther scholar Gerhard Ebeling and agreed with his work to a great extent. Later Rahner was one of my evaluators for my post-doctoral thesis. There he wrote that he could not prove that what I had written was not Catholic.

On the jacket cover of the 6th revised edition of my *Fundamentaltheologie*[13] ("Fundamental Theology"), I have a quote from Karl Rahner, in the way of an advertisement, that comes from his *Theological Investigations* on the question of what can or cannot be an object of revelation. He wrote: "Apart from some reflections in other places, I am aware of this question in Catholic Theology primarily through the work of Fr. Knauer, in his Fundamental Theology.[14] This is precisely the question: Does God's revelation mean that God can inform us about all things possible, for example: on May 25th the world is going to end? Could that possibly be considered as revelation? However, the object of revelation is communion with God and nothing more. The Christian message makes itself intelligible through its content. Only this content makes intelligible how it is possible at all to attribute a human word to God and to speak of him as turning to us. That is the key point in my Fundamental Theology. Therein, it has similarities with the thought of Karl Rahner.

How would you respond to the question: does it still make sense to concern oneself with Karl Rahner?

Basically my answer would be yes. It is profitable to be aware of Karl Rahner's views, even though you might not agree with him on everything. You can always benefit from the good questions he poses.

I think that first and foremost *Foundations of Christian Faith* is a good introduction to his thought, but that is also true of a number of articles in his *Theological Investigations*. I think, for instance of his article, "Theos in the New Testament."[15] On the whole, though, I find that Rahner's more spiritual texts, prayers and homilies are better than many of his theological writings.

There are also a number of issues, it seems to me, that are not very well clarified theologically by Rahner – basically the confusion between the horizon of Being and God.[16] In the final analysis his thinking remains tied to a metaphysics of substance. He characterizes creation as an island in a sea of mystery: that is a very problematic image. I think that, as a matter of fact, Rahner's concept of creation is unclear. There are a whole series of problems. Personally, I believe, to repeat what I already have said, that his spiritual writings are more profound than many of his theological reflections.

Are you thinking of *On the Need and the Blessing of Prayer* or *Encounters with Silence?*

Exactly. I find such texts richer, on the whole, than his academic, theological works. Perhaps this sounds a bit negative, but I think that it's due to an unexplained prior assumption. It is a question of one's presuppositions – take for example, if someone says: God is incomprehensible. Then the question immediately arises: How can one then speak of God at all? I believe that talk about God is only possible in terms of a relational ontology; otherwise God becomes an object among other objects. What we understand about God always is only that which is really different from him, but always points to him.

What I find very significant in Karl Rahner's doctrine of the Trinity is his identification of the immanent and the economic Trinity.[17] There is no way to communion with God other than to be assumed into the eternal love of God for God. That is also the key to the doctrine of justification. No created quality is sufficient to establish communion with God. No matter how gifted or anything else I might be, it would not be enough to establish communion with God.

Is that a criticism of Karl Rahner?

That is a confirmation that God is in God's self Trinitarian; that God's love is an eternal love of God for God in which we are taken up. The economic Trinity is the immanent Trinity. It is out of the question that God's love for us could be determined by anything that is created. To assert this, would be to deny the reality of God's transcendence. If we were not taken up in an eternal, unconditional love of God, we would not have any communion with God. That is an extremely important point, which Fr. Rahner has rightly understood: that God, from eternity, is Father, Son and Holy Spirit and has been revealed as such.

Do you think that Rahner's contribution to theology has already been forgotten?

It sometimes happens with many great theologians that they are forgotten or misunderstood. There are in the history of theology instances of incredible misunderstandings. For example: those having to do with Anselm of Canterbury and his doctrine of redemption. He is not concerned to show that God's alleged anger must be assuaged; but rather to show that God's mercy cannot simply consist in God's closing his eyes to sin. It is much more the case that no created being can establish communion with God: communion with God is only possible in one way and that way is that we are taken up into the love of God for God by God. *Cur Deus Homo?* – so that here can be the Word that says that God loves us. Jesus' death on the cross is for Anselm of Canterbury the witness to that message.

Or in contrast to Luther's doctrine of justification. That faith alone justifies, is, far from declaring that works are superfluous, a battle cry for good works. It is not the fruit which makes the tree good but rather a good tree brings forth good fruit. Whoever wants to do the right thing must live in communion with God. Only the one who knows that one is safe and secure, is the one who lives no longer out of fear for oneself and can do not only the right thing, but in truth, good things.

Can you recall anything that in your opinion was particularly characteristic of Karl Rahner?

His language! Once he even received an award for his German prose, although actually, his texts are very complicated and involve long sentences.[18] But when you read Rahner, and especially when you read Rahner aloud, and are aware of his intonation, it is easier to understand him. Also his books and articles are, strictly speaking, I believe, actually spoken language: a somewhat complicated, spoken language. It can appear to be bafflingly complicated if not read aloud.

Is that any different with his spiritual writings?

They are written in a simpler language and without doubt are more accessible; I believe that they are also his best work. There is also something else that has to be considered: Rahner will typically write in his footnotes: "We cannot treat this or that problem in this context ..." You can almost sense that he suspected that in reality that was exactly the point that mattered. To say something somewhat critical: I reviewed many of the volumes of his *Theological Investigations*[19] and I recall that in volume 10 he discusses what the tradition says about Mary – her sinlessness, her perfection and her freedom from every desire.[20] Her freedom from concupiscence consisted in the fact that Mary was a fully integrated personality. In my review, I asked at that time, whether or not it was perhaps the other way around, and that such a conception of the ideal person is itself highly questionable and thus a form of "concupiscence."[21]

NOTES

1 Cf. K. Rahner, Selbstmitteilung Gottes, in: *Lexikon für Theologie und Kirche* (= LThK), vol. 9 (1964) 627, now in: ibid., *Sämtliche Werke*, vol. 17: Enzyklopädische Theologie. Die Lexikon beiträge der Jahre 1956-1973. Bearbeitet von Herbert Vorgrimler (Freiburg: Herder, 2002) 409; *Sacramentum Mundi* (= SM), vol. 4 (1969) 521-526; now in: K. Rahner, *Sämtliche Werke*, vol. 17, 1280-1284; ibid., Herbert Vorgrimler, Selbstmitteilung Gottes, in: K. Rahner, ibid., *Kleines Theologisches Lexikon* (Freiburg: Herder, 10th edition, 1976) 333; now in: K. Rahner, *Sämtliche Werke*, vol.17, 806-807.

2 Cf. K. Rahner, Existential, übernatürliches, in: *LThK*, vol. 3 (1959) 1301; now in: K. Rahner, *Sämtliche Werke*, vol. 17, 225-226; ibid., Existential, II. Theologische Anwendung, in: *SM* 1 (1967) 1298-1300; now in: ibid., *Sämtliche Werke*, vol. 17, 1038-1039; ibid., Herbert Vorgrimler, Existential, übernatürliches, in: ibid., *Kleines Theologisches Lexikon*, 107, now in: K. Rahner, *Sämtliche Werke*, vol. 17, 565.

3 Rahner's Theologumenon is the object of an ongoing debate; cf. e.g., Nikolaus Knoepffler, *Der Begriff "transzendental" bei Karl Rahner. Zur Frage seiner kantischen Herkunft* (Innsbruck: Tyrolia, 1993); Hansjürgen Verweyen, Wie wird ein Existential übernatürlich? Zu einem Grundproblem der

Anthropologie K. Rahners, in: *Tübinger Theologische Zeitschrift* 95 (1996) 115-131; Paul Rulands, *Menschsein unter dem An-Spruch der Gnade.* Das übernatürliche Existential und der Begriff der natura pura bei Karl Rahner (Innsbruck: Tyrolia, 2000); ibid., Zur Genese der Theologumenons vom "übernatürlichen Existential." Ein Versuch zur exemplarischen Erhellung der Bedeutung der Newscholastik für die Theologie Karl Rahners, in: Roman A. Siebenrock (ed.), *Karl Rahner in der Diskussion.* Erstes und Zweites Innsbrucker Karl-Rahner-Symposion: Themen – Referate – Ergebnisse (Innsbruck: Tyrolia, 2001) 225-246; ibid., Das übernatürliche Existential. In der Taufgnade begründeter Beginn der Gleichförmigkeit des Menschen mit Christus. Ein neuer Blick auf die Genese eines Grundaxioms Karl Rahners, in: *Zeitschrift für Katholische Theologie* 123 (2001) 237-268; David Coffey, The whole Rahner on the supernatural existential, in: *Theological Studies* 65 (2004) 95-118; Thomas P. Flössel, *Gott – Begriff und Geheimnis.* Hansjürgen Verweyens Fundamentaltheologie und die ihr inhärente Kritik an die Philosophie und Theologie Karl Rahners (Innsbruck:Tyrolia, 2004); ibid., Warum ein Existential *übernatürlich* ist: Anmerkungen zur kontroversen Diskussion um Karl Rahners Theologumenon vom "übernaturlichen Existential," in: *Theologie und Philosophie* (= *ThPh*) 80 (2005) 389-411.

4 Cf. K. Rahner, Die ignatianische Logik der existentiellen Erkenntnis. Über einige theologische Probleme in der Wahlregeln der Exerzitien des heiligen Ignatius, in: Friedrich Wulf (ed.), *Ignatius von Loyola.* Seine geistliche Gestalt und sein Vermächtnis. 1556-1956 (Würzburg: Echter, 1956) 345-405; later published under the slightly altered title, Die Logik der existentiellen Erkenntnis bei Ignatius von Loyola, in: K. Rahner, *Das Dynamische in der Kirche* (Quaestiones Disputatae 5) (Freiburg: Herder, 1958, 3rd edition 1965) 74-148; see also ibid., *The Dynamic Element in the Church*, translated by William Joseph O'Hara (New York: Herder and Herder, 1964). – See now, in: K. Rahner, *Sämtliche Werke*, vol. 10: Kirche in den Herausforderungen der Zeit. Studien zur Ekklesiologie und zur kirchlichen Existenz. Bearbeitet von Josef Heislbetz und Albert Raffelt (Freiburg: Herder, 2003) 368-420.

5 Cf. Ignatius von Loyola, *Das Geistliche Tagebuch*, edited by Adolf Haas, Peter Knauer (Freiburg: Herder, 1961); Ignatius von Loyola, *Grundtexte der Gesellschaft Jesu* (Deutsche Werkausgabe 2), translated by Peter Knauer (Würzburg: Echter, 1998) 343-428.

6 Cf. *Spiritual Exercises* 330 and 336; cf. Peter Knauer, Die Wahl in den Exerzitien von Ignatius von Loyola. Vom Geistlichen Tagebuch und anderen ignatianischen Schriften her gesehen, in: *ThPh* 66 (1991) 321-337, esp. 332-334.

7 Rahner's letter is dated February 27, 1959.

8   At the age of 63, Rahner was called from Munich (Romano-Guardini-Lehrstuhl: 1964-67) to Münster (1967-71); cf. Karl H. Neufeld, *Die Brüder Rahner*. Eine Biographie (Freiburg: Herder, 2nd edition, 2004) 279-284; Heribert Woestmann, Ordinarius für Dogmatik und Dogmengeschichte in Münster 1968-1971, in: Paul Imhof, Hubert Biallowons (eds.), *Karl Rahner – Bilder eines Lebens* (Freiburg: Herder, 1985) 84-88.

9   In 1964, Karl Rahner received an honorary doctorate degree in Münster. Following the designation of Hermann Volk (1903-1988), Professor of Dogma in Münster, who became the Bishop of Mainz (1962), there were already in 1962 and then in 1963 attempts to gain Rahner for Münster; cf. Herbert Vorgrimler, *Karl Rahner verstehen*. Eine Einführung in sein Leben und Denken (Freiburg: Herder, 1985), 129f. – See also, ibid., *Understanding Karl Rahner*, translated by John Bowden (New York, Crossroad, 1986) 104 f. Cf. as well Karl H. Neufeld, *Die Brüder Rahner*, 278; cf. in addition: K. Rahner, A Brief Correspondence from the Time of the Council, in: Herbert Vorgrimler, *Understanding Karl Rahner*,141-184,174:"Kötting again made me an urgent offer of the dogmatics chair at Münster." (Letter of September 27, 1963.)

10   Eugen Iserloh (1915-1996), 1954 Professor for Church history at the University of Trier, 1964, Professor for Ecumenical Theology, 1967, Professor for Church history – Medieval and Modern – at the University of Münster.

11   Cf. Peter Knauer, *Verantwortung des Glaubens*. Ein Gespräch mit Gerhard Ebeling aus katholischer Sicht (Frankfurt: Knecht, 1969).

12   Gerhard Ebeling (1912-2001), 1946 Professor for Church history, then for Systematic Theology and Hermeneutics at the University of Zurich; cf. Peter Knauer, Ebeling, Gerhard, in: *LThK*, vol. 3 (Freiburg: Herder, 3rd edition 1995) 425.

13   Cf. Peter Knauer, *Der Glaube kommt von Hören*. Ökumenische Fundamentaltheologie. (Graz: Styria, 1978, 6th edition 1991); cf. ibid., *Unseren Glauben verstehen* (Würzburg: Echter, 1986, 6th edition 2001).

14   K. Rahner, Über Engel, in: ibid., *Schriften zur Theologie*, vol. 13 (Zürich, Benziger, 1978) 381-428, 388. – See also, ibid., On Angels, in: ibid., *Theological Investigations*, vol. 19, translated by Edward Quinn (New York: Crossroad, 1983) 235-274, 241: "Is it possible to answer the question of whether there is a formal principle permitting a priori a distinction between objects that from the very outset simply cannot be regarded as an object of revelation and those which can be the object of a supernatural revelation? Is it possible perhaps to say of certain propositions on the existence and nature of particular realities that they could never be revealed because their content from the outset could never be the object of revelation? Unless we are completely mistaken, this is the sort of question that

is scarcely or never raised in Catholic theology. (This assertion may be due to my own ignorance; apart from touching on the question elsewhere in my own reflections, I have come across it in Catholic theology only in P. Knauer's fundamental theology ...)."

15   K. Rahner, Theos in the New Testament, in: ibid., *Theological Investigations*, vol. 1, translated by Cornelius Ernst, OP (London: Darton, Longman and Todd, 1961) 79-148. – See K. Rahner, *Schriften zur Theologie*, vol. 1 (Einsiedeln: Benziger, 1954) 91-167; now in: ibid., *Sämtliche Werke*, vol. 4: Hörer des Wortes. Schriften zur Religionsphilosophie und zur Grundlegung der Theologie. Bearbeitet von Albert Raffelt (Freiburg: Herder, 1997) 346-403.

16   Cf. Peter Knauer, *Der Glaube kommt vom Hören* (Bamberg: Schadel, 5th edition 1988) 56, footnote 59.

17   Cf. *ThPh* 45 (1970) 133-136; 46 (1971) 423-426; 50 (1975) 448-451.

18   This had to do with the "Sigmund Freud Preis für wissenschaftliche Prosa" ("Sigmund Freud Award for Scholarly Prose") which Karl Rahner received in 1973; cf. the recollection of Nobel prize winner for literature, Heinrich Böll, Auf der Suche nach einer Neuen Sprache, in: Paul Imhof, Hubert Biallowons (eds.), *Karl Rahner – Bilder eines Lebens*, 97-98.

19   Cf. *ThPh* 45 (1970) 133-136; 46 (1971) 423-426; 50 (1975) 448-451

20   Cf. K. Rahner, Human Aspects of the Birth of Christ, in: ibid., *Theological Investigations*, vol. 13, translated by David Bourke (New York: Seabury Press, 1975) 189-194.

21   Cf. Peter Knauer, Bookreview, in: *ThPh* 50 (1975) 203-208: "In contrast to this Rahner understands the integrity of the Mother of God as freedom from concupiscence, which is seen as the impossibility of integrating the drives of human nature and of the environment in the personal decision of the subject (208). I ask myself, whether one must not define the concept of concupiscence the other way around, namely, as the illusory striving for such as integration, in which one wants to bring everything into one's control. Would not then true freedom from concupiscence consist precisely in abandonment of this illusory demand? That is what Rahner says in relation to pluralism, that it may not ever disappear (112)."

25

A JESUIT WEARING A NECKTIE

IN CONVERSATION WITH FR. JÓZEF NIEWIADOMSKI, INNSBRUCK

*Józef Niewiadomski, Dr. theol., Mag. phil., born 1951 in Poland, 1991-
1996 Professor of Dogmatic Theology at the Catholic Private University in Linz, 1996 Professor of Dogmatic Theology at the University of
Innsbruck, and Dean of the Theology Faculty since 2004.*

How did you get to know Karl Rahner?

The first time I met Fr. Rahner was in Poland. It was about 1970-71,
still in the communist era and he came to the Catholic University in
Lublin to deliver a lecture which he gave in German. At that time I
was in the seminary and we seminarians were always called upon to
attend guest lectures when there was some concern that too few people would attend. In sum, we were 150 seminarians – all in cassocks
and we filled the lecture hall, although there were other people there
as well. For me it was an extraordinary experience; Karl Rahner was
wearing a necktie! Here was Karl Rahner, already well-known, – the
great Jesuit professor – and he appeared wearing a necktie, while we
seminarians had to appear in cassocks. A cassock is, of course, only
a piece of clothing, but we were expected to wear it from morning to
night. Yet, here was Fr. Rahner coming to speak, wearing a necktie.
Our prefect began to perspire because it was feared that the seminarians would now ask why he could speak wearing a tie and they always
had to be attired in cassocks.

The second time I met Rahner was in Innsbruck. I had come to
Tirol in 1972. Fr. Schupp[1] was the professor of Dogma and he invited Fr. Rahner to a lecture on Revelation. It was a great experience;
the Madonna lecture hall (*"Madonnensaal"*) was one of the largest
lecture halls and it was filled to the last seat. My German was not
very good at that time. Fr. Schupp lectured from a prepared text and
then Fr. Rahner was to respond. He began – that's something that I

will never forget – with the following introductory sentence: "If I have understood Fr. Schupp correctly, which I doubt to be the case, then he means ..." Then he continued in his typical Rahnerian style, but always beginning with the same sentence: "If I have understood Fr. Schupp correctly, which I doubt to be the case ..." That was not only coquettish, but in part a recognition that he was going to present a type of theology that comes from a different theological starting point. Fr. Rahner thought highly of Fr. Schupp. When Fr. Schupp lost his teaching position it was understood to be a clear sign that Fr. Rahner would replace him: mine was his last master's degree thesis. My work had already been accepted when he was fired. Fr. Rahner took over the classes in Christology and Soteriology. That was in the winter semester of 1974-75; he traveled from Munich for the lectures. Fr. Schupp always stood at the podium and read his lectures from written notes. What fascinated me about Fr. Rahner was that he would walk back and forth as he lectured. I find myself following his pattern and I walk back and forth and do so gladly; I do not remain at the podium. It just goes to show you how a student can be impressed. Fr. Rahner clearly had a concept in his head that was not a repetition of something old, but it was a newly developing idea. I had the sense of being part of seeing him in the act of formulating his ideas.

In 1981, he returned to the Jesuit residence in retirement. I had been hired as an assistant on the faculty and worked in the Institute for Dogmatic Theology. That was the third time that I encountered Rahner and it was a completely different experience than the other two times. Fr. Rahner had instituted a Wednesday evening Colloquium where God and the world were discussed. A topic would be proposed and Rahner simply would deliver a discourse on it. He regularly came to the Institute, almost daily, and I was able to experience him as a human being. As assistants we still had library duty at that time which entailed sitting in the large reading room "guarding" the books. Fr. Rahner would come in and look at the new books which were on display and would make comments in a low voice, but loud enough for all who were there to hear it.

Let me tell you a story which will give you an insight into Fr. Rahner. There was a book on Fundamental Theology by Adolph Kolping[2] on display, a pretty thick volume.[3] He picked up the book and looked at it from all sides. I was on duty that day, sitting at the desk facing the students and he signaled with his finger for me to come over to him. It seemed that he wanted to say something to me quietly, but he spoke so that the entire room could hear it: "Do you know that Kolping is a big ..." That, too, was Karl Rahner! Fundamentally what he really liked to do was to speak to the young assistants and students, to go out to eat ice cream. As an assistant you naturally revered the great Rahner. In hindsight, I regret that I did not go out with him more often. I always felt that it was expected that you were to speak to him about scholarly issues, but basically, the older he got, the more it was clear that he simply wished to engage in normal human encounters, often completely banal conversations. I realized that only in hindsight.

He felt at home at the Institute; he was happy to come there. He attended all the Institute parties. One unforgettable occasion was the 60th birthday of Fr. Walter Kern, SJ.[4] Fr. Rahner sat at the same table as Fr. Engelbert Gutwenger, SJ.[5] Both of them had been at loggerheads their entire lives and now they sat like two children who had grown old and joked with one another. That was something marvelous to behold. In spite of their past disagreement, I saw simply two human beings, who had lived isolated from one another, two lonely islands. At any rate, at such celebrations, I recognized this quality of his being very human.

Fr. Rahner died then in Innsbruck?

That was at the end of March 1984. Naturally, I attended the funeral. We were told that his scholarly estate would be sent to Innsbruck where it would become his personal archive.[6] Fr. Kern did everything in his power to see that someone was relieved of other duties in order to work in the archive. Since I was an assistant at the Institute he commissioned me to do the preliminary sorting out of the material. Various things had already been sorted out by the Jesuits, especially Rahner's unpublished work. I simply began to organize Fr. Rahner's publications and arrange them in order. We bought a small stamp pad and stamp – "Rahner-Archiv." Fr. Kern was, in actuality, the first archivist and I his assistant. We then had the idea that we should apply for financial support for this endeavor from the "Fonds für Wissenschaftliche Forschung" (FWF: "Funds for the Promotion of Academic Research") in Austria and we were able to obtain a grant. We received enough money to hire someone for a half-time position; the applicant that we selected was Roman Siebenrock. I then was relieved of my

position. But I was the one who first worked on sorting out the material and Fr. Kern was the driving force behind the establishment of
the archive. He also was the one who organized the material so that
a distinction was established between the published and unpublished
material and the letters. The archive was connected to the Institute for
Dogmatic and Fundamental Theology – which was the name of the
Institute at that time. When Fr. Kern became Professor emeritus, Fr.
Neufeld was named his successor. The Karl Rahner Foundation and
the Karl Rahner prize also had been established during this time.

What significance does the Karl Rahner Archive have today?

In my opinion, and I'm speaking critically now, the Jesuits had the
opportunity for years to do something with the Archive, but hardly
anything has been done to systematically develop, cultivate and bring
it to the consciousness of the public. Fr. Kern was not really to blame:
I would say that actually too much was demanded of him. He was not
truly a Rahnerian in the strict sense. That the Archive does function
even in a limited way was due to the work of Roman Siebenrock.[7] He
immersed himself in Rahnerian theology and he developed the skills
that an archivist must have. He consulted with the Karl Barth Archive
in Basel (Switzerland) in order to gain the "know-how" necessary to
run an archive. When Fr. Neufeld came from Rome, he did what was
needed the most. Despite that, I must say, in my opinion, that the
Jesuit province and the Jesuit residence missed many opportunities.
For example, at the beginning they missed the chance to contact some
foundations to obtain stipends so that young scholars could come and
study. They didn't think about that. The same thing occurred with
the Jungmann archive which is now simply stored someplace in the
library.

**To return to your encounters with Fr. Rahner. What do you think
would have occurred if you had the opportunity for more frequent
contact with him?**

What I am now as a theologian is the result of my being a product of a
particular time and milieu: in my case the late 1960's. It was a time in
which there were many great academic- theoretical discussions about
the status of theology as a science which we regarded as the *non plus*

ultra. The topics which are so significant now, such as biography, theology, spirituality, reflection, Church and life, were not the main focus of our concern. Fr. Schupp represents the voice for this generation. His publications were all academic-theoretical reflections, far removed from spiritual and ecclesial life. Fr. Rahner stood for something different. But as a young assistant I saw him first and foremost through this lens: that is, that he was this famous theologian! Of course, we all felt that here was a complete person, not someone who only worked with his brain, but here was someone who "embodied" his theology. Johann Baptist Metz's accusation that Fr. Rahner remains limited to an abstract thinking subject is entirely absurd. I would say that Fr. Rahner first of all began with spiritual experience, with the experience of the individual, which does not originate on the abstract level. Spiritual experiences are very intimate; they are not generalizations and they are not abstract.

What I believe that I missed out on – as someone who had the chance – was the opportunity to foster human contact with Fr. Rahner – to get to know him as a person, in an everyday, banal sense. I see now that to go out to eat ice cream was, for Rahner, a completely spiritual act in the sense that, appreciating his Theology of Grace – grace and nature cannot be separated into two levels, but form a whole. I now can see that integral perspective of the whole. As a theologian Karl Rahner was monumental!

Fr. Rahner was also impatient. Do you think that he complained too much about Rome? Was he too critical?

First of all, I never saw Fr. Rahner become angry, nor did I ever find him to be quick-tempered. He was always very kind. Some impressions do stick out in my mind. But I experienced him more as a kind, older man who was totally imbued with the sense of the enormous seriousness of life. He also had a sense of humor. The second image I have of him was that formed by the public perception of his relation to the institutional Church. It was readily apparent that Fr. Rahner was an incredibly pious person, a deeply pious person, who was supported by his piety to the end of his life. He developed his theology out of this piety. His early publications *Encounters with Silence, On the Need for and the Blessing of Prayer, Holy Hours and Devotion to the Passion,* those were writings that flowed from the exercise of his spirituality.

The question of his understanding of Church can only be answered in the context of his spirituality and not in terms of his relationship to bishops. That would produce only a very limited view of his understanding of Church. I would venture to say that his loyalty to the Church was based first on his piety, which was deeply ecclesial and often very traditional. That is something that struck me as a student. At that time – the beginning of the 1970's – that was not something that was appreciated much. You also didn't hear of Fr. Rahner's constant emphasis on silence and on prayer. I recall a remark he made to me while he was riding with me in the car regarding Church Office and the Pope. He said: "You know, Hans Urs von Balthasar has breakfast with the Pope." So he made one comment that was a bit critical of von Balthasar, but at the same time he said: "Of course, I would also readily have breakfast with the Pope." Karl Rahner as a bishop or as a cardinal – that to me is inconceivable!

The elevation of Henri de Lubac, SJ to the cardinalate; that was a sign from Pope John Paul II of his leanings. I was not happy about that. De Lubac was never an academic teacher because his theological positions were always controversial. But that was a predilection of the Pope. Later Yves Congar, OP, Avery Dulles, SJ, and Leo Scheffczyk became cardinals.

To what extent are today's students influenced by Rahner? Does he still matter, or is, for instance, Pierre Teilhard de Chardin more popular?

I really am not capable of answering that. You would have to ask Roman Siebenrock, as paradoxical as that might appear. Since I have been in Innsbruck no one has begun a dissertation on Rahner for either a doctoral degree or a master's. But there are a few doctoral students from India who have begun master's theses on Teilhard. Fr. Schwager has had a few doctoral dissertations written on Rahner for Fundamental Theology.

You stated that Fr. Rahner worked as a theologian not only with his head, but also with his heart – as a man of the Church, as a priest, as a person of prayer.

I had to teach a course on grace. Naturally I drew upon the wonderful article Fr. Rahner wrote on the experience of grace.[8] In this article everything comes together. On the one hand there is this incredible rigor of thought, and on the other a focus based on experience, that goes beyond all cheap psychologizing or a shallow understanding of experience. The understanding of spiritual experience is broadened. It is here that Karl Rahner is revealed to me in all his dimensions, as a person, as a Christian, as a priest, as a theologian and as a Jesuit.

NOTES

1 Franz Schupp, born 1936, Dr. theol., Dr. phil., 1960-1976 a member of the Society of Jesus, Professor of Dogmatic Theology at the University of Innsbruck, since 1979 Professor at the University of Paderborn; cf. Walter Raberger, Hanjo Sauer (eds.), *Vermittlung im Fragment*. Franz Schupp als Lehrer der Theologie (Regensburg: Pustet, 2003) 211-279: Zum Begriff "Offenbarung." Gemeinsame Vorlesung von Franz Schupp und Karl Rahner im Wintersemester 1972-73.

2 Adolf Kolping (1909-1997), 1949 Professor of Fundamental Theology at the University of Münster, 1962-78, Professor of Fundamental Theology at the University of Freiburg.

3 Cf. Adolf Kolping, *Fundamentaltheologie*, vol. 3: Die katholische Kirche als die Sachwalterin der Offenbarung Gottes (Münster: Regensburg, 1981, 875 pages!); vol. 1: Theorie der Glaubwürdigkeitserkenntnis der Offenbarung (Münster: Regensburg, 1968); vol. 2: Die konkret-geschichtliche Offenbarung Gottes (Münster: Regensburg, 1974).

4 Walter Kern, SJ (1922-2007), Dr. theol., Dr. phil., was Professor of Fundamental Theology at the University of Innsbruck and the first Director of the Karl-Rahner-Archiv.

5 Engelbert Gutwenger, SJ (1905-1985), 1939 teacher in Innsbruck, 1939-1946 Instructor at Heythrop College, Oxford, 1946-47 Professor at the Seminary St. Georgen in Längsee (Carinthia, Austria), then once again teacher in Innsbruck (Fundamental Theology, Dogmatic Theology, Philosophy), 1954 a. o. Professor, 1958 Professor of Fundamental Theology, 1959-60 Dean of the Theology Faculty, 1961-62 Rector of the University of Innsbruck, 1949-50 Vice-Rector of the Canisianum; cf., Emerich Coreth, In memoriam, Pater Engelbert Gutwenger, SJ, in: *Zeitschrift für katholische Theologie* 107 (1985) 249-251; Karl H. Neufeld, Fundamentaltheologie in Innsbruck, in: Walter Kern, *Geist und Glaube*. Fundamentaltheologische Vermittlungen zwischen Mensch und Offenbarung, edited by K. H. Neufeld (Innsbruck: Tyrolia, 1992) 7-30.

6 Cf. Adolf Darlap, Das'Archiv' und der'Preis,' in: Paul Imhof, Hubert Biallowons (eds.), *Karl Rahner – Bilder eines Lebens* (Freiburg: Herder, 1985)
   172-73.

7 Cf. the article by Roman A. Siebenrock in the appendix: Experiences in
   the"Karl-Rahner-Archiv."

8 Cf. K. Rahner, Über die Erfahrung der Gnade, in: ibid., *Schriften zur Theologie*, vol. 3 (Einsiedeln: Benziger, 1952) 105-109; cf. ibid., Reflections on
   the Experience of Grace, in: ibid., *Theological Investigations*, vol. 3, translated by Karl-H. and Boniface Kruger (Darton, Longman & Todd: London,
   1967) 86-90.

26

WE ONLY HAVE PREMONITIONS

IN CONVERSATION WITH GERHARD RUIS, SALZBURG

Gerhard Ruis, Mag. theol., born in 1931, producer for many years of "Nachtstudios" (Night Studios) on Austrian Radio (ORF-Studio Salzburg) and Academic Editor for the Publishing House, Styria (Graz).

Is it correct to conclude that Karl Rahner is slowly disappearing from the Church's consciousness?

Here in the German speaking world and, perhaps, also in the Italian-Roman region he has been – in my opinion – "placed in cold storage," as we say. He is rarely quoted in the most recent theological and philosophy of religion publications. Even by theological faculties, and I am now thinking of the University of Salzburg, it does not happen often that Rahner is chosen as a topic for a seminar.

He spoke of the fact that the general situation of the Church is that of a wintry season. But he said that beneath the blanket of snow the seeds of the future do not freeze, but rather prepare for a rebirth. That is true also for his theology. Whether the *Sämtliche Werke* (*Collected Works*) of Karl Rahner, which are being edited by the prominent editorial board consisting of Karl Lehmann, Johann Baptist Metz, Karl H. Neufeld,[1] Albert Raffelt, and Herbert Vorgrimler can lead to a Rahner renaissance, cannot be predicted. There are individuals who remain true to Rahner, who live with his work in this wintry season, if one may speak of it in those terms. I, myself, have never ceased reading Rahner and I am always, over and over again, impressed with his insights. Albert Raffelt has edited some smaller texts by Rahner, for which he is to be commended; small volumes which enable one to take Rahner in small doses each day. Each day, at breakfast, my wife and I share a short Rahner reading. I very much treasure both of the Rahner-Readers – Rahner's homilies and prayers, which Raffelt has edited.[2]

I find that it is a great act of self-emptying when one "reveals" oneself in one's prayers, when one allows others to share in one's prayers. That is certainly something wholly intimate. Rahner's prayers were re-printed again and again. I use them often, especially at funerals. Rahner could be grumpy in everyday encounters, but basically he had a very profound and sensitive soul. I am convinced that he will again experience a renaissance.

You made several broadcasts with Karl Rahner on German and Austrian radio. How did you choose the topics?

We had several conversations; they were also published.[3] The conversations were always on relevant topics. We would also speak a little about his life. He told me about his childhood and his parents. His mother lived to be more than 100 years old.[4] He loved her very much. There was a commemorative photo of her made when she died complete with a prayer from Pierre Teilhard de Chardin, SJ;[5] he showed that to me. Fr. Rahner asked me to read the prayer written in her own hand and asked me to guess how old the person was who had written it. I didn't have the vaguest notion and guessed and was way off the mark. He said: That is my mother's handwriting and she wrote this when she was 100 years old. And that is a beautiful prayer. His mother always said to Karl: Do you know that if you would write more intelligibly, I would be able to understand you better. Hugo Rahner also often said the same thing.

The conversations which we had always revolved around a theme – for instance we had a conversation about "Why does God allow us to suffer?" We talked about this for an entire hour. Sometimes events or seasons of the Church year such as Christmas or Pentecost were the reason we chose to speak on certain topics. You could discuss problems in depth with Fr. Rahner. He also honestly acknowledged: I can say a good deal about a topic and do so in a responsible way, but in the final analysis we only have premonitions. One should never assume that we truly comprehend totally the mysteries of faith. Thomas Aquinas used the expression: "*Totaliter aliter*" – it is always completely different (than we imagine).

Did Fr. Rahner see the questions prior to your conversations?

No. We had the conversations sometimes at the studio or I had my tape recorder with me and we held the conversation either in his room or in his office; it was done in different ways. This is done live only in the rarest of cases. I began the so-called "Salzburg Night Studios" with my father-in-law. We did that every Wednesday night for one hour; we produced the program in advance and then broadcast it.

And Fr. Rahner always was able to have something to say?

Yes, always. He pursued theology like another would breathe. To think theologically was an ingrained habit for him. He was a profoundly spiritual person. I asked him once whether Christians could not be accused by some of their contemporaries of engaging in the social realm and committing themselves to helping the weak and the poor, embracing initiatives for social reform and fighting for equality, but who did not attribute these actions to the working of the Holy Spirit because they then could be accused of proselytizing. Fr. Rahner answered, and now I am quoting him word for word: "I would say wherever people live selfless lives, whenever they truly make the leap into mystery, into unearned love, into a final and radical truth, they are dealing with God and have received God's Spirit. The question whether they can define it as such or verbalize it may be important humanly speaking – for faith or theology – but in the end it is of secondary importance. Thousands of times people have authentic and basic experiences of the Spirit without recognizing them as such. Thus they misinterpret their experience or even reject correct interpretations of it. Nevertheless, they have had the experience. A psychologist who holds that all human thoughts are merely sense perceptions, or associations, or behavior patterns, and so on, will reject such a spiritual interpretation of experience. Still the experience is there. Due to a lack of a correct theological explanation of faith, the experience is not considered spiritual. Those who love totally and absolutely have already loved God and encountered the Spirit, whether they acknowledge it or not."[6]

Shortly before the Second Vatican Council Fr. Rahner gave a famous speech in Salzburg which brought him directly into conflict with Rome.

That was on Pentecost 1962. On June 1, 1962, Rahner gave a formal address "Do not stifle the Spirit!" (*"Löscht den Geist nicht aus"*) at the Austrian *"Katholikentag."* There he pleaded passionately for Christians, and above all for bishops and priests, to choose the way of "Tutiorism of Risk" (*"Tutiorismus des Wagnisses"*).[7]

What in your view were Fr. Rahner's primary concerns?

Ecumenism was a concern very close to his heart, particularly at the end of his life. The book that he wrote with his friend Heinrich Fries in 1983 I see as a kind of a guide book for further ecumenical progress.[8] There were many concrete proposals in this book which provided a kind of theological line of approach to achieve this end. The book caused a great stir when it appeared. But it has more or less disappeared, relegated to the desk drawer and today you hardly hear about it anymore; hardly anyone refers to it. I know, for example that the great ecumenist from Basel, Oscar Cullmann,[9] has spoken with great respect about this book by Fries-Rahner.

What do you have to say regarding the relationship between Rahner and Balthasar?

That was a difficult relationship. I can remember that Fr. Rahner was repeatedly invited to the summer Salzburg Festivals. In fact, he always expressed a great interest in them, but we would scarcely be seated for the performance when he would fall asleep. He was already hard of hearing. I once took him to an open air performance in the cathedral square to see *"Jedermann,"* (Everyman) by Hugo von Hofmannsthal. I mentioned to him that Hans Urs von Balthasar would soon celebrate an important birthday and I would have to do a broadcast on the event and I asked Rahner if he would tell me a bit of what he thought about Balthasar. He needed a little coaxing and finally said: "Ah, I don't know what I should say about him. He is always against me." Fr. Rahner then finally said that he envied Balthasar because he was a very artistic person. That was a gift that Rahner totally lacked. He also described Balthasar as someone who was much more talented than he.

Fr. Rahner's successor to the Romano Guardini chair was Eugen Biser. What was the relationship between them?

They were friends, but the relationship was somewhat awkward. Biser had a significant birthday and chose Fr. Rahner as *laudator*. That did not please him. The entire celebration took place in the prestigious Siemens Foundation. Rahner said to me: "I don't know what I should say about Biser; as a theologian he is not held in high esteem. How can I say something laudatory about him? I don't know his writings." Then he gave a talk that had nothing to do with Biser,[10] who was bitterly disappointed. That's how Fr. Rahner chose to deal with the incident.

NOTES

1 Karl H. Neufeld, SJ, left the editorial board in 2005 and was replaced by Andreas R. Batlogg, SJ

2 Cf. K. Rahner, *Grosses Kirchenjahr*. Geistliche Texte, edited by Albert Raffelt (Freiburg: Herder, 3rd edition1990); ibid., *Gebete des Lebens*, edited by Albert Raffelt (Freiburg: Herder, 3rd edition 1984). – See also ibid., *The Great Church Year*. The Best of Karl Rahner's Homilies, Sermons, and Meditations, edited by Albert Raffelt. Translation edited by Harvey D. Egan, SJ (New York: Crossroad, 1993).

3 Cf. K. Rahner, Heiliger Geist – Gibt es ihn noch in der Welt von heute? Gespräch mit Gerhard Ruis (Salzburg 1976), in: ibid., *Im Gespräch*, vol. 1, edited by Paul Imhof, Hubert Biallowons (München: Kösel, 1982) 277-281; ibid., Der Tod als Vollendung. Ostergespräch mit Gerhard Ruis (Salzburg 1980), in: ibid., *Im Gespräch*, vol. 2, edited by Paul Imhof, Hubert Biallowons (München: Kösel, 1983) 122-125; ibid., Aggiornamento ist nicht vollendet. Gespräch mit Gerhard Ruis, Salzburg, über die Berufung von Kardinal Ratzinger nach Rom (1982), in: ibid., 239-244; Erlösung und Emanzipation. Gespräch mit Gerhard Ruis (Salzburg 1982), in: ibid., 278-283; Auf den Spuren priesterlicher Existenz. Gespräch mit Gerhard Ruis zum 50jährigen Priesterjubiläum (Salzburg 1982), in: ibid., 283-295. – See also K. Rahner, How Is the Holy Spirit Experienced Today? Interview with Gerhard Ruis of the Vienna *Presse*, Salzburg, (June 5-6, 1976) in: *Karl Rahner in Dialogue*, 1965-1982, edited by Paul Imhof, Hubert Biallowons. Translation edited by Harvey D. Egan (New York: Crossroad, 1986), 141-143; ibid., Death as Fulfillment, Interview with Gerhard Ruis for *Die Furche*, Salzburg, (April 2, 1980) in: *Karl Rahner In Dialogue*, 1965-1982, 238-240; ibid., Aggiornamento Is Not Finished, Interview with Gerhard Ruis for the *Süddeutsche Zeitung*, Munich, (January 6, 1982) in: *Karl Rahner In Dialogue*, 1965-1982, 316-319; Salvation and Liberation, Interview with Gerhard Ruis for *Landesstudio Salzburg* of Radio Austria, Salzburg, (April 7, 1982) in: *Karl Rahner In Dialogue*, 1965-1982, 342-345; What Does It Mean to Be a Priest Today? Interview with Gerhard Ruis on the occasion of Karl Rahner's fiftieth jubilee as a priest

for *Landesstudio Salzburg* of Radio Austria, Salzburg, (April 7, 1982) in: *Karl Rahner In Dialogue*, 1965-1982, 346-352.

4 Luise Rahner, born Trescher (1875-1976).

5 Facsimile printed in: Paul Imhof, Hubert Biallowons (eds.), *Karl Rahner – Bilder eines Lebens* (Freiburg: Herder, 1985) 163.

6 K. Rahner, Heiliger Geist – Gibt es ihn noch in der Welt von heute? Gespräch mit Gerhard Ruis (Salzburg 1976), in: ibid., *Im Gespräch*, vol. 1, 277-281, 280 f. – See ibid., How Is the Holy Spirit Experienced Today? Interview with Gerhard Ruis of the Vienna *Presse*, Salzburg, (June 5-6, 1976) in: *Karl Rahner In Dialogue* 1965-1982, 141-143.

7 K. Rahner, Löscht den Geist nicht aus! in: ibid., *Schriften zur Theologie*, vol. 7 (Einsiedeln: Benziger, 1966) 77-90, 85. – See ibid., Do Not Stifle The Spirit, in: ibid., *Theological Investigations*, vol. 7, translated by David Bourke (New York: Seabury Press, 1971) 72-87,81: "We live in an age in which it is absolutely necessary to be ready to go to the utmost extremes of boldness in our attitude towards the new and the untried, to that point at which it would be, beyond all dispute, simply inconceivable for one who accepts Christian teaching and has a Christian conscience at all to go any further. In practice the only admissible 'tutiorism' in the life of the Church today is the tutiorism which consists in taking risks. Today, when we are struggling to solve the real problems which confront us, we should not, properly speaking say: 'How far *must* I go?' because the very nature of the situation itself absolutely compels us to go at least as far as possible. We should be asking ourselves, rather: 'How far *can* we go by taking advantage of all the possibilities in the pastoral and theological spheres?' The reason is that the state of the kingdom of God is certainly such that we must be as bold as possible in taking risks in order to hold out in the manner demanded by God."

8 Cf. Heinrich Fries, Karl Rahner, *Einigung der Kirchen – reale Möglichkeit* (Quaestiones Disputatae 100) (Freiburg: Herder, 1983). An extended special edition which also contains critics on the theses of Fries and Rahner was published in 1985. – See now: ibid., *Sämtliche Werke*, vol. 27: Einheit in Vielfalt. Schriften zur ökumenischen Theologie. Bearbeitet von Karl Lehmann und Albert Raffelt (Freiburg: Herder, 2002) 286-396. See also Karl Rahner, Heinrich Fries, *Unity of the Churches*, An Actual Possibility. Translated by Ruth C. L. Gritsch and Eric W. Gritsch, (Philadelphia: Fortress Press, 1985).

9 Oscar Cullmann (1902-1999), was since 1938 Professor for New Testament and the History of the Early Church at the University of Basel, Switzerland. He was an advisor to Popes Pius XII, John XXIII, and Paul VI in ecumenical questions.

10   Cf. K. Rahner, Realistische Möglichkeiten der Glaubenseinigung?, in:
Horst Bürkle, Gerhold Becker (eds.), *Communicatio fidei* (Festschrift for
Eugen Biser), (Regensburg: Pustet, 1983) 175-183.

27
LIKE A WAKE-UP CALL

IN CONVERSATION WITH WALTER STROLZ, INNSBRUCK

Walter Strolz, Prof. Dr. phil., born 1927; 1954-1958 Editor at Tyrolia Publishing Company in Innsbruck, Austria; 1959-1964 on the editorial staff at Herder Publishing, Freiburg, Germany; 1965-1987 Academic Director of the Institute for the Promotion of Dialogue, "Weltgespräch" and the Ecumenical Foundation, "Oratio Dominica," for the promotion of dialogue between Christians and other World Religions; a free-lance writer in Innsbruck and since 1972 a member of the International Association of Poets and Playwrights, Essayists and Editors, and Novelists, the Austrian branch of the P.E.N. Club.

In an article that you wrote about your encounter with Martin Heidegger you mentioned that you had developed a very personal relationship with Karl Rahner.[1] How did that come about?

When I am asked now to speak about my relationship with Karl Rahner, after a period of more than 50 years, such a question acts like a wake-up call. His stature and his personality remain unforgettable. He had a decisive influence on me during the years 1949-1959. I first became aware of him when I was beginning my study of German language and literature, philosophy and history while he was a preacher at the University Church, the Jesuit Church, in Innsbruck.[2] At the time I was reading his book, *On the Need and the Blessing of Prayer.*[3] What made an impression on me was the unique tone of his language, as well as the penetrating force with which he explored the meaning of hardship and pain, at the same time being consistent with philosophical insights.

In 1953 my visits to the Sillgasse[4] began, precipitated by his book on the philosophy of religion, *Hearer of the Word.* I, already at that time, found the question of the relationship between reason and revelation, philosophy and faith unsettling. Rahner's exposition of this relationship, together with my continued study of his book *Spirit in the World*, proved to be normative for my further faith development up to the publication of my first philosophical book, *Der vergessene Ursprung*,[5] "The Forgotten Source." In our conversations Fr. Rahner encouraged me and gave me the confidence to think for myself, convinced that I already recognized the inseparable relationship between philosophy and revelation. He entrusted me with the task of revising a manuscript of his lecture "*Chancen des Christentums,*" "Chances for Christianity"[6] for a radio broadcast commissioned me to write an article in his place for the *Rheinischer Merkur*[7] on the cosmology of Pierre Teilhard de Chardin and accepted the invitation to lecture at the Tirol conference of Scholars on "*Wissenschaft als Konfession,*" "Science as Confession."[8] Rahner invited me to his "*Privatissimum*" for theology students working directly under his supervision. I participated in his seminar on "Nature and Grace," as well as the one on the mystery of the world.

His style and his method in these seminars will remain in my memory forever: his candid questions venturing into unexplored territory. Fr. Rahner began the discussion, walking back and forth, responding to the questions of Johann Baptist Metz, who was the student moderator at that time, with a well reasoned, and penetrating inexorability. An intellectual fervor flashed from his downcast eyes when a possible answer to the proposed question began to emerge. By that experience, together with studying the first three volumes of *Theological Investigations*, I learned that philosophy and Christian faith can neither be separated nor equated, but rather must be understood in such a way as to be seen in relation to one another.

In 1959 Tyrolia Publishing House published Karl Rahner's *Mission and Grace*. The introduction to the 1989 edition states that the twenty-four essays of the first publication "opened a series of new perspectives that would become important to the work of the Council."[9] Why did a Professor of Dogmatic Theology take up Pastoral Theological questions at all?

Mission and Grace should be seen as a prelude to the *Handbook of Pastoral Theology*.[10] I know, from my role as a publisher involved in the conversations regarding this project around 1962-63, that it was Karl Rahner's intention to establish a new, theological foundation for ministry. Therefore, among the first contributions to his collection, is a reflection on the relationship between the "reality of redemption and the reality of creation."[11] Ecclesial praxis thus avoids the danger of short-lived practices. Fr. Rahner insistently argues that creation must be seen as absolutely necessary if the Christian message of salvation is to address the human person in his creatureliness.

Why he, as a Professor of Dogmatic Theology and the History of Dogma, became so involved in Pastoral Theology has to do, in my opinion, with his way of thinking.[12] The philosophical-anthropological background of his metaphysics involves the question of Being as a whole, incorporating the major categories of worldliness and historicity, derived from Heidegger's *Being and Time*. The human person, as he actually exists, is the subject of Rahner's questioning, anxious, concerned purview.

Fr. Rahner writes in the foreword to *Mission and Grace* that his book intended to be "nothing other than a modest collection of essays, which, perhaps, contributes, in a small way, to the connection of 'theory' and 'praxis,' to their mutual advantage. The title of the book seeks to provide support for the conviction that mission to the apostolate and to pastoral service is a saving event made possible by the grace of God." Did he have too high an expectation for pastoral ministry?

Pastoral service was always seen by Rahner as something that involved the person in his totality. It had to be freed of every dualistic conception of the world and God. Rahner's understanding of Pastoral Theology is surprisingly concrete, earthly, temporally oriented, commonplace and festive, depressing and joyful: all existing together as one. It is situated in the over-arching temporal horizon of the world and salvation history, creation and redemption. The integrative power of Rahner's thought, up-to-date, tried and true, proven, pulsates through the foundational essays in the first volume of the *Handbook of Pastoral Theology*. A Pastoral Theology which does not support this great design is mere psychotherapy and an esoteric word of consolation and has no future.

The new edition (1989) appeared in the same format as the *Theological Investigations* which were published beginning in 1954 by the Benziger Publishing Company. Fr. Rahner once wrote that the

essays could just as well have been published in *Schriften zur The-ologie* (*Theological Investigations*).[13] Herbert Vorgrimler expressed a similar opinion.[14] Why was *Mission and Grace* published by Ty-rolia?

We never discussed that. Tyrolia Publishing alone received the pub-lishing rights as a result of my discussions with Fr. Rahner in his office in the Sillgasse. I also met Emerich Coreth, whose *Metaphysics* was published in 1961 by Tyrolia, through my contacts with the Jesuits in the Jesuit residence.

The "Rahner Year, 2004," was a manifestation of the continued in-terest in Karl Rahner, the man and his writings. How do you ex-plain the fact that publications like *Encounters with Silence*, from 1938 or *On the Need and the Blessing of Prayer*, from 1949 still find an audience today?

It has to do, without a doubt, with the needs of the present time. Karl Rahner comes with his spiritual counsel to provide a fitting response to the present, widespread fundamental need for meditation. It is a possible response to a totally rationalistic world that has lost the ability to appreciate its fundamentally mysterious nature. Fr. Rahner understands how to guide people restlessly searching, surrounded by the tireless predictability of things, to a place of calm and consolation. Whoever listens to him becomes aware of a different use of language. The author of *Encounters with Silence*, on the occasion of the publica-tion of the new edition of the book in 1972, felt "that in the interven-ing time period religious language had changed."[15]

This new use of language can be seen in his book *On the Need and the Blessing of Prayer*. In its specifically incarnational approach to hu-manity it replaces an entire raft of psychotherapeutic literature. There is a move away from addressing God solely from the perspective of one's state of existential confusion. Not mystical seclusion, but the ac-ceptance of our fundamental creatureliness is what counts. Rahner's profound understanding of the care of souls has lasting value. In his article *Priest and Poet* published in 1955[16] he reflects on the relation-ship of the thinker and the theologian. He articulates, in a spiritually masterful way, some sense of the forgotten dignity and honor of lan-guage stemming from its divine source. Because of that, the Word of

God, in light of the revelation of the eternal Word, is alive and active in a variety of ways, in every generation, taking us beyond the concrete world that we see.

Does the theology of Karl Rahner have a future?

I am, of, course, not a prophet, but Karl Rahner is and continues in his work, with its insight and faith, to be the advocate of Being in its totality, affirming the unity of creation and history, reason and revelation. His theological phenomenology of human existence is fundamentally unsurpassable and flows from the axiom he formulated later in life in *The World in God*.[17] Thus a dualistic separation of the created world into a godless world and a worldless God is categorically excluded. Because of this insight it is necessary to rethink the status of spirituality. Karl Rahner's way of thinking and his mode of expression are decisively shaped by the transcendental argumentation process. A linguistic analytical investigation of transcendental philosophy with regard to the prophetic tradition of Israel is still to be attempted. That remains a goal for further research on Rahner. What is the relationship of the historical concretization of this promise to salvation to metaphysics of the human spirit?

I believe that a critical look at the spiritual and religious work of Karl Rahner must include, for instance, the problem of the lack of a study of the Jewish people and their post-biblical history of faith up to the present day within the context of the reference in Romans to the "unbroken Covenant" with Israel, (Rm 9-11). It shall also include a study of the clash between the Christian claim to "Absolute Truth" with the contention of Islam that it is the last, most complete and highest grade of Religious expression. Thirdly, it should include the continuation of Rahner's masterful and courageous dialogue between theology and the natural sciences, the need for which is made even more critical in light of the conflict on the nature of free will in the face of the naturalistic reduction of the human person. There needs to be continued reflection on the history of suffering in creation, be it in nature or in human history with its ever increasing number of catastrophic events and the resulting consequences for the understanding of redemption and the shadow which lies over the Judeo-Christian message of hope due to the irresolvable problem of theodicy. I, for my part, cannot judge what ideas can be mined from Rahner's theological writings to address the question about how to speak of God in light of the severest challenge to the certainty of Christian faith –the experience of the Holocaust. From my limited knowledge I can only venture to say that for this great theologian of unsurpassable integrity, the explanation for the human failure to justify God in the face of the continual growth of evil lies hidden in the hopeful mystery of creation.

NOTES

1 Cf. Walter Strolz, Meine Begegnung mit Martin Heidegger (1889-1976) – Denker des Seins. Ein autobiographisches Wegstück, in: *Jahrbuch Franz-Michael-Felder Archiv der Vorarlberger Landesbibliothek* 3 (2002) 31-43, 32: "At the same time, through events sponsored by the Catholic youth organization, in which I had a leadership role, I became acquainted with Karl Rahner. Then there developed in the 1950's a personal relationship so that I became a welcome guest in his office in the Sillgasse until the move to Freiburg."

2 Cf. Herbert Vorgrimler, in: K. Rahner, *Biblische Predigten* (Freiburg: Herder, 1965) 5-6, 5; ibid., *Biblical Homilies*, translated by Desmond Forristal and Richard Strachan (Dublin: Herder and Herder, 1966) 5-6,5: "Karl Rahner has asked me to say a few words by way of introduction to this book. For nearly ten years he preached Sunday after Sunday in the University Church at Innsbruck, mostly on biblical texts. ... without any show of knowledge, they attempt to bring the age-old familiar texts home to men (sic) here and now; to those who are prepared to listen and to admit their shortcomings; to those who will not take fright at simple, concrete demands – for these sermons do not speak the language of easy optimism – to those who will let mystery show them their true selves, who are prepared to understand that to be Catholic is to be brotherly." Cf. ibid., *Karl Rahner verstehen*. Eine Einführung in sein Leben und Denken (Freiburg: Herder, second edition 1988) 30-32; ibid., *Understanding Karl Rahner*. An Introduction to his life and thought (New York: Crossroad, 1986) 18-20.

3 Cf. K. Rahner, *Von der Not und dem Segen des Gebetes* (Innsbruck: Tyrolia, 1949) (many editions!); ibid., *On Prayer* (Collegeville, Minnesota: Liturgical Press, 1993); cf. K. Rahner, *Prayers for a Lifetime*, Albert Raffelt (ed.), Introduction by Karl Lehmann, (New York: Crossroad, 1984); the German edition was last published together with *Gebete des Lebens* under the title, *Beten mit Karl Rahner*, 2 vols. (Freiburg: Herder, 2004).

4 Meant here is the Innsbruck Jesuit residence which is in the Sillgasse; cf. Emerich Coreth, Das Jesuitenkolleg Innsbruck. Grundzüge seiner Geschichte, in: *Zeitschrift für katholische Theologie* 113 (1991) 140-213.

5 Cf. Walter Strolz, *Der vergessene Ursprung. Das moderne Weltbild, die neuzeitliche Denkbewegung und die Geschichtlichkeit des Menschen* (Freiburg: Herder, 1959). – *Hörer des Wortes (Hearer of the Word)* first appeared in 1941, *Geist in Welt (Spirit in the World)* in 1939. Now both of these works are readily available (in their first and second edition) in: K. Rahner, *Sämtliche Werke*, vol. 2: Geist in Welt. Philosophische Schriften. Bearbeitet von Albert Raffelt (Freiburg: Herder, 1996); ibid., *Sämtliche Werke*, vol. 4: Hörer des Wortes. Schriften zur Religionsphilosophie und zur Grundlegung der Theologie. Bearbeitet von Albert Raffelt (Freiburg: Herder, 1997).

6 Cf. K. Rahner, Die Chancen des Christentums (1952), in: ibid., *Das freie Wort in der Kirche* (Einsiedeln: Benziger, 1953) 37-78; now in: ibid., *Sämtliche Werke*, vol. 10: Kirche in den Herausforderungen der Zeit. Studien zur Ekklesiologie und zur kirchlichen Existenz (Freiburg: Herder, 2003) 160-183, cf. ibid., *Free Speech in the Church* (New York: Sheed & Ward, 1959).

7 Cf. Walter Strolz, Der "Punkt Omega" – Teilhard de Chardin und die Leidenschaft zur Erde, in: *Rheinischer Merkur*, Beilage (section) "Echo der Zeit," June 14, 1959.

8 Cf. K. Rahner, Wissenschaft als "Konfession"? in: ibid., *Schriften zur Theologie*, vol. 3 (Einsiedeln: Benziger, 1956) 455-472; ibid., Science as a 'Confession'? in: ibid., *Theological Investigations*, vol. 3, translated by Karl-H. and Boniface Kruger (London: Darton, Longman & Todd, 1967) 385-400.

9 Karl H. Neufeld, Einleitung zur Neuausgabe, in: K. Rahner, *Sendung und Gnade*. Beiträge zur Pastoraltheologie (Innsbruck: Tyrolia, 5th edition, 1988) I-VI, I.

10 K. Rahner, together with Franz Xaver Arnold, Viktor Schurr and Leonhard M. Weber, was the editor of the four volume work, *Handbuch der Pastoraltheologie*. Praktische Theologie der Kirche in ihrer Gegenwart that appeared between 1964 and 1969 (Freiburg: Herder). As a 5th volume there the *Lexikon der Pastoraltheologie* in 1972 that K. Rahner edited along with Ferdinand Klostermann and Hansjörg Schmid. In comparison with the other editors, of whom he alone survived the completion of the project, the contribution of K. Rahner comprises more than 500 pages (in comparison: F. X. Arnold 25, L. M. Weber 20, V. Schnurr 63, F. Klostermann 150). Most of his contributions were collected in K. Rahner, *Sämtliche Werke*, vol. 19: Selbstvollzug der Kirche. Ekklesiologische Grundlegung praktischer Theologie. Bearbeitet von Karl H. Neufeld (Freiburg: Herder, 1995), therein also the instructive editorial report of the editor, Karl H. Neufeld, with much valuable information, (ibid., XXV-XXXV). Cf. also Herbert Vorgrimler, *Karl Rahner verstehen*, 105-107; ibid., *Understanding Karl Rahner*, 83-85; ibid., *Karl Rahner*. Gotteserfahrung in Leben und Den-

ken (Darmstadt: Wissenschaftliche Buchgesellschaft, 2004) 74-79; Walter Schmolly, Pastoral verantworten: Praktische Theologie, in: Andreas R. Batlogg, Paul Rulands, ibid., Roman A. Siebenrock, Günther Wassilowsky, Arno Zahlauer, *Der Denkweg Karl Rahners. Quellen – Entwicklungen – Perspektiven* (Mainz: Grünewald, 2nd edition, 2004) 242-261.

11   K. Rahner, *Sendung und Gnade*, 51-87; ibid., The Order of Redemption within the Order of Creation, in: ibid., *The Christian Commitment. Essays in Pastoral Theology*, translated by Cecily Hastings (New York: Sheed and Ward, 1963) 38-74. The essay appeared very much revised in the second volume of *Handbuch der Pastoraltheologie* (Freiburg: Herder, 1966) under the title: Grundsätzliches zur Einheit von Schöpfungs- und Erlösungswirklichkeit (208-228); now in: *Sämtliche Werke*, vol. 19, 375-394.

12   Cf. Herbert Vorgrimler, *Karl Rahner* (2004) 78: "Characteristic for Karl Rahner's practical-theological engagement is also the fact that for years he directed for the international periodical *Concilium*, which he co-founded, the section 'Pastoral-theology,' not the section 'Dogmatic.'"

13   Cf. K. Rahner, *Schriften zur Theologie*, vol. 4 (Einsiedeln: Benziger, 1960) 7 (Preface): "Given the objective connection which exists between dogmatic investigations and considerations on Pastoral Theology based on dogma, it is not surprising that some of the essays which I collected in my book, *Sendung und Gnade*, Beiträge zur Pastoraltheologie (2nd edition, Innsbruck 1959), would have fitted just as well into this volume – and vice versa ('Mission and Grace: Contributions to Pastoral Theology'). The relevant pieces there are chiefly: 'Redemptive reality in created reality,' 'The meaning of the individual Christian in the history of salvation,' 'Thanksgiving after Mass,' 'On Visits to the Blessed Sacrament,' 'Primacy and Episcopacy,' 'Dogmatic preliminaries for a proper discussion of the reform of the diaconate,' 'On the Theology of secular institutes.'"

14   Herbert Vorgrimler, *Karl Rahner verstehen*, 97; ibid., *Understanding Karl Rahner*, 76: "The theological foundation of these articles is so strong that they would also have fitted well into the *Schriften zur Theologie*, just as that series also contains numerous articles which document Rahner's major ideas for church praxis and his pastoral inventiveness."

15   Cf. K. Rahner, Vorwort, in: ibid., Hugo Rahner, *Worte ins Schweigen. Gebete der Einkehr* (Freiburg: Herder, 1973) 7-8, 8: "In both texts it can be noticed that in the interim, religious language has changed. But since language arises out of a particular awareness of life, it was not possible to change all those passages which today one would formulate differently."

16   K. Rahner, Priester und Dichter, in: ibid., *Schriften zur Theologie*, vol. 3 (Einsiedeln: Benziger, 1956) 349-375; ibid., Priest and Poet, in: ibid., *Theological Investigations*, vol. 3, translated by Karl-H. and Boniface Kruger (London: Darton, Longman & Todd, 1967) 294-317; cf. Karl H. Neufeld,

Theologie und Dichtung. Über Karl Rahner, in: Peter Tschuggnall (ed.),
Perspektiven einer Begegnung am Beginn eines neuen Millenniums (Anif/
Salzburg: Müller-Speiser, 2001) 56-65.

17 Cf. K. Rahner, Welt in Gott. Zum christlichen Schöpfungsbegriff, in:
Andreas Bsteh (ed.). *Sein als Offenbarung in Christentum und Hinduismus.*
Beiträge zur Religionstheologie, vol. 4 (Mödling: St. Gabriel, 1984) 69-
82.

28

IS NOT THE MYSTERY OF GOD GREATER?

IN CONVERSATION WITH PAUL WESS, INNSBRUCK

Paul Wess, Dr. phil., Dr. theol., born in 1936, is a Lecturer in Pastoral Theology at the University of Innsbruck. From 1962-1996, he was in parish ministry in Vienna and completed his post-doctoral work in the area of Pastoral Theology in Innsbruck. Since retiring as a Pastor he teaches at the Universities of Graz, Würzburg and Innsbruck.

Would you speak about your experience of Karl Rahner? What did you appreciate about him? In what ways were you critical of his thinking in the area of theology?

In 1954, I came to the Canisianum in Innsbruck, immediately after completing my qualifying exams and began my studies in philosophy with Fr. Coreth. In the fall semester of 1957-58, I attended a course on the concept of mystery that included a seminar.[1] Along with a colleague I took the minutes – I still have that manuscript today. Later on I wrote my licentiate in theology under the direction of Karl Rahner. At that time I already began to formulate my first critical thoughts about Fr. Rahner's work, which in fact still basically play a decisive role in my thoughts. For example, I raised the question as to whether you can really say that God is the "Thou," the other, the goal of the human spirit; whether God is not greater; whether the "Thou" of the human person is rather another person? And is not God rather the greater mystery; can the human person as a created entity have such an infinite horizon, does this not then contradict the principle *agere sequitur esse*? ("action follows being"). I raised these questions at the end of my licentiate paper and Fr. Rahner still gave me, in spite of that, nine of ten possible points.[2]

I then studied dogma with Fr. Rahner and took my exams with him. Following that, I did a doctorate in philosophy with Fr. Coreth. In 1961, I returned to Vienna for my pastoral internship. I always had problems with Karl Rahner's starting point – the transcendental anticipation of the infinite (*"Vorgriff"*). But I could not refute his argument for this infinite horizon. It can already be found in *Spirit in the World*: Everyone who even as much as suspects a limit has already transcended it.[3] Karl Rahner, while he appeals to Hegel in his lectures, does not do so in his books. It is the classical argument put forth by idealistic metaphysics: everyone who acknowledges a limit to the human spirit has already contradicted themselves, because in that acknowledgement they have already gone beyond that limit and thus transcended it.

I want to say something else. My philosophical dissertation treated the question of knowing and willing in the human spirit and the issue of the relationality of the human person – that is that the human person is essentially relational and not only self-aware. That, too, was already a kind of criticism of Rahner, because he does not understand the human person as fundamentally relational. In his mind there needs to be a "supernatural existential" to link the human person to a God who speaks. To stand before a silent God would be hell if the human person is constitutively relational and God is humanity's actual partner.

I thus tried, in the fundamental theological question "transcendence of God – relation of the human person to God" to refute Fr. Rahner's argument, but failed, though I always had problems with it, a deep uneasiness. With these questions and reservations still on my mind, I began my career in pastoral ministry. Since I was so critical of Rahner's positions at that time, I did not have any chance of being appointed to any theological faculty.

After three years in pastoral ministry as an assistant pastor in a city parish in Vienna, my 13 year old sister, (a child born to my parents after my father had returned from being a prisoner of the Second World war for eleven years and therefore much cherished) became ill with leukemia and died. I comforted her during her illness. She died with the words:"My God, my God, why have you abandoned me?" She said that in the original version, in Aramaic, presumably, so as not to shock our parents who were present. To me she said: "Paul, do you know what those words mean?" The death of my sister with these last words so hurt me that all the theology and the language about God once more became questionable.

Following her death I asked our Archbishop, Cardinal Franz König, for a one year study sabbatical. I needed to begin again, to consider anew how one can speak of God at all. I went to Amras, near Innsbruck, as an associate pastor and lived in the parish house. Every evening I went for a walk near the construction site of the Brenner Highway ("*Autobahn*"). While doing that I went over and over in my mind trying to find the missing link in the argument as to why Fr. Rahner could not be correct. I was convinced in my heart that he was not correct. And then, one night, the answer came to me – it was like a revelation! This is how I understood the solution: Karl Rahner makes an illegitimate transition, from that which is conceptually possible, to that which is existentially possible. When I think of a limit, I have not yet really transcended it. We cannot conclude that because we can conceive of the possibility in our minds the possibility of its existence in fact is true.

I then wrote a theological dissertation based on this insight. It was devoted to the question: How can we speak of God when theology itself asserts that God is an absolute mystery? I cannot treat this statement of the mystery of God as if it were one property of God alongside other properties, because it calls into question everything that I say about God. The subject of my dissertation was "The Incomprehensibility of God and its consequences for the knowledge of God in Thomas Aquinas and Karl Rahner."[4] I wrote the dissertation under the direction of Fr. Engelbert Gutwenger, SJ. He was the only one in Innsbruck who would accept a work critical of Rahner. I asked Fr. Coreth to be my second reader. He esteemed my work as a philosopher; he gave me his *Metaphysics*[5] before it was published and allowed me to read it, when it was in manuscript form so as to solicit my opinion, but when I gave him my theological dissertation, he said to me: "Mr. Wess, you never did understand me!"

I had radically questioned his transcendental starting point which he had taken over from Fr. Rahner which assumed that by already knowing the question you could derive the answer. My thesis is that I cannot derive a real answer from a question, if it exists only in the mind and has no basis in reality. Fr. Coreth did not agree to be the second reader. Fr. Gutwenger, however, accepted the dissertation and my criticism as an unresolved question. The second reader and evaluator was Fr. Marlet, SJ.

The distinction between the possibility of being as opposed to the possibility of thought seems to be the decisive question.

Klaus P. Fischer in his dissertation *Der Mensch als Geheimnis*[6] defends the philosophical anthropology of Karl Rahner. He is one of the few who went into my dissertation in any depth, but his reaction was totally negative. The first thing that he accused me of, which hurt me deeply, is that I had plagiarized Hansjürgen Verweyen.[7] Naïve as I was, I had listed his book in my bibliography; it takes the same tack as my dissertation. Because Verweyen, although he did not influence me, comes to similar conclusions, Fischer accused me of copying from Verweyen, without documenting that charge. Then, he goes on to say that I go far beyond Verweyen. That is certainly contradictory! I challenged Fischer's criticism in my post-doctoral paper.[8]

It seems to me that Fr. Rahner would welcome having someone to speak with who does not simply repeat everything, but who nevertheless is a thinker.

Here, I must disagree a bit. I sent Fr. Rahner my book, *Wie von Gott sprechen?*[9] with a personal note, because I knew that he appreciated me as a person. I did not receive an answer. I then heard from Professor Gerhard Larcher, (Graz) who studied with Rahner in Münster, that Karl Rahner allegedly said, that I didn't understand him. In conversations with a few others it came out that Fr. Rahner very clearly grasped that my criticism of his work questioned his basic presuppositions. Later on I sought to initiate a conversation with him; this was in the 1980's, but he felt that he was too old and that his strength was diminishing. He proposed that I express my reservations in a periodical. I published an article, *Wie kann der Mensch Gott erfahren? Eine Überlegung zur Theologie Karl Rahners* ("How can the human person learn about God? A reflection on Karl Rahner's Theology") in the Innsbruck periodical *Zeitschrift für Katholische Theologie*. He also did not respond to this article. At least Fr. Rahner mentions me twice in *Theological Investigations*.[10] Johann Baptist Metz also in his time criticized Rahner extensively and Fr. Rahner was especially upset with the parable of the hedgehog and the rabbit. That was a very polemical way to distance himself from his teacher.[11] Perhaps, my criticism will be appreciated today, because the euphoria of the 1960's no longer exists.

Do you still hold fast to your fundamental criticism of Karl Rahner?

My chief criticism remains; abstracting from his philosophically untenable idealistic metaphysics, that Fr. Rahner reduces the mystery of God to God's incomprehensibility. I often go to his grave in the crypt of the Jesuit Church and pray for him. I apologize too, for the fact that I criticize him. And I also say in addition, that if, however, my criticism is justified, then you must now help me. Karl Rahner was a person of piety, a believer, who worshipped God, for whom God was always greater. But in his systematic writings his starting point was the establishment of a method to show the unbeliever, or the critical person of today, an approach to faith; he placed all his bets on the idealistic card. With that he set in motion a process from which he himself would recoil, namely the leveling of Christianity. He had, so to speak, placed humanity on a level with God, especially with his thesis of identifying the love of God with the love of neighbor.[12] Do I not then, put the human person in the place of God? Is then God not reduced to the innermost mystery of the human person? That is a consequence that Fr. Rahner did not want.

I believe that this type of theological thinking has been the cause of the crisis we experience in theology and faith today. I once had a conversation with Cardinal Ratzinger. He had seen my post-doctoral work and observed that it contains a criticism of Rahner. That pleased him very much. In response, I said to him that Fr. Rahner should not be criticized for drawing the logical consequences out of the traditional doctrine on grace. Fr. Rahner did nothing more than to say that grace, the divine life, should not be placed on top of nature as if it were the second floor of a building. That is why the recipient must have a capacity for God. That means that if we should be, can be divinized, as Alexandrian Theology argued, then we must have the capacity for the divine, otherwise divinization would necessitate the imposition of a foreign substance. The concept of a loss of transcendence did not first occur in modern theology; it happened long before that! If an Athanasius can say that God became human, so that humans can become gods, although the Bible states, to want to be like God is the very epitome of sin, then here is where the undoing has occurred! Therefore, no one should criticize the modern theologians who are drawing the logical conclusions from this and thereby – unintentionally, have given up the transcendence of God completely; they are simply thinking logically.

Classical, traditional theology used the model of the ennoblement of something wild: nature is the "something wild" and the divine life is grafted on to it. But the use of the term "grafted on" already implies a critique, because what is grafted on to me, remains something foreign. What is wild is not changed. *Nouvelle Théologie* wanted to point out this problem. Among the French it was Henri de Lubac, SJ, and in the German speaking world it was Karl Rahner who most effectively brought this to public attention. They declared that the human person was a partner of God. No one should present this "horizontalization" as something evil, as it is only the latest consequence of our forgetfulness of transcendence, which had its roots in Hellenistic theology. Rather it should cause us to ask ourselves: where does the guilt lie in us? That Cardinal Ratzinger did not want to hear!

Does not the critique of George Vass, SJ, go in a similar direction in regard to the loss of an appreciation for transcendence?

Vass quotes me in his books.[13] He was one of the few whom I sensed understood me or that he at least took my criticism seriously and supported it. I should, perhaps, once more emphasize that I always esteemed Fr. Rahner as a human being very much. That, I believe, was completely mutual. When we would meet at some conference he would always come up to me.

NOTES

1   Cf. K. Rahner, Über den Begriff des Geheimnisses in der katholischen Theologie, in: ibid., *Schriften zur Theologie*, vol. 4 (Einsiedeln: Benziger, 1960) 51-99; now in: ibid., *Sämtliche Werke*, vol. 12: Menschsein und Menschwerdung Gottes. Studien zur Grundlegung der Dogmatik, zur Christologie, Theologischen Anthropologie und Eschatologie. Bearbeitet von Herbert Vorgrimler (Freiburg: Herder, 2005) 101-135. – See ibid., The Concept of Mystery in Catholic Theology, in: ibid., *Theological Investigations*, vol. 4, translated by Kevin Smyth (Baltimore: Darton, Longman & Todd 1966) 36-73.

2   The best grade was ten on a scale of one to ten; nine was "very good."

3   K. Rahner, *Geist in Welt*. Zur Metaphysik der endlichen Erkenntnis bei Thomas von Aquin (Innsbruck: Felizian Rauch, 1939) 20 (2nd edition:

Munich: Kösel, 1957, 51.). – See also: ibid., *Spirit in the World*, translated by William Dych, SJ (New York: Herder and Herder, 1968) 37-38: "As a matter of fact, how can the human intellect establish itself within its own limits and at the same time give evidence of a remarkable knowledge about a possible 'beyond' of these limits, which knowledge is always included in the knowledge of limits as such?" – Now in: ibid., *Sämtliche Werke*, vol. 2: Geist in Welt. Philosophische Schriften. Bearbeitet von Albert Raffelt (Freiburg: Herder, 1996) 39 f.

4   Cf. Paul Wess, *Wie von Gott sprechen?* Eine Auseinandersetzung mit Karl Rahner (Graz: Styria, 1970).

5   Cf. Emerich Coreth, *Metaphysik* (Innsbruck: Tyrolia, 1961) (3rd edition 1980); see also the English translation, by Joseph Donceel (New York: Seabury Press, 1968).

6   Klaus Peter Fischer, *Der Mensch als Geheimnis*. Die Anthropologie Karl Rahners (Freiburg: Herder, 1974, 2nd edition 1975).

7   Cf. Hansjürgen Verweyen, *Ontologische Voraussetzungen des Glaubensaktes*. Zur transzendentalen Frage nach der Möglichkeit von Offenbarung (Düsseldorf: Patmos, 1969).

8   Cf. Paul Wess, *Gemeindekirche – Ort des Glaubens*. Die Praxis als Fundament und als Konsequenz der Theologie (Graz: Styria, 1989) 132-135. This book – Paul Wess' habilitation – contains his attempt at providing a new, post idealistic foundation for theology that "aims" at speech about God that rests on the corresponding interpersonal praxis, practical experiences, and their interpretation; thus aiming at a proof for God's existence (Gotteserweis) not in the manner of Rahner, of a transcendental proof for God's existence (Gottesaufweis), but rather out of a pre-thematic knowledge about God.

9   Paul Wess, *Wie kann der Mensch Gott erfahren?* Eine Überlegung zur Theologie Karl Rahners, in: *Zeitschrift für Katholische Theologie* 102 (1980) 343-348. – This article is reprinted in the collection: ibid., *Und behaltet das Gute*. Beiträge zur Praxis und Theorie des Glaubens (Thaur: Druck- und Verlagshaus, 1996) 225-232.

10   Cf. K. Rahner, Fragen zur Unbegreiflichkeit Gottes nach Thomas von Aquin, in: ibid., *Schriften zur Theologie*, vol. 12 (Zurich: Benziger, 1975) 306-319, 306, footnote 2; ibid., Die theologische Dimension der Frage nach dem Menschen, in: ibid., 387-406, 392, footnote 8. – See: ibid., An Investigation of the Incomprehensibility of God in St. Thomas Aquinas, in: ibid., *Theological investigations*, vol. 16, translated by David Morland, O. S. B. (New York: Seabury Press, 1979) 244-254.

11   Cf. Johann Baptist Metz, *Glaube in Geschichte und Gesellschaft*. Studien zu einer praktischen Fundamentaltheologie (Mainz: Matthias Grünewald,

3rd edition 1980) 143-145; cf. also: K. Rahner, *Bekenntnisse*. Rückblick auf 80 Jahre, edited by Georg Sporschill (Vienna: Herold, 1984) 37: "Metz has, of course, always and at all times admitted that he was my student and that he owes me a great deal, but he has emphasized even more strongly, that he has a critical relationship to my theology. Actually, we have never discussed this. He has gotten me upset because in several of his lectures, he brought up the comparison between the hedgehog and the hare: a hedgehog and a hare make a bet on who can run the fastest. They run in two burlap sacks next to each other and are able to see one another only at the finish line. The hare runs like crazy, however, the hedgehog places his wife at the end of the course and so as the hare crosses the finish line, the hedgehog's wife cries out: I'm already here! Then Metz explained I am the hedgehog who allegedly, with his transcendental, apriori theology, has anticipated in advance the theological results, whereas Metz, with his Political Theology, must struggle terribly. In the *Festschrift* in honor of my 75th birthday, Vorgrimler asked: where then is the second hedgehog? A Transcendental Theology, which always reflects back on itself, struggles, perhaps, much more than a Political Theology, which confidently and happily races into the future – more or less." See now in: K. Rahner, *Sämtliche Werke*, vol. 25: Erneuerung des Ordenslebens. Erneuerung für Kirche und Welt. Bearbeitet von Andreas R. Batlogg (Freiburg: Herder, 2008) 59-84, 73 f.

12   Cf. K. Rahner, Über die Einheit von Nächsten- und Gottesliebe, in: ibid., *Schriften zur Theologie*, vol. 6 (Einsiedeln: Benziger, 1965) 277-298; ibid., 282 f. and 295; Rahner declares the unity to be an identity. – See also ibid., Reflections on the Unity of the Love of Neighbor and the Love of God, in: ibid., *Theological Investigations*, vol. 6, translated by Karl-H. and Boniface Kruger (London: Darton, Longman & Todd, 1974) 231-249 (ibid., on pages 236 f. and on 247: unity to be an identity).

13   Cf. George Vass, *Understanding Karl Rahner*, 5 volumes (London: Sheed and Ward, 1985-2001); ibid., *Understanding Karl Rahner*, vol. 1: A Theologian in Search of a Philosophy (London: Sheed and Ward, 1985) 63f.

APPENDIX I

HUGO RAHNER, SJ

"FROM BROTHER TO BROTHER"

In her editorial (XI-LVI) to volume 9 of the Complete Works ("Sämtliche Werke") of Karl Rahner, the editor, Regina Pacis Meyer, quotes "almost in its entirety" a letter written by Hugo Rahner on February 18, 1955 to his younger brother Karl. The letter, composed while Hugo Rahner was in Rome, where as a Church Historian and Patristic Scholar he did his research on Ignatius for the Jubilee year 1956, bears the letterhead of the "Istituto Storico della Compagnia di Gesu Roma, Via dei Penitenzieri 20" where he often stayed. In the letter, Hugo Rahner writes to encourage a deeply upset Karl (who, at that time, was on the Theology Faculty in Innsbruck). "Of course, it cannot be ascertained whether or to what degree Hugo's perspective on things was accurate."(XLIV) The problem was the delay of publication of Karl Rahner's manuscript "Assumptio Beatae Mariae Virginis." The publication was scheduled to coincide with the dogmatization of the Assumption of Mary, which took place on November 1, 1950. The delay was due to its being held up in the internal censure process of the Jesuit order. Karl Rahner already had been asked to rewrite his manuscript several times. The fact that this delay had dragged on for years depressed him greatly. Hugo Rahner, on the other hand, was very well acquainted with "Roman practices." "The letter clearly shows evidence of the sincere and earnest frankness with which Hugo dealt with his brother and the high regard he had for their relationship; it is no less to the point, nor unambiguous than the letter Hugo wrote to the Assistant General, but it does show his brotherly affection and love. At the same time the letter makes clear how deeply Karl Rahner was affected by the events surrounding his work and the risk of his becoming bitter." (XLIV) A short time later, Karl Rahner led the students of the Collegium Germanicum et Hungaricum in the Spiritual Exercises at San Pastore, the country estate of the college in Palestrina and came for the first time, at the age of 51, to the eternal city. That manuscript is catalogued in the Rahner studies under the title "Assumptio Arbeit" and was first published posthumously in 2005.

The letter must be seen as an example of Hugo Rahner's interpretation
of the situation. It shows clearly the relationship between the older and
the younger brother. Hugo Rahner's letter reveals to us a man with a
defiant character, but also reveals Karl Rahner's wounded heart and a
man who was apparently very frustrated with how things were going.

[Reprint from: R. P. Meyer, Editionsbericht, in: K. Rahner, *Sämtliche Werke*, vol. 9: Maria, Mutter des Herrn. Mariologische Studien. Bearbeitet von Regina Pacis Meyer. (Freiburg: Herder, 2004) XLIV-XLVII.]

[Rome, February 18, 1955]

Dear Karl,

I want to write this letter to you before Fr. Malmberg and Fr. Tattenbach come to see you.

The matter is serious. If you felt in my recent conversation with you in Freiburg that I seemed to have aligned myself too much with the "other side," I want to beg you with all my heart to believe that this was not a "giving in" or anything like that, and forgive me, for saying this, but, I believe that I have better insight into the situation than you do, who are so passionately involved. Perhaps, this is not a very diplomatic introduction, but it is certainly preferable that I say directly what I think. I tried recently in Freiburg to explain things to you, but of all the things you said in response, only one thing hurt me very much: When you alleged that I had abandoned you already in the question of the censure of your book. Please, let me tell you once more how I view the matter and please, allow me to request a couple of brotherly favors.

All of us are convinced that with regard to this matter, the prevailing mood of the Holy Office is one of extreme nervousness; from where that comes and to what extent that justifies what they do, does not concern us right now. Some people from Germany or Austria have let it be known that they don't trust you. Fr. General has to deal with that attitude. Now, I beg you to accept that fact that Fr. General, himself, and his assistant, value to the utmost what you have accomplished and they know that you are the last person, who (under normal circumstances), would act in such a way as to confirm what those who are attacking you are saying. But now, because you are being attacked – without any cooperation on their part – they are required to deal with you in this unpleasant way. You must also take into account the fact of the unfortunate matter with regard to the past censure of your book and that your refusal, with reference to other and more pressing matters to respond to the Roman censure, has made a bad impression. Then you must try to summon a little understanding that every superior who truly wants to help you and wants to defend you must, first of all, present the *punctum elenchi* and that is not possible by means of long letters (which you might not wish, nor have the right to answer). The only possible way for you to respond would be in a personal conversation here in Rome and you would have interpreted that requirement as a summons. Therefore, Fr. General is sending you a reasonable and informed person who will determine what is – or, and of this I am convinced – what is not wrong. At the same time he can deal with some odd attacks on Fr. Jungmann and finally, also a few questions that have been raised about our faculty in general and speak to the Jesuits in charge in a reasonable way.

The day before yesterday, and yesterday, I spoke at length with Fr. Malmberg; he is a very dear, quiet and pleasant man with whom one can speak easily. The *elenchus* of issues of which you have been accused does not need to upset you further. In my opinion, the accusations are *quoad rem dogmaticum*, farfetched and absurd. But because this is so you should not speak to him in a sarcastic tone, not rant and rave, but rather speak to the point at hand so that he can return to Rome and bring to Fr. General the assurance that the Rahner doctrine is completely orthodox. This speaks to the issue of the alleged *"factual"* or doctrinal objections which have been brought forward. More important, in my opinion, is the other issue as it relates to Fr. General and the Curia itself. Your manner of ignoring, without a word, the Roman process of censure, giving no word of explanation, is self-destructive. Your defense, that you don't have time for this, is seen as insulting in the face of everything you have written and done since. It is easily deduced that you do not want to cooperate, and it is assumed, and rightly so, that anyone who will not submit to a cross examination cannot be right. With a little more flexibility, even on the issue which is challenged the most – the Theology of Death – a middle way might have been found. In short, I truly believe, Karl, that you soon must deal with the question of your book on Mary without anger and must re-examine the issue. Do this for the sake of the beautiful content which even was recognized by the censor so that you can be defended against the laughable, but still dangerous accusations made by the Holy Office. This can be done more easily when they are convinced of your fundamental good will, without a suspicion that you have become stubbornly anti-Roman.

And I ask you, in a very brotherly way, because it matters greatly to me, matters to the extent that I sometimes wake up in the middle of the night and begin to pray fervently for you; please revise your increasingly sclerotic antipathy to what is "Roman." You be the nobler one here, just as de Lubac was. Try it, without always going over and over again the unfortunate events that led to the censure of your book, or all the tragic errors of judgment with regard to the "*Nouvelle théologie*" and satisfy yourself that those in authority truly want what's best for you. They know, precisely, what a prominent position you hold in German Theology, how hard you have worked and what you have accomplished, and they are attempting to do everything possible to defend you from "outside" charges that have reached the Curia from the Holy Office.

I told Fr. Malmberg that he will have achieved his goal if he could bring back three things: 1. a signed statement testifying that the doctrinal accusations brought against you are simply without any basis and are nonsense and that can be supported by the fact that you "*palam locutus es*" (spoke publicly) without anyone until now making any kind of objective and legitimate attack; 2. that your "anti-Roman" attitude in no way rises to the level of an actual "conviction" and that you, in light of all the confusion and misunderstanding which have resulted, would handle these matters more intelligently and more carefully; 3. that you, honestly and sincerely are ready to seek a way to resolve the issues relating to the book on Mary in such a way that a compromise can be reached that would not be interpreted as a dogmatic lack of principle.

That is what I wanted to write to you, perhaps, in too hurried a fashion, but Tattenbach is going to Innsbruck tomorrow. I know, even when you grumble, that you are, at any rate, convinced of *my* good will and my understanding and it would be unbearable for me, if I were to learn that you no longer have any trust in me. Things like this pass, but at this moment (*hic et nunc*) here and now, this must be discussed openly and we do that at best in a spirit of trust. I ask you this, from my heart, not only for myself, but also for Fr. General, who has affection for you and who speaks of you only in the finest way. Don't make it difficult for him and, therefore, be good to the Jesuit Father that he sends to you.

Consider, please, whether it might be useful if you were to write a brief and concise assessment to Fr. General and take it upon yourself to testify that everything that you have written is not only thoroughly orthodox, but was written precisely to clarify what had been left unclear in theological disputation. So, for example, everything that you have written on monogenism was a defense of *Humani Generis* and not a clandestine attack and that those who attack this work, probably did not read the entire argument correctly, just as was the case with "The Many Masses." I would think that such a letter to Fr. General would be very valuable so that he doesn't imagine that you are sitting, despairingly, in a corner sulking, feeling that you have been completely misunderstood.

But that's enough for now. I will write as soon as I know how things look. And be convinced, Karl, that I think of you, in these days of trial, as fervently and as lovingly as I possibly can.

Hugo[1]

NOTES

1 Names mentioned in the letter: Piet van Gestel, SJ, (1897-1972), 1946 Assistant to the German Secretariat of the Jesuits in the Roman Central Office; Johann Baptist Janssens, SJ, (1889-1964), 1946-1964 General Superior of the Society of Jesus; Josef Andreas Jungmann, SJ, (1889-1975), Professor of Catechetics and Liturgy at the University of Innsbruck; Henri de Lubac, SJ, (1896-1991), Professor of Fundamental Theology and Dogma at the Institut Catholique in Lyon, (France), 1950 forbidden to teach in the wake of the encyclical, "*Humani Generis.*" 1962 *Peritus* at the Second Vatican Council, 1983 Cardinal; Felix Malmberg, SJ, (1903-1979), theologian and author in Amsterdam, 1954 *Visitator* for the Jesuit Residence in Innsbruck; Franz Tattenbach, SJ, (1910-1992), 1953-1959 Rector of the College Germanicum et Hugaricum in Rome.

APPENDIX II

ROMAN A. SIEBENROCK
EXPERIENCES IN THE
"KARL-RAHNER-ARCHIV"

[Reprint from: *Stimmen der Zeit* spezial 1-2004, 31-42.]

Which Karl Rahner did I get to know in the "Karl-Rahner-Archiv"?[1]
I was not unfamiliar with Rahner when Walter Kern, SJ, brought me
to Innsbruck in 1985. At various lectures at the College of Philosophy (*"Hochschule für Philosophie / Berchmanskolleg, SJ"*) and in evening
talks in St. Michael's (the Jesuit Church) and in the student community in Munich, I had previously seen and experienced Karl Rahner. I
also knew his books and publications through my religious education
classes in school, and then through my study of philosophy with Karl-
Heinz Weger, SJ, who supervised my master's thesis on Karl Rahner.
When I was studying theology, Karl Rahner was, as far as I was concerned, someone, with all due respect, I avoided. So I must ask precisely, how did my image of Karl Rahner change and develop during
my years in the archives? When I came to Innsbruck, I entered the
archives with a sacred respect: like a "sanctuary." That such an aura was
quickly dispelled by working there every day, was a good thing.

Naturally, in the archives, I did not come to know Karl Rahner,
whom innumerable people had heard in lectures and homilies; nor
did I experience him as many did through personal conversations with
him. I also did not experience him like his listeners, his classmates or
his "victims" in debates and disputations during his time in formation
as a Jesuit, or as a scholarly professor, or in the debates at the Second
Vatican Council or at the Synod in Würzburg. Certainly, I did not
encounter him in the way his colleagues and co-workers did, nor as
his assistants did, who appreciated or tolerated him as their "boss." I
did not have to chauffeur him, driving as fast as the car could go. I also
was never in danger of being consumed by his daily work regimen; he

took for granted what he himself gave: total commitment. I did not get to know him in everyday life, like his Jesuit colleagues did, those who lived with him in his changing moods: not only cheerful and sensitive, but also taciturn and sullen, at times "highly volatile!" Least of all could I get to know him in the internal forum in which he was, for so many people, a Spiritual Director, a friend, a support in time of need, a confessor and counselor. I did not get to know him in that way; even "modern technology" cannot substitute for the encounter – person to person. As archivist I could not look into his eyes and he could not answer me, when I sometimes caught myself in a monologue, in which I asked him, "virtually," where I should catalogue this or that draft he wrote.

And yet, that seems to me to be what is so special about my encounter with him; all these dimensions of his life are encoded in the archives. The varieties of collected papers, the numerous photos and the few personal memorabilia, together with all the silent witnesses, form a tapestry for me; a collection of stories, traditions, interpretations and remembrances. The Karl-Rahner-Archiv is also a reservoir for the "oral tradition."

I have gotten to know Karl Rahner as future generations will get to know him: by means of witnesses who point to the drama of his life, his struggles, his formative experiences as well as his helplessness and his silence in the face of the mystery of death and the eternity of an incomprehensible God. The Karl-Rahner-Archiv reflects, also, the history of faith and the Church of the 20th century. Archives are what they are officially called; the legacy of Karl Rahner that was entrusted by the Southern German province ("*Germania Superioris*") of the Jesuits to the Theology Faculty of the University of Innsbruck for scholarly research. Gradually I learned, and it is still my practice, to introduce interested patrons, from all over the world, how to listen to the silent history of his legacy, to allow it to speak to them. In the Karl-Rahner-Archiv it is as quiet as a mouse, but precisely because of that, the stories cry out from all corners of the archives.

If I describe all the facets of my encounter with Karl Rahner, I can only do so by telling them in sequence, one after the other. In reality they reciprocally illuminate one another. Even so, I am not certain whether I might fail to mention what is really most important, because it remains fully hidden. In an impressionistic or pointillist work of art, the spot of paint first becomes an image at the proper distance from the eye of the observer. I am aware of the fact that I, who manage the archives, do not always have the proper perspective. Perhaps, the proper perspective is discretion and respect when it comes to regarding another person; that is the proper form of encounter.

First and foremost I have met *the Jesuit* Karl Rahner. Originally the archives were housed in Rahner's office, which he used until the time of his death: two small rooms, previously storage rooms, located directly above the receptionist area of the Jesuit residence, not far from his bedroom. In one room he arranged his books on bookshelves which reached from floor to ceiling. He also had two desks and a small cupboard. There was not room for much more than a chair or two for his visitors. The adjoining room was designated the storage area and it was filled with folders, and with small and large cardboard boxes. He liked to collect special reprints of his articles in the pages of the *Lexika*. Archive materials from Leipzig or Dresden, which he had purchased during the Second World War when he gave lectures there, were included, as were boxes of stationery from the Zuccalistrasse in Munich-Nymphenburg; this he used for note paper. Rahner, himself, used an old typewriter, like the one I found in my room in the student wing of the Jesuit residence. His typewriter was ripe for the museum. His furnishings reminded me of the stark environment which so impressed the young Karl Rahner during his first visit to the novitiate.[2] He did not have his own house, nor an office and library, as I saw in Basel at a visit to the "Karl-Barth-Archiv." Even less could the Karl-Rahner-Archiv be compared to the library and archive of John Henry Newman, in the oratory in Birmingham: a cathedral of scholarliness and a place of reverence. That is rather foreign to the sober way of the Society of Jesus. On the part of his Jesuit colleagues, who remembered him, I observed gratitude, respect, but also criticism and even some repressed smiles about his "idiosyncrasies." Rahner, it seems, was not always easy to live with.

Alois Neururer, the receptionist at the Jesuit residence, who held that position since the 1950's, told me a wonderful anecdote. Obviously quite moved, he described how Karl Rahner, in the last years of his life in Innsbruck, sat down in the receptionist area for a little chat and surprised Alois with little signs of appreciation; he discovered a side of Rahner which he had not seen before.

The special aura of the archives lies in its total lack of extravagance. The furnishings are simple: above the desk a cross with a palm branch, a painting of a rose, and a photo of the stained glass window of the Anglican cathedral in San Francisco,[3] in which Karl Rahner, together with Martin Buber are depicted, following in the tradition of the Oxford movement, the current Catholic tradition of the Anglican Church, which began with Richard Hooker. That Rahner had his own work rooms was already seen as a privilege.

On Rahner's desk was the German translation of the Bible, a Greek New Testament, a Denzinger-Schönmetzer, a telephone book, and a series of foreign language dictionaries. Were these his daily theological tools? What other books he may have used were returned to the in-house library. The new typewriter and the comfortable chair he had, Ms. Oeggl, his secretary and a "good soul," obtained for him. He would not have purchased such "luxury" on his own initiative.

I did not simply get to know a Jesuit, I got to know a Jesuit of the "old school." He kept his notes from his days in the novitiate; all neatly organized. He kept a copy of his final vows as a Jesuit, written in his own hand. Documentation of his first attempts at philosophical disputation as a scholastic was preserved. In addition, there are the Latin manuals in which he drew cartoons and wrote humorous comments, all of which point to that world which characterized the houses of formation of the Society of Jesus, in the German speaking world after the First World War.

"Cloister children," Karl and Hugo (1900-1968)[4] called themselves in the Festschrift for their father in the year 1928.[5] The milieu and the Jesuit formation in Latin were so natural that there never appears a word of criticism from this period in his life. Karl Rahner was a diligent and bright student, yet he accepted the given system unquestioningly. The record he kept of books he borrowed from the library indicates that he could not simply choose, on his own, to take books off the shelves, but that he could read the books, which were kept under "lock and key," only with express permission of his superiors. In this world, which has sunk into the past, his universal perspective matured.

These things were seen to be a matter of course; Karl Rahner always characterized this as "normal;" to us, today, they appear less than "normal." Rahner's attitude was rooted in an openness and a readiness to dialogue, to be of service, and this also accounts for his criticism. Is that possible for us today, who lack his rootedness? Karl Rahner appears to have sensed that when he later spoke about "Courage for an

Ecclesial Christianity":[6] he spoke somewhat interminably of "loyalty" and of "matters of course." I, myself, have observed him being quite taken back and believe that I have heard some anger in his voice when he responded to a question about the Church from someone in the student community in Munich. He said: "In the face of negative experiences the question is very quickly asked: Shall I still remain in the Church? The question drives me 'crazy.' For me as a believer it is in the last analysis meaningless. What can the word 'still' mean here? It is like asking whether I will 'still' be a human being, or whether I will 'still' live in this pitiable twentieth century. With such basic realities of life, there are really only two alternatives: either a radical protest that carried to its extreme would have to end in suicide, or an acceptance and living through of life with all its negative aspects. The point for me is that Christians remain in the Church in spite of all the anger that they might feel about it."[7]

Church is the existential reality of his life and of his theology in the course of the changing times. A change can also be seen from looking at his passport photos: Until the Second Vatican Council, studio quality photos feature him in a roman collar; after that in a suit. Finally one sees a pale photo of him taken in a passport photo booth labelled "gangster." Is this a protest against a bourgeois lifestyle, is it thriftiness, or perhaps a testimony to his curiosity in the advances in technology?

The contemporary form of self-introspection and autobiographical attention to self remained foreign to him. There is no diary from which I could follow the process of his intellectual maturation. In the few documents which provide autobiographical information, he records what he did, in addition to his teaching, certainly as a basis for his report to the Father Provincial. In the early years he counted the number of confessions he heard and the catechetical instructions he gave. He was always engaged in pastoral activity, even during his time of studies in Freiburg. His "notebook" was the only key I had to help me catalogue the materials packed away in boxes. How little he was interested in reflecting on his theological development I concluded from the fact that handwritten drafts of his first essays were found buried in boxes, which later were translated from the French back into German. The only document of a biographical nature is the list of ancestors, which he could follow all the way back to Tirol. I recognized the Jesuit of the old school also in the collection of old, well-worn prayer books in the tradition of Ignatian spirituality, the relic of Saint Ignatius of

Loyola, and his practice, simply taken for granted and practiced to the end of his life, of rising very early in the morning and beginning each day with meditation and a quiet Mass and ending the day with a similar meditation.[8] That daily schedule, which he describes in one of his early high school essays, shaped his entire life.

His daily routine was much different from mine because I have to manage my own living arrangements. I smile when I recall the experiences of Herlinde Pissarek-Hudelist and Elfriede Oeggl, when they spoke of their experiences with Karl Rahner, being with him on a Sunday morning or on Christmas Eve.[9] They spoke of his attempt at driving a car with manual transmission which ended abruptly with his banging into the front wall of the garage, or how after several failed attempts he resigned himself to the fact that the modern electric egg cooker needed water These stories seem to come from an alternate universe. Rahner lived in another world. He did not have any "Tirolean hobbies" and a "Tirolean proof for the existence of God," which, according to the former Bishop of Innsbruck, Reinhold Stecher, leads one beyond the mountains, one does not find in Karl Rahner.[10] Everything was subordinate to his work. Of primary importance was his interest in people. Here, he was always contemporary.

The stories of Herbert Vorgrimler make abundantly clear to me the traditional Jesuitical lifestyle: only later in life could Karl Rahner give up his reserved demeanor. The rules learned early in life, also with regard to how to relate to women, he internalized for his entire life. When the letter exchange with Luise Rinser was one-sidedly published, it was clear to me, as a married man, how incredibly naïve and without reservation he entered into this friendship: probably as he had done with so many others, as a true spiritual guide and caring human being. I visited Anita Röper personally. She helped me understand many things.[11] Why had he not, as John Henry Newman felt it necessary to do, left behind a dossier for his Jesuit colleagues, in which he addressed possible future accusations? Perhaps he was so little concerned about himself because he entrusted himself more to the judgment and grace of God. I never encountered a Karl Rahner who was concerned about his place in Church History or in theology. That was for him, I believe, something about which he could care less. He allowed himself, time after time, to be drawn into new situations and new questions from a countless circle of people, in order to do justice to his vocation as a priest and a Jesuit. I soon took at face value his own sober assessment, which he saw as the summation of his life: "I don't know what to say about my life. I did not lead a life, I worked, wrote, taught, tried to do my duty and earn my keep; I tried, in this everyday ordinary routine, to serve God, period."[12]

Today all visitors to the Karl-Rahner-Archiv meet him as an author and theology teacher, as *Professor Dr. Karl Rahner, SJ*. Both aspects are connected because in the Archives the Innsbruck "aura" is present. His thinking and writing appear, until the late 1960's, to be actually of a piece. There is a handwritten version of practically all of the essays and books from that period, with dates written in the margin every now and then – a personal record of productivity? There are handwritten versions even of his very first publications. Rahner kept a "poet corner" until it expanded to fill all four walls of his office and then found a place in the basement and in storage areas.

To be sure, Rahner's ideas developed at the Council and afterwards became known worldwide when translations and new editions were published in all the world languages; even Chinese, Japanese and Korean. Compared to Thomas Aquinas, the effect of his work in the year 1954 is not as far reaching. Even in the later, thoroughly organized and comprehensive collection by Karl Lehmann, a remarkable, lax attitude is noticeable. No printed copies can be found of *Hearer of the Word* (1941) and *Spirit in the World* (1939), although there are numerous drafts and the manuscript of the philosophical dissertation must have still been available in the 1950's. His conciliar drafts were loaned out or made their way into others' hands. Therefore only from the drafts provided by Cardinal Franz König was I able to discern the twofold approach of the conciliar theologian: publicly to dampen all expectations, privately, with total self investment, to work for the highest degree of success. How profound this conciliar teamwork was, how many drafts and texts needed to be revised and conceived anew, is unknown. It is surprising that Karl Rahner ignored reviewing the schema based on the concept of the Church sacrament, which had been developed by a team of German Bishops and theologians, found in the Constitution on the Church, as if he had no investment in it.[13]

Besides being an author, he was a teacher of theology and an editor of academic works. Previously unknown to me was the strict regimen of theological tracts which Karl Rahner taught on the faculty, a fixed rotation: grace, reconciliation, creation, sometimes also courses on the sacraments, and Mariology. His colleagues presumed students would study the manuals of theology, the "*Institutiones*," of Ludwig Lercher, SJ.[14] Karl Rahner composed his own class notes: codices. Adolf Darlap, who at times worked on the production of these, has preserved his personal copy of the grace-codex from 1950. Of course, these were written in Latin; later they were replaced by German editions. That change brought with it, prior to the Council, ecclesiastical criticism. He wrote Latin as well as he did German (some maintain, even better Latin); once his Latin text was published in the German translation of his assistant.[15]

Many of the manuscripts impress me still today; the handwritten versions of numerous articles for the *Theological Dictionary* ("*Kleines theologisches Wörterbuch*") among them.[16] They were composed while he was on "vacation," while he worked on the *Lexikon für Theologie und Kirche* and on the preparation for the Council. Karl Rahner must have, without any great preparation, written these "directly" into the typewritten version. The handwritten versions show little in the way of corrections and additions. He was a master of the tradition of the manuals over which he had absolute control, including the relevant "Denzinger numbers." In the students' notes from seminars in the late 1950's, one can see his theological methodology in its original form: formulating the question; circling the question and the theological data, which was second nature to him and at his finger tips; analyzing all these materials for their possible contribution to the challenges of the present day. The scholarly editor, who planned series and *Lexika*, and who edited them, was only able to do this with the help of loyal co-workers. It is obvious that in addition to work on the *Lexikon für Theologie und Kirche* he had various other responsibilities and did not always act in the most appropriate way. He acted at times informally, with "sleeves rolled up," under the pressure of deadlines, seeking to master hopeless situations, and, in all honesty, it was inevitable that he could not manage to do all this any differently than he did.[17] The *Lexikon für Theologie und Kirche* would have been a disaster without him. During this period the quantitative output of his work amazes me. His approach to different topics is not only still worth reading today, but also unsurpassed in many ways. This must also be recognized. How was this possible?

After the Council there appeared to develop in Karl Rahner's office a "factory of theological texts." The handwriting of Karl Lehmann is to be found on almost every manuscript during the time he was an assistant. The Foreword to volume 12 of *Schriften zur Theologie*, was typed on the typewriter (and composed as well), which Karl H. Neufeld, SJ, uses to this very day. And there are not a few texts, which I characterized in the inventory with "m. korr. u. Erg. fd. Hand:" *"mit Korrekturen und Ergänzungen von fremden Hand,"* (with corrections and additions from someone else's hand). Karl Rahner often appeared to give his co-workers a free hand so that the interpretation flowed into the text of the work. Under this mutual influence, he dealt with the keywords and themes of his students and his men and women co-workers: the concern for Political Theology of his student and friend, Johann Baptist Metz; the Theology of Liberation; Feminist Theology; the dialogue with the Jews and with non-Christian religions; the charismatic movement, and many others. Until the very end of his life, he attempted to answer the questions and challenges put to him, even though his assertion that he belonged to the "old school," was not an understatement, he also attempted to safeguard the agenda of the new generation.

This theological generation which grew up under him did not have an easy time stepping out from under his shadow. Some of the criticisms appear to me to be a father-son conflict. On the one hand, I see a radical break with the tradition in Systematic Theology in the German speaking world, which could not be blamed completely on Karl Rahner. In only one generation theology has changed so dramatically that today's theologians can hardly comprehend any of the early essays. The theme "nature and grace," which strongly occupied the preconciliar period, is today hardly able to be communicated. It appears to be unimportant. But when one takes a closer look, it is present in almost all the debates. I always see new sides of Karl Rahner and I've come to appreciate them.

Today, I believe I can say that I know what a theological genius is: one who reflects on the challenges and the distress of the age, conscious of the entire tradition of the followers of Jesus Christ, seeking the hidden face of God. It is someone who meditates, who in prayer and with a self-consuming passion, mostly alone and abandoned, insures that the faith does not disappear in the transiency of the present moment; it is a person who learns to respond to the call of God in a continually changing situation and does all this with a heart for the present and a mind open to the future. That, thereby, an immense amount of stress accrues and in the final analysis, everything one has

accomplished seems worthless, is unavoidable. I conclude this from
reading his self-reflection, existentially expressed in his Theology of
Death: "In any event, theological scholarship as such was actually always of no interest to me ... How long is it before it is forever night?
I don't know. So one goes on, so long as it is still day. In the end one
departs with empty hands, I know that. And it is good so. Then one
looks at the crucified, and departs. What follows is the blessed incomprehensibility of God."[18]

The statement by Thomas Aquinas that everything that he wrote is
so much straw, Karl Rahner quoted often as a description of himself
as well.

In his writings, during and after the Council, Karl Rahner the
"Church politician" comes into view, long before that he wrestled with
the capacity of the Christian faith to address current needs. This can
be seen in his writings for the *Paulus-Gesellschaft* and the *Görres-Gesell-
schaft*. However, even prior to the Council, Karl Rahner emphasized
that at that time, the Church needed a "tutiorismus of risk-taking," as
the only appropriate option for the Church; only after the Council did
this come to be a public conflict. It occurred to me that Karl Rahner
did not come to this conclusion by his own initiative. In the background of almost all his essays and lectures, there is a question, a problem, a request. Karl Rahner's work is radically rooted contextually. He
often became the advocate for the concerns of others, of their actual,
or, at times, perceived needs. Not infrequently, he made public the criticisms that others felt but did not express. His struggle to enable the
Church to be more capable of living into the future did not always win
him new friends. I cannot argue that Karl Rahner always had a sound,
"prudent judgment," or an adequate assessment of the situation, or an
appropriate feel for the proper way of responding, but his diagnoses
are shockingly accurate. A story that was told to me in Münster from
the "wild 1960's," I still find amusing and typical: One time he took
a chair and placed it in the street in front of his residence, to protest
there against the traffic noise, although he could hardly hear the traffic,
due to his being hard of hearing. He did so "out of solidarity."

Occasionally Rahner could be manipulated to invest in something
about which he knew little or nothing. Often, however, he entered into
the "thorny" situations or attempted with a mighty "shove," to get things
back on track. Sometimes, as an Alemannian, he spoke frankly even if
at times somewhat coarsely, of "starting a fight," or he announced that

soon the "bomb would explode." I did not take offense at that manner of speaking because I was used to it from childhood days: in the south-western region of Germany, one's emotions frequently are on the tip of one's tongue. That he could also admit to his mistakes and did not hide that in a closet somewhere, I found admirable. Was he also somewhat unpredictable? How does the saying go: "Whoever works a lot, makes a lot of mistakes, whoever doesn't work hard, makes fewer; some people don't make any." Also that Karl Rahner could be self-deprecating and not take himself too seriously, should not be forgotten. At the end of an interview, part of a series of interviews that sought to showcase prominent people "up close and personal," in which he was asked about his leisure time activities, he responded: "A final comment: As for the things you have begun to address in your questions, I hold to that which my brother Hugo, who was also a Jesuit, once said – 'You know Karl, I am not normal, but I pretend to be...'"[19]

Many disagreements had to do with integrity. The argument with Hans Küng was no accident. According to Karl Rahner it came down to a matter of relinquishing the principles of Catholic Theology. How he responded to those who praised him, although only a short time prior to that, had branded him a heretic, impressed me. The attack of Hans Urs von Balthasar, to which he hardly ever made reference, must have hurt him deeply. Perhaps the fact that he belonged to the "old school" played a role here. How can someone who leaves the Society of Jesus because of an individual mystic (Adrienne von Speyr), de-mand obedience and loyalty to the Church? Sometimes, Karl Rahner must have been bewildered by all the literature and pamphlets which denounced him as a destroyer of the Church and its faith. He kept a copy of many of the attacks. Almost all of them brought forth argu-ments, which in the scholastic tradition, under which he grew up, and which he always presupposed, would not have had any merit. Many expressions of contemporary theology were completely foreign to him: the suffering of God, or the inner view of the Trinity, which Hans Urs von Balthasar takes for granted, and which today leads to talk of three subjects in God. That's why he was immensely pleased that Pope John Paul II sent him greetings for his 80th birthday – personally signed.[20] Only at the very beginning of my days in the archives did it surprise me that Karl Rahner, in composing his public letters to the pope, al-ways insisted on the appropriate address which expressed respect and recognition: "Holy father." Only gradually did I truly come to realize that often his criticisms of developments in the Church sprang from his radical identification with it. When he spoke of the Church he always meant "I" or "we."

I believe I came to have a special connection to *Father Karl Rahner* as a result of the archives. Not only from various stories about Karl Rahner, but also from the daily calendar of events and from occasional notes I received, I was again and again pointed to Karl Rahner the priest, the pastor, the teacher, the spiritual guide in faith and life. I came to see this great service, unpretentiously rendered, without fanfare, and the real help he provided others, If he did not wish to speak about that, I will also not do so at length here. At the *Salzburger Hochschulwochen*, 2003, a priest who had studied with Karl Rahner in Münster, told me how he, to the present day, still remains moved by the way Karl Rahner presided at Mass, at community prayer, and gave spiritual guidance. Karl Rahner, the Professor, was truly a *confessor*: Fr. Rahner was remembered as much for his life witness as for the precise content of his words.

My overview would not be complete if I failed to speak of Karl Rahner, *the preacher*. Since even his practice homilies, from the time he was a theology student, are preserved, and since for the greater part of his life he continually made himself available in service to the proclamation of the Word, I may thus take him simply at his word when he writes: "I have always done theology for the sake of proclaiming the gospel, preaching God's word, for the sake of pastoral ministry."[21] How important his preaching was for many people, can be seen from the fact that many of his homilies were written down in shorthand or tape recorded. This is the Fr. Karl Rahner I meet in the crypt of the Jesuit Church. I have always found a candle burning or fresh flowers at his grave: silent thanks from people whom I do not know. But I, too, need to thank him; this I must not fail to mention, for a very personal reason: I met my future wife, when she came to the Karl- Rahner-Archiv seeking assistance with her master's thesis – "Karl Rahner on Prayer." So I am not truly "objective." Still: Can one really speak about Karl Rahner, in light of eternity, other than with gratitude?

Which Karl Rahner did I get to know in the archives? – Karl Rahner, the theologian, the author, the "workaholic," the priest, a person with contradictions, rough edges, limits and missteps, also someone who never wanted people repeating what he said, in parrot-like fashion, imitators, but as one who later in life simply said: "Do it better!"

All these, yes, but above all I met a person of faith, who spent himself, and at the end of his life – at the very end, in his address in Freiburg for his 80th birthday celebration, "Experiences of a Catholic theologian," falteringly, asked those assembled to say to God a little prayer for him, so that at the end, God would grant him love and mercy. Because that sounds so strange to us today and even in theological circles can be cause for ridicule, I hope that his combination of deeply personal, ecclesial piety with a universally broad, supreme intellectual effort, remains a dangerous memory.

NOTES

1 For an introduction to the archive see Roman A. Siebenrock, Mitteilungen aus dem Karl-Rahner-Archiv (KRA), in: *Zeitschrift für Katholische Theologie* 110 (1988) 310-312.

2 K. Rahner, Im Jesuitennoviziat des Jahres 1919. "Ein Tag im Exerzitienhaus Feldkirch," in: *Geist und Leben* 58 (1985) 81-82.

3 Pictured in: Paul Imhof, Hubert Biallowons (eds.), *Karl Rahner – Bilder eines Lebens* (Freiburg: Herder, 1985) 116; cf. also Günther Wassilowsky, Kirchenlehre der Moderne: Ekklesiologie, in: Andreas R. Batlogg, Paul Rulands, Walter Schmolly, Roman A. Siebenrock, Arno Zahlauer, *Karl Rahners Denkweg*. Quellen – Perspektiven – Entwicklungen (Mainz: Grünewald, 2nd edition 2004) 223-241.

4 Cf. Andreas R. Batlogg, Hugo Rahner als Mensch und Theologe, in: *Stimmen der Zeit* 217 (2000) 517-530.

5 Cf. Karl H. Neufeld, *Die Brüder Rahner*. Eine Biographie (Freiburg: Herder, 2nd edition 2004) 40 f.

6 Cf. K. Rahner, Courage for an Ecclesial Christianity, in: ibid., *Theological Investigations*, vol. 20, translated by Edward Quinn (New York: Crossroad, 1981) 3-12.

7 Cf. K. Rahner, Our Relationship to the Church, in: *Faith in a Wintry Season*. Conversations and Interviews with Karl Rahner in the Last Years of his life, edited by Paul Imhof and Hubert Biallowons. Translation edited by Harvey D. Egan (New York: Crossroad, 1991) 141-153, 143.

8 What he writes in "Gebet im Alltag," indicates a practice in his own life. Cf. K. Rahner, *The Need and the Blessing of Prayer*. A new translation of Father Rahner's book on prayer; translated by Bruce W. Gillette; introduction by Harvey D. Egan (Collegeville, Minn.: Liturgical Press, 1997). Andreas R. Batlogg provides a comprehensive look at his pious practices in light of the meditations on the mysteries in the life of Jesus: *Die Mysterien des Lebens*

Jesu bei Karl Rahner. Zugang zum Christusglauben (Innsbruck: Tyrolia, 2nd edition 2003).

9 Cf. Roman A. Siebenrock, "Die Frau ist der Frau aufgegeben." Ihre Assistententätigkeit im Dogmatischen Institut bei Karl Rahner, in: Günther Bader, Martha Heizer (eds.), *Theologie erden.* Erinnerungen an Herlinde Pissarek-Hudelist (Thaur: Kulturverlag, 1996) 45-55.

10 Cf. Reinhold Stecher, *Botschaft der Berge* (Innsbruck: Tyrolia, 14th edition 2002); also Oswald Wörle, Reinhold Stecher und seine Bergwochen, in: Andreas R. Batlogg, Klaus Egger (eds.), *Dank an Reinhold Stecher.* Perspektiven eines Lebens (Innsbruck: Tyrolia, 2002) 181-183.

11 Anita Röper addressed the topic of Karl Rahner's pastoral ministry several times, first of all using the pseudonym: F. M. Schäfer, *Es ist Licht genug.* Gespräche über den Glauben und seine vergessene Tiefe (Innsbruck: Tyrolia, 1959); then under her own name: Anita Röper, *Karl Rahner als Seelsorger* (Innsbruck: Tyrolia, 1987).

12 K. Rahner, *Bekenntnisse.* Rückblick auf 80 Jahre, edited by Georg Sporschill (Vienna: Herdold, 1984) 58. – Now in: ibid., *Sämtliche Werke,* vol.: 25: Erneuerung des Ordenslebens. Zeugnis für Kirche und Welt. Bearbeitet von Andreas R. Batlogg (Freiburg: Herder, 2008) 84.

13 Cf. Günther Wassilowsky, *Universales Heilssakrament Kirche.* Karl Rahners Beitrag zur Ekklesiologie des II. Vatikanums (Innsbruck: Tyrolia, 2001).

14 The course notes for his lectures in Dogmatic Theology were edited by students in theology in Innsbruck both during and after World War II. Thus there are many editions of the class notes. Karl Rahner was not involved in any of this.

15 One can see this clearly in the essay "Das Gebet im Namen der Kirche." Herlinde Pissarek-Hudelist translated the text from the Latin original; cf. K. Rahner, "Some Theses on Prayer 'In the Name of the Church,'" in: ibid., *Theological Investigations,* volume 5, translated by Karl.-H. Kruger (New York: Seabury Press, 1966) 419-438, as well as KRA I, A, 175.

16 KRA I, A, 176; Karl Rahner, Herbert Vorgrimler, *Kleines Theologisches Wörterbuch* (Freiburg: Herder, 15th edition 1985); cf. ibid., *Theological Dictionary,* edited by Cornelius Ernst, OP, translated by Richard Strachan (New York: Herder and Herder, 1965).

17 Cf. the report on the edition and the documentation in the appendix by Herbert Vorgrimler, in: K. Rahner, *Sämtliche Werke,* vol. 17: *Enzyklopädische Theologie.* Die Lexikonbeiträge der Jahre 1956-1973. Bearbeitet von Herbert Vorgrimler (Freiburg: Herder, 2002) 20-63, as well as ibid., 1395-1436.

18   Karl Rahner (curriculum vitae), in: W. Ernst Böhm, (ed.), *Forscher und Gelehrte* (Stuttgart: Battenberg, 1966) 21.

19   In: tip. Innsbrucker Zeitung 9 (1984) Nr. 2, 6-7, 7. The last sentence was not added in *Faith in a Wintry Season*.

20   Facsimile in: Paul Imhof, Hubert Biallowons, (eds.), *Karl Rahner – Bilder eines Lebens*, 140.

21   K. Rahner, *Im Gespräch*, vol. 2, edited by Paul Imhof, Hubert Biallowons (Munich: Kösel, 1983) 146-152, 150.

NAME INDEX

SUBJECT INDEX